Encyclopedia of
Ships and Seafaring

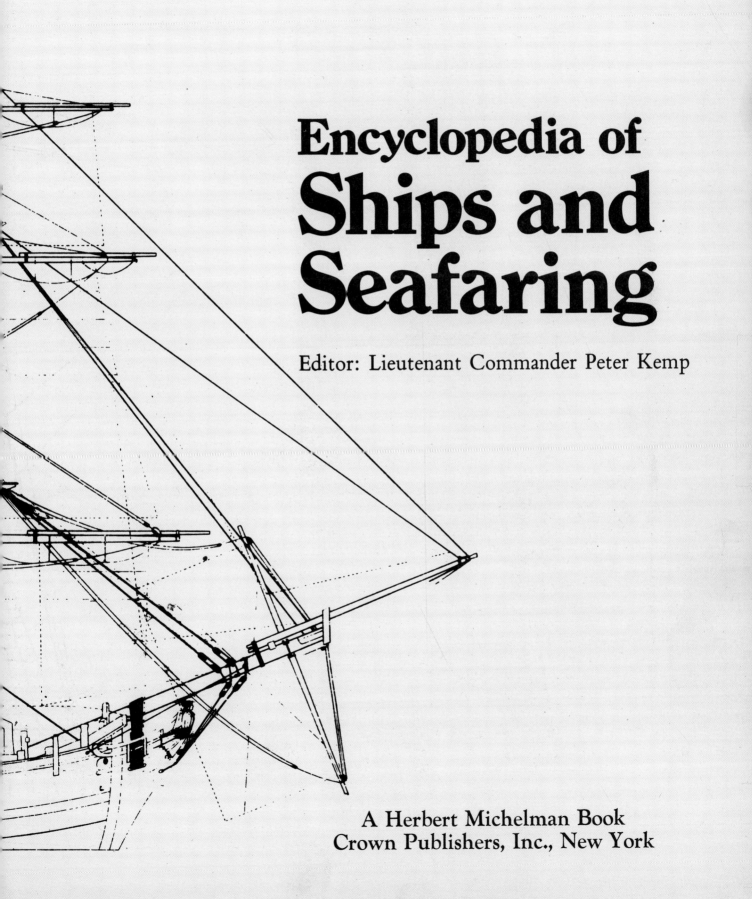

Encyclopedia of
Ships and
Seafaring

Editor: Lieutenant Commander Peter Kemp

A Herbert Michelman Book
Crown Publishers, Inc., New York

Picture Acknowledgments

British Library Board; British Museum; British Tourist
Authority; Chantiers de l'Atlantique; Decca Navigator
Company Ltd; Esso Petroleum Company Ltd; Exeter
Maritime Museum; Ambrose Greenway; Hong Kong
Government Office; Imperial War Museum, London;
Magdalene College, Cambridge; National Maritime
Museum, Greenwich; P & O Photo Library; Rolls-
Royce Ltd; Royal Navy; Royal Norwegian Embassy;
Science Museum, London; Shell Petroleum Company
Ltd; Skyfotos Ltd; Spanish Tourist Office; Standard
Telephones & Cables Ltd; Supramar AG; Town Docks
Museum, Kingston upon Hull; United States Navy;
Universitets Oldsaksamling Oslo; Yachting World.

Created, designed and produced by Reference International
Publishers, Ltd.

Editorial Director, Martin Self; Managing Editor, Sandra Jones;
House Editor, Stephen Jones; Designer, Julian Holland; Artists,
Richard Benson and John W. Wood.

First published in the United States by Crown Publishers, 1980.

Printed in the United States of America.

Library of Congress Cataloging in Publication Data
Main entry under title:

Encyclopedia of ships and seafaring.

Includes index.
1. Ships—Dictionaries. 2. Navigation—Dictionaries.
3. Naval art and science—Dictionaries. I. Kemp, Peter.
V23.E47 1980 387   78-23661
ISBN: 0-517-537389

Contents

Authors

Raymond V. B. Blackman, MBE
A fellow of the Royal Institute of Naval Architects, Raymond Blackman has spent much of his life associated with ships and ship design. He succeeded Francis Macmurtrie as Editor of the authoritative *Jane's Fighting Ships* to become a leading expert in all aspects of the world's warships. Since his retirement he has lived at Portsmouth, one of Britain's principal naval bases, where he keeps in touch with maritime affairs.

Rear Admiral Edward F. Gueritz, CB, OBE, DSC
After a distinguished career in the Royal Navy, in which his last appointment was Admiral President of the Royal Naval College, Greenwich, home of the Naval Staff College, Rear Admiral Gueritz has become one of the foremost experts in Britain on the problems of defense in all its aspects. He is at present the Director General at the Royal United Services Institute in London, and often broadcasts on naval and military history.

Lieutenant Commander Peter Kemp, OBE
Educated at the Royal Naval Colleges of Osborne and Dartmouth, Peter Kemp served in submarines and naval intelligence during World War II and subsequently become Head of the Royal Naval Historical Branch, Ministry of Defence. He has written widely on naval, military, and yachting subjects, and was Editor of *The Oxford Companion to Ships and the Sea.*

Captain John Moore, RN
A naval historian of note, Captain Moore served in submarines and in the fleet air arm. He succeeded Raymond Blackman as Editor of *Jane's Fighting Ships*, and his knowledge of warships and their operational capabilities contributes greatly to the worldwide authority of that publication. He has both written and broadcast widely on naval subjects.

Jonathan Rutland
Freelance writer, author of a number of books on maritime subjects including *Ships* (Samson Low), *The Amazing World of Ships* (Angus and Robertson), and *Hydrofoils and Hovercraft* (Franklin Watts).

Vice Admiral Brian B. Schofield, CB, CBE
After a long career in the Royal Navy, in which he specialized in navigation, Vice Admiral Schofield has written many books about naval affairs, including a history of the Royal Navy's Navigation School at Portsmouth. He has a wide knowledge of current maritime development, in the mercantile as well as the naval world, and takes an active part in the work of the Royal United Services Institute in London.

Foreword

'Whoso commands the sea commands the trade of the world; whoso commands the trade of the world commands the riches of the world . . .' The words were written by Sir Walter Raleigh in his *History of the World* nearly 400 years ago. What was true then has been true throughout succeeding generations up to the present. Ancient peoples made some remarkable voyages in the interests of trade and exploration. The Phoenicians are reputed to have sailed around Africa in 600 BC, while some 1,500 years later Polynesians crossed the Pacific to New Zealand, and Vikings took their longships across the Atlantic to North America. Remarkable as they were, these voyages were limited in their implications for society and the world in general. By contrast, the great voyages of discovery of the 15th and 16th centuries, made possible by the development of more effective rigs, stronger construction, and greater size, vastly extended man's horizons, his knowledge of the world, and his contact with other cultures. The growth of sea transportation brought increased and wider trade and communication, and it brought long-distance sea warfare and colonization.

Technologically this revolution in transportation by sea was complete by about 1600. Thereafter there were no significant advances in shipping for over 200 years, when man's impatience and competitive instincts led to the creation of the clipper ships. Sailing over twice as fast as earlier freighters, clippers transported valuable cargoes across oceans, and they carried determined prospectors to the gold rushes in California and Australia. But their day was short, because by then the modern mechanical world had arrived. Steam power had been invented, and was to bring an unprecedented revolution in transportation at sea and on land.

Today, the sea and the air are the two great highways of the world. The growth of air traffic over the last 30 years has made personal travel between nations easier and faster, but the airways have little part to play in the trade of the world, either now or in the foreseeable future. The key to commerce and power which Walter Raleigh recognized so long ago remains with the world's ships as they make their way across the waters. When we remember that 70% of the earth's surface is covered by oceans and seas, some idea of the magnitude of the ship's daily job, and her importance in the whole modern scheme of life, may become apparent to even the most land-locked.

These thoughts are the genesis of this book. It is quite impossible, of course, to tell the whole story of the ship and of man's endeavors on the seas in a single volume. One of the world's largest maritime libraries, in which I happily spent many years of my life, already contains over a quarter of a million books and adds another thousand or so every year. What this book tries to do is to encapsulate some of that immense story, showing how the primitive boats which man fashioned in the dawn of history have developed into the huge variety of sophisticated ships of today; how the technology of ship design and development has kept pace with the demands of modern living; how men sailed out into the unknown in search for new wealth — or just to find what was there. The *Encyclopedia of Ships and Seafaring* has nine major sections on the development of ships and of man's ability to use and exploit the oceans. These are followed by three major alphabetical sections dealing with the famous ships of all times, all the varieties of ships and boats developed over the centuries and, lastly, all the great men who have figured in the history of seafaring. The first nine sections carry many words in small capitals, which indicate that the subject is featured in one of the three alphabetical sections.

I am deeply indebted to many helpers in the task of compiling this book: Vice Admiral Schofield, Rear Admiral Gueritz, Captain John Moore, and Raymond Blackman. Their willingness to contribute to this book in spite of their many other commitments, and the benefit of their advice and expertise, have been of more value than I can readily express. To their names I must add those of Martin Self and Sandie Jones who, in ways too numerous to specify, have given me constant encouragement and advice in producing this encyclopedia.

Peter Kemp

The Prehistoric Boat

No one can know when, where, or how man first took to the water as a means of transportation. But somewhere in the world, in the dim recesses of prehistory, a man stood on the bank of a river and looked across at the other side. Maybe he came to the same spot many times and began to wonder what lay beyond on the far shore. Slowly the wonder developed into an active curiosity, and one day, perhaps, a fallen tree or a tangled mass of reeds floated down the river before him and drifted into the bank near where he stood. His urge to discover what lay on the opposite shore may have given him the courage to try whether the tree trunk or the tangled weeds would support his weight on the water. Later, no doubt, he discovered that by paddling with his hands he could impart motion to his improvised vessel, and so he set off on his first voyage over the water.

It must all have started something like this, but when and where will never be known to us. Almost certainly the problem of how to cross over the water was being pondered in many different places, not necessarily simultaneously but more probably over a span of thousands of years, for in those prehistoric times there was no way of spreading knowledge beyond the confines of the tribe.

A primitive raft of logs.

The First River Craft

This first floating vessel was not yet a boat, and it would take thousands of years before man acquired the skills needed to produce a watergoing craft which we today would recognize as a boat. The first steps were taken along this road only when man learned through long years of experience and experiment that his tree trunk became more efficient and manageable in water if he pointed its ends, however crudely, or that he could bind together branches of trees or bundles of reeds to form a crude raft, which he could paddle along with his hands. This conscious adaptation of locally available materials signals the true birth of the boat.

Hollowing out a tree trunk with fire.

We can readily imagine that the early development went something like this. Primitive man began to acquire possessions: spears and darts for his hunting, cooking pots for his food, clothing for his warmth, and perhaps some sort of a tent made from skins for his family to live in. He discovered that his tree trunk or bundle of reeds was not buoyant enough to support both him and his possessions, but that he could carry the additional load if he hollowed out the tree trunk or bound up the reeds into a shape like a saucer. Gradually, over the centuries, he discovered that a long narrow shape with pointed ends moved forward better than a square or circular shape. He discovered, too, that he got much more leverage, and thus better speed and control, with wooden paddles than with his bare hands. As his possessions and his confidence grew he began to build larger craft. He learned how to hew out rough planks from tree trunks and how to hold them together either with wooden pegs or with leather thongs. If there were no logs he bound up masses of reeds into a craft that would carry not only him but also his family or his fellow hunters. He learned that by using a paddle over the back end of his boat he could more easily control its direction. This imagined sequence of events in the development of the boat corresponds well with the picture we get from the earliest Egyptian rock carvings and pottery decorations depicting boats. Most of them show some sort of long thin craft with pointed bow and stern, a steering paddle over the stern, and men paddling amidships. The majority of boats depicted are made of papyrus reeds bound together, since wood suitable for boatbuilding was scarce

Palm log dugout from Bengal.

along the Nile. However, some of the early rock carvings do illustrate boats constructed of many short wooden planks, or blocks held together with pegs or rope binding.

It is certain that these carvings show boats in a relatively late stage of their development. The earliest rock carving can be dated to about 4000 BC. Archeological evidence can take us back a further 3,000 years with remains of very early boats uncovered in Sjaelland, Denmark, and in Yorkshire, England, but even this total span of 9,000 years must be minute in relation to the whole period of evolution. Some idea of this long gestation period can perhaps be derived from the Brigg boat, which was unearthed in Lincolnshire, England, in 1886. The primitive construction of the boat is made evident by the lack of an internal frame and separate stempiece and sternpiece, features that were already present in boats of at least 5,000 years ago. However, her unusually large size of 48 ft. 8 in. by 4 ft. 6 in. (14.83 m × 1.37 m) indicates that she came fairly late in the sequence of prehistoric boatbuilding. Lateral strength was achieved with wooden struts wedged at intervals across the shell, and with leather thongs threaded through a series of holes bored along each side and then lashed across the boat to hold the sides firmly against the struts. This implies a skill in boatbuilding that can only have evolved after several hundreds or thousands of years.

Above: Egyptian pot of the 4th millennium BC showing boat with racked truss.

Below: models of Egyptian papyrus boats, c. 2000 BC.

The excavation of the Brigg boat in 1866. This early boat was made from a single immense oak tree.

The Search for Stability

One can imagine the dilemma which faced primitive man as his needs for waterborne transportation grew. He had by now two alternative methods of crossing water: the original raft of reeds, which he had developed into a raft of branches or tree trunks bound together with vines or strips of hide; and the original tree trunk, which he had learned to hollow out, by burning or cutting away the central wood, and to point at both ends. Each had advantages and disadvantages. The raft could easily be increased in size to carry greater loads, but it was difficult to propel through the water or steer, and it could not keep its load dry. The dugout tree trunk was reasonably watertight and easier to steer and propel, but it had a comparatively small load-carrying capacity and was unstable. Simply because the dugout more closely resembles the boat as we know it today does not mean that primitive man chose it, rather than the raft, as the type of boat to develop and improve. It seems much more likely that both raft and dugout were developed more or less simultaneously in different locations, depending on what construction materials were locally available. Eventually the two separate lines of evo-

lution converged, although many boats retain to this day some signs of their primitive origins.

The development of the crude prehistoric raft can be imagined from the account in the *Odyssey* of the vessel constructed by Ulysses. From the wealth of details he

Bamboo rafts from Taiwan.

10

Indian raft of clay pots.

introduced into his description, Homer must have known a good deal about contemporary boatbuilding. He wrote the *Odyssey* around 850 BC, and so the vessel he describes is far along the path of development, no doubt some hundreds of thousands, or even millions of years since the first crude raft ventured on water. Homer tells us that Ulysses collected floating timber and, by means of axe and adze, both of them very ancient shipbuilding tools, carefully shaped thick planks of equal length so that they fitted closely edge to edge. The planks were fastened together with dowels and treenails to form a platform, and above this was constructed a second similarly designed platform, so that the two formed more or less an upper and a lower deck. Along the sides he fitted bulwarks of osiers to give protection from breaking waves.

In this form of construction can be seen the genesis of the modern flat-bottomed punt or lighter, and indeed of many other similar craft of today. It did not need much imagination on the part of ancient man, now that he had the tools, to cut planks, build up the sides, and turn up the ends, and so create a vessel that would go easily over the water. This is the basic construction of the ubiquitous SAMPAN of eastern waters, and indeed of the JUNK itself. According to Virgil, Charon's boat, in which he conveyed his passengers across the Styx, was constructed to this general pattern. The ferryboats that used to ply across the Tiber, certainly within living memory, were also flat-bottomed and built on this simple principle. Their generic name was *codicariae*, derived from *caudex*, a plank.

The problems of development facing the user of the dugout were considerably more complex than those confronting the raft builder. The first dugouts were unstable, and one can imagine primitive man's reactions as he watched them roll over to spill their contents and crews into the water. Perhaps he watched some of his neighbors with rafts and wondered why their craft were so stable in comparison to his; he must have realized that if he could

increase the breadth of his tree trunk in relation to its length there would be a better chance of avoiding these distressing accidents.

The problem of increasing the breadth of a finite tree trunk was solved differently in different parts of the world. In eastern waters boatbuilders fitted another tree trunk or a similar piece of timber parallel to the dugout, held in place by two or three poles or beams at a distance of about three times the breadth of the original dugout. This was an outrigger; it did not greatly interfere with the speed of the boat and it acted as a counterpoise weight

Sampans in Hong Kong.

Outrigger used in a fishing village in Sri Lanka.

when the dugout showed any tendency to roll over. It provided the stability hitherto lacking and enabled the dugout to make quite long voyages in the open sea. There are no records to suggest when an outrigger was first fitted to a dugout, but such dugouts were certainly seen by Egyptian and Phoenician seamen some time during the 1st millennium BC. That these experienced boatbuilders did not adopt the outrigger for their own boats argues that they had already solved the problem of stability and considered their own solution less unwieldy.

Here again one has to depend on conjecture, but the remains of several hundred ancient boats which have been found throughout the Scandinavian countries provide a clue to the solution adopted by western boatbuilders. These boats take many shapes, some being dugouts with horizontal planks attached in the manner of modern bilge keels. They could almost be called outriggers, except that the planks were attached directly to the hull and not held away from it at the ends of horizontal poles. Another form from Scandinavia is that of two dugouts joined together to form a double hull. Both these methods of building provided the additional breadth necessary for

stability. A third example, uncovered at Bjorke in Sweden, consists of a shallow, hollowed-out tree trunk cut to taper towards each end and fixed to shaped bow and stern pieces cut from solid blocks of wood held in place with iron rivets. Two overlapping planks are fastened to the sides of the dugout to increase the internal capacity, in much the same way that a clinker-built dinghy is planked today. The hull cross section is a gentle curve, like that of a shallow dish. These Scandinavian boats all date from about the 1st century AD and therefore come almost at the end of the prehistoric line, but they probably indicate how the western sea people overcame the stability problem.

A double dugout held together with crossbeams.

One feature common to all these Scandinavian boats is a longitudinal projection on the insides of the dugout and side planks, used to extend the freeboard and provide a base onto which the internal ribs of the boat could be stitched. By this time early seafaring man had learned that any boat capable of being taken to sea needed some form of internal strengthening, and he provided this by a series of ribs bent to the internal hull shape and stitched onto the protruding lugs with leather thongs. Some of the larger boats were additionally strengthened by crossbracing, sometimes in the form of thwarts which also provided seats for the rowers. One boat of this type, dug out of a bog on a farm called Hjortspring on the Danish island of Als, had ten of these crossbraces which were more or less semicircular. This was one of the larger boats, with a length of 44 ft. (13.4 m) and a beam of nearly 7 ft. (2 m). The hull was made from five overlapping planks cut to a width of 20 in. (51 cm) and to a thickness of ⅝ in. (15.88 mm), an indication of the carpentering skills of these early boatbuilders. The Hjortspring boat had the typical longitudinal projection along the inside faces of the planks to which the ribs could be bound or stitched.

The Evolution of Seagoing Craft

As these prehistoric boats developed in size, early man discovered that the old unstrengthened form of hull could not stand up to conditions likely to be encountered at sea, even if he rarely ventured out of sight of land. The first voyages beyond the mouth of his local river taught him the great strength of the waves and the wind, and he slowly realized that the only solution was to meet strength with strength. He took to bracing his boats with internal ribs and crossbeams, and he discovered through this new structure that it was easier to paddle a boat sitting down than standing up, and his crossbeams thus developed into thwarts. Later still, if we can take our evidence from some of the Scandinavian boats, he discovered that, if sitting down, it was as easy to pull an oar as it was to work a paddle, and that this substitution gave him greater speed and more control of the boat. Some of these early boats had holes bored in the upper planks through which the looms of the oars were threaded.

In all these early Scandinavian boats the method of construction was first to plank up the hull and then to add the ribs and crossbeams for additional strength. There is no evidence, at least in these northern waters, of when this sequence of construction changed into the more logical method of first putting together the internal framework of ribs and crossbeams and then attaching the side planks to it. Yet, paradoxically, there was a model to hand in the CORACLE, a very ancient type of boat widely used in these northern waters. There is only one method of constructing a coracle: to make the internal wickerwork frame first and then to cover it with animal hide. We know of its

A coracle, constructed of a wickerwork frame covered with hide.

antiquity from the fact that Julius Caesar described it in his account of the conquest of Gaul, and it can be reasonably assumed, if only because of its essential simplicity, that it was in wide use long before that.

It is probably necessary to leave Scandinavia and return to the eastern Mediterranean to discover how and when ships began to be built by the method of first constructing a framework and then attaching side planks to it. If it can be assumed that the ship developed out of the boat, it is possible to determine approximately when the building of the internal frame came to be accepted as the initial step in construction. We have to make one further assumption, that the builder needing larger vessels took as his model the boats he knew and simply built them to a larger scale. It was naturally a very gradual process of increasing the size, maybe foot by foot in overall length, until the boat grew into the ship.

The earliest ship of which we have definite knowledge, because she still exists, is the funeral ship of Pharaoh Cheops, built about 5,000 years ago. Although she was designed specifically as a funeral ship and was never intended as a seagoing vessel, she was built as meticulously as any ship of that period; indeed, more than 600 pieces of timber were used in her construction. The elements of her design begin to approach the traditional framing of a ship in that she was built with a long, made-up timber resembling a keel to which were attached a curved stempiece and curved sternpiece, much as one would start to build a ship today. However, there were as yet no ribs or timbers to which the hull planking could be fastened. The bottom timber, or keel, was made up of several pieces of wood instead of one long baulk because of the lack of suitable trees in the Nile valley. Later, when Egyptian shipbuilding flourished, it was only as a result of extensive imports of suitably long timbers from Lebanon.

The funeral ship of the Pharaoh Cheops, c. 3000 BC.

If we move forward 1,000 years to the reign of the Pharaoh Thotmes II and his sister and co-regent Queen Hatshepsut, we find a long series of reliefs in the rock temple at Deir-el-Bahari that tells the story of the queen's expedition of five ships to the 'land of Punt,' thought to be present-day Somalia. The reliefs are exceptionally detailed and show quite clearly a row of deck beams carried through the hull planking to provide the necessary athwartships strength. The next stage of conventional internal framing had been reached, and all that was now missing were ribs rising at intervals from the keel and bent or sawn to form the shape of the hull. Longitudinal strength, apart from that provided by the combination of keel, stemhead, and sternpost, was provided by a racked double-roped truss around the top strakes of the hull, binding them in firmly to hold the general hull shape.

The last step in the evolution of conventional framing can be seen in the wall reliefs of Ramses III's temple at Medinet Habu, which commemorate his great naval victory over 'the northerners of the isles.' These date from about 1200 BC and, most interestingly, they depict the Egyptian ships without the racked truss that was so marked a feature of the Deir-el-Bahari reliefs. This must indicate a new method of giving longitudinal strength to the hull, a method that could only have taken the form of shaped ribs with stringers attached, a logical and easily understandable development away from the crudity of the rope girdle. The introduction of ribs into a ship's internal framing may have come even earlier than this, for there is evidence that in building his ships Ramses III copied the designs of captured enemy vessels.

The Final Development in Boatbuilding

What was right for the ship was equally right for the boat, and it must be a reasonable assumption that these early shipbuilders applied the same basic principles to boatbuilding that they did to shipbuilding. It is quite possible

that this final development in the eastern Mediterranean, that of first constructing a rigid frame and then attaching the hull planking to it, was of more distant origin, for there had been well-established trading links between the Mediterranean seafaring nations and the peoples bordering the Indian Ocean. The Arabs were widely recognized as skilled boatbuilders from a very early period of man's maritime endeavors, and they may possibly have brought this advance in design to Egyptian ports.

This change in construction was slow to spread to more distant parts of the world, simply because there were virtually no maritime contacts between the hub of development in the eastern Mediterranean and the countries lying beyond the normal areas of seaborne trade. As we have seen, Scandinavian boats built between 1,000 and 1,500 years after the time of Ramses III were still con-

structed on the ancient principle of planking up a hull first and then adding internal stiffening to hold it together and provide extra strength. The northern development of the boat, and subsequently the ship, followed a pattern entirely different from that of Mediterranean and Far Eastern boats and ships, mainly because northern ships had to be built to operate effectively in entirely different conditions of stormy seas and unpredictable weather patterns.

Away from the Mediterranean, where expanding trade naturally brought with it developments in ship size and design, early man remained understandably slow to advance beyond the achievement of his forefathers. In the more inaccessible parts of the world there was little call for progress since there was virtually no trade, except perhaps on a small, intertribal basis. Primitive man was thus content to rely on the indigenous boatbuilding material to hand and the methods of construction handed down from his ancestors. He had no cause to improve or improvise; what already existed served his limited requirements adequately. This is undoubtedly the reason for the survival into comparatively modern times of the ceramic boats of the Ganges Delta, the reed boats of the Euphrates, the bark CANOES of the American Indians, and the KAYAKS of the Eskimos. All these relied on the ready availability of local materials and their suitability to local needs. The ceramic boats of the Ganges were made from the abundant clay along the river bank turned on a potter's wheel and left to bake under the hot Indian sun. About 3 ft. (91 cm) in diameter and roughly hemispherical, they were reasonably well adapted for local trade and navigation along that slow-flowing river, and they were incredibly cheap and easy to manufacture. What more could the local boatman want in such circumstances?

The only tangible records of boatbuilding in prehistoric times are the funeral ships unearthed from burial grounds and the working boats recovered from bogs and lakes. They must all date, even the earliest of them, from a fairly recent stage in the long story of man's need for transportation over water; the last few thousand years of a story perhaps a million years old. Yet, if we look at some of the remoter parts of the world today, there is still evidence to be found of how our distant forefathers first conquered the problem of carrying themselves and their possessions across water. On some of the lakes and rivers of Africa men still bind together the branches of trees to make crude rafts; in South America there are still Indian tribes who take to the rivers in tree trunks hollowed out with knives and axes or burned out with fire. It seems that time has stood still for them, and has thus preserved for us a living picture of primitive man's first efforts to conquer the world's waters.

Reed boat from Lake Titicaca in the Andes.

Oared Ships

Until man learned to harness the wind to move his ships he had only his own muscles to provide motive power. Originally he used these muscles to work paddles, but the transition from paddles to oars must have come quite early. The power obtainable from an oar with a fixed fulcrum was far greater than that supplied by a hand-held paddle, and this improvement became a necessity as ships increased in size and weight.

Egyptian Oared Ships

The oldest ship of which we have tangible evidence is the funeral ship of the Pharaoh Cheops, believed to be some 5,000 years old, which was fitted for rowers, not paddlers, though they stood up to pull on their oars. Further records of early Egyptian oared ships are to be found in the reliefs at the rock temple of Deir-el-Bahari, which depict Egyptian trading vessels of about 1500 BC, showing them with 15 rowers on each side. These were fairly large ships, about 100 ft. (30.5 m) in length, and although they also set a single square sail on a mast stepped amidships, the principal motive power was the oars, not the sail. With a mast stepped in this position it would be possible, by bracing the yards, to use the wind if it blew from either beam, for with no depth of keel under the ship the leeway would be very considerable, far too much for any sort of accurate navigation. So we are forced back to the belief that the sail, wherever the mast was stepped, was looked upon purely as an auxiliary means of motive power when the wind served, and that the rowers represented, so to speak, the main engines of the ship. This remained the general pattern of seafaring in Mediterranean waters for thousands of years.

These early oared ships represent quite an advance on primitive shipbuilding techniques. They demonstrate a more or less standard method of construction based upon a strong keel to which were fixed a curved stempiece and sternpost. The degree of curvature of these terminal additions varied considerably; sometimes they were quite tall structures reaching high out of the water, sometimes squat and turning in upon themselves. The hull planking varied according to locality; in Egypt, where there was a shortage of trees suitable for shipbuilding, it consisted of a large number of short pieces of wood either sewn or pegged together into a fairly full-bodied hull shape. It was not until about 1250 BC, when Egypt had become the major trading country of the eastern Mediterranean, that she began to import timber for shipbuilding in substantial quantities. Until then, her ships had been at a disadvantage because they lacked the strength and robustness that only long hull planking could give.

Egyptian ship of the Punt Expedition, c. 1600 BC.

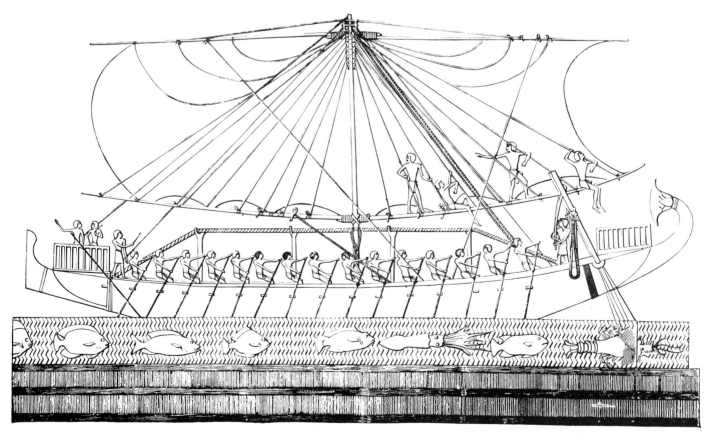

On the evidence of many rock carvings and temple reliefs, the hull planks were held rigidly in position by a racked truss passed right around the top of the hull. This arrangement consisted of two stout ropes about 1 ft. (30 cm) apart, with a thinner rope passed in a zigzag fashion over and under the two ropes, so that the tension could be increased by hauling taut the racking line. Additional longitudinal strength was achieved by a similar hogging truss from bow to stern, raised well above upper deck level on three or four forked wooden supports. The truss was tensioned by a wooden bar in much the same way that the Spanish windlass is used today in ropework to produce tension and power.

In its original form the oared ship of Egypt was without decks; as yet no way had been found to support them. Even though the earliest of these ships carried a single square or rectangular sail on a central mast, they relied for their motive power principally on rowers who stood to their oars since there were no thwarts on which to sit. But quite soon, certainly by 1500 BC, deck beams had made their appearance, for they are clearly shown in the Deir-el-Bahari reliefs of the ships which formed Queen Hatshepsut's expedition to the 'land of Punt,' probably modern Somalia. These deck beams protruded through the hull planking, indicating that they were supported on the hull strakes themselves and not yet on timbers or ribs rising at intervals from the keel. It is not easy to ascertain from these reliefs whether the rowers are standing or sitting to their oars — they are depicted in a sort of half-and-half position — but certainly they are on an upper deck and not on the ship's bottom as was the case before the introduction of deck beams. Once deck beams were fitted, ribs, timbers, and stringers followed quickly as a matter of course; as evidenced by the absence of the racking truss in ships depicted in temple reliefs of about 1200 BC.

The reliefs in the temple at Deir-el-Bahari provide details of another remarkable Egyptian ship of very early date, a vessel specifically built for transporting granite obelisks hewn out of the rock at Aswan down the Nile to Luxor. These massive obelisks stood about 95 ft. (29 m) high and weighed about 350 tons, and it was intended that the ship should carry two of them at a time. One of the scribes at the court of the Pharaoh Thotmes recorded

that the ship was 180 ft. by 50 ft. (55 m × 15 m), but this must be a very rough estimate, for a vessel of these dimensions would be hardly able to support the weight of two obelisks. She might just do so with a reasonable margin of safety on a length of about 200 ft. (61 m) and a beam of about 75 ft. (23 m), but this would be a very large ship for 1500 BC. This particular ship had deck beams on three levels, which implies a measure of design skill remarkable for so early a date.

The depictions of these very early ships all come from Egypt, although she was by no means the only great seafaring nation. It is known that the Arab peoples east of Egypt were also extensive maritime traders, and although they left no pictorial records, it is reasonable to assume that they had progressed at least as far as the Egyptians, particularly since a large part of Egypt's trade at this time was along the shores of the Indian Ocean. The Arabs were also known to be skilled navigators from ancient times, more advanced in this field than the Egyptians — another indication that they must have built ships capable of fairly long sea voyages.

Mycenae and Crete

There were, of course, other nations in the Mediterranean with long seafaring traditions: Phoenicia, the Minoan Empire of Crete, and the Mycenaean civilization of mainland Greece. In the temple of Medinet Habu there is a large relief celebrating a naval victory in the 12th century BC achieved by the Pharaoh Ramses III over the 'northerners of the isles,' who probably came from Greece and possibly from Crete, and certainly the ships of the enemy are shown to be as large and as advanced in construction as the ships of Ramses.

On the island of Thera near Crete is a fresco dating from about 1500 BC that provides the earliest detailed representation of Minoan warships. They are of a similar overall pattern to the warships of Egypt, with a single rectangular sail on a mast stepped a bit forward of amidships and with 44 rowers, 22 each side, probably sitting to their oars on benches below the upper deck level. The earliest picture of a Greek ship is of a much later date, but if, as seems probable, the Minoan Empire was overthrown by the Mycenaeans around 1450 BC, the invading force must have come by sea, and its ships must have been at least as large and as powerful as the ships of Crete. The Minoan war fleet had been the most powerful in the Mediterranean, and had protected Crete's trade effectively against the many pirates of that region. There is evidence that much of Egypt's seaborne trade was also carried on under the protection of Cretan sea power, for only very occasionally do we find evidence of Egyptian warships. Almost all the Egyptian records which still exist, with the exception of the temple carvings at Medinet Habu, represent trading ships.

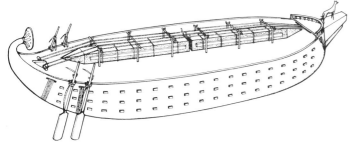

Ship built to transport obelisks down the Nile, c. 1500 BC.

The Phoenician Empire

The time was approaching in the Mediterranean when a single pattern of ship, used both for trade and for war, would begin to be supplanted by two distinct and separate types. There were two reasons to account for the division. The first was man's increasing ability to adapt the sail to differing wind directions and strengths and so to make it the prime mover in place of the oar. The second was the emergence of two new sea powers in the shape of Phoenicia, at the eastern end of the Mediterranean, and the city-states of classical Greece. Both were largely reliant on seaborne trade for their growth and prosperity, and a growing rivalry for control of the established Mediterranean trade routes led the two powers into the development of pure warships to protect their interests and attack those of their enemies.

The Phoenicians were the first in the field by some three or four centuries. Tyre, the principal city-state of Phoenicia, was at that time the richest city in the world, built and maintained almost entirely on seaborne trade. Sidon and the smaller Phoenician ports of Gebel and Arvad came close behind Tyre in wealth and seafaring skills. Bronze was the most important metal of the age, and the Phoenicians had a skill in working metals above that of all other nations. It was the need to import copper and tin, the basic constituents of bronze, which lay at the root of their remarkable seamanship. Finding copper was relatively easy, for the mines of nearby Cyprus could provide all they needed, but the nearest source of tin lay in Spain at the other end of the Mediterranean, and when the Spanish mines were exhausted the Phoenicians had to go even further afield, to Cornwall and the Scilly Islands at the southwestern extremity of Britain.

The Phoenicians developed two types of merchant

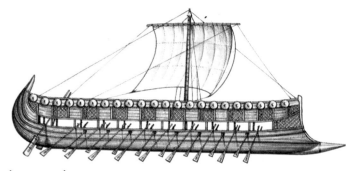

Phoenician bireme.

ships: the small *gaulus* for local trade in the eastern Mediterranean and the larger *hippo* for more distant voyages. These hippos were the vessels that became known throughout the maritime world as ships of Tarshish. No one has ever discovered the site of Tarshish after which these ships were named, and it is possible that the Phoenicians never reached it or even that it was a mythical city. Yet the prophet Ezekiel knew of it, for when prophesying the fall of Tyre he wrote: 'The ships of Tarshish did sing of thee in thy market; and thou wast replenished and made very glorious in the midst of the seas.'

In the early stages of their development both the gaulus and the hippo were generally oared ships, with the single mast and sail providing rest and relief to the rowers when the wind served. It is not known when this pattern changed in merchant ships, but at some period during the years of Phoenician maritime supremacy a second mast with a sail made its appearance and the rowers ceased to supply the main motive power of trading ships. The evidence for this is in the carving that decorates a marble sarcophagus recovered in 1914 from the Old Harbor at Sidon in Lebanon. The ship in the carving has the normal mast stepped amidships together with a second mast, or possibly a very high-steeved bowsprit, right forward in the bows of the ship. Each mast carries a sail laced to a yard. Both yards are shown with braces so that they could be trimmed to the wind, indicating that the two sails were expected to do the main work of driving the ship through the water. The carving shows no oars, nor any provision for rowers, and this is very unusual for a ship of this date.

In the early days of their maritime greatness the Phoenicians had a relatively peaceful passage for their trading ships, needing only to defend them against pirates. But with the emergence of Greece as a sea power, and an adventurous and belligerent Greece at that, they had the wit to realize that their whole prosperity would now depend upon their ability to build ships whose sole purpose was devoted to war, in order to clear the seas of marauding Greek fleets. They set about this new task with all the skills they had developed in building their merchant ships and evolved an entirely new design: they

Phoenician hippo, also known as a ship of Tarshish.

began to build galleys propelled by two banks of oars and armed with a bronze or wooden beak or ram.

These were the first true galleys, forerunners of the Greek BIREMES; indeed the later Greek designs copied them almost exactly. This is in fact the moment at which the warship and the merchant ship begin their separate lines of development. In place of the single, unspecialized ship manned by rowers and using sail whenever the wind served, two distinct types of vessels came into being. To the old design a second mast was added and the result was a merchantman, a sailing ship relying on rowers only when she became becalmed or required precise movements for entering or leaving harbor. The new warship was designed for speed, which only rowers could give, and although she carried a single square sail on a centrally stepped mast, its only purpose was to provide periods of rest to the rowers when the wind blew from abaft the beam. Both sail and mast were invariably lowered before battle, and the galley depended entirely on her rowers to give her speed and maneuverability.

One of the earliest representations of the new type of ship is in a relief from the palace of Sennacherib at Nineveh, dated around 700 BC. It clearly shows the two banks of oars staggered one above the other, while projecting from the bows on the waterline is the ship's main weapon, the long beak. A central bridge superstructure above the hull was manned by archers, who provided a longer-range means of attack.

The design of this original galley is of particular interest because it reveals the knowledge of ship construction and hydrodynamics which these early Phoenician shipbuilders possessed. The length-to-beam ratio of all the trading ships which the Phoenicians had built so far was about 2½ or 3 to 1; in their galleys it was about 6 to 1 and in a few extreme cases 8 to 1. This ratio gave the galley the long, slim hull with which she could achieve the speed necessary to protect the merchant ships under her charge. However, with so little lateral stability there was always a danger of capsizing through excessive rolling, and to avoid this risk the Phoenicians built their galleys with fully planked outrigger extensions on either side, in which sat the slaves pulling the upper bank of oars. When the galley was on an even keel, both these outriggers were above the waterline and so produced no additional skin friction to slow the vessel down, but when she began to roll the outrigger extensions provided the additional beam needed to keep her stable in the water. It seems unlikely that this method of producing reserve stability came about by chance, for there was room within the actual hull to accommodate the two banks of rowers; it was almost certainly a deliberate design feature devised by these skilled shipbuilders of more than 2,600 years ago.

Greek vase found at Vulci in Etruria. The tubby vessel on the left is a merchant ship, on the right is an oared warship with a ram.

The Greeks

The period of Phoenician mastery of the seas lasted for seven centuries. It came to an end in 333 BC, when Alexander the Great attacked Tyre, breached the city walls after a seven-month siege, and scattered the inhabitants, selling 30,000 of them into slavery. For a few years the Phoenician trading empire fell under the sway of Carthage, a city-state originally colonized by the Phoenicians, but it was to Greece rather than to Carthage that dominance of the Mediterranean eventually passed. With the Phoenician galley as their model the Greeks built their famous *penteconters*, and with these, and later with their TRIREMES, which were larger developments of the penteconter, they dominated the Mediterranean until they, in their turn, succumbed to the advance of Roman sea power a few centuries later.

The story of Jason's search for the Golden Fleece in the *Argo* provides us with a contemporary account of the appearance and construction of a penteconter. In a description of the Greek fleet, Homer wrote that these ships were 'black,' 'hollow,' and 'benched.' This is clarified in the account of the *Argo*'s construction. Apparently she was built of pine planks shaped with axes and was coated inside and out with pitch, which would have given her a 'black' appearance. Since she had no deck she was 'hollow.' Her top strake was pierced for 50 oars and her

rowers sat on thwarts; so she was 'benched.' She was therefore typical of a Greek galley of the 6th century BC, with an overall length of about 80 ft. (24 m) and a beam of about 14 ft. (4 m). She was built mainly for trade, and her voyage was to the Euxine (Black) Sea for the 'Golden Fleece': probably sheepskins weighted down on the bottom of the rivers to catch the grains of gold washed down in the fast-running water. There was nothing unusual in using a galley for trade, and Herodotus reports that on many of the Greek trading voyages the ships employed 'were not the round-built merchant ship but the long penteconter.' The Greek maritime traders of this period were always aggressive, and if they happened to cross the path of another merchant ship, they had no hesitation in attacking her, seizing her cargo, and capturing her crew to sell as slaves at the next port of call. For this they needed speed to overtake their victim, and a penteconter gave them all the speed they needed.

War was never far away during the time the Greeks held sway in the Mediterranean. There were wars between individual Greek states, wars against Carthage, wars against the Persians, and finally wars against the Romans. In its original form the penteconter was too light and fragile a vessel to stand up to the strains of pitched battle. Again the Greeks followed the Phoenicians' example and adopted the arrangement of two

Greek trireme: inset shows alternative positions of rowers.

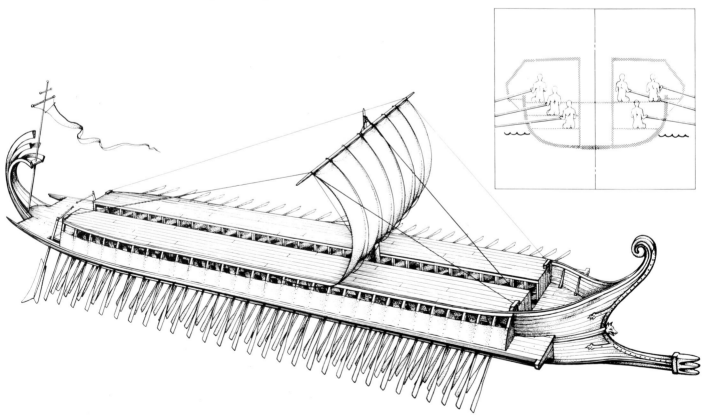

banks of oars for their galleys. The result was the bireme, but it was built lighter than the Phoenician model and the two outriggers were used not to accommodate rowers but merely to provide a fulcrum for the upper bank of oars. The main attack weapon was the ram projecting from the bow, and above the rowers was built a longitudinal bridge, known as the *kakastroma*, for the archers and stone slingers. The bireme was evolved at the beginning of the 6th century BC, and for the next 100 years or so it fulfilled the Greek requirements for attack and defense at sea. But in the course of time, and with the ever-increasing severity of sea warfare, the bireme became a poor match for the heavier warships being produced by other nations, and consequently the design was expanded into the trireme, the most formidable ship of war which the Mediterranean had yet seen. The trireme was a remarkable fighting ship, concentrating a great amount of offensive power into what was still a relatively small hull.

The uncovering of dry docks at Munychiam and Zea, which were used for the repair of triremes damaged in battle, provides the best information on this galley's dimensions. The docks measured approximately 150 ft. by 20 ft. (46 m × 6 m), which means that the galley herself must have measured about 130 ft. (40 m) in overall length including the ram, and 16 ft. (5 m) in beam. Since the ram extended for 10 ft. (3 m) beyond the stem, the length of the actual hull structure would have been about 120 ft. (37 m). We know from contemporary records that the hull accommodated 170 rowers divided into *thranites*, who pulled the top bank of 14-ft. (4.3-m) oars, *zygites* pulling the middle bank of 10½-ft. (3.2-m) oars, and *thalamites* pulling the lower bank of 7½-ft. (2.3-m) oars. With a hull of this size and with this number of rowers, the galley would be able to achieve a maximum speed of about 8 knots in calm waters, when the rowers were encouraged, probably with whips, to produce their utmost effort. In addition to the rowers, a trireme carried five officers and 25 petty officers, making a total crew of 200. When mobilized for battle, extra marines in heavy armor were stationed on the upper deck to form boarding parties for the capture of enemy galleys.

The hull design was remarkably well conceived to produce a maximum of stability, strength, and speed. It incorporated the Phoenician principle of outrigger compartments running nearly the full length of the hull. These were pierced for the top bank of oars, providing the fulcrum for the thranite rowers. The galley was steered with two vertical steering oars at the stern, one on each side, and was further maneuverable by backing the oars on one side for a very quick turn. To absorb the force of ramming an enemy, the keel was extended to form the basis of the ram and was further strengthened by two thick wales running the whole length of the galley at the turn of the bilge and similarly extended to join the keel at the base of

the ram. This was a three-toothed projection covered in metal, usually bronze. Above this main ram was another, formed by bringing the upper wales together on the bow, and this too was covered with metal. The object of the upper ram was to push the enemy over once the hull had been pierced by the main ram. All the rowers were positioned below the deck to give them protection from enemy arrows.

The Greek biremes and triremes proved their superiority at the Battle of Salamis in 480 BC, when they fought a much larger Persian fleet. The Greek fleet, under the command of Themistocles, was drawn up in the bay of Eleusis, which is open to the sea only through two narrow channels. Here they were found by the Persian fleet, commanded by Xerxes, and with his considerable superiority in numbers he decided to attack at once, confident of success. But he had not reckoned with the speed and maneuverability of the Greek galleys. In such narrow waters, the Persian ships, jammed together in their eagerness to attack and unable to use their oars, were easy targets for the Greek triremes. The more lightly built Greek galleys swiftly drew alongside, sheared off the enemy's oars with their rams, and then pushed them over, demonstrating the classic tactics of galley warfare. The Greeks sank over 200 Persian ships for a loss to themselves of just 40 vessels.

Inevitably, the great success of the trireme led both the Greeks themselves and other maritime nations to build yet larger warships. For the next five centuries Greece, Carthage, and Rome fought for control of Mediterranean trade routes, and since the oared galley was the only form of warship in existence, the only possible development was an increase in size. The trireme evolved into the quadrireme and the quinquireme, and there is mention in contemporary records of warships being built with up to 16 banks of oars, which is at the very least highly unlikely. There is also an account of a *tesseraconteres*, a huge Roman galley with 40 banks of oars, built for Ptolemy Philopater of Egypt, and it is said that it used 4,000 rowers.

How these multibanked ships could have operated has long been a puzzle. In one of the great tesseraconteres, for example, a simple calculation can demonstrate that the rower on the top bank would have needed an oar of the impossible length of 53 ft. (16 m) to reach the water, if in fact there were 16 banks of oars. The puzzle arises because of the long-held belief that each oar had only one man to pull it. What is far more probable is that these galleys were described by the number of rowers used on each set of three oars. A quinquireme, for example, would have had two men on both the longer top and middle oars and one pulling the short bottom oar, five men in all on the set of three oars. This is the only possible solution of the puzzle which will fit the galley's known dimensions.

Throughout almost the whole of the Carthaginian and

Roman eras war galleys grew progressively larger in size and more massive in construction. While they all relied on the ram as their principal weapon, some had additional means of attack mounted on board. Many of the larger Roman galleys, for example, carried catapults that hurled great stones and rocks a considerable distance. Many were also fitted with a hinged wooden gangway or bridge, known as a *corvus*, which was secured vertically to the mast and could be dropped on the deck of an enemy ship in order to board her.

The Battle of Actium, a galley action fought in 31 BC between the Roman fleet of Octavian and the Egyptian fleet of Mark Antony and Cleopatra for control of the Roman world, proved that the heavily built, multibanked galley, for so long considered the acme of oared warships, could be outmaneuvered and defeated by more mobile vessels of lighter construction. While the Romans continued to build a few of the huge multibanked galleys because they had faith in the effectiveness of their long-range catapults, they also built large numbers of the lighter galleys,

known as *liburnians*, from a design evolved in the Adriatic. From this model they developed two sizes of galleys called *dromons*, of which the larger pulled two banks of oars and the smaller a single bank. What these two types lacked in weapon power — they were too small to carry a catapult or a corvus — they more than made up with their speed and ability to turn almost in their own length. In an attempt to combine the speed of a dromon with the weapon power of a heavy galley, the Romans introduced longer oars with as many as seven men on each, hoping that this extra leverage on the water would produce the additional speed required, but these huge oars were too cumbersome even for seven men to handle efficiently.

The galley remained the principal warship of Mediterranean nations long after other navies had discarded the oared ship in favor of sail; its use lasted in fact well into the 17th century. The famous Battle of Lepanto, which took place in 1571 between a Turkish fleet and a combined Christian fleet, was probably the last great naval engagement fought between galleys. Six GALLEASSES, or

The Battle of Actium (31 BC), showing Cleopatra withdrawing from the fighting.

sailing galleys, figured among the Christian fleet, but these heavy and unwieldy hybrids were of little importance in a collection of more than 200 galleys rowed by 43,000 oarsmen, facing an even larger Turkish fleet.

One of the best known builders of galleys during the middle and late 16th century was the Venetian Per Theodoro de Nicolo, and in the Biblioteca Nazionale in Venice are preserved his manuscript instructions for building war galleys. They show that even at this late stage of warship development three sizes of galleys were still being built. The smallest of the three was the *fusta*, 88 ft. 6 in. (27 m) in overall length, with a beam of 13 ft. (4 m) and a depth of 4 ft. 6 in. (1.4 m). The largest had an overall length of 151 ft. (46 m), a beam of 24 ft. 6 in. (7.5 m), and a depth of 10 ft. (3 m). All the Mediterranean galleys from first to last were carvel-built, with the hull planks laid edge to edge, so that the outside of the hull formed a smooth curve from keel to gunwale.

The Oared Ship in Northern Waters

The development of the oared ship in northern waters took a different direction from that of her Mediterranean counterpart. Like the galley, she was used mainly for fighting, or more accurately, raiding, but also for coastal and river trade. The early examples are best represented by the funeral ship discovered in a burial mound at Oseberg Farm, near Tonsberg in Norway, in 1904. This famous ship, dating from about AD 800, has an overall length of 70 ft. (21.3 m), and is constructed of oak planks overlap-

Galley of 1625, with guns mounted in a platform on the bow.

ping each other in the fashion that would today be called clinker building. She is pierced to row 15 oars each side, but there are no built-in thwarts, which suggests that the rowers sat on sea chests when pulling on their oars. She drew very little water and had a considerable beam for her length. A square sail set on a single mast helped her along when the wind served, and she was steered by means of a steering oar operated by a short inboard tiller. She was probably a ship of the type known as a *karfi*, a lightly built

Papal galley from Cressentio's Nautica
Mediterranea, *1601.*

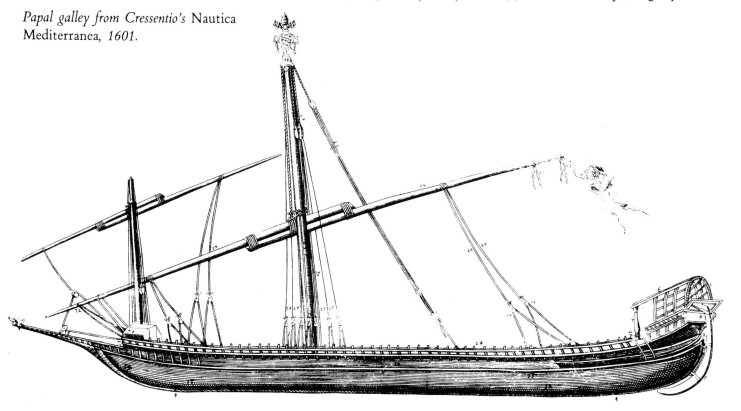

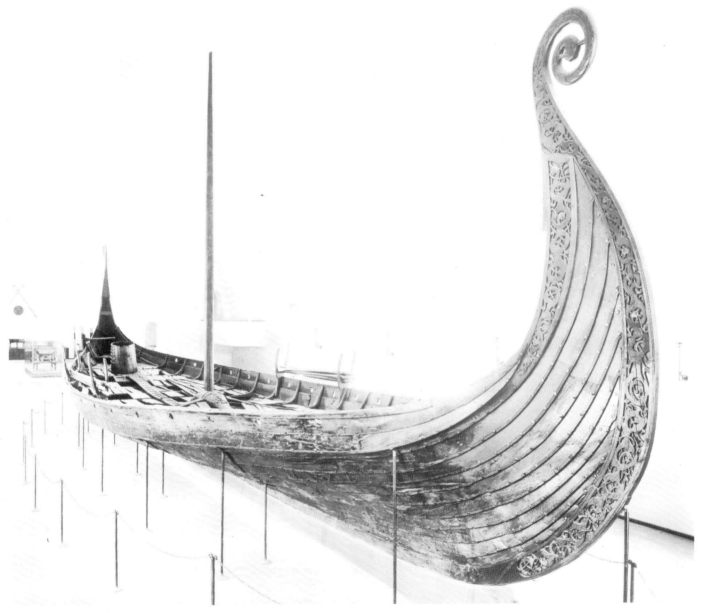

The Oseberg ship (AD 800), discovered in a burial mound in Norway and now housed in Oslo Museum.

vessel used on estuaries and lakes and capable of being carried across marshes or sandbanks when necessary.

Similar development was taking place in England, as illustrated by the royal burial ship excavated at Sutton Hoo, near Ipswich, Suffolk. She is earlier than the Oseberg ship, dating from about AD 650. Unlike her Norwegian counterpart, she had no mast or sail and was propelled solely by oars. She follows very much the same general lines of construction with the hull planks overlapping each other. No doubt this departure from the Mediterranean pattern was dictated by the fact that Mediterranean waters are generally smooth, while those of the North Sea and eastern Atlantic are mainly rough and choppy, conditions in which the overlapping of the hull strakes would provide a stabilizing effect.

The period of Norwegian dominance of northern waters which we loosely call the Viking era began in about AD 800 and lasted for nearly five centuries. It was based on the LONGSHIP, one of the most famous warships or raiding ships of early ship history. The longship was clearly developed from the earlier trading ships of which the Oseberg ship is an example. A prototype of the longship was discovered in a burial mound on Gokstad Farm, near Sandefjord, but though the construction shows all the typical features, she is too small to have been used for distant raiding. Her keel, sternpost, and stempost are cut from a solid block of timber and her 16 strakes of oak planking are fixed together with rivets. She is 76 ft. (23.2 m) long, with a beam of 16 ft. (4.9 m), and is built with a relatively high freeboard of 6 ft. (1.8 m), and with the typically elegant high curved bow and stern of the longship. She is pierced for 16 oars a side and again there

The Gokstad ship (AD 900), constructed of 16 oak strakes riveted together.

are no fixed thwarts for the rowers. However, the oars are set too low down in the hull for the rowers to have stood to them and, like the Oseberg ship, the assumption is that the rowers sat on their sea chests or else had removable benches. The hull planking is caulked with tarred rope, and there is a pine mast 40 ft. (12.2 m) long which would have set a single square sail with a spread of about 16 ft. (5 m). When she was uncovered in the burial mound she had 32 circular shields on each side, and this perhaps explains why so many modern drawings of galleys show these shields arrayed along the gunwales. In fact, they were displayed only in harbor, probably for recognition purposes, and were never mounted at sea.

Although the Gokstad ship is too small to be considered a true longship, she shows the path Norse boatbuilders were taking in their search for an ideal ship for war and distant raiding. She also demonstrates the high degree of constructional excellence that always characterized the longship. The urge to develop larger ships was largely attributable to the long series of internecine wars fought in the Baltic during the 10th century AD, and also to the

Norwegian's increasing reliance on the sea as a source of plunder and profit.

There is much information to be found about these longships in the writings of the *Skalds*, whose long poems, or sagas, tell us so much about the period. We know, for example, that the *rum* was a basis of ship measurement, one rum being the amount of space between two adjacent crossbeams. There was one thwart to each rum, and in the larger longships, those of 30-32 rum, two rowers sat each side of the centerline to man the oars, pulling two to each oar. These big longships, built to a length of about 150 ft. (45.7 m) and a beam of 20 ft. (6.1 m), were known as *skeids* or *drakars*, and carried a total complement of 180 men. In the smaller longships, known as *skutas*, only one rower pulled on each oar.

The sagas of the Skalds even record the names of the men who built these longships. One of them, named Torberg, was the builder of perhaps the best known of all the longships, Olaf Tryggvesson's *Ormrinn Langi*, or *Long Serpent*, a drakar of 34 rum. 'Of all the ships in Norway,' wrote Snorre the Skald, 'she was the best made and at the

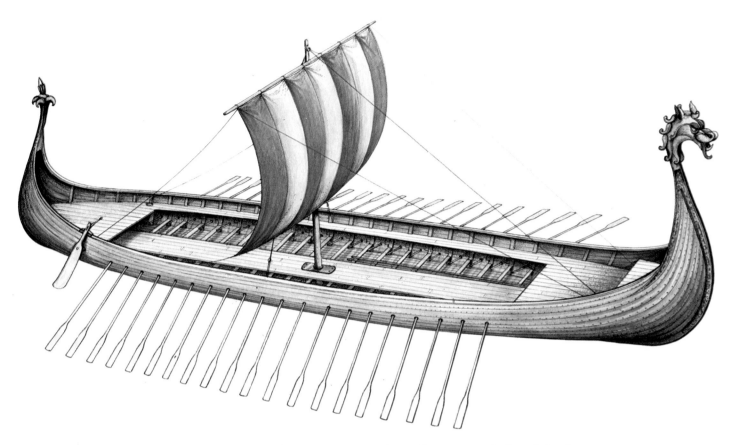

A Viking longship. Ships of this kind reputedly sailed across the Atlantic five centuries before Columbus.

greatest cost.' Other famous longships of this period were Harald Hardrada's *Buza*, King Haakon's *Kristsuden*, and Olaf Haraldsson's *Visunden*.

The great series of northern voyages which began with Eric the Red in 984 came about almost accidentally. For nearly 200 years the Vikings had terrorized western Europe, crossing the North Sea and passing through the English Channel to the coasts of France and Spain, plundering and holding the local inhabitants to ransom as they went. They were virtually unopposed, for no other northern nation had ships which could match their longships for speed. But in time the English, French, and Scottish kings realized that only by engaging the Vikings at sea with equal or superior ships could they break free of the intolerable burden of their raids. So they too built longships, even bigger and faster than those of the Vikings, and for a time they kept these enemies at bay. The Viking answer was to add additional strakes to their hulls and raise the freeboard of their longships by about 2 ft. (60 cm), so that the archers carried on board could fire their arrows downwards into any enemy longship that tried to deny their passage.

It was this increase in the freeboard of the longship that made possible the new voyages into the more distant waters of the Atlantic. They started when Eric the Red was arraigned for murder in 984 and fled to Iceland to escape the charge. There he heard from a trader that land

had been sighted further west, and when he found this new land he called it Greenland. In the summer of 985 he set out with a small group of settlers, rounded Cape Farewell, and set up a colony near what is now the town of Julianehaab. In 999 his son Leif ERICSSON went to Norway and obtained from Olaf Tryggvesson a commission to established Christianity in Greenland. On his return there in 1000 he heard tales of how a trader named Biarni Heriulfsson had been blown off course and sighted land even further to the west. He decided to set out in this direction and in 1001 returned with an account of having reached the land sighted by Heriulfsson, landing at Helluland (now believed to be Baffin Island), Markland (probably Labrador), and Vinland (reputedly Newfoundland). All this is set out in the saga known as the Flatey Book, and we have little reason to doubt its veracity. There is, moreover, tangible evidence to support this story in the Norse runes which were found on rocks in these locations. And it was not only across the Atlantic that they made these tremendous voyages; Viking fleets were reported in Barcelona, Pisa, Rome, Venice, and even Constantinople during the height of their maritime supremacy, when they held much of Europe to ransom.

These were remarkable voyages for longships to make, particularly when we remember that they were undecked vessels, or at best possibly half-decked. But with the longship's strong construction and long flowing lines, and the fine seamanship of the crews, these voyages were well within the compass of these magnificent ships and experienced seamen. Unquestionably they used their single square sail whenever they could to rest the rowers, and this sail had been improved by the invention of the *beitass*, a wooden boom attached to the foot of the mast and used to stretch the tack of the sail forward, enabling it to be used even with the wind slightly ahead of the beam. However, the longship remained essentially an oared ship.

The longship was not solely a Scandinavian ship, even though the design originated there. The ships which King Alfred of England built to stop the Danes invading England were longships, and so too were the ships which William of Normandy used to transport his army across the English Channel in 1066. The Venetian gondola, which was mentioned in records as early as 1094 and is still in use today, owes something to the original longship design in her flowing lines and general configuration.

Something of the longship influence can also be seen in the ceremonial barges which used to be so colorful a feature of national days of celebration. Perhaps they originated on the Nile with the voyages made by the pharaohs; certainly Cleopatra had a barge of great magnificence, rowed, if we can believe Shakespeare, with silver oars. In England such barges were first known as snakes, a phonetic translation of the Scandinavian *esnecca*, an 8th-century longship, and both Henry I and Henry II are recorded as having their own snakes for use on ceremonial occasions during the 12th century.

Probably the most famous of all state barges was the *Bucentaur*, the great barge in which the Doge of Venice made his annual ceremonial wedding of the sea. Her name was a contraction of *buzino d'ore*, barque of gold, and she was indeed a golden ship, much of her hull and upper wales gilded with gold leaf. She was rowed with 21 oars each side, each oar being pulled by four workmen from the Arsenale. There is a model of the second and last *Bucentaur* in the Arsenale Museum in Venice, and she occupies a prominent place in Canaletto's famous picture of the Venetian scene on the day of the Doge's symbolic annual wedding ceremony.

During the 17th century the use of ceremonial barges spread from royalty to various guilds and livery companies as well as to the East India companies of a number of countries. By then they were essentially river craft used in processions, water pageants, carnivals, or any other occasion requiring a parade of splendor or ostentation. As a rule they were magnificently decorated, with a large canopied cabin in which sat the exalted owners, as often as not with a feast spread before them, while the rowers, dressed in scarlet or cloth of gold, pulled at their oars in the forward half of the barge.

Their day ended when steam was brought to river traffic, the black smoke from early boilers proving unpalatable to the lordly travelers in their decorated barges. One of the last occasions when barges were seen in profusion on the River Thames in England was when the body of Lord Nelson was brought up the river from Greenwich to Whitehall on January 8, 1806, in a stately procession of 17 ceremonial barges.

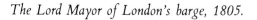

The Lord Mayor of London's barge, 1805.

The Development of Sailing Ships

The desire to use the wind to drive a vessel over the water must be nearly as old as the boat itself, and even before sails were invented men would hold up leafy branches to catch the wind and impart motion to their primitive craft. The earliest illustrations of ships under sail (and indeed of any boats) come from rock carvings and pottery decorations found in the Nile valley. A pottery bowl of 3100 BC, for example, clearly shows a boat with a single square sail set on a mast positioned forward in the bows. These very early ships relied on oars for their motive power, although a sail was sometimes used when the wind served to assist the rowers.

It is possible, and even probable, that the Egyptians were not the first to use sails made of cloth or animal skins. Further east, Chinese and Arab civilizations, which certainly coexisted with and possibly predated that of Egypt, were both well known in ancient history as seafaring peoples. We have to take Egypt as our baseline simply because it is there that the earliest records exist.

Early Egyptian illustrations show the mast and single sail of ships set well up in the bows, which proves that initially the sail was used only when the wind blew from astern. If the ship needed to go in any direction other than directly before the wind, she could do so only under oars. But in the later rock carvings, certainly in those of 1500 BC at Deir-el-Bahari, the mast is shown stepped amidships, and there are braces on the yard from which the single square sail was set. It is certain, therefore, that by this date Egyptian seamen had discovered that if a sail is set at an acute angle to the wind the ship will move forward, even when the wind is blowing from abeam or slightly forward of it. The Deir-el-Bahari reliefs also show rowers pulling on oars while the sail is set, which was

Model of the earliest seagoing ship, taken from an Egyptian relief of 3000 BC.

probably the recognized method of ship propulsion in those days. Slaves in Egypt were plentiful, and if their labor could provide an extra turn of speed above that achieved by the sail alone, it would make sense from the shipmaster's point of view to use them to the full. (For further discussion of Egyptian ships see the preceding chapter on *Oared Ships*.)

Sailing Merchant Ships of the Ancient World

It is to the Phoenicians that we must turn to find the first real sailing ship. They were great traders and workers in metal, and their expeditions for raw materials took them not only across the whole of the Mediterranean from east to west but also, particularly in their search for tin, as far afield as Cornwall, the Scilly Islands, and the Canary Islands. To accommodate their ever-growing trade they built two types of ship, a small ship known as a *gaulus* for trade in the eastern half of the Mediterranean and a bigger ship known as a *hippo* (or 'Ship of Tarshish') for more distant voyages. The earliest development of the hippo can be seen in a 13th-century BC mural painting on a tomb at Thebes, which shows a fairly large ship with a square sail set between an upper and lower yard on a centrally stepped mast. The painting shows a ship fully decked from bow to stern with a hull built fairly deep to give considerable cargo stowage. She had no bulwarks but was fitted with a rail set on stanchions along her gunwales, probably to prevent any additional deck cargo from sliding overboard when the ship rolled. The length-to-beam ratio was about 2 to 1 and there were two cargo hatches on deck for access to the holds, which ran the full length of the ship. She was pierced for oars, which is what one

Model of a Roman cargo ship, 2nd century AD.

would expect in a vessel with a single square sail on a centrally stepped mast, for oars would certainly be required for going directly to windward or for entering or leaving harbor. She was steered with two steering oars, one on each quarter.

The next significant development of the hippo came some three or four centuries later. The evidence of this change is a carving on a marble sarcophagus which was recovered in 1914 from the Old Harbor at Sidon in the Lebanon. This shows a ship with two masts, one centrally placed in the normal position, the other stepped right forward in the bows and raked steeply forward, much in the fashion of a very high-steeved bowsprit. The forward mast is shown to carry a square sail, similar to the spritsail set below the bowsprit on most sailing ships up to the 17th century. The central mast carries the normal square sail of the time, although both this and the spritsail are laced to a single upper yard and not between an upper and lower yard as in the earlier hippo. The usual two steering oars are shown, but in this carving the ship is not pierced for rowers. This may be an omission on the part of the carver, for although it might just be possible to sail such a two-masted rig without oars, it is most unlikely at this very early stage of ship development that any ship would have gone to sea without them.

An interesting detail in this carving is that the ship is shown with what looks like a low aftercastle which projects beyond the sternpost. It reminds one of the built-up sterns of the Spanish carrack design of 2,000 years later. Another modern feature is the raising of the cargo hatch above deck level, and yet another is the way the shrouds of the mainmast appear to lead to deadeyes, presumably so that they could be drawn taut. In the face of all this apparent modernity it is perhaps no surprise to see that the ship carries a small boat, perhaps a lifeboat, on deck.

The Phoenicians were by repute exceptionally skilled seamen; they were the first western seamen to use the Pole star for navigation and regularly to make long voyages out of sight of land. In addition to their well-authenticated voyages to the Canary Islands and to southern England in search of tin, they are credited with a circumnavigation of Africa in about 600 BC during the reign of Pharaoh Necho II, who commissioned them to man an Egyptian expedition for this purpose. Herodotus later cast doubt on the truth of the story when he wrote, 'They told things believable perhaps for others but unbelievable for me, namely that in sailing around Libya (Africa) they had the sun on the right side.' In fact this remark of Herodotus seems to confirm that the voyage actually did take place, for south of the equator the sun would be on the right side as the expedition sailed westward around the southern tip of Africa.

After the fall of Tyre the Phoenician trading empire fell mainly into the hands of the Greeks and Carthaginians, then the Romans. So far as we know neither Greece nor Carthage adopted the two-masted rig of the later Phoenician hippo but continued to rely on the single centrally stepped mast with its one square sail. The evidence for this rests mainly on the decoration of a number of contemporary Greek vases which show their merchant ships under sail, sometimes pursued by a galley bent on capture. These ships, if one can judge by the length of yard and the size of the sail, were a good deal smaller than the Phoenician hippos, perhaps about 50 ft. (15 m) in length and with a beam of about 14 ft. (4 m). Most of them are shown with a curved overhanging bow, high bulwarks, and a long light bridge running the full length of the deck. They were fairly deep-draft vessels, able to carry a considerable cargo in their holds as well as an additional load on deck.

Although this is the type of ship most often depicted in pottery decoration, it would be wrong to assume that all Greek and Carthaginian sailing merchant ships followed the same pattern. Shipbuilding was still very much a local trade and each district, and probably each individual port, had its own characteristic features. The most one can say is that the Mediterranean sailing merchant ship of the period was a solidly built, short, tubby vessel designed to carry the maximum cargo with the shortest possible keel. Interestingly, the curved overhanging bow of this design closely resembles the clipper bow of later centuries; the same bow shape is still to be seen in many Mediterranean fishing boats today, particularly around the coasts of Greece and Italy.

After the defeat of Greece and Carthage, the Roman Empire covered almost the whole of the Mediterranean from north to south and from east to west, and in order to keep this vast area in subjection and supplied with food and materials a powerful fighting navy and an extensive merchant fleet were required. We know quite a lot about these ships because when Lake Nemi in the Alban Hills near Rome was drained in 1932, two large hulls were found lying in the mud at the bottom. One was of a war galley and the other of a merchant ship. The galley was enormous, about 235 ft. (72 m) long with a beam over the outriggers of 110 ft. (34 m). It is thought to have been a 15-banked ship, i.e., a trireme with 15 rowers on each set of three oars. The merchant ship was equally large, 240 ft. (73 m) in overall length with a beam of 47 ft. (14 m), which gave her a remarkable length-to-beam ratio of 5 to 1. Her hull was more damaged than that of the galley and there were no clues as to the number of masts, though certainly she would have needed more than one on a hull of that length. The mystery about these ships is why they should have been built on a lake high up in the hills, and it has been suggested that they were constructed there as playthings of the Roman court. This might perhaps explain the high length-to-beam ratio of the merchant ship in days when the normal ratio was 3 or 4 to 1; she was more slimly built to give a little extra speed to thrill the courtiers. But what does emerge from the discovery of these two hulls is the great skill of the Roman shipbuilders, particularly in judging the dimensions of beams and timbers necessary to provide adequate strength for ships of this size. Both ships were of a highly sophisticated design considering their antiquity. Roman coins found inside them suggest that they were probably built during the reign of the Emperor Caligula in the 2nd century AD. Sadly, both ships were destroyed during World War II.

We also have a description of a Roman grain ship of about this date written by Lucian, the Greek satirist, after a visit to the harbor of Piraeus. 'What a tremendous vessel it was!' he wrote, '120 cubits long, as the ship's carpenter told me, and more than 30 cubits across the beam, and 29 cubits from the deck to the deepest part of the hold. [This would make her dimensions about 150 ft. by 45 ft. by 44 ft. (46 m × 13.7 m × 13.4 m).] And the height of the mast and the yard it bore, and the forestays that were necessary to keep it upright! And how the stern rose in a graceful curve ending in a gilt goosehead, in harmony with the equal curve of the bow and the forepost with its picture of Isis, the goddess who had given the ship her name! All was unbelievable, the decoration, paintings, red topsail, the anchors with their windlasses, and the cabins in the stern. The crew was like an army. They told me she could carry enough grain to satisfy every mouth in Athens for an entire year. And the whole fortune of the ship is in the hands of a little old man who moves the great rudders with a tiller no thicker than a stick.'

This is the first mention of a topsail, and although Lucian mentions only one mast, it is probable that she had two at least, and possibly three. There is a relief at Ostia which shows a two-masted merchant ship with the triangular topsails set above the square mainsail, and other evidence shows that in the larger merchant ships a third mast was appearing abaft the other two. Indeed, these Roman trading ships were so large that they would have

been difficult to manage without a three-masted rig.

In the years preceding the downfall of the Roman Empire in the Mediterranean there was a considerable trade in the import of marble and obelisks to beautify the imperial city. Vessels even bigger than the grain ships were required, and there is a 3rd-century mosaic in Rome which shows one of them entering harbor. One interesting feature of the illustration is a stern galley built out beyond the sternpost and shaded by an awning for the use of important passengers or the captain. But more significant is the sturdy three-masted rig with a square sail on each mast and the sail on the central mast surmounted by a triangular topsail which was known as a *supparum*. These were the ships which introduced the three-masted rig which was to hold sway among the big sailing ships of the world for the next 1,600 years.

Developments in Northern Waters

It is difficult to know for certain when the sailing ship first appeared in northern European waters. The pictorial stones at Gotland in Sweden, which are thought to date

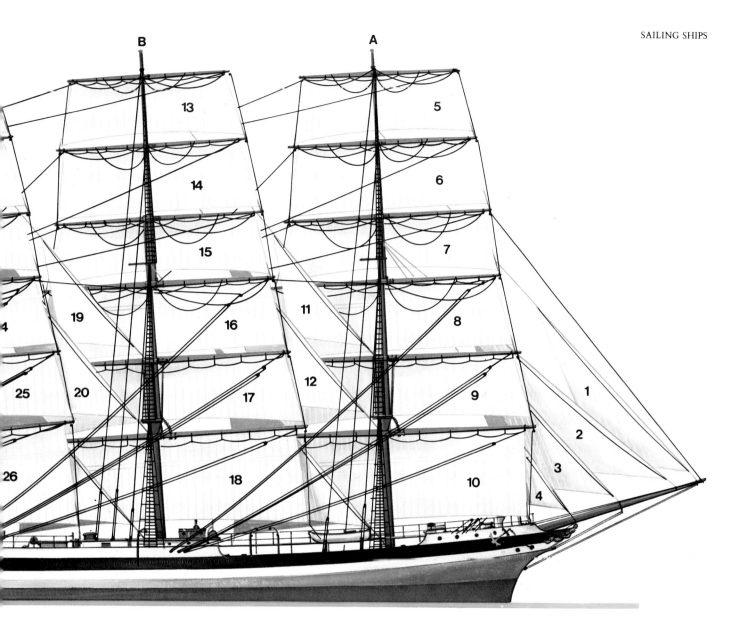

from about the 7th century AD, show a sailing vessel of a different shape from normal Scandinavian construction, with a bow and stern rising at almost right angles from the keel. She is shown with a square sail set on a short mast in the center of the vessel and laced to an upper and lower yard. Two sheets lead to bridles on the lower yard, one on each side of the mast. The sail has a diamond pattern; we know that the reason for this is that the sail was made from a homespun cloth which, because it became loose and baggy when set, was reinforced diagonally in both directions with strips of animal hide. Julius Caesar, in his account of his conquest of Gaul, noted that the English and Veneti ships with which he had to do battle 'used skins and a sort of thin pliant leather for sails, either because they lacked canvas and were ignorant of the art of making sailcloth or more probably because they believed that canvas sails were not so fit to bear the stress of tempests . . . and to drive ships of that bulk and burden.'

However, these were not sailing ships but GALLEYS using the traditional single square sail. Nor can we be sure that the ship pictured on the Gotland stones was a true

The sails of the four-masted bark Herzogin Cecilie:

(A) foremast; (B) mainmast; (C) mizzenmast; (D) bonaventure mizzen or jigger; (1) flying jib; (2) outer jib; (3) inner jib; (4) fore staysail; (5) fore royal; (6) fore upper topgallant sail; (7) fore lower topgallant sail; (8) fore upper topsail; (9) fore lower topsail; (10) foresail or forecourse; (11) main topgallant staysail; (12) main staysail; (13) main royal; (14) main upper topgallant sail; (15) main lower topgallant sail; (16) main upper topsail; (17) main lower topsail; (18) mainsail or main course; (19) mizzen topgallant staysail; (20) mizzen staysail; (21) mizzen royal; (22) mizzen upper topgallant sail; (23) mizzen lower topgallant sail; (24) mizzen upper topsail; (25) mizzen lower topsail; (26) mizzen sail or mizzen course; (27) jigger topmast staysail; (28) jigger topgallant staysail; (29) jigger staysail; (30) spanker topsail; (31) upper spanker; (32) lower spanker.

sailing ship and not an oared ship with a sail, although the novelty of her design does indicate that she was not a longship. It is certain that as early as the 9th century AD sailing ships embarked on voyages in northern waters without the use of rowers, for it was then that two Danish seamen, Oddr and Wulfstan, were sent by King Alfred of England to discover the northern limits of Scandinavia. Apparently they reached the mouth of the River Dvina in the White Sea before turning back, and claimed to have seen sailing vessels hunting whales off the north Norwegian coast. While we have no details of their ships, nor of the whaling ships they encountered, we can be certain that they were not oared ships.

The Cog of the Middle Ages

As was the case in the Mediterranean, the northern sailing ship developed in design and grew in size to cope with a growing seaborne trade. The first great stimulus for northern merchant seafarers was the formation of the Hanseatic League in about 1240. This began as a loose federation of German towns along the Baltic coast with the aim of centralizing trade in that sea, but it soon spread westward to embrace towns on the North Sea coast, including some in Holland, England, and then Norway, in order to gain control of the growing trade there in iron, copper, timber, and fish. As the Hanseatic League expanded during the 14th and early 15th centuries, it was able, by virtue of its federated strength, to bargain for preferential treatment and even for monopoly in some of the trade it handled. However, towards the end of the 15th century industrial growth in Europe led to the establishment of companies of merchant adventurers that effectively broke the League's monopoly of trade.

At the height of its powers, this centralization of trade in the hands of the Hanse towns encouraged the building of larger and better ships. While there was no central

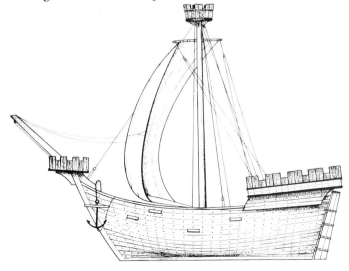

Hansa cog of the mid-14th century.

direction as to the design of ship each Hanse town should build to carry its particular goods, there was a general exchange of information about the kind of ships being built and their performance in the conditions of the North Sea and the Baltic. From this information evolved a type of ship particularly adapted to the rough waters of the North Sea, and although each individual town probably incorporated some small feature that it considered important, in its general lines the ship became more or less of a standard design that spread beyond the Hanse towns to all the nations which bordered the North Sea.

This ship was the Hansa COG and she is depicted on most of the town seals of ports in which she was built. The cogs built in the Hanse towns had a long straight keel from which a straight stem rose at an angle of about 60°, with a similar straight stern rising at an angle of about 75°. This is a distinct departure from the curved bows and sterns which were prominent features of the longship and, of course, of all the ships built in the Mediterranean. It is also a somewhat surprising design feature as it would tend to make a ship hard-headed and apt to hang when tacking against the wind. When the cog design was taken up by English shipbuilders they gave it a curved bow that joined the keel a good deal further aft, and this no doubt made the ship much more weatherly as a result. The straight bow and stern certainly made construction more simple and cut building time, but the consequent lack of sailing qualities, particularly when the sea was rough, was a heavy price to pay. As in the early Egyptian ships, the deck beams were carried through the hull planking to provide additional structural strength.

Though there is little recorded evidence of the dimensions of the Hansa cog, it would seem that the average trading cog built to cross the North Sea was about 100 ft by 25 ft. by 10 ft. (30.5 m × 7.5 m × 3 m), which in modern measurement terms would give her a tonnage of about 280. The average English cog was slightly smaller and a good deal broader, with a tonnage of about 240. The somewhat tubby design of the English cog gave her another generic name of 'roundship,' and in time this name spread to most of the ships built in England, which at this period were usually much wider in the beam than the ships of other northern nations. All cogs had a single central mast with a square sail about 2,000 sq. ft. (186 m²) in area; they are depicted fitted with a set of reef points along the foot of the sail. This shows that in heavy weather demanding a reef, the foot of the sail was bunched up and secured by the reef points instead of the more normal method of square-sail reefing, which was to tie the reef in to the yard from which the sail was set. Sails were tanned with a dressing made from bark to inhibit rot, and by now hemp rope had replaced the original strips of hide used for the rigging.

Although the first of the Hansa cogs, if we take our

evidence from the older of the town seals, were simple straightforward ships without external embellishments, they soon began to incorporate castles at the bow and stern, and eventually a third castle at the masthead. It has been suggested that these castles were used as observation platforms, but a more likely purpose would be to provide protection from the pirates who still roamed the seas during those years. Pirates would attack by boarding over the ship's waist, the lowest point of her gunwales, and the fore- and aftercastles would enable defenders to fire their arrows or throw their darts down onto the attackers. It is probable that the third castle on the masthead served as a lookout, although a miniature in an illuminated manuscript produced for Queen Eleanor of Castile in 1279 shows fighting men even in this masthead castle. But this was an illustration of a fighting ship during the Crusades; a merchant ship in peacetime would not carry fighting men, or certainly only a few in order to man the fore- and aftercastles as a defense against pirates.

It was about this period that the hanging rudder replaced the steering oar to mark the next major step forward in ship development. The actual date is uncertain, but a carving on the font in Winchester Cathedral appears to show a ship with a rudder attached to its sternpost. The date of this carving is believed to be 1180. Fide Church in Gotland has a representation of a ship carved into the wall plaster which shows the rudder clearly hung from the sternpost and worked by a tiller which is curved to go around the upper part of the sternpost. The carving is dated to the early years of the 13th century. This evidence confirms that the hanging rudder preceded the design of the Hansa cog, though whether it was incorporated in the design from the start is uncertain.

It is surprising that ships in northern waters were for so long single-masted, for in the Mediterranean the two-masted and three-masted ship was the rule rather than the exception. There could have been no lack of this knowledge in the north, for a whole series of Crusades had been fought in which northern armies had taken part. Richard the Lionheart, King of England from 1189-99, had led his army to the Crusades in his own ship, the *Trenchemer*, which was a two-masted dromon, a big, heavily built ship of deep draft with capacious holds to carry the knights' horses. The English equivalent of the dromon was the *buss*, which retained, however, the single mast and sail. The large size of the buss is borne out in a description of 1195 by Richard of Devizes; he notes that she could carry, besides her crew, up to 80 knights with their horses, 80 footmen, and 28 servants, with enough provisions to last for a year. It seems strange that such a big ship relied on a single mast and sail to drive her through the water, particularly when so many northern seamen must have seen the rigs of Mediterranean ships.

The first mention of a two-masted English ship is to be

Relief from Winchester Cathedral, England, showing hanging rudder, c. 1180.

found in the Rolls (medieval accounts kept on long strips of paper rolled up on a stick), at Carton Ride in Norfolk. The date is about 1350 — more than 1,000 years after this rig was introduced in the Mediterranean. The second mast was probably added to counteract the effect of the forecastle built up on the bows, for the wind acting on this would tend to blow the bows of the ship down to leeward and make her almost impossible to sail to windward. The Norfolk Rolls give no details of the second mast but it was probably positioned aft of the mainmast to provide the necessary sail area to counterbalance the force of the wind on the built-up bow. The third mast probably appeared soon afterwards, as seamen discovered the extent to which extra masts added to the ease of handling.

By the 14th century ships, in both northern and Mediterranean waters, were beginning to approximate to a design which was to become almost standard during the course of the next three centuries. This was a large and heavily built ship with a long keel, a curved bow with a large built-up forecastle, fairly low in the waist, and with a high rounded stern with two or three additional short decks built up to form a poop and quarterdeck. She had a length-to-beam ratio of about 2 or 2½ to 1 and was three-masted, setting two or three square sails on the foremast and mainmast and a single lateen sail on the mizzen. The bows had no flare and were very bluff. A large tiller, often needing three or four men to operate it, worked a rudder fixed to the sternpost with gudgeons and pintles. The sails were made of heavy canvas and all the cordage, including the anchor cables, were of hemp. The Mediterranean countries also began to adopt this design as a result of northern trading voyages, which introduced seamen there to the merits of the cog as a robustly built ship with a large carrying capacity for its size.

The Carrack and the Caravel

The lateen rig, which is essentially a fore-and-aft rig, had been introduced into the Mediterranean probably by the Arabs and for many years had been in use as the standard ship rig for all types of sailing vessels. It was much more efficient than the square rig, particularly to windward, and although it needed a larger crew to handle it, because the yards had to be dipped around the mast when tacking, labor in those days was plentiful and cheap. But as trading voyages grew longer, particularly in the rougher waters beyond the Mediterranean, the advantages of a square rig in ease of sail handling became apparent even to those who had known nothing but the lateen rig. It was sturdier and entailed no dipping of the yards around the masts. Only on the mizzenmast was a lateen sail set, and this was because, being a fore-and-aft sail, it presented a square surface to the wind and thus produced a larger force to counteract the effect of the wind on the high bow.

This reversion to square sail in the Mediterranean marks the birth of the CARRACK, which became the generic name for most of the large Mediterranean sailing ships irrespective of their nationality. They were originally two-masted ships — square-rigged on the fore and lateen-rigged on the main — but soon became three-masted as the ships increased in size. Like all northern ships, the carrack was built bluff in the bow and had a rounded stern which ended in a square counter. Her extensive forecastle projected some distance beyond the stemhead and an aftercastle was built up on the poop quarterdeck. As the carrack gradually increased in size these two castles were extended by adding extra decks to them until they towered up to a considerable height above the waist of the ship. Some of the biggest carracks, which were built to a tonnage of over 2,000, had as many as four separate decks

A carrack of the early 16th century.

built up over the quarterdeck.

The CARAVEL, a ship always associated with the great voyages of exploration in the 15th century which began to open up the hitherto unknown world, was a contemporary of the carrack. She was originally designed for fishing, but the name was later used as a generic term to describe any small sailing ship. Caravels became the favorite ships of the great explorers of the late 15th and early 16th centuries mainly because they were small, commodious, easy to handle, and drew so little water that they could approach unknown shores with little danger of running aground. Although COLUMBUS, in his first voyage across the Atlantic to the New World in 1492, sailed in the largest of his three caravels, the SANTA MARIA of about 90 tons, he confessed in his journal that his favorite was the smallest, the *Niña*, of about 65 tons. The other great explorers of his era echoed his sentiments.

The caravel was of a simple design, lacking the carrack's embellishment of fore- and aftercastles. She was built with a length-to-beam ratio of about 3 to 1 and with a fairly pronounced sheer from bow to stern. There was no forecastle as we know it, the gunwale continuing in a gentle upward curve to the stemhead. A fairly long quarterdeck aft, perhaps extending to about one-third of the overall length, was the sole modest acknowledgment of the contemporary concept of the built-up stern, and this simple hull outline promised a weatherly ship. Initially caravels were lateen-rigged on all three masts, but as soon as they began to be used for ocean voyages the labor-intensive lateen rig was changed to square rig on foremast and mainmast, retaining a lateen sail only on the mizzen. This mixture of square and lateen rig was known as the *caravela redonda*, as opposed to the *caravela latina*, which described the all-lateen rig.

Actual dimensions of these caravels have not been recorded, but if we take the evidence of Bartolomé de las Casas in his *Historia de las Indias*, which he wrote between 1550 and 1563 with the aid of Columbus' own journals, the *Santa Maria* had an overall length of about 80 ft. (24 m) on a keel length of about 60 ft. (18 m) and a beam of about 27 ft. (8 m). She drew 6 ft. 6 in. (2 m) of water, which on a modern calculation would make her about 90 tons. She was one of the larger caravels — smaller ones like the *Pinta* and *Niña* were 50-60 tons. It is interesting to note that some of the pinnaces, which were the contemporary English equivalent of the Spanish and Portuguese caravels and were also used for voyages of exploration, ranged from around 60 tons down to as little as 12 tons. Sir Humphrey GILBERT's *Squirrel*, one of the five ships used in his attempt to colonize Newfoundland in 1583, was a tiny vessel of only 10 tons.

A great deal of this 15th-century development of the ship can be attributed to Prince Henry of Portugal, better known to seamen as HENRY THE NAVIGATOR. In about AD

The rig of the caravela redonda.

The all-lateen rig of the caravela latina.

150 Claudius Ptolemaeus (Ptolemy), an Egyptian of Greek extraction, had drawn a map of the world and incorporated it in a book known as his *Geographia*. This work was lost on his death and remained unknown until in 1400 a Greek manuscript copy of the work was discovered in Constantinople. It was quickly translated into Latin and although all the maps were distorted because of an error in calculation, the book had a tremendous impact on a maritime world anxious to extend the bounds of contemporary

navigational knowledge. In 1420 Henry the Navigator established a naval 'arsenal' at Sagres on the Atlantic coast of Portugal, to which he invited geographers, astronomers, mathematicians, and navigators to study astronomy and cartography and to teach the art of navigation to Portuguese seamen. Although Prince Henry did not live long enough to see the full realization of his dreams of maritime expansion, Portuguese seamen trained at Sagres had by 1490 rounded the southern tip of Africa and broken into the Indian Ocean. Within another year or two they had reached India itself and had begun to push down the long chain of islands which we know today as the East Indies. Almost simultaneously Spanish seamen successfully crossed the Atlantic Ocean to discover a new world which promised a great flow of riches through trade and exploitation.

This sudden doubling or even trebling of the extent of the known world presented shipbuilders with a new and challenging problem. Ships had to be sturdy enough to endure long ocean voyages lasting weeks or months, with no sheltered harbors in which to reprovision. They had to be designed and built not only to carry a bigger crew and the food and water necessary for a prolonged voyage but also with a hold large enough to transport a worthwhile cargo. What in 1400 was a big ship (250-300 tons) was in 1500 too small for these transocean trade routes.

There was, too, another problem. The new discoveries to the east and to the west had been made by the seamen of Portugal and Spain respectively and, naturally enough, they claimed these new lands and all the trade that they involved as their sole property. The other major seafaring nations of Europe — France, England, and Holland — were forced to dispute this claim, even to the extent of fighting for the right to trade, and this entailed the building of large warships to protect their home waters and large merchant ships armed with guns and manned with fighting men to enforce their right to trade when they

A Spanish carrack of 1496.

reached their journey's end. The design of these two types went hand in hand: the big warship providing the model for the big merchant ship. As we have seen, Spain and Portugal built their largest carracks up to a tonnage of about 2,000, though the average tonnage was then about 1,500; the other European nations, more wisely perhaps, did not exceed about 1,000 tons, which gave them a much more nimble, weatherly ship to match against the unwieldy bulk of a slow, lumbering carrack, particularly when it came to a fight over the right to trade.

The basic design of the ship did not alter, although a significant change was to come in the late 16th century. It was still what was known as the 'high-charged ship,' built up forward and aft with massive 'castles' for the wind to work on. It was these big wind areas which made the ships so difficult to maneuver and which forced them down to leeward when sailing on a wind. In an attempt to counteract this drift away to leeward, the shipbuilders increased the sail area by setting more sails, which called for higher masts. So we begin to find topmasts added to lower masts and square topsails set on them above the lower sail. A fourth mast stepped right astern also appeared; it was known as a bonaventure mast and was designed expressly to counteract the effect of the wind on the high-charged bow. During the 16th century masts were again increased in height to match the growth in tonnage of ships. This was by the addition of topgallant masts fixed to the topmast and with topgallant sails set above the topsails. In the four-masted ship the fore- and mainmasts were square-rigged, the mizzen had a square topsail above the lateen course, and the bonaventure carried a single lateen sail. It was a reasonably efficient rig for a ship of this design, though extremely labor-intensive. Nevertheless, for the whole of the 16th century these ships carried the trade of the world to and from its most distant corners, at an average speed of no more than 2 or 3 knots.

The Galleon

A radical change in hull design was introduced in England by Sir John HAWKINS during the decade 1570-80. This came about after he had witnessed the loss of an English warship through Spanish treachery on his third 'triangular' voyage in 1567. These voyages were known as triangular because they involved three trips: trade goods were carried from England to Sierra Leone where they were exchanged for slaves; the slaves were then taken to the West Indies and the Spanish Main and sold; the money thereby obtained was invested in a cargo of sugar or other produce to be brought home and sold in England. It was a profitable trade and Queen Elizabeth I, who was always short of cash, adventured one of her ships, the *Jesus of Lubeck*, in the round voyage with Hawkins in command of the expedition. After he had sold his cargoes of

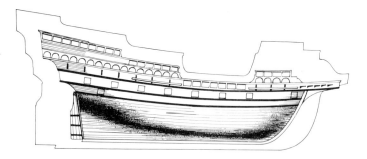

The development of the galleon from the high-charged ship (outer outline): the massive fore- and aftercastles are lowered, the forecastle moved further aft, and the length-to-beam ratio increased.

slaves in the West Indies, a heavy storm and shortage of provisions forced Hawkins to seek shelter in the Spanish port of San Juan de Ulúa where the governor agreed to provide shelter and sell provisions to the English ships. But on a sudden signal the Spaniards attacked and captured the *Jesus of Lubeck*, slaughtering her crew almost to a man. The two other smaller ships of the squadron, the *Judith* and the *Minion*, escaped through their speed and weatherliness. The captain of the *Judith* was a young man named Francis DRAKE, and both he and John Hawkins swore vengeance on the Spaniards for their treachery. Francis Drake redeemed his vow by becoming the most feared English sailor among Spanish seamen, causing an immense loss of Spanish shipping in all his future voyages; John Hawkins redeemed his by studying why the *Jesus of Lubeck* was too slow to escape the Spanish assault when the smaller ships had managed to win free. When Elizabeth I made him treasurer of her navy, a position of great authority, he put his thoughts and plans into action to try to produce a superior design of ship.

He took two small ships of the Queen's navy, the *Tiger* and the *Bull*, which were due to return to the dockyard for rebuilding, a frequent necessity in wooden ships at that time, and had them taken apart. Replacing any timbers affected by rot, he proceeded to lengthen their hulls from a length-to-beam ratio of 2½ to 1 to one of 3 to 1. He lowered the high sides of the ships so that they would lie lower in the water and completely removed the high forecastle which overhung the stem, replacing it with a lower structure which he placed several feet further aft. At the same time he lowered the aftercastle, though it remained higher than the forecastle, and replaced the traditional round stern with a square one.

The result of all these design changes produced a ship that lay more snugly in the water, and, with the increased length-to-beam ratio, was easier to sail. But the big dividend came from the lowering and repositioning of the forecastle. The effect of the wind on the original high structure, which in the past had always blown the bows down to leeward, was removed, and its effect on the remodeled aftercastle was to give the ship a small degree of weather helm which helped to hold her bows up into the wind, always a desirable property in any sailing ship. The new Hawkins design created a ship that was faster, sailed a little closer to the wind, and was easier to tack to windward. With the success of the *Tiger* and the *Bull*, his design was used in all new naval building, and the result was to be seen a few years later when a great Spanish fleet was defeated mainly by the superior speed and sailing qualities of the English ships. The general description given to these ships was 'low-charged,' to distinguish them from the former 'high-charged' ships, i.e., ships with a high castle at each end. There was no basic change in the rig, which remained square-rigged on the foremast and mainmast and lateen-rigged on the mizzen, sometimes with an additional bonaventure mizzen for the larger new-design warships.

It may well be that John Hawkins was assisted in his new design by Matthew Baker, a notable Elizabethan shipwright who wrote a treatise on shipbuilding, entitled *Fragments of Ancient Shipwrightry*, which is now in the Pepysian Library in Magdalene College, Cambridge. Written in about 1585, it is the earliest extant technical treatise on shipbuilding and has drafts of many of the new ships built for the Elizabethan navy. In several of the profile designs Baker added the drawing of a large fish, often recognizable as a cod, covering the underwater part of the hull, presumably to indicate the shape and proportions he wanted the hull to take below the waterline.

This new type of ship became known as a GALLEON, though not in England where it originated. Sir William Wynter, who during the Spanish Armada campaign of 1588 commanded the *Vanguard*, one of the Hawkins-designed ships, wrote of them: 'Our ships do show themselves like gallants here. I assure you it will do a man's

heart good to behold them.' And the Duke of Stettin, who inspected the new design, wrote: 'I found them all built very low at the head, but very high at the stern, so that it made me shudder to look down.' Nevertheless, the other maritime nations of Europe soon discovered the superiority of this new design and were not slow to adapt it to their own particular building processes. There is a model of a Flemish ship of 1593 in the Museo Navale in Madrid which shows that the Dutch had adopted the new hull within seven or eight years of its first appearance in England, and French, Spanish, and Portuguese warships were using it by the first decade of the 17th century.

Where warship design led, merchant ships were quick to follow. Spain and Portugal, which had both invested heavily in large carracks to carry their burgeoning trade from the newly discovered lands to the west and the east, were the last to discard the high-charged design, but the impossibility of defending these comparatively sluggish and unwieldy ships against attack by their smaller and nimbler opponents finally convinced them. There was still an enormous amount of piracy in all the world's oceans, and international trade rivalries were more often than not an adequate excuse for attack on a merchant ship sailing singly without escort. A large cumbersome ship that kept drifting away to leeward was inevitably a 'sitting duck' target to a determined marauder. News traveled slowly in those days, and months could go by before details of such attacks reached the ears of authority, especially if they were committed in distant seas.

Most of the aggression throughout the 16th century took place in the new trade areas in the Far East. Spain, whose new lands lay to the west, was still at this time the world's major naval power and no other nation was yet strong enough to challenge her supremacy, although the defeat of Philip of Spain's Invincible Armada in 1588

One of Matthew Baker's galleon designs, from Fragments of Ancient Shipwrightry, *c. 1585.*

signified the writing on the wall. But Portugal, whose discoveries in India and the East Indies had opened an even more valuable new market in spices, silks, and precious stones, had no such naval invulnerability. Ships from England, Holland, and France made determined but fruitless attempts to find a new sea route to the east via the northwest of America and the northeast of Russia, but their lack of success did not deter other ships of these countries from using the sea route first discovered and opened by the Portuguese. A state of unofficial war was developed in these distant oceans, with each country establishing areas of local maritime superiority and defending them against all comers.

Model of an Elizabethan galleon of 1600. These low-charged ships were used both for trade and for warfare.

The East Indiamen

Inevitably, at so great a distance from the restraints of home governments, these national trade areas in the east had to become largely autonomous, their administration nominally in the hands of home-based East India Companies but practically in the hands of local governors who were appointed by the companies. Eight European nations established East India Companies at around the turn of the 16th century in attempts to win this valuable trade but only three of them — England, Holland, and France — managed to form their companies into permanent and powerful entities. As well as being granted a monopoly of all trade in the areas they controlled, they also had authority to mint their own money, establish their own code of justice, and raise their own armies and navies. Even more important, they constructed their own dockyards and built their own ships: the English at Deptford on the River Thames; the Dutch at Rotterdam and Amsterdam; and the French at Lorient, named especially for this particular trade.

In the course of their trading history these European East India companies became immensely wealthy and built some of the finest ships to be seen on the oceans. It was an age when ship decoration was entering its most ornate and expensive period, and the various East India Companies, to whom expense was always a minor consideration, carved and gilded their ships to the extreme of fashion. Yet they were exceptionally sturdy ships beneath their decoration, soundly constructed of the finest timber available and to the best contemporary design. They were, of course, armed for defense — and sometimes for offense — against local pirates, the ships of rival companies, and on occasion, the warships of competing nations, and so were designed to a large extent on warship lines but with a large cargo capacity beneath their gundecks. The term East Indiaman was coined as a generic name for these merchant ships which were instantly recognizable at sea and in harbor both for their size and for their magnificence of decoration. In general, the design followed that of the English

Replica of the Nonsuch, *which sailed to Hudson Bay in 1668.*

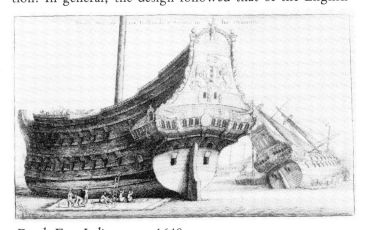

Dutch East Indiamen, c. 1640.

British merchant figurehead, the Golden Cherubus, 1660.

galleon introduced by John Hawkins and Matthew Baker, though with a tall three-masted rig in place of the four masts of the larger naval ships. By about 1700 all had adopted the ship rig of square sails, up to topgallants, on all three masts, with a gaff-rigged spanker below square topsails on the mizzen. This had by then become the traditional rig for large ships throughout the world, and lasted through the remainder of the sailing era. As merchant ships, they were the aristocrats of the oceans throughout the 17th and 18th centuries, the epitome of all that was best in western merchant shipbuilding. With the expanding eastern trade and ever-increasing wealth, the size of the East India Companies' ships grew from around 1,500 tons in 1750 to about 2,000 tons in 1800, very much in line with the growth in size of warships.

The decoration of ships, which reached the heights of extravagance during these same centuries, had started as superstition among seamen of the ancient world. The ships of the Greeks and Romans had the heads of gods and goddesses carved on their prows to invoke divine protection during voyages, or the head of a bird — frequently a swan — to encourage the ship to float as proudly and safely on the water as that aquatic fowl. They had an eye painted on each bow to enable the ship to 'see' her way across the seas in the dark. These were understandable decorations in those very early days when navigation, as we know it, was an undiscovered science and every voyage a venture into unknown and uncharted seas. Some of the later ship decoration is also understandable in the case of royal ships, where monarchs needed to impress their neighbors and their own citizenry with their wealth and power. But during the 17th and 18th centuries every ship was decorated with some form of carving; even the humblest fishing craft had a carved twirl or two on its washboards and stern. Naval ships and the ships of rich companies and individual merchants were decorated in virtually every place where a carver had room to wield a chisel, and even the housing of the ship's bell took the form of a miniature temple or was carved with allegorical figures. No expense was spared: when the *Sovereign of the Seas* was launched in England in 1637 the Pipe Office accounts for that year show that her decoration alone cost £6,691 — as much as the entire ship cost to build.

Such a show of expensive magnificence could not last; by the end of the 18th century most ships were still decorated, but on a much more modest and restrained scale. The urge for economy was first felt in England at the start of the 18th century, and maximum amounts were prescribed for the carving and painting of naval ships. In general, merchant ships were eager to follow the naval lead, and because at that time English ships were recognized by other European countries as models of naval architecture, the new fashion set by England was soon imitated on the continent of Europe.

The Development of the Spritsail and the Gaff Rig

In the late 16th century the different characteristics of northern and southern European ship rig began to merge. The ships of the Mediterranean, previously all-lateen-rigged, began to adopt the typical northern pattern of square sails for their fore- and mainmasts, particularly in larger ships designed to sail beyond the Mediterranean itself. The northern ships, those of Sweden, Holland, France, and England, took up the lateen sail for use on the mizzen- and bonaventure-mizzen masts, chiefly because these sails could be trimmed broader to the wind than square sails and so used to offset the tendency to sag away to leeward through the force of the wind acting on the built-up forecastle. The combination provided a well-balanced rig, though the lateen was an awkward sail to handle since its long sloping yard had to be dipped around the mast on each occasion of the ship tacking. It also necessitated a large crew which added to the overheads.

It seems reasonably certain that it was the difficulty in handling the long lateen yard that led to its replacement by the spritsail in the ships of northern countries. There is some evidence from Mediterranean rock carvings that a sprit — a long spar used to spread a square sail by being led diagonally from tack to peak — was used in those waters as early as the 2nd century BC, but the first evidence of its use in Europe can be seen in a picture of a Swedish ship painted in 1525. There is reason to believe that in fact the sprit originated a few years earlier in Holland for use in shallow-draft barges and fluyts, probably because sailing in shoal waters required a quicker means of tacking than was possible with the lateen sail. The great advantage of the sprit over the lateen was that there was no yard to be dipped around the mast when tacking against the wind.

A few years after the sprit had been introduced the Dutch went a step further by developing it into the gaff

Dutch fluyts in harbor, 1650.

The gaff rig of a Portuguese lighter.

as a result. The taller mizzenmast allowed a square sail to be set above a spritsail, but not above a lateen sail because of its very high peak. For some years, Spanish, Portuguese, and some French ships retained the lateen sail on the mizzen, possibly because they found it more suited to Mediterranean conditions, but in north European waters the advantages of the Dutch half-sprit rig for the mizzenmast were becoming much more apparent, and gradually a spanker set beneath a mizzen-topsail superseded the full sprit rig. By the mid-18th century the Spanish carrack had of course disappeared from the oceans, and the rig of the western sailing ship became more or less standard throughout the whole of Europe: square-rigged on all three masts with the gaff-rigged spanker on the mizzen below a square topsail. Up until the introduction of mechanical propulsion, this remained the standard ship rig for all nations, though in the case of smaller ships, each nation retained the traditional rigs which they found most suitable for their particular waters.

rig, using two small spars at head and foot of the sail in place of one large spar diagonally across the sail. That this was not a new development but the modification of an existing one is shown by the fact that it was called the half-sprit, retaining the name of the rig it replaced. For the first 50 years or so the gaff rig was used only in small coastal vessels of up to 50 tons, until its obvious advantage in ease of handling was recognized as equally applicable to vessels of larger dimensions.

By the late 17th century most of the large sailing ships of northern Europe had replaced the lateen sail on the mizzenmast with the Dutch spritsail, which was easier to handle and less labor-intensive. The ships of Spain and Portugal, mainly carracks and caravels, retained their lateen sails on the mizzen, probably because, at least in the case of carracks, the ships were built bigger and therefore with more crew accommodation for handling this awkward sail. But in both areas, northern and southern, the ship herself was going through a metamorphosis. Not only was she being built larger to meet increasing demands of world trade, but she was also being built taller by stepping a topgallant mast above the topmast. The bonaventure mizzen disappeared simply because a larger area of sail could be spread on three tall masts than on four shorter masts, and it was found that the ship sailed better

Thames barge with large four-sided spritsail.

41

Sailing Ships in Eastern Waters

There are fewer sources available to tell us how the ship was developing in more distant waters. All the early atlases are decorated with cartouches, many of them showing ships, but it is difficult to establish their accuracy. Some very early accounts of voyages to the east — such as the *Itinerario* of the Dutch explorer Jan Huygen van Linschoten — are included in the many volumes of De Bry's *Collectiones*, published between 1590 and 1634. These show various types of native craft in eastern waters, but whether they were drawn from life or from travelers' descriptions is again unknown.

One of De Bry's illustrations of a typical eastern trading ship shows a vessel built up and roofed in from abaft the single central mast, presumably to provide cover and protection for the cargo. There are rowers before the mast, but they are drawn facing the bows and therefore push on their oars instead of pulling on them. A single lateen sail is spread from the central mast. As in all De Bry's illustrations it is difficult to estimate her size as his sense of proportion was sadly lacking, but if one can judge from the number of rowers, the ship could hardly be less than about 120 ft. (36.5 m) in length with a beam of at least 30 ft. (9 m). Other illustrations of eastern ships show vessels without rowers and with more than one mast.

We know from several sources that the Arabian DHOW is of very ancient design. The largest ones had two masts with a lateen rig. They were similar to the sailing dhows of today, except that they had a broader beam and were extensively used for trading. Subsequently the Arab nations developed the *bhagla* and the *ghanja*, both of which were oddities. The bhagla was a comparatively large ship with a hull design copied from the 17th- and

A lateen-rigged bhagla.

18th-century European East Indiamen, but it used a lateen rig on all three masts instead of the European square rig. The ghanja was distinguished by a very long quarterdeck which overhung the rudder head by a considerable distance. She, too, was lateen-rigged on all three masts.

In Chinese and Javanese waters the ancient JUNK, which had been developed as early as the 4th century AD, was still the principal type of vessel used for trade and war. Marco Polo's account of his voyage to China in 1298 gives a description of the junk which conforms closely to the sailing junk of today. The two most noticeable differences between the junk and western ships, if one accepts Marco Polo's account, were the former's subdivision into sepa-

One of De Bry's illustrations of an eastern trading ship.

Small Chinese trading junk.

rate watertight compartments, by the installation of transverse bulkheads, and the use of a single rudder fixed to the stern. The transverse bulkheads were specifically designed to prevent the vessel from sinking if she hit a rock and pierced her hull. The use of a single rudder seems to imply that the hanging rudder replaced the steering oar much earlier in the Far East than in the west.

In addition to the junk, a very early traditional ship of Java was the *fusta*, which in many ways was not unlike the Mediterranean dromon of the Romans, though not so large. It too used a lateen rig, with two masts in the early versions, and was fitted with a hanging rudder. The Chinese also developed the *lorcha* in the mid-16th century. This had a hull built on traditional European lines surmounted by a junk rig. It evolved as a result of the Portuguese occupation and settlement of Macao, which introduced the western hull design to the east. The type name later spread to the Mediterranean and was loosely and erroneously used to describe a variety of small ships using the lateen rig.

Right: a lateen-rigged pearling dhow from Bahrain.

Below: a Fijian proa with a lateen sail and an outrigger.

The rest of the eastern maritime world, centered in the island groups in the southwestern Pacific, remained faithful to its original canoe design which received the generic name of *prahu*, the Malayan word meaning boat or ship. Prahu very quickly became shortened to *prau*, a description still in use today to indicate locally built vessels. They were generally rigged with dipping or standing lugsails on one or two masts. Where larger vessels than single canoes were required to carry large cargoes, the normal solution was to build a platform or deck mounted on two or even three canoe hulls — the ancient forerunners of today's catamarans and trimarans.

Sailing Merchant Ships of the 18th Century

Ship design virtually stood still throughout the whole of the 18th century, the only change being an increase in size. Using the general design introduced at the end of the 16th century, ships were now built up to a tonnage of about 3,000 — very nearly the maximum size possible for ships of all-timber construction. There had been a relatively small development in warship design during the first half of the 18th century with the introduction of the FRIGATE, a small ship built for speed, but this had little effect on the building of general merchant ships where speed was of secondary importance to cargo capacity. The frigate was rigged in exactly the same way as a big ship, with three masts and square sails, and achieved her extra speed simply by an increase in her length-to-beam ratio and the use of lighter scantlings in her construction.

Nevertheless, there were some other small advances. In 1705 jibsails were introduced into the Royal Navy to replace the clumsy and inefficient spritsails formerly set above and below the bowsprit. These were not the same as the spritsails mentioned previously, but took their name from the bowsprit. They were small square sails set on a short pole above and below the bowsprit and were designed to lift the bow a little to give the ship a slightly cleaner run through the water. The small contribution they may have made to sailing efficiency was, however, more than outweighed by the virtual impossibility of keeping the yards trimmed accurately to the wind from a position forward of the stem. Jibs, being fore-and-aft sails, were not only easier to handle and trim to the wind but were also far more efficient in helping to lift the bows.

Another advance was the substitution of the steering wheel for the tiller attached to the rudder head. As ships grew larger, the tiller grew longer and in heavy weather required at times as many as four men to overcome the rudder pressure. Another drawback was that the helmsman's view of the ship's sails was obscured by the poopdeck above him, which meant that he could not work the tiller effectively. This disadvantage had been to some extent overcome by the invention of the whipstaff, which was a vertical attachment by which the tiller could be moved, but the mechanics of the whipstaff were such that it was impossible to get more than about 5° of movement to the rudder, far less than was required for the efficient handling of any ship at sea. The introduction of the steering wheel was a big advance in design since it could be placed forward of the break of the quarterdeck, allowing the helmsman an uninterrupted view of the ship's sails. The gearing, too, reduced the physical effort of moving the rudder which had been such a drawback of the tiller.

These may have been modest refinements in design but they significantly improved the overall handling of the big sailing ship. The better ship control that resulted inspired designers to investigate whether there might not be other improvements that could be made. The leader of this new movement was a Swedish naval architect named Frederik Hendrik af Chapman who was in effect the first man to study the science of hydrodynamics. He did so by building hull models and testing them in a tank in which they were drawn through the water by an ingenious system of drop weights. Among other findings, his studies proved that a hull with a fine entry and a clear run aft could move through the water with much less resistance than those built full and bluff in the bows, which was the almost universal pattern of contemporary shipbuilding. He published his findings in 1768 in his *Architectura Navalis Mercatoria*, illustrated with many merchant ship designs, and seven years later followed it with *Tractat om Skepps Buggeriet* (Treatise on Shipbuilding), two publications which over the next 20 or 30 years were to have a profound influence on shipbuilding throughout the western world. Other naval architects followed Chapman's lead and made yet deeper studies of hydrodynamics in an attempt to find the form of hull with the minimum drag. It all meant a gradual change away from the tubby hull initiated by Hawkins and Baker into much slimmer hull lines with an uninterrupted run from bow to stern. Science and research were beginning to be applied to ship design, replacing the rough-and-ready methods on which all shipbuilders had relied in the past.

There were advances, too, in the design of rigs. The gaff-mizzen was replaced by the spanker, with topsails set above it, and the topsails themselves were split into two: upper and lower. A topgallant mast was stepped above the topmast and, in the larger ships, an additional pole mast was introduced from which to set royals above the topgallant sails. The fore-and-aft rig was coming into much wider use for small craft, again introduced mainly by the Dutch. The first ship type to use a gaff rig on two masts was the Dutch JACHT, a shallow-draft vessel fitted with leeboards for use in inland waters. This was later developed into the *bezaan jacht*, a single-masted small ship, gaffrigged with a triangular staysail and a long bowsprit from which a jib could be set forward of the staysail. It was still a shallow-draft vessel for use in shoal waters, leeboards being used to prevent excessive leeway when sailing on the wind. The bezaan jacht design was copied in England, where, because the coastal waters were not so shoal as in Holland, it was given a deeper draft to obviate the need to fit leeboards. This design evolved into the English CUTTER. A few years later a square sail was added above the gaff-mainsail to provide an increase in speed, and later still it was given a second mast, with gaffsails on fore- and mainmasts, an additional square sail on the foremast, and topsails on both masts. Some of the Dutch marine paintings of the late 17th and early 18th centuries show this rig, though usually without the topsails.

For shorter sea voyages a large variety of new types of ship were developed in northern Europe. The most common type was the BRIGANTINE, or brig in its shortened form, a two-masted ship square-rigged on both masts with a gaff-mainsail or spanker. The name came from the Mediterranean, where it was used in the 16th century to describe a small galleass much favored by pirates for its speed under oars and sail; indeed its origin lies in the Italian word for pirates — *brigantini*. But the north European brigantine, which came a full century after the Mediterranean ship, was a completely different type of ship, designed purely for trade. Until the mid-18th century a brig and a brigantine were the same ship, but from then on, while the brig remained square-rigged on both masts, the brigantine kept its square rig on the foremast but adopted a fore-and-aft rig on the mainmast.

Very similar to the brig was the SNOW, a small vessel popular for coastal and short-sea trade. It differed from the brig in having a short additional mast stepped immediately abaft the mainmast. This was called a trysail mast and the gaff-mainsail was hoisted on it. The advantage of this extra mast was that the gaff-mainsail could be more easily handled, and could be hoisted or lowered without any interference with the main yard from which the course was set. With its separate mast it could also be hoisted higher than the yards to give a better sail balance. In a later development the trysail mast was replaced by a long horse on the mainmast, on which the gaffsail was hoisted.

In the Mediterranean, although brigs, brigantines, and snows were widely used, the more popular types of small merchant ship were the polacres and XEBECS. They were designs typical of the Mediterranean and were never seen in other waters. The polacre was apt to be larger than most other types of small merchant ship, being built up to a tonnage of about 1,200. There were two types of polacre: the smaller brig polacre which was two-masted, usually square-rigged on both masts but sometimes lateen-rigged on the main; and the larger ship polacre which had three masts, square-rigged on the main and lateen-rigged on the fore and mizzen, though on occasions they were to

The Norwegian brig Statsraad Erichsen, *1858.*

be seen with a lateen rig on all three masts. Both types had a foremast with a pronounced forward rake. Their name came from the fact that all the masts were single spars or poles, with no topmast stepped and no crosstrees; another peculiarity was that there were no footropes on the yards for the crew to loosen or furl the square sails. Men stood on the yards themselves to handle the sail next above them, which must have been an awkward and sometimes

The snow, a small coastal vessel of the 16th to the 19th century.

A ship polacre, here square-rigged on all three masts.

A Spanish xebec, derived from the older pirate brigantine.

dangerous method of sail handling. The polacre had a clipper bow fitted with a long bowsprit, though she set no jibs, and a long overhanging stern with a short bumkin to which the mizzensail was sheeted.

The xebec was a direct descendant of the older pirate brigantine, with long overhangs at bow and stern, very similar to the ancient war galley, and a narrow floor to give her a good turn of speed through the water. Above the floor she was built out to a considerable beam with a turtle deck so that any water shipped while sailing would run quickly back into the sea through the line of scuppers. Gratings were rigged above the deck to give the crew members a secure footing and to keep them dry. But the most distinctive feature of the xebec was the variable rig, which could be altered to suit the weather and the point of sailing. She was three-masted and her normal working rig consisted of square sails on the foremast and lateen sails on the main and mizzen. If the wind were abaft the beam, the lateen yard on the mainmast was lowered and an immensely long square yard was swayed up from which a huge main course was set. When sailing close-hauled in a moderate wind, a lateen rig was spread on all three masts with extra long yards; in strong winds these long yards were replaced with ones of normal length. It was a complicated rig calling for a very large crew, and William Falconer in his *Universal Dictionary of the Marine* (1771) reckoned that a xebec needed a crew three times as large as that required for a square-rigged ship of similar size. In spite of her financial disadvantages, the xebec had the ability to outsail any other ship afloat.

The design of smaller ships was still largely local in character, though some basic types were beginning to appear. In the Baltic the *jagt* and the *galeas* were the main small vessel types, used for local trading and fishing, with minor variations in size or design according to locality. The Dutch, who were particularly skilled in building small ships, used the *tjalk*, the *kof*, and the *bezaanschuyt* and their many local derivations. In France the *chasse-marée* was developed into a small, very fast, three-masted ship with lugsails on each mast, and proved very popular for smuggling and, in time of war, for privateering. English coastal trade was carried in a variety of vessels: small brigs; BARGES which maintained their original spritsail rig; KETCHES; KEELS; and, for the coal trade, a distinct type known as a CAT. Portugal had the *fregata*; Spain the FELUCCA and the *tartane*; Italy the *trebaccolo* and a *tartane* similar to the Spanish design; and Greece the *trekandian* and the *sacoleva*. About the only thing they all had in common was their size; their rigs could vary according to the locality in which they were built. Perhaps they can best be described as the small workhorses of the western seas.

Sail versus Steam in the 19th Century

The introduction of the marine steam engine during the 19th century as the motive power for ships was, perhaps, the writing on the wall foretelling the end of the sailing ship's long centuries of service to man's urge to discover and expand. Steam took a long time to establish itself as the prime mover of a ship, simply because it took many years to develop engines and boilers with sufficient power and reliability to be accepted as the main source of propulsion. It also took naval architects a long time to work out how to provide adequate bunker space for fuel without cutting too deeply into a vessel's cargo-carrying capacity. For the first half of the 19th century the steam engine in ships was installed mainly as an auxiliary source of power to the sail, and it was only during the second half of the century that it became established as the primary source of marine propulsion.

The European merchant ship at the start of the 19th century was in general based on the lines of the naval frigate. She had the long keel of the frigate, the same blunt

The Development of the American Clipper

At the beginning of the 19th century a challenge to the European design of a deep-bellied, capacious, but slow merchant ship came from the other side of the Atlantic. The United States, having broken free from British colonial status, was building a new type of small merchant ship designed more for speed than for cargo capacity and used mainly for coastal trade. With an overall length of about 120 ft. (36.5 m) and beam of about 24 ft. (7.5 m), the ship's main characteristic was a long flush deck with no superstructure forward or aft. Instead of the square cross section of the European design, her hull was built with a rounded bottom tapering down to a long keel, and she drew slightly more aft than she did forward. During the War of 1812, unable to match the naval power of Britain, the United States adopted the maritime *guerre de course*, seeking to win the war at sea by attacking British merchant shipping rather than seeking pitched naval battle. The American merchant ships were fitted out as privateers and, since they were designed for speed, they proved an immense success, well able to run down and capture any merchant ship they sighted. In general they were rigged as topsail schooners, though some did appear with a brig or a brigantine rig. But when the war ended their usefulness was more or less at an end. The rounded bottom, though good for speed, was poor in cargo capacity in comparison with the square-bottomed ship, and there were as yet few sea trades where speed of passage was of greater importance than the volume of cargo which could be carried.

There were, however, two such trades and in these the American ships cornered the market. One was the shipping of negro slaves from Africa to the southern states of America. This was known as the 'Blackbird' trade, and a fast ship was essential to avoid the antislavery patrols set up to halt this inhuman traffic. The other was the Chinese opium trade where speed was equally vital. Both these trades were ideal for the American wartime privateers, ships of 200-300 tons built specifically to outrun any other ship at sea. As most of these ships were built in the states of Maryland and Virginia, they were given the name of BALTIMORE CLIPPERS: Baltimore because it was the main center of the southern shipbuilding industry; clippers because it was said that they could 'clip' the time taken on passage compared with any other ship on the same run. It was the first use of this name, although these ships were not clippers in the later sense of the term. Certainly they had the sharp, forward-raked stem of the clipper but not the hollow bow which was always the hallmark of the true clipper design.

In 1832 a larger Baltimore clipper named the ANN MCKIM was built and given a square rig instead of the normal topsail schooner rig. Many people have claimed

Portuguese fregata.

and rounded bow, and the heavy overhanging stern. She had the same full bilge, making her roughly square in cross section, and this gave her the largest possible space for cargo but at the same time made her slow through the water. She was built to the same heavy scantlings to provide a strong and sturdy ship. Ship-rigged on three masts, she made her steady and stately way at an average speed of perhaps 3 or 4 knots across the oceans. With trade expanding across the world at an almost frightening pace, shipowners were more concerned with maximum stowage space than with high speed. Demand was so constant for cargoes of all types that the owners could be assured of a good price all year — the time had not yet arrived when the first ship home with the new season's crop could demand a higher price than those ships which arrived later.

her as the first real clipper because of this change of rig, but she still did not have the hollow bow and so does not truly qualify. But 17 years later an American designer named John Griffiths introduced the hollow bow in a vessel named RAINBOW, which was built by Smith and Dimon in New York. She was the first true clipper, though her length-to-beam ratio of under 5 to 1 was not enough to allow her to achieve the fantastic speeds of some of the later clipper designs.

Nevertheless, the revolutionary design of the *Rainbow* marked a great step forward in the development of the sailing ship. Her appearance marked the end of the bluff-bowed, square-bottomed ship which had held sway for the past 300 years, and naval architects were quick to appreciate the qualities of these new ideas in hull design. Furthermore, she arrived at a moment when everything seemed to conspire to put a premium on speed at sea. She was launched in 1849, the year when gold was discovered in California in large quantities and the year when Britain repealed her deep-sea Navigation Act. Under the terms of this Act all imports into Britain had to be carried in British ships or in ships of the exporting country, and the repeal of the Act opened new and lucrative avenues of trade to the ships of all countries. The most important of these was the China tea trade, and the first consignment of the new season's tea to arrive in London each year could command a doubling of the normal freight rate. In 1850 the first ship to reach London with the new season's crop was the American clipper *Oriental*, and for the next five years American ships dominated this rich trade.

The discovery of gold in California provided another important source of revenue for the new clippers. There was as yet no transcontinental railroad, and the only way of reaching the goldfields was either by sea around Cape

The American clipper Donald McKay, *1855.*

Horn or overland by horse-drawn wagon. Although the distance from New York to San Francisco by sea around Cape Horn is 17,397 nautical miles (32,219 km), it was still quicker to go by sea than overland. In 1851 the new clipper *Flying Cloud* made the voyage in 89 days, 21 hours at an average speed of about 9 knots. The financial rewards for shipowners were fabulous. Everything required in the goldfields, from the prospectors themselves to the machinery they used, the food they ate, the building materials they needed, and even the dance-hall girls to entertain them, had to be carried by sea. Consequently no ship ever needed to sail without a full cargo. The average earnings of a single voyage from New York to San Francisco during the years of the gold rush worked out at $78,000, and most ships made enough money in their first year of trading to cover the whole cost of their building and to provide a handsome profit in addition. Some did even better. The *Sovereign of the Seas*, one of the best known of all the American clippers, is credited with having earned more than $84,000 in freight rates on her maiden voyage alone.

The great name in American clipper history was Donald MCKAY, a naval architect and shipbuilder of Boston, whose clippers became famous throughout the shipping world. His first ship was the *Staghound*, launched in 1850, and she was followed by such notable successors as *Flying Fish, Flying Cloud, Sovereign of the Seas, Champion of the Seas, James Baines,* LIGHTNING, and DONALD MCKAY. These were names which rang around the world and made the name of McKay virtually synonymous with perfection in design. They were real flyers, and the *Sovereign of the Seas* reached speeds of 22 knots at times during a passage of 13 days, 14 hours from New York to Liverpool. The *Lightning*, in a passage from Boston to Liverpool, ran 436 nautical miles (807 km) in 24 hours, an average speed of over 18 knots. This was exceeded by the *Champion of the Seas* on her maiden voyage to Melbourne, when she logged 465 nautical miles (861 km) in 24 hours while running her easting down. Allowing for the difference in longitude, her real time was 23 hours and 17 minutes, which gave her an average speed of over 20 knots. These were phenomenal speeds for sailing ships and remain as a testament to McKay's skill and the quality of his ships.

In Europe, the launch of the *Ann McKim* on the other side of the Atlantic, even though she was not a true clipper, had sounded a warning note of the competition to come. She was faster than any existing European ship and, with her square rig on three masts, was a different proposition from the topsail schooners developed from the privateers. In Britain a new design had been produced, known as a BLACKWALL FRIGATE: Blackwall, because it was there that Green and Wigram built these ships; frigate, because they were built for speed, although they in no way resembled a naval frigate. They were sturdy ships

built with a finer run from bow to stern and were therefore faster than the old design. They were built mainly for the India trade after the East India Company had lost its monopoly, and the first of them was the SERINGAPATAM, a ship of 818 tons launched in 1837. She set a new record of 85 days from London to Bombay, nothing remarkable in view of what was to come but a great deal faster than anything achieved in the East India Company days.

But a Blackwall frigate was nothing like a clipper and though they were very successful ships in their particular trade, the need for greater speed was becoming ever more apparent to the European shipowners if American domination of the carrying trade was to be averted. The *Scottish Maid*, a small ship built by Alexander Hall at Aberdeen, was the first British vessel expressly designed to compete with the Americans. Although she was fast, she did not have the essential characteristics which proclaim the true clipper. The first real clippers built in Britain were the *Stornoway* and the *Chrysolite*, both coming from Hall's yard in Aberdeen, and they were built in the decade 1845-55 for the prestigious and profitable China tea trade.

British Clippers

It was the American civil war between North and South in 1861-65 which opened the door to European, and particularly British, shipowners. Clipper building in the United States had to take second place to the needs of the war, and this gap in American production gave British designers time to work out the details of rig and hull form best suited to all the requirements of worldwide trade. Just as the United States had produced Donald McKay, so Britain produced Robert Steele of Greenock, Scotland, and from his drawing board were to come some of the most wonderful ships of the whole clipper era.

His ships had the raked stem, hollow bow, and overhanging counter-stern of the true clipper, but had finer lines and a more delicate run from bow to stern than Donald McKay's masterpieces. These clippers also had a much improved sail plan, which enabled them not only to withstand a gale of wind but also to 'ghost' along in light airs which would not be strong enough to move an American-built clipper. Their length-to-beam ratio was higher than McKay's ships — between 7 and 8 to 1 — and their long straight keel gave them a very good grip of the water when sailing close to the wind. They were a little smaller than the American ships, averaging around 1,000-1,200 tons, and they saved a good deal of constructional weight in comparison with the American all-wood construction by being composite-built, with wooden hull planking bolted to iron frames and stringers. Their hulls below the waterline were sheathed with copper as a protection against the teredo worm and marine growth and so produced less skin friction while sailing. It would be wrong to think that these ships were just copies of the

American clippers; they were a distinct type of their own, and though they never quite achieved the staggering speeds of the American ships in high winds, they were much superior in overall performance.

The best known of the early British clippers were the *Fiery Cross*, *Serica*, ARIEL, TAEPING, and *Taitsin*, all built for the China tea trade. In 1866 these five ships raced from Foochow to London, a distance of 16,000 nautical miles (29,650 km), to be the first home with the new season's crop, and the first three reached London within three hours of each other after a 99-day voyage half way around the world. All three of them, *Taeping*, *Ariel*, and *Serica*, had been designed and built by Robert Steele.

In 1868, almost at the end of the clipper era, Walter Hood of Aberdeen built the 991-ton THERMOPYLAE, claimed to be the fastest sailing clipper in the world. She was built to a design by Bernard Waymouth, and on her maiden voyage, with passengers and cargo, she sailed from London to Melbourne in 59 days, a record that no other sailing ship has ever bettered. A year later the CUTTY SARK was ordered from the Dumbarton firm of Scott and Linton

The Cutty Sark, *a British clipper launched in 1869.*

specifically to challenge the reputation of the *Thermopylae*, and she made her first voyage in the China tea trade in 1870. But already she and the *Thermopylae* were too late on the scene. In 1869 the Suez Canal was opened and tea from China could now reach London in a steamship using the Canal much faster than it could in a clipper sailing around the Cape of Good Hope. For a few more years the clippers eked out an existence in the Australian wool trade, but in the end the steamship, with its much greater cargo capacity, made them uneconomic in that trade as well.

Towards the end of the clipper era the composite-built clipper was replaced by one built entirely of iron, an alto-

The 1,795-ton clipper Flying Cloud, *built by McKay.*

The British tea-clipper Thermopylae, *built in 1868.*

The five-masted steel bark France II, *launched in 1911.*

gether stronger and longer-lasting material than wood. The first clipper of wholly iron construction was built by Scott of Greenock and was the *Lord of the Isles*, designed for the China tea trade, and her appearance removed much of the prejudice previously held against iron by many of the world's shipbuilders. The additional strength of all-iron construction also enabled much larger sailing ships to be built, and for several years this delayed the inevitable end of sail trading ships as ocean carriers.

The Last Days of Sail

The opening of the Suez Canal in 1869, as we have seen, marked the end of the China tea clippers. In the year before it was opened, a census of world shipping showed that sailing ship tonnage amounted to 4,691,820 tons and steamship tonnage to 824,614 tons. Only four years later, sail tonnage had dropped by more than 500,000 tons while that of steamships had more than doubled. As the years passed, this rate of decline of sail tonnage accelerated, mainly because of the increase in efficiency and reliability of marine engines and boilers. Consequently, more and more shipowners were attracted to steamships with their much larger cargo capacity.

The largest clipper ever built was the *Sobraon* of 2,131 tons, in her way a remarkable ship as she was initially designed as a steamer and, against the general trend, was completed as a clipper. But she was small in comparison with the sailing ships which were to come. There were still some sea trades which could offer worthwhile cargoes to big sailing ships: for a time the Australian wool trade was one of them, and the South American nitrate trade was another as it meant a return voyage around Cape Horn, waters which all steamships avoided. In 1890 the firm of Henderson of Glasgow built the FRANCE for the A.D. Bordes Line, a five-masted steel bark with a dead-

weight tonnage of 5,900, and in 1902 Ferdinand Laeisz of Hamburg built the PREUSSEN, the only ship in the world to carry a square rig on all five of her masts. Under full sail she spread 60,000 sq. ft. (5,574 m²) of canvas. With a length of 433 ft. (132 m) and a beam of 54 ft. (16.5 m), she could carry 9,000 tons of cargo in her holds. Even bigger was the *France II*, a five-masted bark with a dead-

Gorch Fock II, *a three-masted bark built in Hamburg in 1958 and used as a training ship.*

weight tonnage of 8,000, built by Chantiers de la Gironde.

These big sailing ships prospered for several years, mainly in the South American nitrate trade but also as carriers of coal, steel, rails, hides, and guano. It was a precarious business, for everywhere the competition from steamships was fierce. In the end two events were to hasten the final disappearance of the large sailing ship from the oceans. The first came in 1897 with a big increase in insurance rates for sailing ships, introduced by Lloyds of London. Many owners, crippled by the increasing expenses in an ever-dwindling freight market, sold off half their fleets in an attempt to survive; others tried to economize by the dubious practice of signing on apprentices in place of seamen. The second event to seal the sailing ship's fate was the opening of the Panama Canal in 1914, which meant that steamships could reach the nitrate ports of South America without having to sail around Cape Horn, and so this trade, which had been the chief livelihood of sailing ships, was finally lost. For a few more years some owners held on, competing as best they could for the few freights available to them, but in the end they too were forced to accept the inevitable and had their vessels broken up, or abandoned them in remote harbors throughout the world. Only a few of the big sailing ships survive; as sail training ships, like the *Gorch Fock II* or as museum exhibits, like the *Cutty Sark*.

It was the introduction of steel plate as a shipbuilding material during the last two decades of the 19th century which had the paradoxical effect of temporarily prolonging the life of the sailing ship and also of making it obsolete. It was because of the strength of steel that the sailing ship could be built considerably larger than was possible with wood, giving her the extra cargo capacity with which to earn her keep as a working ship. Without the use of steel, the sailing ship would have been too small to compete in the shipping market as it existed at the end of the 19th century. But at the same time, steel brought to the sailing ship's rival, the steamship, a great saving of weight in construction compared with iron and thus made her a more efficient ocean carrier, particularly when added to the great contemporaneous improvements in the marine boiler.

In hull design, this final version of the sail trading ship was not beautiful as the clipper hull had been beautiful. Cargo capacity was now of more importance than speed, and so the new design tended to be slab-sided to provide a square cross section for the holds. The beauty of the bark or schooner rig, however, to some extent compensated for the box-like hull, and to see one of these great ships under sail with her royals set above double topgallant and double topsails was one of the loveliest sights the sea had to offer. Perhaps it is enough to say that they were worthy ships to bring an end to some 3,000 years of sailing ship history.

Clipper ships moored in London.

Yachting

The word yacht is the past participle of the Dutch verb *jachten*, to hurry or to hunt. It entered the English language in 1660 after Charles II had been restored as King of England and had been presented with the yacht *Mary* by the States General of Holland to celebrate his accession to the throne. *Mary* was a small sailing ship of 100 tons and was given to him for use as a private pleasure vessel. The following year Charles built a second yacht and his brother the Duke of York followed suit. In his diary John Evelyn recorded that on October 1, 1661, he was invited on board the King's yacht *Katherine* for a race from Greenwich to Gravesend and back against the Duke of York's yacht *Anna*. During the 23 years of his reign Charles owned 27 yachts, ranging from the 180-ton *Saudadoes* to the 22-ton *Minion*, which he eventually sold as 'useless.'

Regatta Racing

This royal interest in sailing for pleasure stimulated others to build yachts and to organize races between owners. In 1720 the Cork Harbour Water Club, later to become the Royal Cork Yacht Club, was formed as a center for pleasure sailing, and there are records of races sailed on the Thames by members of the Cumberland Society, later

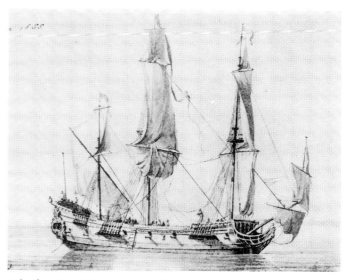

Charles II's 180-ton yacht, Saudadoes, *1670.*

reorganized in 1775 as the Royal Thames Yacht Club. Similar records of races sailed in the Solent, Isle of Wight, date from 1780.

The sport of yacht racing, initially developed in Britain,

Dutch yachts, c. 1710.

A yawl (10-12 tons), c. 1820.

was relatively slow to develop in other countries, with the possible exception of Holland. It began to spread widely during the 19th century, particularly during the industrial revolutions which swept the western world in mid-century, when fortunes were quickly made and rich men looked for new means of spending their money. Ownership of a racing yacht became a social asset, and the desire to shine at this new sport stimulated would-be owners to search out designers who could introduce new hull shapes that could move more quickly through the water. Yacht clubs began to spring up around the coasts of Europe and the United States, initially catering for local yacht owners, but they soon began to organize international competition in the sport.

It was natural during the early years of the new sport that the initial hull design should be based on the fastest existing ships afloat: in most countries this was the

Henrietta, Fleetwing, and Vesta competing in 1865.

revenue cutter, used for the prevention of smuggling. This vessel was fitted with an exaggerated cutter rig with a very long bowsprit and boom and with upper and lower square topsails set above a gaff-mainsail. The hull form was a full forebody and a long, fine run aft, a design which became known as the 'cod's head and mackerel tail' shape. Designed for long and strenuous service at sea, the revenue cutters were constructed to heavy scantlings, but yacht owners quickly learned that, for this particular sport, a lighter construction could provide additional speed. As at that time there was no system of handicapping yachts according to hull size or sail area, an owner anxious to win races merely built a larger yacht so that she could spread a greater area of sail. As an example, Mr. Joseph Weld's racing cutter *Alarm*, which won many races, was built in 1830 to a measurement tonnage of 193. As well as cutters, brigs and barks were popular for racing and, like cutters, were also increasing in size. In many of her races the *Alarm* faced competition from Lord Belfast's brig *Waterwitch*, built to a tonnage of 381, and from Mr. G.H. Acker's bark *Brilliant*, with a tonnage of 493.

By mid-century the sport of yacht racing was spreading rapidly, as much in the United States as in Europe. The competition among a growing number of yacht owners meant an increasing amount of profit for shipbuilders. There was also profit to be made by a designer who could come up with a better hull shape, and one which created less turbulence in the water, than the 'cod's head and mackerel tail' design to which the majority of yachts were still built. The first naval architect to apply his talents to this problem was the British engineer J. Scott Russell. In 1848 he designed an iron yacht, the *Mosquito*, which was a 50-ton cutter, built with a long, hollow bow and with the maximum beam well aft. She was a regular winner at regattas around the coast, but for a time her radical design aroused distrust among owners, and consequently only one other yacht was built to a similar design.

Three years later Scott Russell's design was vindicated when an American syndicate brought the schooner *America* across the Atlantic to compete in British regattas. She had been designed and built by George Steers to a hull shape similar to that of the *Mosquito*, and was a frequent winner in British waters. Her most famous race was in August 1851 when she came first of 16 starters in a race around the Isle of Wight to win a '100-guinea' cup presented by The Royal Yacht Squadron of Cowes. This became known as the America's Cup, a challenge trophy which, in the years since it was first won in 1851, has proved the greatest single stimulus to yacht design around the world, with millions of pounds, dollars, francs, and kroners spent by the many challengers and defenders.

Yacht racing was spreading so fast in popularity that it was now becoming big business. The next major step forward in hull design was achieved by E.H. Bentall, an agricultural engineer of Maldon in Essex, England, who built a yacht to his own ideas on the Blackwater River. She was the *Jullanar*, built in 1875 to, in his own words, 'the longest waterline, the smallest frictional surface, and the shortest keel.' She was narrower in the beam than previous yachts and proved a phenomenal success, virtually unbeatable in a race. Her design was later adapted to produce such famous racing yachts as King Edward VII's *Britannia*, Lord Dunraven's *Valkyrie II* and *Valkyrie III*, Mr. A.D. Clarke's *Satanita*, and the German Emperor's *Meteor II*. All these, and many others, were designed by G.L Watson and were built on the Clyde between 1893 and 1896. And at about the same time the great American designer Nathanael G. Herreshoff built the *Gloriana*, a smaller racing yacht but with a hull form entirely different from anything yet seen. Her main feature was an immensely long overhanging bow with the forefoot cut away to produce a straight line from the stem to a very short keel and terminating in a long overhanging counter stern. There was no other yacht in the United States which could match her for speed, and the basic theory of Herreshoff's *Gloriana* hull form has virtually remained standard racing-yacht design ever since.

A form of handicapping, based on the length of the waterline, had been introduced before the end of the century to enable yachts of different size to race together, but it led to the building of racing yachts designed specifically to beat the handicap rule. It was an unhealthy design, with a very small draft, a wide beam, and a deep fin keel. They were known generally as 'skimming dishes,' and while very fast, were virtually uninhabitable. In order to produce a more sound hull design, an international conference was held in 1906 which was attended by all the nations interested in yacht racing, with the exception of the United States. As a result a new measurement rule was adopted in which the beam as well as the length was a factor, and this produced not only a far more stable hull design but also an excellent seaboat. This was the first of what became known as the 'meter' rules for the design of racing yachts. The largest racing-class yachts were built to 23 meters, while 15-meter, 12-meter, 8-meter, and 6-meter classes were accepted as international classes which could race together at any regatta in the world.

Until 1911 all these meter-class yachts had the gaff-cutter rig, but during that year the Bermuda rig, which substituted a tall triangular sail for the gaff-mainsail and topsail, was introduced for some of the smaller racing classes. When racing was resumed after World War I the Bermuda rig was adopted almost universally for all racing yachts, and indeed for cruising yachts as well, its aerodynamic qualities proving much superior to the gaff rig. A new measurement rule was introduced in 1925 with the object of giving designers some latitude in relation to waterline length, beam measurement, and underbody

Jolie Brise, three times winner of the Fastnet Race.

shape while still remaining within the rule. This new rule produced the J-class yachts, the epitome of big class racing, with permissible variations in waterline length between 75 and 87 ft. (23-26.5 m). This allowed designers to exercise all their skills in the search for hydrodynamic excellence. These were probably the most beautiful racing yachts ever built, but they lasted only until 1937, the ris-

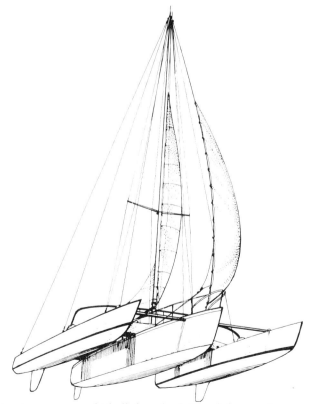

A trimaran, a multi-hulled yacht designed for speed.

The three-masted topsail schooner Sunbeam, *which Lord Brassey sailed around the world in 1876-77.*

ing costs of design, construction, large professional crews, and multiplicity of sails putting them beyond the financial reach of all but the very rich.

Since World War II yachting in all its aspects — racing, ocean racing, and cruising — has expanded at a phenomenal rate. Even the introduction of new building materials and series production techniques has failed to keep up with an ever-expanding demand, and the coastal waters of most maritime countries are today crowded with sailing yachts of varying shapes and sizes. The most prolific of the new building materials is glass-reinforced plastic (GRP), which lends itself to series production in long runs, but ferrocement and glued laminates have also played a big part in the modern yacht-building revolution. Steel and aluminum are also widely used today for racing-

and cruising-yacht hulls. As much research has gone into modern hull design as into aerodynamic research where, again, new materials such as nylon, Terylene, and Courlene have been used to replace the traditional canvas of sails and hemp of rope. In many modern yachts even the wire rope used for mast shrouds and stays has been replaced by mild steel bars. Aerodynamic research has also led to a change in the traditional sail plan, with the foretriangle superseding the mainsail as the main driving power of the yacht.

These postwar years have also seen the development of the multihull yacht, based on traditional Malayan and Polynesian design. The catamaran is a twin-hulled yacht with identical hulls widely spaced and connected with a rigid platform on which the mast is stepped and the accommodation built. The trimaran, a development of the catamaran, has a central hull and twin floats, one on either side. Both are capable of speeds of up to 20 knots in favorable conditions by reason of their low immersion area, but because of the inherent stiffness of the design, which prevents them from heeling over to the wind, they both need different handling techniques under sail than the normal single-hulled sailing yacht.

Ocean Racing

Ocean racing has a shorter history than regatta racing. The first long-distance offshore race was organized by the New York Yacht Club in 1866 when three schooners, *Henrietta, Fleetwing*, and *Vesta*, raced from Sandy Hook, U.S., to Cowes, England, for a prize of $30,000. Similar long-distance races took place during the next four years, and Kaiser Wilhelm II, anxious to convince other countries during the years of German naval rearmament before World War I that Germany was truly a maritime power, took a considerable part in the early organization of the sport. In 1897, in honor of Queen Victoria's golden jubilee, he presented a trophy for a race from Dover to Kiel, which became an annual event. In the same year he organized the Kiel Week regatta, a yearly yachting occasion comprising daily offshore races for cruising yachts to match the famous Cowes Week in England, and in 1905 he presented a silver cup for a race across the Atlantic.

In 1906 the Cruising Club of America started its biennial Rhode Island to Bermuda race over a course of 660 nautical miles (1,222 km). In 1925 the first Fastnet race was sailed in Britain over a 605-nautical mile (1,120-km) course from Cowes to Plymouth, rounding the Fastnet rock off southwest Ireland en route, and it was agreed between the two countries that the two races, the most prestigious in the ocean racing calendar, should alternate with each other.

Yachts which engaged in ocean racing during the early years were mainly ordinary cruising-type boats, sturdily built for a long sea life, generally gaff-rigged cutters or yawls. Many had been converted from working boats, such as fishing craft and pilot cutters, and one of the best known and successful ocean racing boats of these years was E.G. Martin's *Jolie Brise*, which started her life in 1913 as a 44-ton French pilot cutter. But in 1927 William Fife, a noted Scottish yacht designer, produced the 50-ton Bermuda-rigged cutter *Hallowe'en* specifically for ocean racing, and her success began a new era in offshore-racing yachts. This new departure was greatly encouraged in 1931 when the brilliant young American designer, Olin James Stephens, produced his 58-ft. (18-m) ocean-racing yawl *Dorade*, which swept the offshore racing board. There were many who regretted the passing of the old-fashioned cruising yacht, which for so long had been the backbone of the sport, but the new ocean racers were fine

seaboats, sturdy enough to stand up to the heaviest weather yet still able to make headway in even the gentlest of breezes. And with competition in ocean racing now on an international scale, the new boats undoubtedly presented a real challenge to a designer's skill and resulted in steady progress towards the goal of the ideal hull and rig for the ocean-racing yacht.

Early in the sport a handicapping system was instituted in order that yachts of different sizes could compete in the same race with a fair chance of success. It takes the form of a time correction factor, worked out on the basis of hull measurements, sail area, spars, and other design features, measured by officials of each national racing authority, and applied to the elapsed time of completion of the course to produce a corrected time.

The major ocean-racing event of today is probably the Admiral's Cup. It is open to teams of three yachts from any nation which wishes to compete and consists of the Royal Ocean Racing Club's Channel race of 215 nautical miles (398 km), two inshore races of 30 nautical miles (55 km) each, and terminates with the Fastnet race. A similar series is organized in France by the Cercle de la Voile for the One Ton Cup, and other nations, notably the U.S. with its Onion Patch Trophy, have instituted comparable events. The longest ocean race organized as a regular event is the Transatlantic race from Britain to the U.S. sailed every four years; another, very nearly as long, is the 2,500-nautical mile (4,630 km) California to Honolulu race which is held every other year.

There is also private sponsorship which, from time to time, organizes long-distance ocean races. The Round Britain race is a revival of a special race organized in 1887 by the Royal Thames Yacht Club to celebrate Queen Victoria's golden jubilee, but a more spectacular privately sponsored race, held in 1968-69, was the *Sunday Times* Golden Globe race for a single-handed nonstop circumnavigation from Falmouth, England, eastabout by way of the Cape of Good Hope, New Zealand, Cape Horn, and back to Falmouth. It was won by Robin Knox-Johnston who sailed 30,123 nautical miles (55,787) in 313 days in his 12-ton ketch yacht *Suhaili*, which he himself had helped to build in 1964.

Cruising

Cruising, the noncompetitive side of yachting, has become perhaps more a way of life than a form of sport. It reflects a general love of the sea life, and man's efforts to accommodate this love to the rigors and duties of everyday life. Before the days of modern boatbuilding materials and mass production, many of the more popular types of cruising yachts were, like the early ocean racers, conversions of working boats, designed to accommodate an owner and his family or crew in reasonable comfort for voyages lasting anything from days to months. In general these were

Gaff cutter with topsail; a cruising yacht.

stout, well-tried boats, capable of meeting the vagaries of weather and sea conditions.

There had been several instances of extended cruising during the 19th century, but these were generally undertaken by wealthy owners in large, well-found yachts, with professional crews. In 1876-77 Lord Brassey sailed around the world in his 531-ton three-masted topsail schooner *Sunbeam*, a voyage immortalized by Lady Brassey in her book *The Voyage of the Sunbeam*. Lord Crawford made many long cruising voyages in his 1,490-ton *Valhalla*, ship-rigged on three masts with a professional crew of 100 men. There were, of course, many smaller yachts engaged in cruising during these years, but a fairly general opinion among owners was that for prolonged cruising and distant voyaging, the minimum size of vessel needed was something around 100 tons, with a well-trained experienced crew to share the duties of sail changing, maintenance of the vessel, etc.

This general conception was shattered by two well-recorded voyages around the turn of the century, both of them single-handed circumnavigations. The first of them was the round-the-world voyage made in 1895-98 by Captain Joshua SLOCUM in the *Spray*, a 36-ft. (11-m) sloop of 9 tons, which he largely rebuilt from keel to truck with

oak that he felled, shaped, and treated himself. The second voyage, in 1901-04, was made by Captain John Voss in the *Tilikum*, a red cedar dug-out canoe decked over by Voss and fitted with three small masts, setting a small jib, gaff-foresail and mainsail, and jib-headed mizzen. She drew 22 in. (559 mm) of water forward and 24 in. (610 mm) aft, and probably still holds the record for being the smallest vessel ever to have made a circumnavigation. Both these notable voyages gave a considerable impetus to cruising, destroying the old belief that only with a large yacht and a big crew could long voyages and extended cruising be undertaken. Although today circumnavigation by cruising yacht, and single-handed circumnavigation at that, are relatively common, these two voyages are still remarkable because both were made before the days of purpose-built yachts, modern construction materials and man-made fibers, self-steering gear and radio direction finders, simplified navigation methods, new food preservation techniques, permanent radio contact with the shore, and financial sponsorship. They proved beyond all doubt that a small vessel soundly built and handled by an experienced seaman was capable of going in safety anywhere in the world, which is in truth the very essence of cruising. Almost as great an impetus to long-distance cruising in small yachts was provided by the writings of such people as Edward F. Knight, who in 1887-88 sailed a converted ship's lifeboat to the Baltic and back, a voyage described in *The Falcon in the Baltic*; R.T. McMullen, whose classic book *Down Channel* inspired many small-yacht sailors to follow his example; and Erskine Childers, whose novel *The Riddle of the Sands* has remained a best-seller ever since it was first published in 1903.

The great expansion of yachting since World War II, fostered by the introduction of new building techniques, has led to the mass construction of small, sturdy, well-designed, well-equipped yachts which are fully capable of undertaking long voyages in reasonable comfort and safety. There has, in recent years, been an immense growth in long-distance cruising in small boats, evidenced perhaps by such cruising voyages as that of the 20-ft. (6-m) sloop *Sopranino*, which in 1952 crossed the Atlantic with a crew of two, and that in 1958 of *Borer Bee*, a home-built, 24-ft. (7-m), plywood hard-chine sloop with bilge keels, which sailed from Singapore, where she was built, to Britain by way of the Red Sea and the Mediterranean. Since then thousands of equally impressive cruising voyages have been undertaken in small boats, so much so that they have virtually become a commonplace. That today they go mainly unremarked is perhaps the most convincing proof that cruising in all its aspects has become not only a favorite sport, but a way of life for thousands who choose to spend a large part of their lives afloat.

Right: modern racing yacht under parachute spinnaker.

The History of Exploration

Tradition has it that Pythagoras, who lived around 450 BC, was the first man to put forward the theory that the earth was a sphere. About 250 years later Eratosthenes, using the Pythagorean theory, worked out the circumference of the earth by measuring the lengths of shadows cast by the sun in Alexandria and Aswan, on the tropic of Cancer. His calculation differed by less than 4 percent from the figure we know today. He then constructed a world map, using meridians of longitude and parallels of latitude, measured from Rhodes, the seaport which he took as the center of the world. He was followed by Marinus of Tyre, who began drawing charts for seamen during the 1st century AD, and by Ptolemy, who solved the problem of how to project the curved surface of the earth onto a flat chart by a simple conic projection.

By the time of the fall of Constantinople, which brought into sharp focus the need to discover new routes to the east, most geographers and seamen recognized that the earth was a sphere. There were, however, still a few who clung to the belief, made plain in the poems of Homer, that the earth was a flat disk. The flat earth idea implied, of course, that if a ship ventured too far into the unknown seas beyond Europe, it would fall off the edge of the world, and for a time such fears may actually have hindered the pursuit of geographical knowledge.

Early Exploration

It could be argued that the first worldwide explorers were the Phoenicians, who sailed surprisingly far in their search for tin. Certainly they were the first Mediterranean sea people to venture into new and unknown waters; reputedly sailing south to the Azores, and north as far as Cornwall and the Scilly Islands. These voyages were undertaken long before the invention of the magnetic compass, and long before the first crude charts were produced. The Phoenicians relied principally on their ability to navigate by the sun and stars.

An approximately contemporary voyage, made apparently in search of geographical knowledge, was undertaken by Pytheas in the 4th century BC. Pytheas was a Greek navigator and astronomer who lived in the Greek colony of Massilia, now Marseilles. Although his own account of the voyage has been lost, quotations from it survive in the writings of Strabo and Polybius and enable us to map his voyage with reasonable certainty. Setting out from Massilia he sailed around the coasts of Spain and France, up the east coast of Britain until he reached the Orkney Islands, to which he gave the name Thule. He also sailed along the north European coast, probably as far as the Elbe estuary. Some claims have been made that he reached the Baltic, but this appears unlikely as there is no

Ptolemy's first conic projection, 2nd century AD.

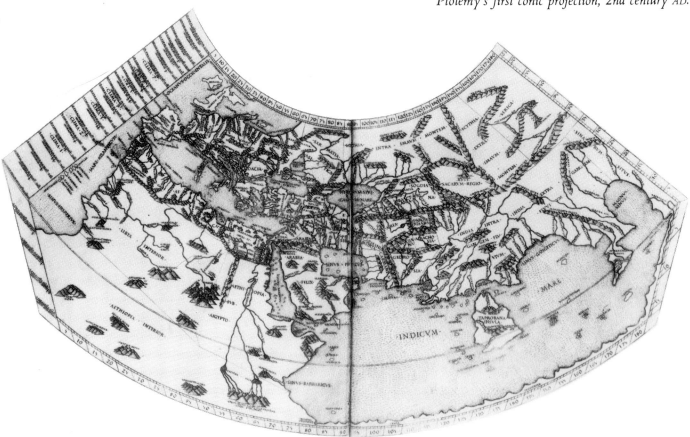

mention of the great peninsula of Denmark around which he would have had to sail. Pytheas' voyage is notable because he used observations of the sun's altitude to work out the latitude of the places he visited, and from his records Greek geographers, like Ptolemy, were able to incorporate these northern discoveries into their maps of the world.

Some of the Norse voyages of the 9th century AD can well be classed as explorations, particularly those of Eric the Red, Biarni Heriulfsson, and Leif ERICSSON. By island-hopping voyages via Britain, the Shetland Islands, and the Faroes, they reached Iceland, Greenland, and eventually Newfoundland, which they named Vinland. As a result, Iceland and Greenland were added to the world maps, although the existence of Vinland never became widely enough known to reach the Mediterranean mapmakers.

The Founding of the Hispanic Empires

The fall of Constantinople to the Turks in 1453 cut off Europe's profitable commerce with India and China and underscored the vital need to discover a new route to those territories. The great name behind this new enter-

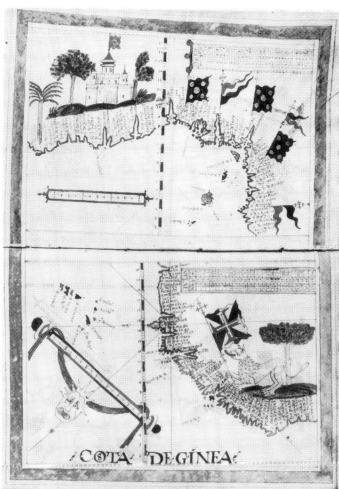

Portuguese map of African coast, c. 1550.

Henry, Prince of Portugal (1394-1460).

prise was Henry, Prince of Portugal, better known as HENRY THE NAVIGATOR, who became Governor of the Algarve and lived at Sagres. Here, in 1420, he set up an establishment for the study of navigation, astronomy, and cartography, which attracted the foremost mathematicians and geographers of the age. Some of them came from as far away as Arabia, which was then leading the world in navigational knowledge.

Henry's ambition was assisted in no small measure by the aids to navigation that had already been developed. The magnetic compass, though still not entirely reliable, was becoming a common instrument at sea; the Arabic *kamal*, for measuring the altitude of heavenly bodies, had been developed into the cross staff; and the astrolabe was in existence for measuring altitudes on land for surveying purposes, and soon came to be adapted for use at sea. One of Henry's recruits was Jafuda, the son of Abraham Cresques, the greatest exponent of the Catalan school of chartmaking. It was Jafuda who founded the Sagres school of hydrography which was to make Portuguese charts the most accurate and most valued throughout the

15th and 16th centuries. Henry was fortunate, too, that around this time the CARAVEL, the ideal small ship for long ocean voyages of discovery, was being developed with a weatherly ocean rig: the *caravela redonda*, square-rigged on the foremast and sometimes on the mainmast as well, in place of the all-lateen rig of the original *caravela latina*.

It is generally held that this adaptation of the traditional caravel rig, which played so great a part in the early history of exploration, can be attributed to the Venetian navigator Alvise da Cadamosto, whom Henry had enlisted in 1455 to take charge of his expeditions down the coast of Africa. In his second voyage of 1456, Cadamosto was driven out to sea by a storm and lamented the absence of square rig, which he considered much superior to the lateen rig in strong winds. As a result of the storm, Cadamosto discovered the Cape Verde Islands, and after exploring them returned to the African coast which he followed down as far as Konakry (10°N) before returning to Sagres. On his return he devised the compromise of part square rig, part lateen, which typified the *redonda* rig.

Henry the Navigator did not live long enough to see the full fruition of his navigational work, though by the time he died in 1460, sea captains trained at Sagres had slightly bettered Cadamosto's achievement and had penetrated down the west coast of Africa as far as Sierra Leone. But the amount of profit to be made from voyages to this coast, with the discovery of gold and the sale of negro slaves, exerted a negative influence on the impetus of exploration. Ship captains preferred to end their voyages there, with the certainty of handsome profits, rather than proceed farther into the unknown, and so for some years Henry's dream of rounding Africa faltered. This lack of incentive was overcome by Henry's successor, Alfonso V, who granted a monopoly of the Guinea trade to a Lisbon merchant named Fernão Gomez, on the condition that each year his ships sailed a further 100 leagues along the coast. Forced ever onward by this stipulation, Gomez's ships rounded the bulge of Africa to discover even greater riches along the Gold and Ivory Coasts, and by the time the monopoly ended, in 1474, he had reached the Island of Fernando Po, only 3°30′ above the equator.

There can be little doubt that Alfonso, like Henry before him, realized the political importance of pushing down the African coast. If, as was hoped and expected, Africa ended in the sea, then a new route to India and China, discovered and pioneered by Portuguese pilots and therefore Portuguese by right of prior discovery, would be opened. The prize, if it could be achieved, would be enormous, and so further voyages of exploration were sent out. By 1484 Diogo Cão had reached the mouth of the River Congo, and four years later the great prize fell into Portuguese hands. In December 1488 three caravels sailed up the Tagus, having earlier rounded the southern tip of Africa. Alfonso had by this date died, but his son, João II of Portugal, was there to witness the homecoming. The leader of the expedition, Bartholomew DIAZ, told the king how they sailed almost to mid-ocean before making enough southing to round Africa, and how they had then been driven even further to the south by a great storm before returning to the land. His landfall had been about 100 miles (160 km) east of the great southern cape of Africa, and he had named the place Agulhas. He had anchored his small squadron in what is now Mossel Bay to make repairs and take on fresh water and had then sailed for some distance up the east coast of Africa until a mutiny among his crews had forced him to return. On account of the great storm, Diaz had named the southern tip of Africa *Cabo Tormentoso*, Cape of Storms, but the king renamed it *Cabo da Bona Esperanza*, Cape of Good Hope, in recognition of the fact that the great prize of India, and perhaps China as well, was now within his grasp. And so it proved. Another Portuguese squadron, under the leadership of Vasco da GAMA, was sent out in the late autumn of 1497 and in May 1498 it reached Calicut on the western coast of India.

This voyage of Vasco da Gama gave Portugal a means of reaching India and China, and of tapping the rich trade which these countries offered. Portugal now had an answer to the Moslem domination of the existing land routes which had until then been the only means of communication and trade with the east. It was the culmination of a long and carefully planned campaign of expansion, founded on the earlier voyages of Diogo Cão, Bartholomew Diaz, and other Portuguese navigators. Only in one aspect did da Gama's voyage fail, and that was in trade itself. He carried the sort of trade goods — brass hawk bells, coral necklaces, and cheap textiles — which had dazzled the natives of West Africa, but which were laughed to scorn by the rich and relatively sophisticated rulers of India. Eventually da Gama managed to purchase a small cargo of spices to take home as samples by selling the shirts of his crew. In the follow-up voyage of 1500, under the command of Pedro Cabral, a very different type of trade goods was carried — the new shipborne gun known as the bombard. When all other forms of negotiation had failed, Cabral was able to enforce his demands and load full cargoes of desirable spices at very low prices. It was in his voyage to India that Cabral, crossing the South Atlantic to make sufficient way to the south to round the Cape of Good Hope, discovered the coast of Brazil and claimed it for Portugal.

Spain, the greatest maritime power in Europe, was also reaching for the same prize, though without the same sense of dedication as the Portuguese rulers. Ferdinand of Spain was a cautious monarch with no liking for risky ventures and he took much persuading that the shortest and easiest route to India lay to the west rather than to the

Right: Columbus leaves Palos on August 3, 1492, and bids farewell to Ferdinand and Isabella. Above: The Santa Maria, *Columbus' flagship.*

east. At this time Christopher COLUMBUS was formulating his 'Enterprise of the Indies,' as he called it, which was founded on the belief that Japan lay only 2,400 nautical miles (4,450 km) west of the Canary Islands (the correct distance is 10,600 nautical miles or 19,650 km) and that India was no more than a few hundred miles farther on. He took his 'Enterprise of the Indies' around the European courts and offered it to João II of Portugal, Henry VII of England, and Charles VIII of France, but they all turned it down. Ferdinand and Isabella, joint sovereigns of Spain, also twice declined to give it their backing. In the end they relented and in 1492 authorized Columbus to make the voyage with three small caravels. Columbus' little squadron sailed from Palos on August 3, 1492, and after a stop at the Canary Islands for repairs and rig alterations, land was sighted in the early morning of October 12. Columbus named the island San Salvador, and after

discovering several more islands and still convinced that India must lie just beyond the horizon, named them collectively *las Indias,* the Indies. It was not until his third voyage to *las Indias* in 1498-1500 that he realized this new discovery was not India, China, or Japan but a new and unknown continent lying across his route.

His voyage to the New World was followed by many others embarking from Spain. In 1513 Vasco Nuñez de Balboa, who had founded the town of Darien in the Gulf of Uraba, climbed the inland peaks of the Isthmus to become the first European to sight the great ocean which lay to the west of America. He claimed possession of it in the name of King Ferdinand of Spain and named it the 'Great South Sea.' It was while exploring in the Isthmus of Darien that he heard from natives of the gold of Peru, as also did Francisco Pizarro, who was one of Balboa's party. Bearing false witness against his leader, Pizarro was instrumental in getting Balboa condemned and executed for treason. He himself led the subsequent expedition to Peru and extracted the gold of the Inca civilization by torture and a ferocity seldom equaled before. Many of the other voyages at this time from Spain to the New World were mounted purely for plunder and exploitation, with no thought of adding to the knowledge of geography.

Following Balboa's sighting of the Great South Sea, new exploratory expeditions were dispatched from Spain to try to find a way through to the new ocean. Only that of Ferdinand MAGELLAN was successful. He was Portuguese by birth and had made several voyages to the Portuguese empire set up in India after the voyage of Vasco da Gama. Falling into disfavor in Portugal, he renounced his nationality and succeeded in interesting Charles V of Spain in a proposal to search for an entrance to the Great South Sea to the south of the new continent. He sailed in 1519 in command of a squadron of five ships, made a landfall near Pernambuco on the eastern coast of South America, and coasted southward to look for an opening through the land. He found it in the strait which now bears his name and reached the Great South Sea, renaming it Pacific because of the gentle weather which greeted him in those waters. He continued westward and after 98 days of near starvation and the decimation of his crews by scurvy, he discovered an island, probably Guam, where his men could rest and recover. With his ships refitted and his crews refreshed Magellan sailed on and reached the Philippine Islands in 1521, recognizing them from his previous voyages under the Portuguese flag. Magellan and many of his crew lost their lives in the Philippines when they mounted an attack on one of the islands in an attempt to convert it to Catholicism. Of the two ships which escaped destruction, one was so leaky that she had to be abandoned in Borneo, but the other, the *Vittoria,* under the command of Juan Sebastian del Cano, finally reached Spain in 1522 with only 31 of the original 270 men who

Magellan's attack on Mactan Island, 1521.

had set out on the expedition three years earlier.

This, the first circumnavigation of the world, is one of the epic voyages of history, stamping Magellan as one of the world's greatest navigators. Although he did not himself live to complete the voyage, Magellan can be described as the first circumnavigator since he had previously reached the Philippines during his service in the east with the Portuguese. But the great importance of his voyage was the discovery of the Magellan Strait, which opened up a new sea route to India and China. Almost equally important was the discovery of the vastness of the Pacific Ocean, first made apparent to the world's geographers when the log of the surviving *Vittoria* was studied after her return. For the first time the true size of the earth came to be realized and consequently new atlases and charts were drawn up which began to approximate the representation of the world as we know it. The new charts were to prove a great boon to the seamen who followed in Magellan's footsteps.

This opening up of the world by the Spanish and Portuguese voyages to the west and the east led both countries to seek to legitimize their claims of monopoly of these routes. The principle of possession by right of prior discovery was already recognized throughout Europe, although this referred to the discovery of land, and had so far never been applied to the sea. Already a papal bull issued by Pope Alexander VI had granted to Spain the possession of all land lying to the west of a line drawn north and south 100 leagues west of the Azores, and to Portugal all land lying to the east. A new application was made to the Pope for a revision of this papal bull to recognize not only Cabral's claim to Brazil but also to cover the seas traversed by Spanish and Portuguese ships. A new papal bull was issued moving the line a further 270 degrees to the west to give Portugal possession of Brazil, and it confirmed Spain's and Portugal's sovereignty of the sea routes linking their new land discoveries to their homelands.

Portugal now set about consolidating her new empire in the east, relying on the revised papal bull to deny the sea routes to all foreign competition. After Cabral's voyage, in which force had been used to assert Portuguese trading interests, another expedition led by Alfonso d'ALBUQUERQUE was sent out in 1503 both to extend the trading empire and to consolidate it against possible attack. Appointed as viceroy to rule the eastern lands in the name of the king, he was perhaps more of a soldier than an explorer, although he did make several new discoveries, particularly in the Red Sea, which he was the first European to enter. On his arrival in the east, he captured Goa and fortified it to serve as the capital and as a main supply and repair base for the empire. He then fought a successful campaign to win Malacca for the Portuguese crown, but while he was thus engaged his ship, containing all the wealth he had accumulated during his career, sank in Goa harbor. He set about amassing another fortune, but died of a heart attack when he learned that he was to be superseded as a result of intrigues in the Portuguese court. Although his discoveries in these eastern waters were perhaps of little importance in the light of the earlier voyages of da Gama and Cabral, to him must go the credit of bringing together Portuguese interests in the east and welding them into a practical and defensible trading empire. That, some 50 or 60 years later, this empire was breached without much difficulty by Dutch and English merchant adventurers was not the fault of d'Albuquerque, who had been remarkably thorough in his work, but was due to Portugal's lack of will to back her new empire with a fleet of warships to protect lines of sea communication. In the existing climate of world trade and competition, reliance on a papal bull was not enough; the initial discoveries and national claims required a backing of naval power if they were to endure and prosper.

The Rival Nations

Although Spain and Portugal never questioned the legality of the papal bull which in effect divided the ownership of the entire world between them, it found no such recognition in Protestant Holland and Britain. Even France, one of the foremost Catholic nations of Europe, decided that the need for trade, which all new discovery engenders, must take precedence over her allegiance to Rome. So far as these three countries were concerned, there was still a tremendous area of the world waiting to be discovered, and in their opinion the sea was an open highway free for all to navigate. China was still believed to be a land of immense and inexhaustible wealth, at least as great as that of India, and if an alternative to Magellan's route could be found to reach it, one which did not entail such a long and arduous voyage, then it might well pay a remarkably handsome dividend.

France was the first of the non-Hispanic nations of Europe to mount the search for an alternative westward passage to China. Two Florentine brothers, Giovanni and Girolamo da VERRAZZANO, who sailed in the service of France, left Dieppe in a ship provided by King François I of France and sailed to America. They reached the coast near the present Cape Fear in North Carolina and sailed north. At first they thought they had found a way through to the Pacific when they reached Pamlico Sound, mistaking the great area of water inside the Outer Banks for the Pacific, but when they realized their mistake they continued northward. They were the first Europeans to enter New York Bay and Narragansett Bay, the site of the present Newport in Rhode Island, and may even have reached the coast of Newfoundland after rounding Cape Cod. They returned home with nothing of value beyond a series of accurate maps drawn by Girolamo, but these were not sufficient to stimulate François I into financing a second voyage. However, the Verrazzano brothers managed to attract enough backing for a second voyage, during which they visited Brazil and returned with a cargo of logwood which was sold profitably. This was

French ships reach Portus Regalis, Florida, in 1562.

65

Map of the New World by Abraham Ortelius, 1570.

used to finance a third voyage in 1528 in which Giovanni Verrazzano proposed a search of the Isthmus of Darien for a route through to the Pacific. The voyage was a tragic failure. They reached the Lower Antilles and, remembering the friendly Indian tribes they had encountered along the North American coast during their first voyage, decided to take a boat ashore, not realizing that the inhabitants of the Antilles were man-eating Caribs. As their boat neared the shore, Giovanni stepped into the water and waded to the beach, to be instantly cut up and eaten by the natives. Verrazzano was not the only explorer to meet this fate. Two hundred and fifty years later the French explorer Nicholas Marion-Dufresne and several members of his crew were eaten by Maoris when

they set foot in New Zealand in 1772.

A second French expedition was sent out in 1534 under the command of Jacques CARTIER. He discovered the entrance to the St. Lawrence River and sailed up it, confident that it would extend to the center of the continent where a west-flowing river would be found leading to the Pacific. There was, of course, no such river, but the land was rich in furs, and the addition of Canada to the French empire was a handsome reward for Cartier's enterprise.

Holland, which at this period was a province of Spain — though actively engaged in a struggle for independence with England's help and encouragement — was slow in starting her empire building. When she did so, she chose the easier and more logical way, looking eastward rather

66

Encounter with a bear on Barents' Arctic expedition, July 1594.

The Elusive Northern Passage

The first two voyages in search of the Northeast Passage set out in 1553, led by Sir Hugh WILLOUGHBY and Richard CHANCELLOR. Both of them failed to find a way through the ice which they encountered in the seas around Novaya Zemlya. These voyages were followed by those of Stephen Borough in 1556, James Bassendive in 1568, Arthur Pet and Charles Jackman in 1580, and Henry HUDSON in 1607 and 1608. Most of these voyages made important geographical discoveries, and one at least resulted in the formation of the profitable Muscovy Company for opening up trade with Russia, but none of them succeeded in finding a new sea route to China. The farthest that any of them reached was the western edge of the Kara Sea where the Arctic ice blocked any further progress. After the failure of the English voyages, the Dutch mounted an expedition in 1594, led by Willem BARENTS, but it too was unable to find a route through the ice.

The English search for a Northwest Passage was a much more prolonged affair. Most world maps of the period showed an open Arctic Ocean to the north of America and there seemed to be no reason why ships should not sail through it to reach China. The first three voyages in 1576, 1577, and 1578 were made by Martin FROBISHER, resulting in the discovery of Frobisher Bay in the southwest corner of what is now Baffin Island. There followed three voyages by John DAVIS in 1585, 1586, and 1587, with Davis taking a more northerly route after passing Cape Farewell on the southern tip of Greenland. This route took him through the strait which separates Greenland and Baffin Island and is named after him. Henry Hudson, unsuccessful in finding a passage to the northeast, now made two voyages to the northwest, sailing through the Hudson Strait and into the huge Hudson

than westward as France had done. Her ships rounded the Cape of Good Hope, struck the southern tip of India, and pushed down to the southeast, colonizing the islands of the East Indies and setting up their local capital in Batavia.

As opposed to the French concentration on a western route and Dutch concentration on an eastern route, England attempted to search in both directions. Her one previous attempt to discover a trading empire in the New World had been disappointing, for John CABOT's voyage across the North Atlantic in 1497 had resulted only in the discovery of Newfoundland, a land of little economic worth. On his way home Cabot had sailed across the Grand Banks off the Newfoundland coast and discovered the immense cod fishery there. The theory of ownership by prior discovery, however, could hardly be applied to an area of sea and defended as a national monopoly, and in any case, Portuguese and Breton fishermen had been fishing the Grand Banks 200 years before Cabot's arrival. So there began for England the heart-breaking search for new sea routes to China westward around the north of America and eastward around the north of Europe. The theory of these sea passages was first advanced in England by Robert Thorne in 1527 as a means of avoiding conflict with the Spaniards and Portuguese, both of whom had resources of naval power to defend their claims far in excess of those of England. As the years advanced, and her searches for a Northeast and a Northwest Passage to China foundered in disappointment, it became apparent that England would have to fight for the right to trade in the new markets of east and west, but she was not in a position to do so until near the end of the 16th century, when the new GALLEON design was introduced.

The Gabriel, *in which Frobisher sailed to Greenland in 1576.*

Bay on his second voyage in 1610. After wintering in what is now known as James Bay, where his ship was frozen in until the spring thaw, Hudson was put ashore with other members of his crew by his mutinous second-in-command and was never seen again.

William BAFFIN continued the search for a Northwest Passage with five voyages made between 1612 and 1616. Following Davis' route, his ships made their way north-westward into what is now known as Baffin Bay, and reached the northern end of it during his last voyage, but he was halted by thick ice. Baffin must, however, have been reasonably close to Lancaster Sound, through which the much-desired Northwest Passage was finally achieved. The last of this series of expeditions was made in 1631 by Luke Foxe and Thomas James. They were successful to the extent that they finally proved that there was no way through to the Pacific from the western shore of Hudson Bay. Foxe Basin, in the north of Hudson Bay, and James Bay in the south, are named after these explorers. Their voyages did, however, achieve the formation a few years later of the great Hudson Bay Company, set up to exploit the rich fur trade.

James COOK, in his third and final voyage, tried to find an entrance to the Northwest Passage from the Pacific end. He sailed round the southwestern extremity of the Alaskan peninsula and through the Bering Strait to reach a latitude of 70°30′ N before being stopped by an ice wall. English attempts to find this elusive Northwest Passage spanned nearly 350 years. In 1745 the British Parliament offered a reward of £20,000 to any British subject, excepting those in ships of the Royal Navy, who could discover a Northwest Passage through the Hudson Strait. However, very few would-be explorers were tempted by this offer, mainly because the earlier voyages had found no way out from Hudson Bay. But when the Parliament Act was amended twenty years later to make the offer open to naval ships, and removed the requirement of the Hudson Strait route in favor of a more northerly one, a long series of British Admiralty expeditions took up the search. The first was in 1818, under the command of Commodore John Ross; followed by Edward Parry in 1819-20, 1821, and 1824-25; George Lyon in 1825; John Ross again in 1829-33; James Ross in 1831; George Back in 1836-37; and Sir John Franklin, who sailed in 1845 and was never seen again. When he failed to return, some 40 search expeditions were sent out to try to discover his fate and it was on one of these, in 1850, that Admiral Robert McClure finally discovered the strait, named after him,

Officers of the 1852 expedition sent out in search of Sir John Franklin.

LIEUTENANT OSBORN, COMMANDER OF THE "PIONEER."   MR. ALLARD, MASTER OF THE "PIONEER."   COMMANDER M'CLINTOCK ("INTREPID.")   MR. PULLEN, MASTER OF "THE NORTH STAR."   COMMANDER RICHARDS ("ASSISTANCE").

THE ARCTIC SEARCHING SQUADRON.—(FROM PHOTOGRAPHS BY BEARD.)

which led into the Beaufort Sea and through the Bering Strait into the Pacific. It is an oddity of history that for the next 50 years this Northwest Passage, which had been so sought after and which had claimed so many lives, remained unused and almost forgotten. The first person to negotiate the Passage successfully was the Norwegian explorer Roald AMUNDSEN who, in 1902, sailed from east to west in the small fishing sloop *Gjøa*. Some 35 years later Henry Larson repeated the feat from west to east in the Royal Canadian police boat *St. Roch*. Finally, in 1969, the 400-year old dream of a commercially viable Northwest Passage from the Atlantic to the Pacific was realized when the Humble Oil Company's 150,000-ton tanker MANHATTAN brought the first cargo of crude oil from the Alaskan oilfield to refineries on the east coast. Unhappily she suffered such severe damage from the ice during her voyage that it was never repeated, and the Passage's commercial prospects withered and died, despite the fact that shortly after the *Manhattan's* passage the 6,000-ton Swedish ship *Trojoland* reached Bathurst Island with oil drilling equipment and returned without mishap.

Terra Australis Incognita

The late 15th-century voyages of Vasco da Gama to India and Columbus to the West Indies had effectively shown that there were few parts of the earth which could not be reached by sea, and the only task remaining was to fill in the gaps still left in the geographers' world maps. Magellan had of course shown that there was another way into the Pacific besides that around the Cape of Good Hope and across the Indian Ocean, but even his great voyage contributed little to the charting of the unknown areas. It was largely through the formation in the first years of the 17th century of the various national East India Companies, particularly the English and Dutch, that many of the gaps in the Pacific Ocean were filled in, with the Dutch company spreading southward down the chain of the East Indies and the English company pushing their interests around the Malay peninsula and up to China.

In 1642 Abel TASMAN, a skilled navigator of the Dutch East India Company, was sent on an expedition to discover the extent of Terra Australis Incognita, a vast landmass which geographers believed must exist somewhere in the southern hemisphere to balance the huge landmass which they now knew existed in the northern hemisphere. Several Dutch navigators had already sighted parts of the northern and western coasts of Australia during the course of their voyages, but it was Tasman's task to discover whether this land was a part of the legendary southern continent. He proved that it was not by a circumnavigation of Australia, during the course of which he landed on what is now called Tasmania and named it Van Diemen's Land in honor of the Governor of the Dutch East Indies. Later he sighted the coasts of New Zealand,

explored the islands of the Tonga group, and returned to Batavia, whence he had sailed, by way of the New Hebrides group, Solomon Islands, and New Guinea. Although his voyage proved that Australia was an island, it still did not solve the problem of Terra Australis Incognita, which continued to be shown on the world maps as a huge and unknown continent.

Magellan's round-the-world voyage of 1519-22 was followed 58 years later by a similar voyage by Sir Francis DRAKE. This, however, was in no way intended as a voyage of exploration; it was more a privateering voyage directed against Spain in which the main object was plunder and a challenge to Spanish claims of sovereignty over the whole of the Pacific Ocean. Yet, unknowingly, Drake made one significant discovery when, after sailing through the straits of Magellan, he was driven south by a storm to about latitude 57°S, proving that Tierra del Fuego was an island and not part of Terra Australis Incognita, as all geographers had concluded after reading the account of Magellan's voyage. In his account of the voyage Drake wrote that south of the island 'the Atlantic and the South Sea meet in a large and free scope,' but the importance of this discovery of yet another and easier way into the Pacific from the west was only realized in 1616 when it was used by Jacob LE MAIRE and Willem Schouten. They were looking for a new way into the Pacific in order to circumvent the regulations of the Dutch East India Company, whereby the use of the Magellan Strait was forbidden to all Dutch ships except those of the Company. Jacob le Maire had read Drake's description and had seen in it a possible means of breaking the Company's monopoly of trade in the East Indies.

Drake's voyage was to set off a whole series of expeditions, particularly when it was learned that he had returned from his circumnavigation with treasure valued at half a million pounds in Elizabethan money. Most of these subsequent voyages made some contribution to the charting of the world, as also did the many buccaneering voyages around the turn of the 17th century, for example those of William DAMPIER.

By the middle of the 18th century only one geographical enigma remained: the position and extent of Terra Australis Incognita, which the mapmakers still insisted must exist if the earth were not to topple over under the predominant weight of landmass in the northern hemisphere. This last unknown was finally solved by Captain James Cook in the course of his three great voyages. On his first voyage Cook sailed from Plymouth in 1768, and after his observations at Tahiti of the transit of Venus across the face of the sun, which he made on behalf of the Royal Society, he followed the Admiralty's directive and set out to the south in search of the legendary continent. He reached the latitude of 40°S without sighting land, and the long southerly swell which he encountered convinced him that the open ocean must persist for a considerable distance in that direction. Sailing west along the parallel he reached New Zealand and proceeded down the length of North Island, surveying the coast as he went. Sailing through the strait which separates North and South Islands and which today bears his name, he was able to demonstrate that New Zealand was in fact a number of separate islands and not a part of the mainland of Australia as had previously been thought by the world's mapmakers.

But he had not yet proved beyond doubt that Terra Australis Incognita did not exist. There was more than enough space south of 40°S to accommodate another continent, and until it was fully explored and proved to be empty there must still be doubt about its existence. The importance of this issue was largely political since, if a great southern continent did exist, the British wanted to

Replica of Sir Francis Drake's Golden Hind.

A typical example of early 17th-century cartography: John Speed's 'new and accurate' map of the world, 1626.

Drake presented with a crown in Nova Albion, 1579.

might be outlying islands of the unknown continent. In the same year Cook embarked on his second voyage and, after rounding the Cape of Good Hope, attempted to find the islands which Kerguelen-Tremarec had reported. He failed to discover them, but by sailing well to the south of their reported latitude, proved at least that they could not be part of Terra Australis Incognita. Turning eastward, he became, in January 1773, the first navigator ever to cross the Antarctic circle. He continued in these latitudes until he was in the longitude of the east coast of Australia and turned north to rest and refit in New Zealand. He spent the remainder of the year in the Pacific and by the start of 1774 was back in the high south latitudes to continue his search. Still steering east he again crossed the Antarctic circle and reached the latitude of 71°10′ S before being turned back by ice. His ship passed well south of Cape Horn and finally completed the circumnavigation in these high latitudes. Whenever he attempted to steer farther to the south he encountered ice, which convinced him that although there might be a continent in the far south, it must be inhabitable and of no great value to Britain.

The Scientific Quest

Beyond a few island groups in the Pacific, South Indian Ocean, and South Atlantic, there was little of the habitable world left to discover after Cook's three voyages. The emphasis in exploration now turned towards science, and a whole succession of voyages was made to every part of the world to study flora and fauna, to investigate the physical effects of the earth's magnetism, and above all to survey the world's coastal waters and ocean depths with the same degree of meticulous accuracy which had so characterized Cook's work. The United States and most of the European nations took part in this new quest, which produced many accurate and detailed records and charts. Most of these expeditions sailed fully equipped with teams of draftsmen, painters, hydrographers, biologists, botanists, and other scientists.

Typical of these scientific voyages were those of George Vancouver, a fine navigator and marine surveyor in the Cook tradition. His first surveys in 1791 were in the waters around Australia and New Zealand; a year later he carried out the work for which he is best known, in Puget Sound and Vancouver Island on the west coast of North America. Another of these voyages was that of Matthew Flinders, who circumnavigated Australia in 1801-03, surveying as he went. His scientific studies on the deviation of the compass caused by the iron components of ships were perhaps his major contribution to navigation, and the Flinders' Bar, which he devised, is still used in modern magnetic compasses to reduce the deviation error. Another explorer who studied the best methods of compensating magnetic compasses against the residual magnetism of iron ships was the Russian explorer Adam

claim possession of it before the French or Spanish could reach it. Consequently a second voyage was planned for Cook. In 1772 the French navigator Yves Kerguelen-Tremarec had found a group of sub-Antarctic islands, which he named Iles de Kerguelen; he believed these

Captain James Cook (1728-79).

Cook receives an offering from the Polynesians, 1779.

Krusenstern, who was sent on a voyage by the Czar to demonstrate the advantages of opening a sea route from Russia to China via Cape Horn.

In 1817 the French navigator Louis-Claude de Freycinet sailed for the Pacific on a three-year voyage to undertake scientific observations in geography, astronomy, meteorology, and terrestrial magnetism. On his return he spent 20 years preparing and publishing his observations and surveys in an edition of 13 volumes of text and four of charts and plates, regarded today as one of the finest and most detailed descriptions of a voyage ever published. Another French circumnavigation was that led by Jules-Sebastian Dumont d'Urville in 1822-25, devoted to studies of hydrography and natural history, and as well recorded as that of de Freycinet. During a later voyage in 1837-40 d'Urville penetrated the Antarctic ice in the hope of discovering the South Magnetic Pole.

One of the best known scientific voyages of the 19th century was that of the BEAGLE, commanded by Robert Fitzroy with the naturalist Charles Darwin on board. The main objective of this voyage was the surveying of the southeast coast of South America and the Straits of Magellan, and Fitzroy's survey still stands as one of the most accurate and detailed ever made — although outside the circle of navigators it was overshadowed by the naturalist studies of Charles Darwin. Like James Cook before him, Fitzroy was a man who always had the welfare of his crew at heart. When he retired from active sea life he spent much of his time in meteorological studies to try to determine a method of forecasting storms at sea and a means of warning sailors of their dangers. He was the first man to draw synoptic charts in a study of weather patterns, and devised a system of storm-warning signals by means of cones hoisted ashore that is still used today.

Finally, although he was not an explorer, the U.S. naval officer Matthew MAURY deserves a mention for his detailed and prolonged studies of the North Atlantic winds and currents. He was a navigator who earned a worldwide reputation in the science of oceanography and hydrography. His charts and sailing directions were used by seamen of many nations to save time and distance on ocean voyages by the most advantageous use of currents and favorable winds. Today he is recognized as the true father of oceanography, and his system of recording oceanographical information was adopted in naval and merchant ships of all maritime countries.

Arctic Exploration

The long and fruitless searches for the Northeast and Northwest Passages to China had brought a number of navigators to the fringe of the Arctic Ocean. The Arctic circle itself is drawn along the latitude of 66°33'N, a circle with a diameter of 3,300 nautical miles (6,100 km) and enclosing an area of 5,400,000 square miles (14,000,000 km^2). Within this area lie the northern tips of the European, Asian, and North American landmasses. The remainder is ocean, most of it permanently covered with ice which varies in thickness, according to the season, from 5 to 30 ft. (1.5-9.0 m). It is a solid mass in winter, but breaks up into floes in the summer. The ice drifts in a northwesterly direction from about the middle of the Siberian coast towards the northeast tip of Greenland.

The early navigators, in their searches for an alternative sea route to China across the top of the world, reached Novaya Zemlya in the east and Baffin Bay in the west, both in about latitude 71°N. Henry Hudson reached a latitude of 80°23' N in one of his four voyages, the farthest north that man had yet penetrated, and on his return voyage he discovered Jan Mayen Island. A large number of the islands lying to the north of the main landmasses were discovered and charted during these early voyages, with the exception of some lying to the north of Canada, which were not known to man until the great series of naval voyages made in the 19th century which finally solved the riddle of the Northwest Passage. Their names, and the names of the straits which separate them, sound almost like a roll call of the leaders of the expeditions which went in search of the Passage.

In 1648 the Russian explorer Semyon Dezhnev sailed around the northeastern tip of Siberia, through the strait which separates it from Alaska, and into the ocean beyond. This strait was rediscovered in 1725 by Vitus Bering, a Russian naval officer who gave it his name. Bering charted Kamchatka and the Anadyr peninsula. Another Russian expedition, known as the 'Great Northern,' charted the northern coast of Siberia in 1733-43. The expedition sailed in two parts, one starting from the west and sailing east, and one from the east and sailing west. Fyodor Menin explored the west coast of

Taymyr as far north as 75° while Khariton Laptev surveyed the west coast. By the end of the expedition the gap between the two parts was less than 500 miles (800 km), although the most northerly point of the Taymyr peninsula, lying in about 78°N, was only reached on foot. The man who made this final trek was Semyon Chelyuskin, who gave his name to the Cape. This 'Great Northern' expedition almost achieved the Northeast Passage, its near success being due to the fact that in the summer much of the Passage is free from ice; in winter conditions the ice not only extends farther to the south but also thickens to form an almost impenetrable barrier.

That the Northeast Passage was a reality was proved in 1878-79 when the Swedish explorer Nils NORDENSKJÖLD made his famous circumnavigation of Europe and Asia in his ship *Vega*. He very nearly completed the Northeast Passage in a single season, being within 100 miles (160 km) of Bering Strait before ice brought the *Vega* to a halt. When the ice retreated in the following summer he completed both the Northeast Passage and his circumnavigation. Between the two world wars the Soviet Union, as the largest occupier of Arctic territory, became interested in these northern waters and in 1932 set up a government department, known as the *Glavsevmorput*, to administer the 'northern sea route,' their name for the Northeast Passage. After three years of surveying the route, laying buoys, and assembling icebreakers, two ships were passed through in each direction, and in 1936, the first full year of operation, more than 100 ships used the route. During World War II, before the German attack on the Soviet Union, the German merchant raider *Komet* reached the Pacific with the assistance of the Russian icebreaker *Josef Stalin*. After the war the Soviet Union built the 16,000-ton nuclear icebreaker LENIN for use on the northern sea route, following her with the larger and more powerful icebreakers of the *Arktika* class.

The first real attempt to reach the geographical North Pole as distinct from the Northwest and Northeast Passages was made in 1773 by the British navy with the ships *Racehorse* and *Carcass*. Led by Commodore Phipps, it is chiefly remembered because the young Horatio NELSON served in the expedition as a midshipman and showed some signs of his outstanding qualities in a spirited and well-publicized encounter with a polar bear. The latitude of 80°40' N was reached before the ships were turned back by ice. Another attempt, which was John FRANKLIN's first voyage of Arctic exploration, was made in 1818 but was equally unsuccessful. At this time there was in Britain a strong revival of interest in Arctic exploration due largely to the influence of Sir John Barrow, the Secretary of the Admiralty. With his active support a whole series of naval voyages was made to the north, most of them still searching for that will-o'-the-wisp, the Northwest Passage, although some took as their goal the North Pole itself.

The Erebus *in James Ross' Antarctic expedition, 1839-43.*

They all shared, however, the same dedication to scientific research regardless of their geographical destinations. James Ross took part in an expedition led by his uncle, John Ross, in search of the Northwest Passage, and in the course of the voyage he discovered the North Magnetic Pole in 1831. Another major achievement was that of William Parry during his fourth Arctic voyage: in an attempt to reach the Pole across the ice from Spitsbergen, he reached latitude 82°45' N, the highest yet achieved.

Although none of the expeditions for the Northwest Passage was successful, they all added considerably to the mapping of the northern territory and islands of the North American continent. In 1848 James Ross penetrated Lancaster Sound and surveyed Somerset Island. Two years later a British naval expedition succeeded in linking the Prince of Wales Strait and Melville Sound. The American expeditions of 1850 and 1853, led respectively by Henry Grinnell and Elisha Kane, discovered much new territory in the north. Another British naval expedition of 1852, under Sir Edward Belcher, rescued Robert McClure and his men, who had been forced to abandon their ship in the ice off Banks Island after their discovery of a Northwest Passage through to the Pacific.

Most of the expeditions to the Arctic in the years between 1848 and 1859 were sent out to search for Sir John Franklin and his crews, who had led an expedition of two ships into these waters in 1845 and had never returned. In all, no fewer than 39 expeditions were sent out in search of him, mainly from Britain, the United States, and Canada, and it was not until 1859 that Captain McLintock, in the steam yacht *Fox*, discovered a cairn containing the log of the expedition up to April 25, 1848. It told how Franklin's two ships, *Erebus* and *Terror*, had been made fast in the ice near King William Island just as the expedition was about to discover a new passage through Peel Sound. After 18 months in the ice the ship had been abandoned and the survivors had set out to march to safety. None survived.

Arctic Exploration

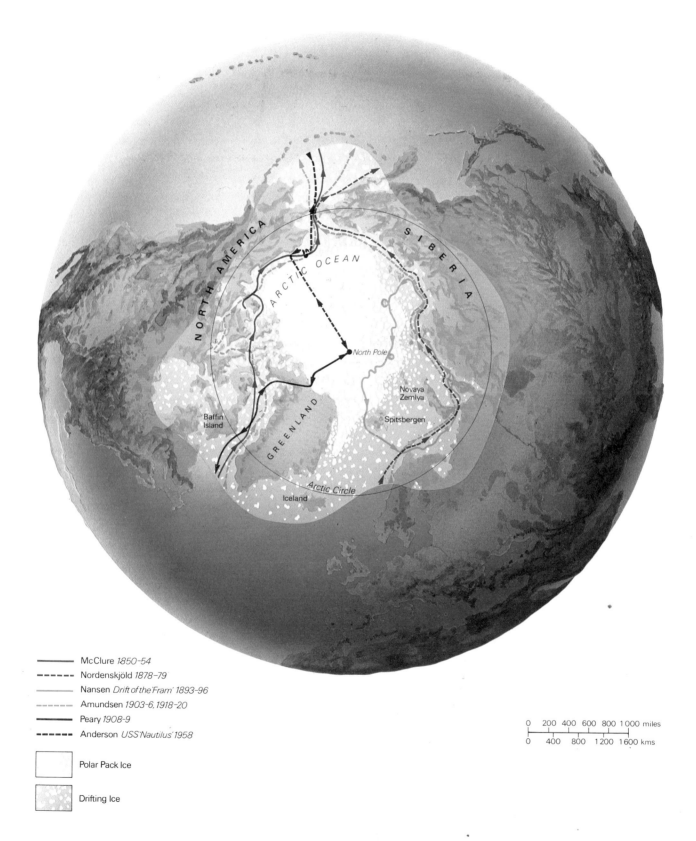

NORTH AMERICA

SIBERIA

ARCTIC OCEAN

North Pole

Novaya
Zemlya

Spitsbergen

Baffin
Island

GREENLAND

Arctic Circle

Iceland

McClure *1850-54*

Nordenskjöld *1878-79*

Nansen *Drift of the 'Fram' 1893-96*

Amundsen *1903-6, 1918-20*

Peary *1908-9*

Anderson *USS 'Nautilus' 1958*

Polar Pack Ice

Drifting Ice

0 200 400 600 800 1000 miles

0   400 800 1200 1600 kms

Antarctic Exploration

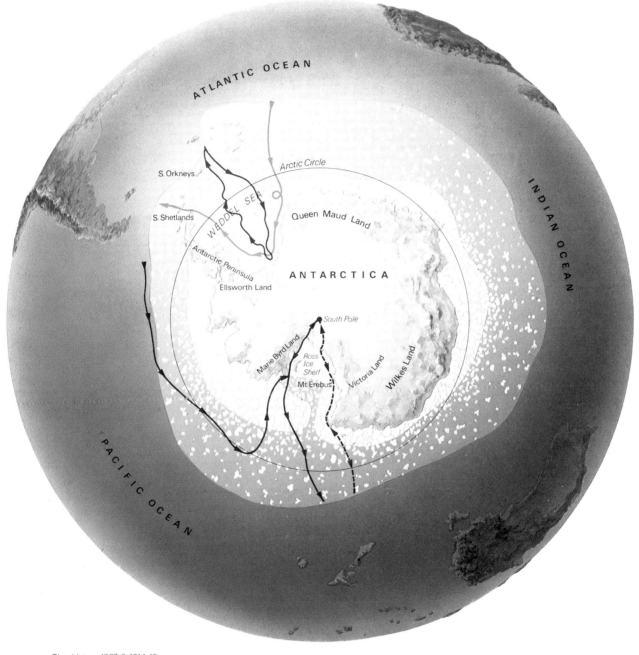

ATLANTIC OCEAN

S. Orkneys

Arctic Circle

WEDDELL SEA

Queen Maud Land

S. Shetlands

Antarctic Peninsula

ANTARCTICA

Ellsworth Land

INDIAN OCEAN

South Pole

Marie Byrd Land

Ross Ice Shelf

Victoria Land

Wilkes Land

Mt Erebus

PACIFIC OCEAN

Shackleton *1907-9, 1914-15*
Amundsen *1910-12*
Scott *1911-12*
Filchner *1911-12*

Polar Pack Ice

Drifting Ice

| 0 | 200 | 400 | 600 | 800 | 1000 miles |
| 0 | 400 | 800 | 1200 | 1600 kms |

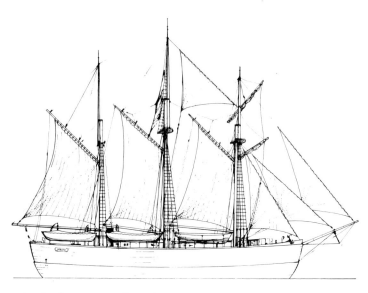

Fridtjof Nansen's ship, the Fram.

After McClure's success in establishing the existence of the Northwest Passage, most attention in Arctic exploration was directed towards achievement of the Pole itself. Captain Hull, making his third Arctic voyage in 1871, reached a point 412 miles (663 km) from the Pole; in 1875 Lieutenant Markham, a member of the British expedition led by George Nares, reached a latitude of 83°20′ N. The American explorer G.W. de Long led an expedition in 1879 but his ship, the *Jeanette*, was crushed in the ice off the New Siberian Islands. The wreck was discovered some years later off the southeast coast of Greenland, a proof of the existence of the north polar drift. This information was used by the Norwegian explorer Fridtjof NANSEN on his second polar voyage in 1893 when he deliberately sailed his specially strengthened research ship FRAM into the pack ice near the place where the *Jeanette* had been crushed. Three years later, after drifting across the polar icefield, the *Fram* reached open water northwest of Spitsbergen, and during the drift Nansen sledged to a point 227 miles (365 km) from the Pole. This record was bettered by 20 miles (32 km) four years later by an Italian expedition led by the Duke of Abruzzi.

Some ten years later, in 1909, Captain Robert PEARY claimed to have reached the North Pole on April 6 of that year. Less than a week earlier, another American, Dr. Frederick Cook, had claimed to have reached the Pole on April 21 of the previous year. He was a member of an expedition sent out in 1907 but as nothing had been heard of him, it was assumed he had died of exposure during the attempt. A scientific investigation later upheld Peary's claim and discredited that of Cook.

In the following years various attempts were made to reach the North Pole by air, by such men as the Swedish scientist Andrée, Roald Amundsen, Admiral Richard Byrd, Umberto Nobile, and Hubert Wilkins, and they met with varying degrees of success. On August 3, 1958 a new way of reaching the North Pole was achieved by Commander W.R. Anderson, who made the first successful submerged transpolar voyage in the nuclear submarine NAUTILUS. On March 17 of the following year polar history was again made when the nuclear submarine *Skate* broke through the ice to surface at the North Pole.

Antarctic Exploration

The early search for a rich and fertile continent in the extreme south of the globe ended with the view of icy desolation that James Cook's second circumnavigation of 1772-75 had found. As far south as 71°10′ S, Cook had not yet sighted a continent, only the islands of South Georgia and the South Sandwich group.

South Georgia, however, was discovered to be the home of a huge colony of fur seals, a valuable commodity which quickly attracted a rush of British and American sealers to the Antarctic waters south of Cape Horn. Exploitation of the fur seals of South Georgia led to their virtual extinction in a matter of years, and the search was on for new seal colonies. In 1819 a British sealer, William Smith, discovered the South Shetland Islands, with an even richer seal colony, and in 1820 Edward Bransfield and the American sealer Nathaniel Palmer sighted mountains in the northern tip of the Antarctic peninsula, the first actual sighting of the continent of Antarctica.

Further voyages engaged in the discovery of new sealing and whaling grounds, notably those of James Weddell in 1823, John Biscoe in 1830, Peter Kemp in 1833-34, and John Balleny in 1834, began to map the outline of the new continent, and a search for the South Magnetic Pole led to three national expeditions: by France under Dumont d'Urville, by the United States under Charles Wilkes, and by Britain under James Ross. All three made fairly extensive discoveries of the continental coastline, and all three confirmed that the land was barren and without economic importance. The search for new seal colonies also failed, and public interest in Antarctica waned.

It was briefly revived during the last decade of the 19th century when a Scottish and several Norwegian expeditions made a fruitless search for whales, but the major new impetus to Antarctic discovery and research came in 1895 when the Sixth International Geographical Congress urged the scientific examination of the continent. A whole series of expeditions converged on the area during the next 20 years, led by such distinguished explorers as the Belgian, Gerlache de Gomery; the Swede, Otto Nordenskjöld; the Scot, William Bruce; the Frenchman, Jean-Baptiste Charcot; the German, Wilhelm Filchner; and the British explorers, Robert Falcon SCOTT and Ernest SHACKLETON. Between them they mapped most of the Antarctic coastline and discovered the rest of the small islands which lie off the continental landmass.

CAPTAIN SCOTT (COMMANDER) MR GEO MURRAY MR SHACKLETON (3RD LIEUT)
(CHIEF SCIENTIST)

MR SKELTON (ENGINEER)

MR ARMITAGE (NAVIGATING OFFICER)
MR RHOYDS 1ST LIEUT PILOT

The officers of the British Antarctic expedition 1901-04, led by Scott.

The achievement of the South Pole became the next objective. In his 1901-04 expedition Scott made the first sledge journeys to the south, reaching the foot of the great glacier system which leads up to the polar plateau. Shackleton, in the 1907-08 British Antarctic Expedition, discovered 500 miles (800 km) of new mountain ranges flanking the Ross ice shelf and sledged to within 47 miles (76 km) of the Pole itself. Scott returned in 1911 in the *Terra Nova* determined to reach the South Pole, and in the same year Amundsen arrived in the *Fram* with the same ambition. Scott and his small party reached the South Pole on January 17, 1912, only to discover that Amundsen had reached it a month earlier. Scott's whole party perished in a blizzard on the return journey when within a day's march of safety.

More expeditions to Antarctica between the two world wars continued to map the continent, and the few major geographical gaps left were filled in by international expeditions after World War II. Scientific observation has now replaced discovery, and postwar technical advances, particularly in motorized transport and load-carrying aircraft, have removed much of the hardship and danger which so characterized the earlier expeditions. Antarctica itself, by virtue of an international treaty which was signed in Washington in December 1959, now enjoys the unique status of being open territory available for peaceful scientific investigation by any of the world's nations. And this is, perhaps, a fitting end to the whole long history of exploration, so much of it designed and dominated by the urge of national aggrandizement and greed.

The History of Powered Ships

Although it is generally accepted that the development of powered ships properly dates from the late 18th century, there is no lack of evidence that the search for alternatives to oars and sails as means of ship propulsion began many centuries earlier. The early Egyptians experimented with hand-operated paddle wheels but discovered that a slave on a paddle wheel was less efficient in terms of ship movement than a slave on an oar. Comparable experiments were made by the Romans and the Chinese, with similar results. Attempts to use horses or donkeys to turn paddle wheels in place of slaves were equally unsuccessful. The paddle wheel was turned by a treadmill operated by the men or animals, but since there was no means of gearing to increase the speed of the wheel in relation to the treadmill, the speed of revolution was not enough to move the ship through the water.

Other methods of turning paddle wheels, including clockwork, were put forward from time to time as ships grew in numbers and trade around the world increased, but none proved able to produce sufficient power to propel a ship of any size through the water. Steam was first used as a source of power at the end of the 17th century, long before the technical problems of adapting it to turn a paddle wheel could be solved by contemporary engineers. There were certainly plenty of engineers in those days who dreamed of ships driven over the seas by steam engines, but the difficulties of building an engine to fit into a ship defeated them all.

The First Marine Engines

The first man to build a steam-powered engine is believed to be Thomas Savery, an Englishman who built an engine which worked a water pump. The date was 1698. Nine years later a French inventor, Denis Papin, constructed a steam-driven pump for raising water, an improvement on Savery's model, and later built a second engine which he attempted to couple to a paddle wheel for ship propulsion. His experiment failed, partly because the mechanical difficulties of transforming the reciprocal motion of the engine into rotary motion for the paddle wheel defeated him, and partly because in any case his engine could not generate sufficient steam pressure to get the paddle wheel moving. These difficulties also defeated several other inventors working on similar projects.

Thomas Newcomen was the next inventor to take a hand in the ship propulsion problem. In 1711 he designed a steam engine in which a piston, working inside a cylinder, was connected by a piston rod to a beam which worked a separate pump. This was designed for lifting water, and did so in considerable quantities. But when he tried to adapt his engine for ship propulsion he found the same difficulty as Papin in producing steam at sufficient pressure to drive a paddle wheel. He did finally overcome the problems of converting reciprocal motion into rotary

motion, but by that time his engine and its associated machinery was too heavy and too bulky to fit into a ship. The most important factor in his failure, however, was the lack of steam pressure; had he been able to increase it appreciably above the 15lb/sq. in. (1.05 kg/cm²) which he achieved, his clumsy machinery might have succeeded, though very inefficiently, in providing motion through the water.

The first important name in the development of the marine steam engine is that of James Watt. In 1765 he took out a patent for an engine with a double-acting cylinder, using steam both above and below the piston, combined with a separate steam condenser, and using a crank action invented by John Steed to convert the reciprocal motion of the piston into the rotary motion of a shaft. At the same time he developed a more efficient boiler with an internal flue which produced steam at a pressure sufficient to drive his engine with reasonable efficiency and power. In 1768 he went into partnership with Matthew Boulton, the owner of an engineering workshop in Birmingham, and between them they produced steam engines specifically designed for particular purposes. One of these purposes was the propulsion of ships and most of the world's early steamships were operated by means of Boulton and Watt engines.

The first vessel to move through the water under steam power alone was a large clinker-built wooden boat built in France by the Marquis Claude de Jouffroy d'Abbans, an eccentric aristocrat with an inventive mind. His single-cylinder engine turned a pair of paddle wheels by an ingenious method, using a toothed wheel operating inside a cylinder with engaging slots cut in the inside walls. The cylinder was attached to the end of the piston rod of the engine and thus moved backwards and forwards in time with the engine. A series of pawls inside the slotted cylinder ensured that the central wheel revolved in one direction only in spite of the backwards-and-forwards motion of the cylinder. The central wheel was attached to a shaft which turned the paddle wheels. The Marquis' ingenuity went even further than this: as well as operating the two paddle wheels, the engine could drive a large shaft fitted across the boat which was used to weigh the anchor in much the same way as a capstan. His boat was named PYROSCAPHE and he tested it out on the River Saône, near Lyons, in 1783. The engine ran for 15 minutes before breaking down, and during that time the boat moved through the water for a distance of about 400 yards (365 m). De Jouffroy did not develop his idea further.

Other experiments in steam propulsion for ships were being carried out at this time, most notably by John FITCH in the United States. Fitch's invention was an engine which, by means of linking beams, operated six vertical oars on either side of a vessel built like a barge. She was called *John Fitch* after her inventor and was tested on the

Pyroscaphe, *the first steam-driven boat, 1783.*

Delaware River in 1786, moving a short distance through the water. But, like the *Pyroscaphe*, the engine broke down too soon for it to be regarded as a valid means of ship propulsion. He built a second steam-powered vessel in 1787 and tested it on the river between Philadelphia and Burlington in 1789, but could find no one in the United States to back his invention with the capital necessary for its development. He was equally unsuccessful when he tried to interest the maritime authorities of Britain and France. He committed suicide in 1794, having written in his journal: 'The day will come when some more powerful man will get fame and riches from my invention, but nobody will believe that poor John Fitch can do anything worthy of attention.'

Early River Steamboats

The world's first successful steam-driven ship, in terms of reliability, was the CHARLOTTE DUNDAS, which made her appearance on the Forth and Clyde Canal in Scotland in March 1802. She was built by William Symington, an engineer with a workshop on the River Clyde, to the order of Lord Dundas of Kerse, a governor of the Canal company, and named for his daughter. She was designed to operate as a tug and replace the horses which towed the barges up and down the canal. The *Charlotte Dundas* was a wooden vessel 56 ft. (17 m) long, with a maximum beam of 18 ft. (5.5 m) and she drew 8 ft. (2.4 m) of water. Symington's design was a single-cylinder steam engine which developed about 12 hp and drove a single paddle wheel mounted at the stern between two rudders. On her

Symington's Charlotte Dundas *(1802), the first reliable steamboat, used on the Forth and Clyde Canal.*

maiden trip she towed two 70-ton barges for a distance of 20 miles (32 km) along the canal at an average speed of 3 knots against a strong headwind. For the next three or four months she continued to work as a tug on the canal without breaking down, but had to be withdrawn because it was feared that the wash from her paddle wheel would cause the canal banks to fall in.

On board the *Charlotte Dundas* during one of her canal trips was an American engineer, Robert FULTON; indeed, he had been an observer of John Fitch's earlier attempts at steam propulsion. Fulton was connected not only with

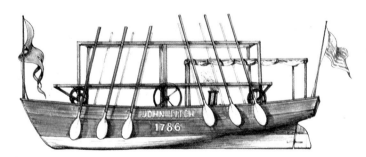

One of John Fitch's earliest designs, featuring steam-driven oars. In her trials (1786) her engine proved unreliable.

Henry Bell's River Clyde steamer Comet *(1812), which achieved average speeds of over 6 knots.*

The P & O paddle steamer Lady Mary Wood *(1842), which carried the first sea mails to the Far East in 1845.*

the birth of steam propulsion but also with early experimental SUBMARINES (see the section on *The Development of Submarines* later in this chapter). In August 1803 he demonstrated a steam-driven vessel on the River Seine in France, but his name is better remembered for his ship CLERMONT, which operated a passenger service on the Hudson River. The *Clermont* was more than twice as large as the *Charlotte Dundas*, with an overall length of 133 ft. (40 m) and a displacement of 100 tons. Her engine was built by Boulton and Watt in England and shipped across the Atlantic. It had a single vertical cylinder with a diameter of 24 in. (60 cm) and a stroke of 48 in. (122 cm) and it drove two 15-ft. (4.6-m) diameter paddle wheels through bell cranks and spur gearing. On her maiden voyage in 1807 *Clermont* steamed from New York to Albany and back, a distance of approximately 240 miles (390 km) in 62 hours at an average speed of 3.9 knots. This passenger service, which cut the normal travel time between the two cities by half, was so popular that the *Clermont* was

not large enough to accommodate all the passengers who wished to take advantage of the new service. Encouraged by this success, Fulton built a larger vessel, which he named *Phoenix*, to operate a similar passenger service on the Delaware River. She was built at Hoboken, also with a Boulton and Watt engine imported from England, and to reach her operating station had to steam down the coast of New Jersey from New York to Philadelphia, a voyage which makes her the first steam-propelled vessel to be used in the open sea.

Fulton's financial successes with his river steamers did not go unnoticed in Britain. In 1812 a Scottish engineer, Henry BELL, who had watched the *Charlotte Dundas* make her first trip on the Forth and Clyde Canal and who had met Fulton during one of his visits to England, designed a small steamship which he ordered from the shipyard of John Ward and Sons with an engine built to Bell's design by John Robertson. The small 45-ft. (14-m) vessel was named COMET and her engine, a single cylinder driving two four-float paddle wheels, one on each side, was installed with the boiler below deck. She operated a passenger and freight service on the River Clyde between Glasgow, Greenock, and Helensburgh and achieved an average speed of 6.8 knots, a considerable improvement on the *Clermont*. Her engine is still preserved today in the Science Museum in London.

After six years' service on the Clyde, Bell extended *Comet*'s route up the west coast of Scotland to Tarbert and Oban in the Western Highlands, but in December 1820, while returning from Fort William, the *Comet* was driven ashore in a gale and wrecked. Bell lived on for another ten years to witness many spectacular advances in steamship development but was himself too poor to build another steamship, and died penniless in Glasgow in 1830. He was not the first, nor indeed the last, inventor to suffer by public neglect of an invention which was to make the fortune of later developers.

Bell's *Comet* on the Clyde and Fulton's *Clermont* on the Hudson served as twin triggers for a spate of steamboat building for service on the rivers of Europe and America. A passenger service on the River Thames from London Bridge to Margate and Ramsgate was started in 1814 with the small paddle steamer *Margery*, and within a couple of years there were several small paddlers operating above and below London Bridge, from Teddington in the west to Margate in the east, and since the cost of a ticket from one landing to the next was one penny, the service became known as London's Penny Steamers. Similar developments were taking place on the River Seine in France and on the great rivers of the United States where the distances covered were immensely greater. One of the steamboats on the Mississippi had a regular run of over 2,000 miles (3,200 km).

Seagoing Steamships

It was only a matter of time before steamships plying up and down the major rivers developed into steamships serving coastal routes and later into cross-sea, and indeed, cross-ocean vessels. In 1818 a regular steamship packet service was inaugurated across the Irish Sea between Greenock and Belfast, and in the same year the first steamship service between Leith, the port for Edinburgh, and London was started. Two years later the Leith-London service could boast the largest steamship yet built, the *James Watt*, with an overall length of 141 ft. (43 m) and a beam of 47 ft. (14.3 m) over her paddle boxes. She was a remarkable ship in her way, not because of her size but because she was fitted with two single-cylinder engines, one for each paddle wheel.

A regular steamship line in the United States between New York and New London was inaugurated in 1816, and also in that year a passenger service was started across the English Channel from Brighton to Le Havre.

The next notable advance in development came in 1822 with the AARON MANBY, the first iron steamship. Hers was not the first hull to be built of iron instead of wood — an iron lighter had been built some years earlier — but she was the first iron ship to be driven by steam propulsion. She had an engine designed by Henry Bell which gave her an average speed of 9 knots, and she began her life with a regular service between London and Paris. After a few successful months she was bought by a syndicate of French shipowners who used her to run pleasure trips on the Seine. After 15 years on the Seine she was transferred to the River Loire for similar services and continued to work there until 1855 when she was broken up.

That steam propulsion for seagoing ships was well established by 1822 is evidenced by an official return made to the British Parliament comparing the times taken on 30 coasting routes by steam and sailing vessels. In no case was the saving in time by using steam propulsion less than one-half; in some instances the time saved was as much as five-sixths.

It was at this time that the carriage of mail at sea came under new scrutiny, with tremendously important consequences for the expansion of steamship operation. The carriage of mail had been until then a government responsibility, with the various nations operating their own mail packets. In 1821, in order to improve the service across the Irish Channel, which had been irregular when using sailing packets (sometimes taking as much as nine days when the weather was bad), the British government purchased two steamships, the *Royal Sovereign* and *Meteor*, to carry the Irish mail. They proved so successful that more steamships were purchased for use on the continental mail routes. All these mail ships were owned by the British government, but in 1833 the mail to and from the Isle of Man and between Britain and Holland was entrusted to private companies, with a twofold result. Not only was the carriage of the mail quicker and more reliable in the hands of private shipowners, but the competition among them for the lucrative mail-carrying contracts stimulated innovations in marine engineering and hull design that produced more efficient ships. For a short period this divided carriage of mails, partly in government-owned ships and partly in private vessels, continued, but within a very few years the British government retired completely from the scene, entrusting the sea mail wholly to private contractors. This was to have a profound effect both on the technical development of the steamship and on the rapid growth of their numbers, and in many cases the granting of a mail contract led directly to the formation of some of the best-known shipping lines of today. The Cunard Line, for example, owes its inception to a contract for carrying British mails across the Atlantic, as did the Collins Line of the United States, which began by carrying the American transatlantic mails.

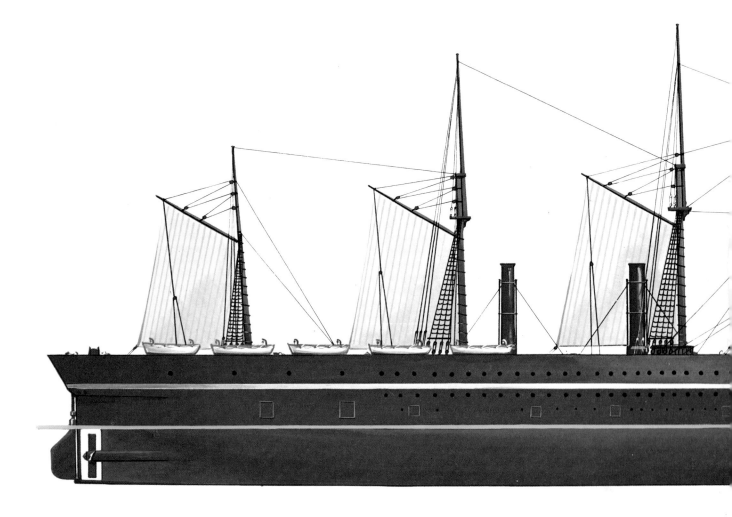

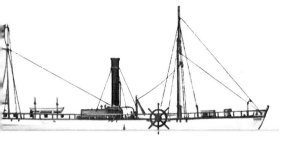

These four 19th-century steamships illustrate the development of powered ships over the first 60 years of their history. The Charlotte Dundas (center), launched in 1802, was 56 ft. long and 17 ft. in the beam, and her 12 hp single-cylinder engine drove a single stern paddle wheel. The Clermont (top), launched in 1807, was 133 ft. long and 18 ft. in the beam. She was of about 100 tons and had two side-mounted paddle wheels. Brunel's iron-hulled Great Britain (far left) featured screw propulsion, and was by far the biggest ship in the world when launched in 1845 (3,270 tons gross, 322 ft. long, 50 ft. in the beam). But the giant Great Eastern (bottom), also designed by Brunel and launched in 1858, was over three times larger (18,914 tons gross, 692 ft. long and 83 ft. in the beam); despite sail, screw, and paddle propulsion she was underpowered.

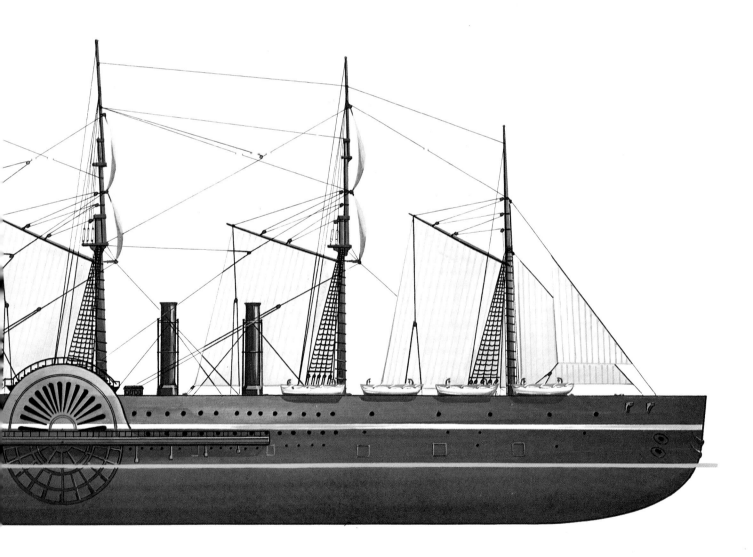

The iron-hulled screw steamer Chusan *(1852), which inaugurated the P & O mail service to Australia.*

Oceanic Crossings

The Atlantic had actually been crossed by a steamship in 1819 when the SAVANNAH, a ship built in the United States, made the crossing from west to east. She was built as a full-rigged ship, but as an afterthought she was fitted before her launch with an engine and detachable paddle wheels which could be unshipped and carried on deck when not in use. Certainly she made the passage from Savannah to Liverpool in 25 days, but as she was under sail alone, without using her engine, for more than 90 percent of the passage, she can hardly be claimed as the first ship to cross an ocean under steam.

The *Savannah's* feat of crossing the Atlantic under sail and steam in 1819 was followed in 1825 by that of the *Enterprise*, a 470-ton ship, which sailed from London to Calcutta, a distance of 11,450 nautical miles (21,205 km) in 103 days. She was under steam for 64 days and under sail for 39 days. Other notable voyages were made by the Dutch *Anacas* which plied between Holland and the Dutch West Indies in 1827-29, and the *Royal William* which operated a regular service between Quebec and Halifax for two years before crossing the Atlantic in 1833 to be sold. Most of these, however, were essentially sailing ships with auxiliary steam engines, and none was able to use her engine continuously for long passages.

The main difficulty in producing a ship to cross an ocean with her engine working throughout the voyage was the stowage of sufficient coal on board to feed the boiler. It was a problem partly of size, for there had to be enough space not only for coal but also for passengers and cargo to make the ship an economic possibility, and partly of internal design, for adequate bunker space had to be

The Savannah, *which crossed the Atlantic in 1819.*

provided in the vicinity of the boiler. The marine engine and boiler had proved themselves reliable enough for long ocean passages; if the problem of fuel storage could be solved the oceans could be crossed under steam power.

The problem was in fact solved in somewhat dramatic fashion. At a meeting of the directors of the newly founded Great Western Railway in Britain in 1835, one of those present complained that a planned extension of the railroad track to Bristol would make the line too long. The Company's engineer, Isambard Kingdom BRUNEL, retorted that it was too short, and that it ought to be extended to New York by building a passenger steamship. As a result Brunel received a commission to design a ship to be named GREAT WESTERN.

At about the same time, impressed by the growing reliability of steamships, an American lawyer, Dr. Julius Smith, came to Britain to organize a transatlantic shipping line, the British and American Steam Navigation Company. It ordered its first ship, originally to be named *Victoria* but later changed to *British Queen*, in 1837. But while the construction of the *Great Western* in William Patterson's shipyard in Bristol went steadily ahead without difficulty, that of the *British Queen* was delayed to such an extent that it became certain that she would be overtaken by the *Great Western*. Anxious to be the first across the Atlantic under steam power, Dr. Smith approached McGregor Laird of Birkenhead for advice and he recommended the chartering of the 703-ton SIRIUS, which had a 320-hp engine and a designed speed of 10 knots. She had not been designed for an ocean crossing, and the only way of providing her with enough coal for the passage was to fill her existing bunkers and every other available space below deck, and also to carry two large heaps of coal on the upper deck.

The *Sirius* was the first away, leaving Cork in southern Ireland on April 4, 1838, with 40 passengers on board. Out in the Atlantic she ran into a severe storm which not only slowed her passage but increased her consumption of coal to such an extent that it was all exhausted before she could reach New York. She completed her voyage only by burning most of the wooden cabin furniture, her yards, and one of her masts. She reached New York, greeted by cheering crowds, after a passage of 18 days, 10 hours, at an average speed of 6.7 knots.

The *Great Western* left Bristol on April 8, four days after the departure of the *Sirius*. Unlike the *Sirius*, she had been designed specifically for the Atlantic. She sailed with full bunkers, but with no extra spaces filled with coal, and reached New York a few hours after the *Sirius*, again to a tumultuous welcome. Her Atlantic crossing took 15 days, 5 hours at an average speed of 8.8 knots. On arrival she had 200 tons of coal left in her bunkers, and this removed any doubt about the feasibility of steam propulsion across any of the world's oceans, given proper ship design.

The Expansion of Transoceanic Traffic

The years following this first transatlantic race saw a tremendous growth in ocean traffic. A number of technical improvements contributed to this upsurge of activity, not the least of which was the introduction of iron in the construction of steamship hulls. Both *Sirius* and *Great Western* were wooden ships, but already the advantages of iron as a more satisfactory building material were becoming obvious. The *Aaron Manby*, built of iron in 1820, was still in profitable service, and in 1838 the 400-ton *Rainbow* was built of iron to carry cargoes between London, Ramsgate, and Antwerp. The use of iron, a much stronger material than wood, made unnecessary the massive timbers required to give a wooden ship sufficient hull strength, and thus increased the available cargo space within the hull to twice the capacity of the wooden ship. In addition, an iron hull did not 'work' in rough seas like a wooden hull, and so did not give rise to the persistent small leaks, due to the small movements of the hull planking (its 'working'), to which a wooden ship was liable. When the Great Western Company decided to follow the *Great Western* with a second ship, Brunel persuaded the directors to have her built in iron. And at the same time the propeller was being introduced as a more efficient means of driving a ship through the water than paddle wheels.

The keel of the new ship was laid in 1839 and she was named GREAT BRITAIN. She was nearly three times as large as the *Great Western*, with a gross tonnage of 3,270 compared with the 1,340 tons of the earlier ship. Brunel's design gave her four single-cylinder steam engines which were connected to the same shaft and developed 1,500 hp. She was originally designed with paddle-wheel propulsion, but during her construction Brunel attended the trials of the propeller-driven *Archimedes* and, halfway through building, changed the *Great Britain*'s design to give her a six-bladed propeller of 16 ft. (5 m) diameter in place of the paddle wheels he had originally intended. One of the features of her iron construction was the use of five transverse bulkheads extending the full width of the ship, dividing the hull into six watertight compartments. She was built in the same Bristol shipyard as her predecessor and was launched in 1843 in the presence of the Prince Consort; she made her maiden voyage from Liverpool to New York in 1845. At the time she was the largest ship in the world. Today she lies preserved in Bristol in the same dock in which she was built, a permanent memorial to the skills of early Victorian shipbuilding.

The *Sirius*, *Great Western*, and *Great Britain* proved beyond all doubt that the way was open for a great surge in steamship building. The time, too, was ripe for such an expansion, for the industrial revolution of the mid-19th century was bringing wealth to nations and to individuals, and with it a demand for travel, both for business and pleasure. Brunel estimated that the time had arrived for a ship which could carry 4,000 passengers, 6,000 tons of cargo, and sufficient coal for a nonstop voyage to Australia and India. The reason for his belief was the great surge of emigration from Europe which began in the second half of the 19th century, and he looked to the relatively empty spaces of Australia to satisfy their land hunger. He worked on his design in close association with John Scott Russell, a marine engineer who owned a shipbuilding yard at Millwall on the River Thames and had a deep interest in the best hydrodynamic design of hull form. He had made many experiments in tank-testing models of various shapes and with full-sized vessels on a canal, and his results had given rise to the wave-line theory of hull design, a theory still very much in use in ship design today.

Between them they produced plans for a ship to be named the *Leviathan*, with an overall length of 692 ft. (211 m), a beam of 83 ft. (25 m), and a draft of 29 ft. (9 m). Her designed tonnage by measurement rule was 18,914 and her displacement tonnage 27,700 — more than seven times as large as the *Great Britain*, herself at that time still the largest ship in the world. Brunel and Russell sold the design to the Eastern Steamship Navigation Company, which changed her name to GREAT EASTERN. Because of her great size she was equipped with both paddle wheels and a propeller, and her engines were designed to give her a speed of 15 knots. She was built with a cellular double bottom and fitted with a steering engine, the first ship to embody these features, which are now universal in all ships of any size. Her keel was laid in 1854 and she was launched, after many constructional difficulties and delays, in 1858 and fitted out as a passenger liner in great luxury and at great expense. On her maiden voyage across the Atlantic she attracted no more than 36 passengers instead of the 4,000 for whom she had been built. After failing as a passenger ship she was converted into a cable carrier and in this capacity laid four cables across the Atlantic and one from Aden to Bombay. She was finally broken up in 1888 after lying abandoned and unused for 20 years.

The *Great Eastern* was a failure because she represented an attempted short cut. She was built before the advance in engineering design and technology could match her advance in size. Had she been constructed 20 years later, by which time the current single-acting marine steam engine had moved forward into triple expansion, she might well have been one of the most economically successful ships of her generation.

The Development of the Passenger Liner during the 19th Century

The development of steamship traffic was helped by two factors: the improved and still improving efficiency of machinery and new ideas about passenger accommoda-

tion. The traditional importance of the afterpart of a ship, the poop or aftercastle, from which the captain controlled his ship in the days of sail, was incompatible with passenger comfort in screw-driven ships and in rough weather. The *Oceanic*, commissioned in 1871, had a new layout for passenger accommodation with saloons placed athwartships and cabins forward and aft of them. She was one of several vessels built by Harland and Wolff of Belfast for the Oceanic Steam Navigation Company, known to later generations as the White Star Line. At the same time Samuel Cunard, whose name is so closely associated with the transatlantic passenger service, was collaborating with Robert Napier, one of the most brilliant marine engineers of the period, in putting ships such as the *Britannia, Acadia*, and *Persia* on to the Atlantic run. The latter was the first iron Cunarder.

The basis of the competition in the transatlantic service for the next century was the conveyance of passengers across the ocean in the shortest possible time and with the minimum of discomfort. In fact, for a proportion of the

The luxury transatlantic liner Queen Mary, *launched in 1934.*

passengers — a proportion which increased sharply as the years went by — the emphasis was on comfort, and even on luxury, reflecting the standards accepted and expected in European and North American high society. Right up until the mid-20th century the decor and appointments of the passenger ships still in service continued to maintain the standards of the more prestigious European first-class hoteliers. The United States' contribution to the competition was pioneered by E.K. Collins, who ran a service subsidized by Congress in the 1850s with ships named *Atlantic, Arctic, Pacific,* and *Baltic* — large vessels of over 3,000 tons each.

In the Pacific, the American Pacific Mail Steamship Company operated from 1847, and in 1887 obtained the U.S. government mail contract for the run between San Francisco and Hong Kong, calling at Yokohama. The ships employed were wooden paddle-ships, indicating the lag in development in North America, but they proved economical over the great distances of the Pacific Ocean. On the Atlantic, the Collins Line failed after the loss at sea

of the *Arctic* and *Pacific*, but the later *City of Paris* and *City of New York* pioneered a new development in marine engineering, being fitted with two engines and two propellers. The smoother passage which twin screws provided made both ships very popular on the Atlantic run.

The continuously increasing demand for transocean passages, coupled with the rapid technological advances in engine and boiler design of the last quarter of the 19th century, heralded the dawn of the era of the big liner. It was an immensely profitable trade, and most nations with traditions of maritime importance boasted at least one, and frequently several, prestigious steamship lines operating across the world's oceans. The Atlantic was the most profitable ocean, mainly because of the industrial strength and wealth of the United States and Britain, whose citizens could afford to travel across the ocean that divided them in great luxury. But there were also good profits to be made from regular liner services to South Africa, South America, India, China, and Australia, and they too carried an ever-growing number of passengers.

Competition was naturally fierce, particularly at the top end of this traffic where passengers were prepared to pay a premium for speed and comfort. By the end of the 19th century the design of the big ocean liner was becoming more or less standardized, not only to fulfill the demands of the passengers, but also to compete with the ships of rival companies. In order to attract a sufficient clientele to produce the revenue required to run the ship, the liner needed to have cabin- and steerage-class capacity for some 2,500 passengers, at least two passenger decks above the upper deck to provide the public rooms and cabins which the travelers expected, facilities for deck games and sports, a small army of stewards and stewardesses to minister to their comfort, a minimum speed of about 20 knots, and an engineering installation that did not produce undue vibrations when at full speed. All this called for a ship of about 25,000 tons displacement, and the trend towards bigger ships was accelerating. The speed of this growth in size can be judged by the tonnage figures of the 12 years between 1893 and 1905, covering the turn of the century. In 1893 the largest liner afloat was the Cunard Company's *Campania* with a displacement tonnage of 21,000; in 1897 North-German Lloyd's KAISER WILHELM DER GROSSE displaced 23,760 tons; in 1899 White Star's *Oceanic* increased the figure to 26,100; in 1901 White Star commissioned the *Celtic* of 37,900 tons; and in 1905 the Hamburg-Amerika Line produced the *Königin Augusta Victoria* with a displacement tonnage of 43,000.

An important element in the competition on the transatlantic service was the upsurge of German activity, epitomized by the capture of the 'Blue Riband' of the Atlantic by the *Kaiser Wilhelm der Grosse* in 1897 with a crossing of 5 days, 17 hours, and 8 minutes at an average speed of 22.35 knots. Her record was later taken by the *Kaiser Wilhelm II*, which was built in 1902. (In 1909 the title was won by Cunard's MAURETANIA with a speed of 26.06 knots. Amazingly, she held the record for 22 years.)

But the glamor of the big ocean liners of this period concealed another aspect of transatlantic trade, equally profitable and in some cases sadly exploited — emigration, mainly from eastern Europe and the Mediterranean to North and South America. Many of the big ocean liners, in addition to their first- and second-class passengers, provided space for a steerage class into which were crowded as many would-be emigrants as possible, who paid a small sum for their passage. They brought with them on board their own food and bedding, the ship providing two or three cooking stoves on deck and bunks erected in tiers below decks with the sexes segregated. By the turn of the century the stream of emigration, which had begun in the mid-19th century, had developed into a flood, stimulated at both ends by the desire of the underprivileged in Europe to escape to a new life rich in opportunities in America and by the needs of industry on that side of the Atlantic

for cheap labor. Some good ships were built specifically for this trade, such as the 8,000-ton Italian ship *Ancona* with space for 2,500 emigrants and 8,000 tons of cargo. But many more were old ships due for the scrapheap, bought cheaply and given a few more years of life with a sketchy refit, into which were packed men, women, and children in conditions of extreme squalor. The profits were immense, and as yet there was in the world little sense of social responsibility. It took a world war to eliminate these worn-out ships, and international agreements on minimum standards of safety and accommodation to prevent their return when the next spate of emigration began in the 1920s.

The big ocean liners may have been the most glamorous ships of the late 19th century, but equally important progress and developments were being made in other ship types. It was during this period that the specialized cargo ship appeared: the first ship fully refrigerated to carry meat in bulk, the *Timaru*, was launched in 1870; the first ship specifically designed as a tanker to carry crude oil in

First-class dining saloon of the liner Laconia, *1922.*

bulk, the GLÜCKAUF, was launched in 1886. The first train ferry was operating before 1900, and other specialized ships were designed and built to carry bulk cargoes of mineral ores, coal, fruit, and grain.

Also at about this time, great progress was being made in the development of SUBMARINES, especially by John P. HOLLAND, who designed and built a number of experimental craft between 1878 and 1900 and eventually won orders from the U.S., Russian, and British navies. Of course, the idea of submarine warfare had already existed for many centuries and numerous ingenious designs had been tried out. The full story of the long years of the submarine's evolution into an effective fighting vessel is told in the section *The Development of Submarines*.

20th-Century Trends

A major technical advance which occurred at the turn of the century was the introduction of the Parsons steam turbine, which superseded the reciprocating engines with triple- or quadruple-expansion cylinders of earlier vessels (see *Engines and Propulsion Machinery* later in this chapter). The first transatlantic ship to be fitted with turbines was the Allan Line's *Victorian*. The fitting of Parsons turbines in the *Mauretania* and in her ill-fated sister, the LUSITANIA, stemmed from an agreement between the British government and the Cunard Company for the construction of two vessels to reestablish British superiority on the Atlantic. In the same period the great milestone in modern naval history was the construction of the battleship DREADNOUGHT (see the following chapter on *Warships and Sea Warfare*). She was driven by turbines, and this, together with other design innovations, rendered all existing battleships obsolete.

Another advance was the development of the liquid-fuel engine, deriving from work by Lenoir in 1860, and then Dr. Rudolf Diesel invented his engine in 1892. Early motor vessels were mainly oil tankers employed on inland waterways. Four were built for Russia in 1908. The first oceangoing diesel ship, which began operating in 1912, was the Danish East Asiatic Company's SELANDIA, and by the beginning of World War I the world tonnage of motor ships had reached 230,000 tons. During the interwar period more motor vessels were built than steam vessels, and by 1939 they represented 22.5 percent of the total world tonnage. Noteworthy examples between the wars are *Adventure*, the only major British warship to be fitted with diesel propulsion, and the Dutch passenger ship *Oranje*, which was the world's fastest motor vessel.

The developments in the period from 1918 to the end of World War II were evolutionary rather than revolutionary. The Blue Riband of the Atlantic passed from the *Mauretania* to the German BREMEN in 1929 and to the French NORMANDIE in 1932 before it returned to Britain with the QUEEN ELIZABETH in 1938. The *Normandie* was an

Stern view of the Lusitania *(1906) in dry dock.*

outstanding example of turbo-electric propulsion; engines of this type were also fitted by the Peninsular and Oriental Steam Navigation Company in their *Strathaird* and *Strathnaver*. Tonnage and overall length increased from the *Mauretania*'s 37,938 tons gross and 790 ft. (240 m) to the *Bremen*'s 51,656 tons and 938 ft. (287 m), and from the *Normandie*'s 83,432 tons and 1,029 ft. (313.6 m) to the *Queen Elizabeth*'s 83,673 tons and 1,031 ft. (314.2 m).

The End of the Passenger Liners

In 1952 the new liner UNITED STATES crossed the Atlantic in 3 days, 10 hours, and 40 minutes and captured the Blue Riband with a speed of 35.59 knots. She was a smaller liner of only 53,329 tons gross, but was already setting a pattern for diminishing size, the first evidence of the effects that transatlantic air travel was to have on these one-time queens of the ocean. There were some slight hiccups in this pattern — the French liner FRANCE, which made her maiden voyage in 1962, and the British QUEEN ELIZABETH 2, launched in 1970, were both slightly larger

Queen Elizabeth 2, *the last great passenger liner, at Southampton.*

than the *United States*. Neither has been a success as a transatlantic liner: the *France* was eventually taken off the North Atlantic run because of increasing losses and later converted into a Caribbean cruise ship under the name *Norway*, and the *Queen Elizabeth 2* sails across the Atlantic only a few months of the year, earning her keep as a luxury cruise liner.

And this indeed, so far as can be seen ahead, is the only future left for the great ocean liners. Both the *France* and the *Queen Elizabeth 2* are miracles of modern marine engineering, but the jet aircraft which cut the Atlantic crossing time to a few hours has put them, and all others like them, out of business as passenger-carrying ships on regular routes. Many liners have only survived by becoming cruise ships for the tourist industry; often by becoming part of a fly/cruise holiday package.

Post-World War II Developments

The years since the ending of World War II have seen immense changes in the pattern of world shipping and the design and construction of ships. The decline in the passenger liners has been matched by the growth of BULK CARRIERS — ships designed for a particular cargo instead of the mixed cargoes which were the mainstay of most merchant shipping until only a few decades ago. The dimensions of tankers and bulk dry cargo carriers have increased enormously, largely as a result of the closure of the Suez Canal at various times since 1956; this has forced ships to use the sea route around the Cape of Good Hope and the increase in ship size has been an inevitable economic consequence. There are already supertankers ranging from 150,000 tons to 540,000 tons, and plans have been drawn up to construct similar ships of up to 800,000 tons. As in the case of the *Great Eastern* in her day, there are likely to be some problems over berthing such monsters, and the hazards of navigation are a source of increased concern, with large-scale pollution a grave and ever-present possibility.

Many of the bulk carriers are purpose-designed with appropriate handling equipment for rapid unloading and loading of their particular cargo — ore, grain, and so on. A similar development for a mixed cargo is the CONTAINER SHIP, in which the cargo is packed into metal containers which are loaded or unloaded by dockside gantries. As the containers are of uniform size, the holds and decks of ships can be designed exactly to accommodate them so that there can be no danger of the cargo shifting in rough weather, which in earlier days was a frequent cause of ships sinking at sea. Further development of these new types of cargo ship will probably concentrate on ship propulsion and the use of new lightweight materials.

War experience in landing tanks on enemy coasts has paid a useful dividend in the postwar development of roll-on, roll-off ferries (RORO), a huge improvement on the prewar method of loading cars, in which they were lifted by dockside crane with a four-point chain bridle and lowered into the ferry's hold. The first roll-on, roll-off ferries were fitted with stern doors opening onto a ramp so that cars could be driven straight on board; a more recent development is the hinged bow, which simplifies the process.

Another type of vessel to emerge after World War II, with far-reaching military consequences, is the nuclear-powered submarine. Nuclear propulsion enables submarines to remain underwater almost indefinitely and to cover vast distances without returning to the surface, and this, together with their fearsome nuclear armament, means that today's submarines are an extremely potent factor in naval strategy and the world balance of military power. (See the chapter on *Warships and Sea Warfare* and also the section on *The Development of Submarines* in this chapter.)

Other recent developments in the design of ships include AIR-CUSHION VEHICLES, such as hovercraft, and HYDROFOILS and hydroplanes, all of which fall into the general category of surface-effect vessels — vessels which travel above the surface of the water. (These are discussed in more detail later in this chapter in the section on *Engines and Propulsion Machinery*.)

As far as cargo ships are concerned, one area in which development is still being actively pursued is the concept of self-propelled 'mini' cargo carriers accommodated in a mother ship's hull. To some extent the basic idea originated in the infantry-landing ships developed for amphibious operations during World War II, and its modern application lies in the LASH (Lighter Aboard Ship) and BACAT (Barge Aboard Catamaran) systems. LASH found its main opening in the Middle East trade boom which began in 1973 with the five-fold rise in the price of oil, operating chiefly in the smaller ports unable to handle bulk cargoes. BACAT operates mainly in Europe and Africa. In both these concepts the main advantages are quicker cargo transhipment and a reduction in port dues, since the mother ship can float out her barges or lighters off the ports of delivery without herself incurring port dues. Deliveries can be made to different ports in the neighborhood more or less simultaneously, and the barges or lighters loaded with return cargoes ready to be reaccommodated in the mother vessel. These systems also enable cargoes to be delivered to small inland ports along the banks of rivers and canals.

New Trends in Ship Design

With the strength and flexibility of modern shipbuilding materials and the versatility of modern marine engineering, there are not many new demands that an experienced naval architect in conjunction with a good shipbuilder cannot meet. In the years since World War II they have produced the BATHYSCAPHE, a development of the prewar bathysphere, which is a small free-moving submarine capable of penetrating the extreme depths of the ocean. One of these, the *Trieste*, reached a depth of 36,000 ft. (11,000 m) in the Guam Deep Trench in 1960. They have built passenger- and car-carrying hydrofoils and hovercraft which can achieve a sea speed of more than 60 knots by lifting the vessel's hull onto or above the surface of the sea. They have also built self-propelled oil-drilling rigs and fixed production platforms for the exploitation of oilfields under the seabed. (See the chapter on *The Sea as a World Resource*.) However, there are of course always some limitations facing designers and builders when considering any new departure in marine development which modern technology may have made possible. The most important limitation is always cost, and if this were not a criterion in the introduction of new developments, there would certainly be many desirable changes in the design and con-

The bathyscaphe is a postwar deep-diving vessel; in 1960 the Trieste *(above) reached 36,000 ft. (11,000 m).*

struction of ships which could be put into operation almost at once.

One would surely be the substitution of aluminum alloy for steel as the main shipbuilding material; its advantages would be a considerable saving in weight and a great improvement in resistance to corrosion, yet it also has sufficient strength and resilience to absorb the normal strains on a ship in a seaway. Aluminum has already been introduced for the building of some small warships, where economy is not the final consideration, and for the construction of the superstructure of large liners, where the weight saving makes an important contribution to the ship's stability, but in general it is too expensive a material in comparison with steel to be used for hull plating in ships which must earn an adequate financial return on their construction costs. There are other new building materials developed during the last few years which may have some application for commercial shipping, particularly glass-reinforced plastic (GRP, or fiberglass) and ferrocement, but in their present stage of development these are generally confined to small craft such as harbor

launches and Chinese sampans. Similarly, if cost were no criterion, small ships would be powered with gas turbines because their power-to-weight ratio is so much more favorable than that of the normal ship's diesel installation. And large ships would use nuclear propulsion in place of steam, if only because one fueling of the reactor would be sufficient to take the ship twice around the world. But again, as with aluminum alloy, both these types of power installation are too expensive for general commercial use, and nuclear power has the added problem of radiation hazards. The time may come when improved production methods or volume production can bring unit costs down to a commercial level, but certainly that time is a long way off, though it may be closer in the case of the gas turbine for smaller ships.

Looking further into the future, the achievement of the Russian nuclear icebreaker *Arktika* in reaching the North Pole in August 1977 may well herald a new generation of specially strengthened and equipped ships to exploit a shorter sea route between east and west across the polar seas. Another possible avenue of development lies with the new generation of supertankers. But very few of the world's major oil terminals have the depth of water to accommodate these immense ships, and to adapt them would incur a very large and costly program of dredging and port rebuilding. It would not be beyond the skill of modern naval architects to design very large tankers to be built in detachable sections which could be floated off and towed into the terminals while the ship herself lies off, anchored in deep water and, incidentally, saving very heavy harbor fees.

These are possible directions in which ship design and shipbuilding could develop in the future. That there will be others, adapted to the special requirements of the day, is certain. Yet over all modern shipbuilding and development there hangs a new question-mark: the continued availability of liquid fuel given the current rate of extraction and the climate of international relations. The world demand for the movement of new materials and manufactured goods continues to grow, and the sea remains the only highway along which that demand can be satisfied. As will be seen in the next section, nuclear propulsion can only be an answer if the economic problems of installation and operation and the radiation hazards can be overcome. Another area of active possibility is the fuel cell; yet another may be some method of using hydrogen as a fuel.

Engines and Propulsion Machinery

The Evolution of the Steam Engine

All the early marine steam engines were adaptations of steam engines designed for use on land. Newcomen's engine was designed to pump water out of tin mines, Savery's and Papin's were the same, and although we associate the name of James Watt with the first effective marine engine, his original designs were, like those of Newcomen, for mine work and for driving machinery. Watt's designs incorporated his ideas of a separate condenser in which the steam could be condensed without cooling the cylinder, a stuffing box to enable the piston rod to move through the cylinder cover, and the entry of steam above and below the piston. The exacting technological demands of Watt's design brought him into partnership with Matthew Boulton, a combination of inventor and engineer. Boulton and Watt engines were extensively used ashore and also in several of the early steamships, and once the patent had lapsed in 1801, the double-acting beam engine was adapted by others for marine purposes.

Robert Fulton's claim to have operated the first steamboat, in spite of the earlier experience of the *Charlotte Dundas*, was based on a cylinder condenser and pump ordered from Boulton and Watt. The generally accepted marine engine was at that time the vertical-beam or walking-beam engine, where the piston of a vertical cylinder

By 1838 steam engines were reliable enough for ships to attempt Atlantic crossings, and the Sirius *(above) was the first to make the trip under steam power alone.*

was connected to a diamond-shaped walking beam mounted on an A-shaped frame. The beam pivoted in the center, its other connecting rod running down to a crankshaft and from there to the paddle wheel. In Fulton's DEMOLOGUS the engine cylinder was 46 in. (117 cm) in diameter with a 5-ft. (1.5-m) stroke which gave a speed of 6 knots on 120 hp. The *Chancellor Livingston* of 1817 was fitted with a 40-in. (101-cm) cylinder having a 5-ft. (1.5-m) stroke to drive flywheels and, in turn, paddle wheels. Her speed approached 9 knots.

Other names associated with the development of the marine steam engine are John Stevens, John Hall, who is credited with the first passage of a steamship at sea instead of on a river or canal, and his two sons, Robert and Francis, who introduced some engineering refinements to the basic marine engine of James Watt.

The early steamships were all relatively small vessels, and their engines, which were also small, were very much in their infancy. Before significant advances in engine and ship size could be made, more efficient engineering techniques — especially in forging pistons and crankshafts and casting cylinders — had to be learned. Joseph Maudslay, head of the firm Maudslay Sons and Field, is notable for the invention of a screw-cutting lathe which, coupled with Wilkinson's boring machine, made possible the rapid manufacture of steam engines. John Penn, an engineer of Greenwich, England, was another who introduced design improvements, and his trunk engine was selected to power most British warships.

Another area in which technical development was of

The launch of the Great Britain *at Bristol by Prince Albert, 1843.*

prime importance was in the design and construction of marine boilers. The earliest ships' boilers were little more than square water tanks heated by a furnace with a single large flue, and since there was as yet no system of staying them in position, they were restricted to a very low steam pressure, no more than 3 or 4 lb./sq. in. (0.21 or 0.28 kg/cm^2) above atmospheric pressure. But while ships' boilers were still something of an engineering after-thought — any rough and ready means of supplying steam to an engine was thought to be good enough — the rail-roads were beginning to develop and some first-class engineers, such as Richard Trevithick, William Hadley, George Stephenson and his son Robert, were turning locomotives into efficient mobile power plants. They developed light boilers with interior fireboxes and any-thing up to a hundred small firetubes to carry the hot gases to the funnel exhaust, providing a quick and effi-cient means of generating steam. Marine engineers were quick to see the advantages of this type of boiler and even improved upon it by incorporating additional firetubes returning through the boiler from a forward combustion chamber, thus obtaining the same heating surface in a boiler half the length of the locomotive's. At around the

same time a reliable marine condenser was invented; exhaust steam from the engine, instead of being wasted, was condensed back into water by passing it through tubes cooled by seawater and returned ready for re-use in the boiler. This combination of efficient boiler and marine condenser enabled shipowners to raise their sights beyond short-sea passages and contemplate transoceanic voyages.

Marine engines took a further step forward with Brunel's GREAT BRITAIN, whose power installation incor-porated several interesting new features. Her engines, which had four oscillating cylinders with a bore of 88 in. (224 cm) and stroke of 72 in. (183 cm), were placed low down in the bilges, two on either side of the engine room; they worked upwards onto a large sprocket wheel, from which four chains drove a smaller sprocket wheel on the propeller shaft. The gearing produced 53 rpm of the pro-peller from the 18 rpm of the engines, giving a speed of about 12 knots. Three tubular boilers, each with 8 furn-aces, produced steam at 15 lb./sq. in. (1.05 kg/cm^2). Although it was an ingenious and successful installation, it was still no more than a sophisticated adaptation of Watt's engine.

The next small step forward was the introduction of a

direct-acting engine to replace the side-lever type which had evolved from the beam engine. Instead of the beam there were two levers, one on each side of the cylinder, connected to the piston rod and crankshaft. The first ship to be fitted with the new type of engine was the *Gorgon*, and in her installation the cylinder was placed immediately below the crankshaft.

Brunel followed his *Great Britain* with the GREAT EASTERN, driven by a combination of paddle wheels and propeller, each with separate engines. In many respects she represented a dramatic advance, even though her engines were still the basic single-stage. The engine for the propellers was made by James Watt and Company of Birmingham, England, and the paddle engines by John Scott Russell and Company of Millwall, London, the builders of the ship. The paddle engines stood 40 ft. (12 m) high when completed and they included four oscillating cylinders of 74 in. (188 cm) diameter with steam from four boilers of box pattern operating at 24 lb./sq. in. (1.7 kg/cm^2) pressure. The four screw-engine cylinders were horizontal direct-acting with 84 in. (213 cm) diameter and 48 in. (122 cm) stroke, served by six double-ended tubular boilers at a pressure of 25 lb./sq. in. (1.75 kg/cm^2). The ship achieved and maintained speeds of 14 knots but at that speed her fuel consumption was excessive and uneconomic, and she was a commercial failure.

But the critical breakthrough was near. As long ago as 1781 Jonathan Hornblower had expounded the theory of the compound steam engine, in which the steam is used twice, first in a high-pressure cylinder and then in a low-pressure one, both connected to the same crankshaft. The obvious advantage of such a system is the production of double the power from the same amount of steam. It had been impossible to put the theory into practice during the early years of the marine steam engine, even though it was accepted by every engineer, because the existing technology had not yet solved the problem of producing steam at an initial pressure high enough for it to be used twice over.

John Elder took out a patent for a compound engine in 1853, and by 1868 the Cunard Company had two ships, the *Parthia* and *Batavia*, operating with compound engines across the Atlantic. They showed a saving of nearly 30 percent in fuel costs, and other steamship lines followed Cunard's example, installing compound engines in new ships and also when refitting older ships.

Several events encouraged the development and improvement of the compound steam engine. One was the opening of the Suez Canal in 1869 which, by providing a short cut in the sea route to India and China, opened the profitable Far Eastern trade to the steamship, which until then had remained in the hands of sailing vessels. Another was Robert Whitehead's adaptation of an Austrian invention into a locomotive torpedo, which in turn

called for the development of high-speed naval torpedo boats to carry the new weapon. These and other similar events underlined the importance of refinements in the design of ships' boilers: increased steam pressure was required to provide both economy by the use of the compound engine, vital for the long-distance operators on the Far Eastern route, and the speed needed for the new naval torpedo boat. One immediate solution was to adapt the fire-tube boilers used in railroad locomotives, but a number of distinguished engineers, particularly Nathanael Herreshoff in the United States, and John Thornycroft, Alfred Yarrow, and J. Samuel White in Britain, eventually produced a water-tube boiler, of which the Yarrow three-drum type was generally accepted as the most efficient high-pressure boiler available in the last decade of the 19th century.

It was no more than a logical step forward to advance from the compound engine to the triple-expansion engine, in which steam is used three times in one cycle by the introduction of an intermediate-pressure cylinder between the high and the low. The first triple-expansion engine was fitted by Alexander Kirk into the *Propontis* in 1873, but was a failure because of lack of adequate steam pressure. But a few years later, after the introduction of the Scotch return-tube marine boiler, which was very reliable and worked at pressures of up to 160 lb./sq. in. (11.2 kg/cm^2), triple expansion became the standard marine power installation for every sort of vessel, from the largest passenger liners to the smallest coasters. With the exception of a few giant liners such as the North German Lloyd *Kaiser Wilhem II*, which was fitted with immense quadruple-expansion engines developing 43,000 hp, the triple-expansion principle dominated the marine engine field until Charles Parsons produced the turbine.

Steam and Gas Turbines

The reciprocating steam engine in its triple- and quadruple-expansion forms was extremely reliable, and was in almost universal use in ships around the world; but the reciprocating mechanism — the fact that the pistons in the cylinders had to stop moving at the end of each stroke before starting back again in the opposite direction — embodied an inevitable loss of energy. If the movement of the driving components could be made continuous, the energy gain would be considerable, achieving a much more efficient use of fuel. This is what the turbine promised, and it needed only one or two brave souls to introduce it successfully into their ships for the whole of the shipping world to follow their lead.

The idea of using a jet of steam to spin a rotor set with blades on its circumference was an old concept in engineering, but one which had defied the skill of inventors to adapt for useful purposes. One of the problems was the uneven expansion of different metals under heat; another

Sir Charles Parsons, inventor of the steam turbine.

The British Admiralty was Parson's first customer, ordering two small destroyers with turbine engines, the *Viper* and the *Cobra*. Then came an order for a turbine passenger steamer, the *King Edward*, for use alongside the traditional paddle steamers on the River Clyde. In 1904 the Allan Line ordered the *Victorian* and *Virginian* for the transatlantic run, and their success stimulated the Cunard Company to specify turbine propulsion for their new big liners, the *Mauretania* and *Lusitania*. Their turbines produced 70,000 hp and enabled the *Mauretania* to regain the Blue Riband of the Atlantic with an average speed of 26.06 knots. The final nail in the coffin of the reciprocating steam engine was driven in when the British Admiralty specified turbines for the new battleship *Dreadnought*.

Oil fuel as an alternative to coal for steam turbines was first used in the British *Tribal* class of destroyers in 1907, but it was not until 1920 that the substitution of oil fuel for coal took place on a wide scale, largely as a result of experimental research into the most efficient techniques of burning it in marine boilers. It had many advantages over coal as a marine fuel; not only did it have a higher thermal efficiency than coal but also it was cleaner and much easier to handle, since it did not require an army of stokers to trim the bunkers and shovel coal into the boiler furnaces when the ship's engines were working.

A more modern development of the steam turbine is the gas turbine. It was produced primarily for aircraft but in recent years has been adapted for ship propulsion, though

was how to reaccelerate the steam jet after it had passed through one set of blades in order to reuse it on a second set. These were some of the difficulties facing Charles Parsons (and many other engineers) when he began work on the project, and it took years of patient and concentrated work for him to produce a working model; he also had to await the development of harder metals. But his new marine engine, when built, was so revolutionary that most shipowners recoiled from it in horror, more content with the devil they knew and trusted in the form of the triple-expansion engine than the unknown and untested devil that Parsons was offering them. However, after considerable frustrations following the patent of his invention in 1884, Parsons finally swept aside the opposition by demonstrating his invention in the 100-ft. prototype craft TURBINIA at the diamond jubilee review of the Royal Navy at Spithead in 1897. She achieved a speed of 34.5 knots and opened up a new era of ship propulsion, with particular significance for warships.

Parsons' geared machine steam turbine of 1897.

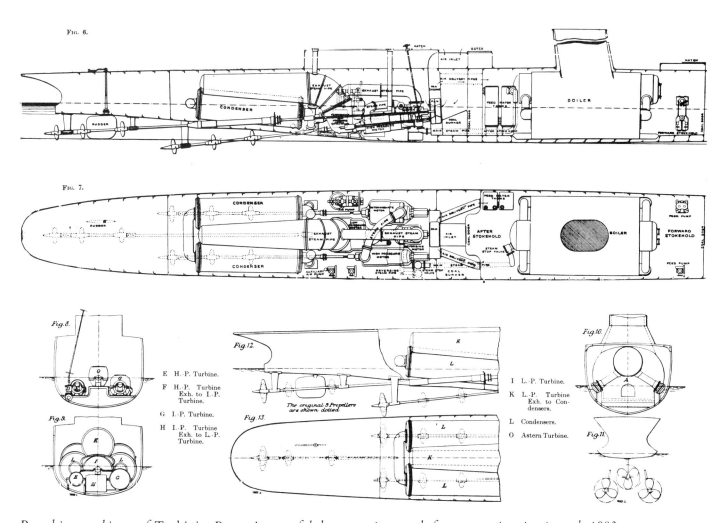

Propulsion machinery of Turbinia, *Parsons' successful demonstration vessel, from an engineering journal, 1903.*

so far only for the smaller warships of frigate size and below. Its main advantage lies in its power-to-weight ratio, unsurpassed by any other form of marine engine; another advantage is that it does not require a period of warming up before use to accommodate the expansion of the metals used in its construction, but can generate full power almost immediately. These are valuable assets for naval use but are not essential in the mercantile world. And, in its present state of development, the gas turbine consumes a disproportionate amount of fuel, a factor which tends to preclude its use in any ship that needs to earn her keep by passenger transport or cargo carrying.

Internal-combustion Engines

The gasoline-driven internal-combustion engine has little application in maritime propulsion apart from in small auxiliary craft such as launches, etc. It was, however, used in submarines in their early development, until the advent of the heavy-oil engine made it possible to abandon the gasoline engine with its ever-present risk of fire.

The genesis of the heavy-oil engine lies in a patent

granted in 1876 to Dr. A.N. Otto for a method of increasing the power in a gas engine. In 1892 Dr. Rudolf Diesel, adopting the Otto four-stroke cycle, designed an engine which ran on oil which burned, and therefore expanded, inside the cylinder. He gave his name to the

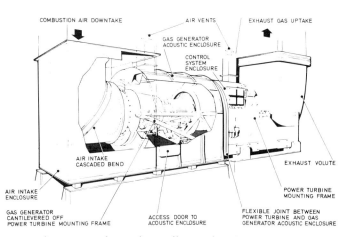

A modern gas turbine, the Rolls-Royce Olympus.

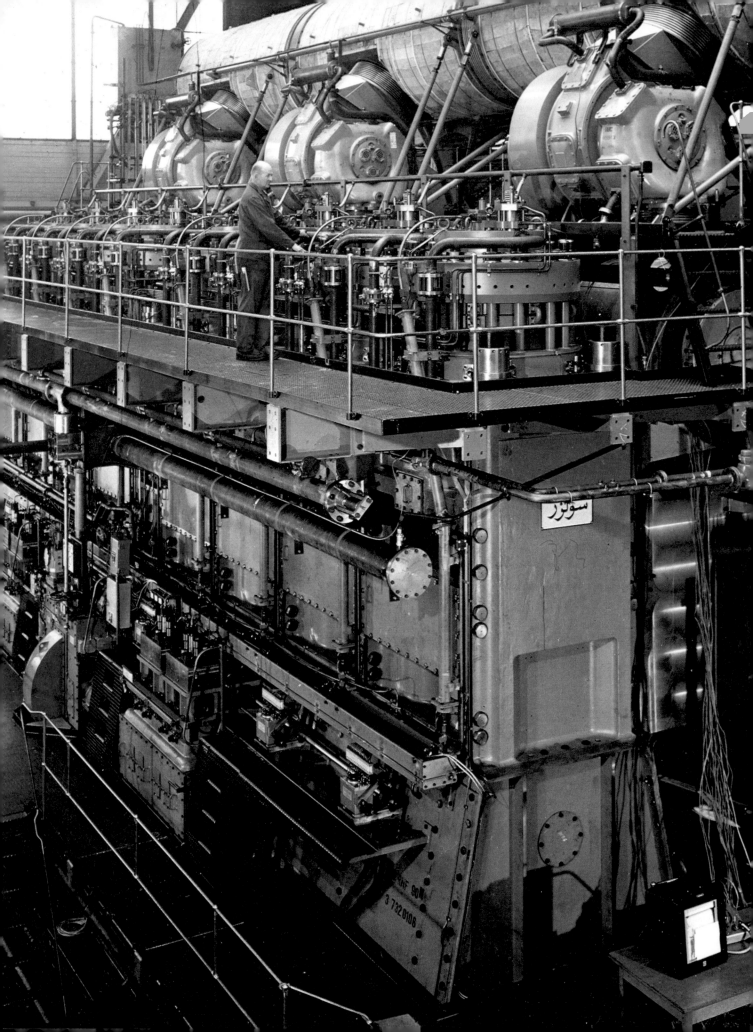

engine, and developed it into a compression-ignition motor which, in time, was to revolutionize ship propulsion as radically as the turbine had done only a few years earlier.

The heavy-oil diesel engine has several advantages for use in ships and one disadvantage. Compared with gasoline, with its low flash point, heavy oil has a high flash point and is safe. Unlike steam engines, it needs no boilers and no steampipes, and saves space in a ship's hull through the elimination of the boiler room, thereby providing additional capacity for cargo. Furthermore, it is very reliable and easy to maintain. All these features add up to make the diesel engine the most economical of all methods of ship propulsion in terms of fuel consumption, running costs, and (with the exception of the gas turbine) occupation of space; one would therefore expect every commercial shipowner to specify diesel propulsion in all the ships he operates. But its one important disadvantage is that there are limitations on its size, principally concerning the crankshaft, which needs to be strong enough to absorb the enormous pressure exerted by a big engine without the risk of fracture. It has been found that, because of these limitations in the size of the crankshaft, the maximum size of a diesel engine is one that can develop about 17,000 shp, sufficient to drive a ship of around 18,000 to 20,000 tons gross. For ships of a larger tonnage, the most economical form of propulsion is the steam turbine, even though this cannot compare with the diesel engine either in running costs or in the space occupied by the installation.

Nuclear Power

Nuclear power represents an enormous advance in ship propulsion. However, it is attended by grave problems of safety and is at present enormously expensive. So far it has been used mainly for naval vessels, though its installation in merchant ships might increase if these fundamental problems can be overcome. The advantages of nuclear propulsion in submarines are obvious; in fact nuclear power has created the first true submarine whose endurance is limited only by human, and not material, considerations (See *The Development of Submarines* later in this chapter). For certain warships, and especially for aircraft carriers, the advantages of independence in terms of main propulsion fuel outweigh the demands on weight and space which nuclear power plants and their associated safety requirements can impose. Indeed, the critical factor of size may not be the propulsion fit, but rather the aircraft and their fuel and armament requirements. In merchant ships, the economics of cargo carrying argue against the heavy initial expenditure on the nuclear propulsion unit, its weight, and the training of the operators. Other con-

Left: a giant Sulzer marine diesel engine.

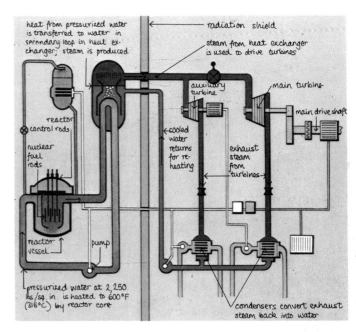

A nuclear propulsion unit: nuclear fission in the reactor vessel (regulated by control rods) heats pressurized water which, via a heat exchanger, produces steam to drive a turbine.

siderations are the problems of refitting at the very few ports where facilities may exist and the considerable risk of restrictions on entry into territorial waters, or even passage through straits, because of public concern about radiation hazards. Commercial arithmetic explains why there are so few nuclear-powered merchant ships. The United States built the SAVANNAH in 1962, a 20,000-ton vessel with a speed of 24 knots, largely as an experiment in nuclear propulsion for merchant ships, but she was not a success. In 1969 the Germans built the *Otto Hahn*, a nuclear-powered ore carrier, and the Japanese, too, are experimenting with nuclear propulsion in a small vessel with a cargo capacity of 2,400 tons. The most successful use of nuclear propulsion in nonnaval ships would appear to be in the big icebreakers built to operate on the northern sea route across the top of Siberia. The first nuclear icebreaker was the LENIN, launched in 1957 and completed two years later, and she has been followed by the *Arktika* and *Sibir*, both of 19,300 tons standard displacement. The *Arktika* penetrated to the North Pole through the ice in August 1977, an indication of her power in the icebreaker role.

In terms of fuel consumption, nuclear power is essentially a more efficient way of boiling water and producing steam. The reactor around which the installation operates takes the place of the normal ship's boilers, furnaces, fuel bunkers, and associated machinery. The fuel is enriched uranium which produces great heat when fission takes place inside the reactor, the periods of fission being regulated by control rods. The heat is absorbed by the coolant

Otto Hahn (1969), a German built freighter with nuclear propulsion.

which encircles the atomic pile, and this is transferred to water contained in heat exchangers surrounding the reactor. The water in the heat exchangers produces steam at high pressure which can be used normally in turbines with direct drive or with turbo-electric drive. The radiation hazards of the reactor and its associated fuel and machinery are enclosed within a massive shield which surrounds the whole installation and may weigh 1,000 tons or more. A single fueling of a reactor can take a ship more than three times around the world.

Paddles and Screws

It has been said that the helical screw, invented by Archimedes, confused later generations of marine engineers who sought to apply it as a logical means of ship propulsion. Archimedes designed it as a means of pumping water, and there seems to our modern minds to be little reason why it could not be used to push a ship through water. The ebullient Leonardo da Vinci, that Florentine mastermind who seems to have dabbled in most of the mechanical problems to preoccupy the world's engineers in later centuries, exercised his mind with drawings of turbines and screw propellers. But be that as it may, the earliest ideas on mechanical ship propulsion centered on mechanizing the movement of oars and paddle wheels. The American John Fitch produced a vessel in which steam power was used to move 12 vertical oars, six on each side of his ship. At about the same time the Marquis de Jouffroy succeeded in propelling his paddle-steamer

Pyroscaphe up the River Saône for 15 minutes before the engine broke down. Right at the start of the 19th century the *Charlotte Dundas* was the true herald of the coming revolution at sea with her successful progress on the Forth and Clyde canal. She was driven by a single narrow paddle wheel mounted in her stern, not in the fashion of the famous American stern-wheelers of the big rivers with a broad paddle wheel astern of their hulls, but set within the hull. In *Clermont*, Robert Fulton made a big step forward by mounting a paddle wheel each side of the ship, a more efficient method of propulsion and one which was to become the standard for paddle wheels.

Because paddle wheels operate half in and half out of the water they are basically inefficient in the conversion of power into movement through the water. But what they lose in efficiency they gain in maneuverability, for the position of a paddle wheel on each side of a ship's maximum beam provides the largest turning movement available in any ship. As a result, paddle-wheel propulsion has continued to exist long after it was proved to be considerably less efficient than the submerged propeller as a propulsion unit, though almost entirely for vessels whose main work lies in narrow or congested waters. For ferries, excursion steamers, harbor and dockyard tugs, paddle-wheel propulsion is often a better means of movement than a propeller because their particular tasks call for extreme maneuverability in restricted spaces. There may also be an element of nostalgia in their survival, particularly in the case of river steamers, where profitability depends on the attraction of large numbers of customers.

For naval purposes the paddle wheel was far too vulnerable to be considered as a means of propulsion. Exposed on either beam of the ship, it was an obvious target for gunfire, and ship designers were forced back to considerations of the Archimedean screw to overcome naval objections to the paddle wheel. There had been a few early experiments along this line, notably by Joseph Bramah who, inspired by the design of windmills, patented an early form of screw propeller in 1785. John Shorter also took out a patent for a screw propeller in 1800, but it was a clumsy affair with a chain drive and a long shaft which needed a buoy at the end to support it in the water; no sensible shipbuilder even considered it as a feasible solution to the problem.

Four engineers are usually credited with the design of the first workable ship propellers, all of them taking out patents between 1833 and 1836. They were Frédéric Sauvage of France, John ERICSSON of Sweden, who was working as an engineer in London at the time, and Robert Wilson and Francis Pettit Smith, both of Britain. Only two of these four were successful in having their designs accepted. Ericsson invented a double screw which was successfully demonstrated in the *Francis B. Ogden* in 1837 and the *Robert P. Stockton* in 1838, and Smith's screw, which had two twins on the Archimedes principle, was fitted in a small 10-ton vessel with a 6-hp engine which made a successful passage from London to Dover in a choppy sea. To satisfy demands from the British Admiralty for trials in a larger vessel he built the 237-ton ARCHIMEDES, which achieved a speed of 10 knots and made successful cruises to Amsterdam and Oporto.

It was as a result of the *Archimedes* trial that the British Admiralty fitted out two similar frigates, the RATTLER with Smith's screw and the *Alecto* with conventional paddle wheels, for a series of exhaustive trials which culminated in the celebrated tug-of-war in which the *Rattler* proved the superiority of propeller propulsion by towing the *Alecto* at a speed of 2.5 knots against the best that her paddle wheels could do.

Archimedes *(1838), designed by Francis Pettit Smith, was the first sizable screw-propelled vessel.*

101

If the British Admiralty opted for the Smith version of a screw propeller, most of the mercantile shipbuilders favored the double screw invented by Ericsson, and Brunel fitted an Ericsson propeller with six blades into the *Great Britain* in 1843. The advantages of the screw propeller over the paddle wheel — economy in fuel consumption for merchant ships and immunity from gunfire damage for warships — led very quickly to its wholesale adoption in the ships of all maritime nations. In the state of marine engine development at that time the early screw propellers were massive affairs of large diameter; the *Great Britain*'s screw had a diameter of 16 ft. (5 m), and the *Great Eastern*'s was a monster of 24 ft. (7.3 m) diameter. This was because the contemporary steam engine was unable to produce sufficient revolutions per minute to get the maximum efficiency from a small, balanced propeller and so had to turn a bigger screw to push as large a volume of water as possible to give the ship motion. The *Great Britain*'s engines turned at a leisurely 18 rpm (gearing increased the propeller speed to 53 rpm); the *Great Eastern*'s propeller engine (she had a separate engine for her paddle wheels) revolved at 39 rpm.

A major initial difficulty with the fitting of propellers in ships was the stern gland, the hole in the ship's stern through which the propeller shaft had to pass to drive the propeller. There was no suitable form of packing to make the stern gland watertight, and the general method in use in the early days was to encase the iron shaft in a brass tube where it passed through the hull. This, however, produced considerable wear on the brass of the tube so that, after quite a short period of running, the stern gland started to leak, and there were many cases where ships had to be beached hurriedly to save themselves from sinking because of the volume of water entering through the worn tube. This particular problem was solved in 1854 when John Penn, whose trunk engines had been adopted for British warships, discovered the properties of lignum vitae, a hardwood from South America. It contains enough vegetable oil to be self-lubricating and proved to be an admirable material for packing stern glands.

As the new marine engines, compound, triple-expansion and turbine, achieved the speeds required for maximum mechanical efficiency, a great deal of thought had to be given to propeller design in order to transfer that mechanical efficiency into maximum propeller efficiency. Over the years a diversity of propeller designs have been used, from the relative simplicity of the single-shaft Smith and Ericsson patents to multibladed propellers with up to five shafts. Variable pitch propellers, which today have reached sophisticated standards, owe some of their modern design to a patent taken out as early as 1844 by Bennett Woodcroft, and Christopher Hayes and Joseph Maudslay also patented pitch-control mechanisms during the 19th century. The contra-rotating combination of propellers, adopted many years ago for torpedoes to give them improved course-holding properties, is another option now under consideration for ship propulsion.

Speed, Economics, and New Developments in Propulsion

It is interesting to reflect that, despite all the tremendous advances made in the development of powered ships, speed has proved an elusive element; whereas in land and air travel advances in technology have produced dramatic increases in speed, no such progress can be seen in marine transportation. It has been said that the Roman forces under Julius Caesar setting out to invade Britain in 55 BC, the Spanish Armada in 1588, and the German invasion force of 1940 (had it ever set out), would all have crossed the English Channel at about the same speed. It is a fact that the British invasion force for the abortive Suez operation in 1956 averaged the same speed as Lord Nelson's fleet on the same passage from Malta to Egypt for the Battle of the Nile in 1801. The presence of landing craft or barges in all these naval expeditions goes some way towards explaining the apparent lack of progress; but merchant shipping too has hardly accelerated over the centuries. Experience with a variety of merchant vessels in two world wars confirms the generally low average speed of merchant ships; in both world wars ships were organized into slow and fast convoys and in each of them slow convoys were lucky if they averaged 5 knots. Some ships were underpowered, some were poorly maintained, some had dirty bottoms, some were poor seaboats, but even if

One of the propellers of the ill-fated Titanic.

these limitations had been removed, the average slow convoy speed would only have improved by a knot or two.

For nonnuclear ships, a vessel's speed is calculated to allow the required passage to be made at the most economical rate of fuel consumption. There is an optimum economical speed below which the total fuel consumed will be increased because the passage will take longer; if the speed is higher than the optimum more fuel has to be burned and above a certain point, even allowing for the shorter time on passage, the total consumption becomes greater. The economical speed thus represents the most favorable ratio between a ship's earning capacity set against her fuel consumption.

Omitting the great ocean liners, in which speed, even if wasteful, was a saleable asset in attracting a full passenger list, the speed of powered ships can be said to have increased, over nearly 180 years of development, approximately from that of the snail to that of the tortoise. The *Charlotte Dundas*, the first recognizable steamship, was credited with a little over 3 knots in 1802. The *Great Britain* in 1838 produced a speed of 9 knots. She was, perhaps, the first of the ocean liners, but speed was not at that time an essential attribute of a liner and the increase represents less than 40 years of marine engine development. For the average cargo steamer during the rest of the 19th century, 9 knots was about the norm. There was an increase of about 1 knot between the turn of the century and the outbreak of World War I, and of about 1 knot more between the two world wars. These speeds, of course, refer to average cargo ships and do not embrace the big passenger liners or warships which, by 1939, were achieving speeds of around 30 knots.

There was a considerable advance in average merchant ship speed in the 30 years following the end of the World War II, due in part to more research into optimum hull form and engine and propeller design, and to the experience of World War II that faster ships were not so vulnerable to submarine attack. Part of the reason, too, was the immense growth in cargo capacity of the modern tankers and bulk carriers which made higher speeds economic in terms of ships' earning power. By 1975 the average speed of cargo ships had increased to around 20 knots. Since then it has fallen, and is still falling. The reason for this is the towering cost of oil fuel, which underwent a five-fold rise during the 1970s. Even with the immense cargoes carried in a single ship today, the economical speed has been roughly halved and is back to the average of the start of the century.

Two new developments are worthy of mention in connection with the interrelated subjects of speed and economics. One is the development of surface-effect vessels (HYDROFOILS and AIR-CUSHION VEHICLES) which are capable of high working speeds at sea. The other is the return to the use of sail power.

Marine boiler for installation in a container cargo ship.

Back to Sail Power?

The enormous increases in the cost of fuel in recent years have, as we have seen, had a significant impact on the economics of merchant shipping, with a general fall in the speed of cargo ships. This has led to the idea of returning to the wind as a source of motive power, using modern technology to provide more efficient ways of harnessing this free and abundant (if unpredictable) resource. Various plans for wind-driven cargo ships are in existence. One such development is the DYNASHIP, a German-inspired project for the reintroduction of square-rigged ships as bulk carriers, using an aerodynamically designed sail plan allied to mechanical means of sail handling directed by a computer. An auxiliary engine is installed to provide the necessary electric power on board and to take the ship out of areas of calm and into areas of predicted winds. Cargo carriers of up to 17,000 tons are planned in this project.

Another wind project, at present under study at Southampton, England, envisages the use of wind turbines or rotors to provide propulsion, possibly by direct gearing to an ordinary marine propeller. This is an adaptation of the Magnus-effect device which was established as an aerodynamic principle some 70 years ago; it was in fact investigated as a means of ship propulsion between the two world wars but was dropped because the then low cost of fuel oil did not provide sufficient incentive to study the project further (see also ROTOR SHIP).

Both these wind projects may or may not succeed, but it appears probable that the use of some sort of sail in conjunction with normal mechanical propulsion will be adopted for many ships. The use of a sail to help a ship on her way makes both economic and ecological sense by reducing fuel costs and pollution from exhaust gases. The new type of sail may well take the form of something like an aircraft wing, with its trimming controlled by a computer to effect the most efficient settings.

Surface-Effect Vessels

The term 'surface-effect vessel' means a craft which operates on or slightly above the surface of the sea, in contrast with conventional ships, whose hulls are partly submerged in the sea. Surface-effect vessels are mainly HYDROFOILS, which skim on the surface, and hovercraft, which operate a foot or two above the surface on a cushion of air (see AIR-CUSHION VEHICLE).

The basic idea behind hydrofoil development is to eliminate the drag of the water by a boat's hull lifting itself clear of the surface by means of planes or foils, using high speed to do so. The idea is not new, the earliest experiments dating back to 1891. In 1905 Enrico Forlanini reached a speed of 38 knots during trials on Lake Maggiore with a small craft of his own design fitted with ladder foils. For the next 20 years hydrofoil experiments continued on the basis of Forlanini's theories, in which the foils remained submerged, but in 1927 a group of German engineers evolved the surface-piercing foil, in which the boat uses her speed to bring the foils completely to the surface so that the vessel skids along on top of the sea.

Hydrofoils did not come into commercial use until after the end of World War II, and then as fast passenger ferries over short passages. The first regular service was between Sicily and Italy, operating at a speed of some 50 knots, in 1956. They were also widely adopted by the Soviet Union for passenger services up and down the main rivers, the Soviet version being built at the Krasnoye Sormovo shipyard. Since then, many countries have introduced hydrofoils for fast passenger-carrying services across short distances.

Hydrofoils divide themselves into two basic types

Hydrofoil passenger ferry with surface-piercing foils.

depending on whether they are fitted with the *Canard*-type foil or the conventional foil. The *Canard*-type is surface-piercing and supports 30 percent of the vessel's weight on the forward foils and 70 percent on the after foils. This type gives a very high speed but is more difficult to control. In the conventional type of foil the percentages of weight support are reversed with 70 percent on the forward foils and 30 percent aft. The whole hull of the vessel is lifted clear of the water but the foils themselves remain submerged, and though this type cannot produce quite so high a speed, it is much easier to control during operation.

Propulsion is by jet engine, which burns fuel at a very high rate. It is this heavy fuel consumption that limits the hydrofoil to short-sea or river passages. Ideas have been put forward for large hydrofoils for fast ocean passages at speeds of 60 knots and over, but the stowage of adequate

Prototype British VT2 *hovercraft car and passenger ferry.*

fuel for such passages would probably need all the available space on board to the exclusion of passengers or cargo.

Like the hydrofoil, the principle of the hovercraft is not new. Emmanuel Swedenborg first put forward the idea of forcing air beneath a ship's hull to reduce the drag of the water in 1716, but was beaten by how this could be done in the then state of technological development. Experiments using compressed air were made during the second half of the 19th century, and early in the 20th century the Austrian engineer Dagobert Müller von Thomamhul used the sidewall air-cushion principle in building a vessel for the Austrian navy which achieved a speed of 40 knots. But it was Sir Christopher Cockerell who produced the first practicable design in 1950, though it took another 8 years to get official recognition of its value and to raise the funds necessary for its development.

The hovercraft produces its own cushion of air by ducted fans, and this cushion is contained beneath the hull within a flexible skirt so that its lifting pressure is not dissipated into the surrounding air. In the *SR.N-4* version, which operates car- and passenger-ferry commercial services, the power unit is four gas-turbine engines which drive four variable-pitch aircraft propellers to provide forward movement and four 12-bladed centrifugal fans to provide the air cushion. As the hull of the hovercraft is lifted a foot or two (30-60 cm) clear of the water, there is no water resistance at all, and speeds of up to 65 knots are easily achievable.

The hovercraft is an amphibious craft, as much at home on the land as it is on the sea. As such it has naval and military capabilities as well as its better-known role as a fast car and passenger ferry. Speed is an asset in itself, but in its amphibious roles, the hovercraft's capacity to pass

Jet Caribe, *a hydrofoil ferry with fully submerged foils.*

over difficult surfaces, underwater obstacles, and through treacherous waters has opened many new possibilities. Applications of the air-cushion principle have been tested over ice and snow, marsh and muskeg, desert sand, and mud; and small hovercraft have been used for search and rescue near airports, for fire services, for emergency medical services, and for relief work in cases of natural disaster. For military purposes the hovercraft is in use with the United States and Soviet forces as an amphibious troop and logistic carrier and a new type is being evaluated in the United Kingdom as a mine-countermeasures vessel.

Like the hydrofoil, the hovercraft burns fuel at a high rate and, in its present state of development, it is limited in its commercial applications to the shorter sea routes. But experiments are currently being made in the United States to see whether it can be developed into an ocean-going vessel by using less fuel-consuming propulsion methods, such as water-jet or super-cavitating propellers. If these experiments prove successful, they will mark yet another milestone in the history of powered ships.

The Development of Submarines

Early Experimental Submarines

Man's desire to find ways of concealed movement by water led to many experiments with submersible vehicles including, according to legend, ventures underwater by Alexander the Great at the siege of Tyre in 332 BC. In more modern times William Bourne, an English physicist in the reign of Queen Elizabeth I, was the first to make public ideas on how a vessel could be made to dive underwater by suppressing its positive buoyancy. In 1620 Dr. Cornelis van Drebbel, a Dutchman, demonstrated to King James I that it was possible to submerge a vessel and propel it underwater by the use of oars. At Rotterdam in 1653 a Frenchman named de Son built a submarine incorporating a paddle wheel rotated by clockwork, but when it was launched the clockwork was not strong enough to turn the paddle wheel. In the next century a ship's carpenter named Day invented a submarine which was forced underwater by weights hung below the hull. It reached a depth of 30 ft. (9 m) in Plymouth Sound, England, in 1773, but in a second dive the mechanism for releasing the weights failed to work and the boat continued down until it was crushed by the pressure of the water.

A significant step forward was made by the *Turtle*, which was the invention of David BUSHNELL, who was studying at Yale University in 1775. He was interested in explosives, particularly in underwater explosions and in ways of delivering the explosives to a chosen target. The latter requirement was met by the construction of an egg-shaped craft which could be submerged and propelled by its operator. The propulsion and diving mechanism, operated by hand and foot with cranks, drove two screw propellers, one horizontal and one vertical. The operational use of this vessel nearly justified Bushnell's hopes when, piloted by a Sergeant Lee, it was successfully propelled to a position beneath Admiral Lord Howe's flagship *Eagle* in New York Harbor during the American Revolution. The means of attaching the 150-lb. (68 kg) explosive proved inadequate, and the charge eventually exploded harmlessly after being released by Lee to scare off pursuers.

The principle of underwater warfare, whether by submarines or mines or a combination of both, was well recognized in the 19th century. The grounds for alarm were voiced by William Pitt, Prime Minister of Britain during the Napoleonic War, when he witnessed a demonstration of the next stage of submarine development by the engineer John Fulton: 'This remarkable invention of yours seems to go to the destruction of all fleets.' Fulton's new boat, the *Nautilus*, was of about 9 tons and 25 ft. (7.6 m) long, propelled by a hand-cranked propeller. Some time before, Fulton had demonstrated her to the French authorities at Brest. His proposals were rejected by the French, but Pitt saw possibilities for the use of his device against them. John JERVIS, Lord St. Vincent, was less enthusiastic; he opposed Pitt's support of a

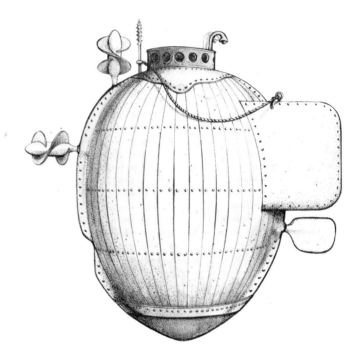

Bushnell's experimental submarine Turtle, *1775.*

submarine project, claiming that it represented '. . . a mode of warfare which they who command the seas do not want and which, if successful, will deprive them of it.' Fulton, whose name is also closely connected with the development of steam propulsion, returned to his native land in disgust when the British eventually rejected his

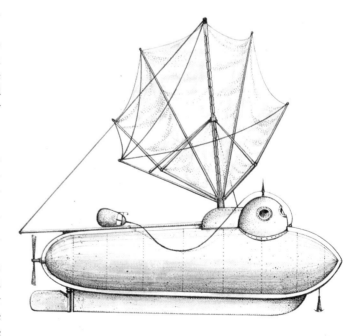

Fulton's Nautilus *(1801), rejected by France and Britain.*

proposals. Nonetheless, 50 years later the threat of underwater attack, or at least fear of the unknown, was sufficient to give an initial success to Wilhelm Bauer when he maneuvered a submarine of his invention, driven by a four-bladed propeller, against a Danish blockading squadron off Kiel in 1850. Bauer's next submarine almost met with disaster, however, when it dived to the bottom in 60 ft. (18 m) of water and began to break up under the water pressure. Bauer's understanding of the pressures involved and the confidence which he inspired in his two companions enabled them all to escape. Realizing that he could only open the hatch from the inside if he equalized the pressure inside the boat with that outside, he began flooding the submarine to compress the air inside, and he and his crew came up in a bubble of air. This method of free escape is a standard modern submarine escape procedure.

Like many other inventors, Bauer was rebuffed in his search for financial support successively by governments in Germany, Austria, the United States, and Britain. Finally, in St. Petersburg, he received support from the Czar and in 1855 built *Le Diable Marin*. In his craft, while submerged in the harbor, Bauer celebrated the coronation of Czar Alexander II by playing the Russian National Anthem with a small orchestra on board. The sound carried through the water and was clearly heard ashore and in other ships in harbor.

The American Civil War provided another stimulus for invention as Confederate officers sought means of breaking the Federal blockade. Initial efforts were directed at the use of small surface hand-operated or steam-driven craft nicknamed *Davids*, equipped with spar torpedoes to attack the Federal *Goliaths*. These were TORPEDO BOATS rather than submarines, although they were designed to operate fractionally below the surface. The best remembered of the hand-operated *Davids* is the *H.L. Hunley*, which in 1864 sunk the Federal sloop *Housatonic* with a spar torpedo, though she herself also went down in the explosion.

Advent of the Modern Submarine

The next significant name in the history of submarine development is one of the best known and is in fact the true father of the modern submarine. John P. HOLLAND was an Irish schoolteacher who emigrated to the United States. A Fenian in politics, he worked on designs of submarines, possibly with the idea of using them somehow against the hated British. His first two boats, *Holland I* and *Holland II*, later renamed the *Fenian Ram*, were built in New York in 1878, their construction financed by the Fenian brotherhood. The *Fenian Ram* was 31 ft. (9.4 m) long and of 19 tons displacement, powered by a 16-hp two-cylinder Brayton gasoline engine. She performed reasonably well as a submarine but had difficulties over her weapon system, designed to fire a 6-ft. (1.8-m) projectile using compressed air. He then built a third craft, a 15-ft. (5-m) working model of a new design. Rivalry among the Fenian group resulted in the *Fenian Ram* and the new

Early Royal Navy submarine built by Holland's Electric Boat Company.

model being stolen, in the course of which both were accidentally sunk.

Five years later, in collaboration with the U.S. Navy, Holland founded the Holland Torpedo Boat Company to build a new submarine. She was named *Plunger* and built to an overall length of 85 ft. (26 m) and a displacement of 168 tons. Her armament was five Whitehead torpedoes, which by that time had been developed into formidable underwater weapons. However, the *Plunger* was not a success and the company was wound up.

But by 1900 events were moving in the submarine's favor. The internal-combustion engine, still gasoline-powered, was the most satisfactory means of surface propulsion for a submarine, while a battery-driven electric motor provided underwater propulsion. The batteries could be recharged with the gasoline engine driving the electric motor as a dynamo to provide the charging current. With the new Whitehead torpedoes the submarine could well become a formidable warship, and many navies were now more than ready to investigate the possibilities.

With the financial backing of the firm which had made the *Plunger*'s batteries, Holland formed a new company, the Electric Boat Company. In 1900 *Holland VIII* was built and was bought by the U.S. Navy for trials. The Company's next submarine was the *Fulton* and was sold to the Russian navy. As the result of the *Holland VIII* trials, the U.S. Navy placed an order with Holland for six new boats, and the British navy bought five.

Meanwhile, also in the United States, Simon Lake was designing and building submarines. His first was the *Protector*, a well-designed submarine with hydroplanes forward and aft to control the angle of dive and a tear-drop hull, today the most advanced hull shape for submarines. Lake's idea of submarine warfare was for a boat to lie on the seabed and report the movements of passing warships or to cut the moorings of mines, and for this purpose he fitted a pair of large wheels amidships so that the boat could run along the seabed. By the time he was dissuaded from this odd idea, the U.S. Navy was contracted to Holland, and Lake had lost the market in his home country. However he sold the *Protector*, without her wheels, to Russia and in fact lived in that country for the next seven years, selling some of his designs to Austria and Germany.

European designers, too, were active in this new underwater world. In Sweden, Thorsten Nordenfeldt, working from ideas of propulsion pioneered in Britain by the Rev. G.W. Barrett, built a number of submarines which he sold to Greece, Turkey, and Russia. Gustave Zédé in France produced the *Gymnote*, electrically propelled and notable for being fitted with extra hydroplanes, and his work was followed by Maxime Laubeuf, who in 1900 commissioned the *Narval* which incorporated many features that became standard in later submarines, including a double hull and periscopes. She had steam surface and elec-

tric underwater propulsion, and one of her novelties for the period was an oil-fired boiler. She represented a significant advance and an important European contribution to submarine design.

The advent of diesel propulsion to replace the gasoline engine brought the submarine into her final form until nuclear power revolutionized the whole conception of submarine warfare. Over the next 40 years there were occasional variations in design and many improvements in construction and weapon fit, but in its essentials the 1950 submarine was no more than a sophisticated version of the 1910 boat. They all suffered from the fact that their batteries needed to be recharged after a period of submerged use, and there was no way of recharging them underwater. On the surface a submarine is obviously very vulnerable, particularly since the invention of radar and other refined detection devices during World War II.

Both world wars were fought with this basic type of submarine, and in both of them losses of submarines were considerably heavier than losses of any other type of warship. Towards the end of World War II there were two major developments which, in their ways, lessened the main area of vulnerability of the submarine, although neither was more than a halfway house. The first was the Schnorkel breathing tube, developed by Germany from an invention discovered in Denmark when that country was overrun in 1940. It was a 30- to 35-ft. (10-11 m) tube attached to the hull of a submarine, allowing air to be drawn in and exhaust fumes to be released when sub-

The Royal Navy's patrol submarine Olympus, *1962.*

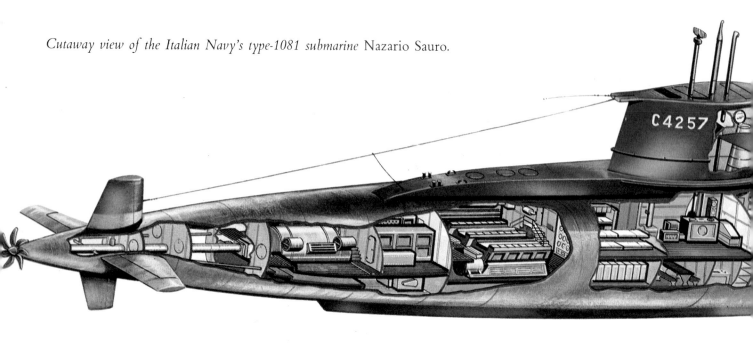

Cutaway view of the Italian Navy's type-1081 submarine Nazario Sauro.

merged at periscope depth so that the diesel engines could be operated without affecting the air in the boat. The Schnorkel could therefore reduce the amount of time a submarine needed to stay on the surface to recharge her batteries, and indeed prolong the capacity of the batteries by making it possible to use the diesel engines for submerged propulsion at periscope depth. But it did not reduce the dependence of the submarine on the atmosphere because the top of the Schnorkel tube had to project above the surface of the sea.

The second development was the introduction of a closed-cycle engine with an internal supply of oxygen so that the diesels could be run with the submarine submerged. This was achieved by using high-test peroxide in the engine ignition circuit so that, as with the Schnorkel tube, the internal air in the boat did not have to be used for the engine. One of the principal objects of the closed-cycle engine was high submerged speed, an important feature of all submarine warfare. The engine was developed by Dr. Walther in Germany but, perhaps fortunately for the Allies during World War II, it reached fruitition only during the very last days of the war, too late to affect the issue in any way.

For years, the dream of the true submarine, one which could operate for long periods at high speeds completely independent of the sea's surface, had animated all submariners. The problem to be solved was how to generate energy by burning fuel without the use of oxygen. The closed-cycle engine using high-test peroxide was approaching the answer, but still had some limitations in

endurance because of fuel-supply problems and was therefore not entirely independent of the sea's surface throughout the whole of a patrol. Further development of the system after the end of World War II produced underwater speeds in the region of 25 knots, very satisfactory in submarine warfare terms.

The Nuclear Revolution

The great advance in submerged speed and the advent of the true submarine came with the successful achievement of a nuclear-powered submarine. On January 17, 1955, the U.S. Navy's NAUTILUS signaled that she was under way on nuclear power. From that moment submariners could have at their disposal (at a considerable cost) boats with submerged speeds in excess of 30 knots whose underwater endurance was limited only by consideration of human factors. Long-distance deployments, lengthy patrols, and high-speed tactical maneuvering all became possible for submarines with a nuclear propulsion unit. The United States, the Soviet Union, Britain, and France all moved into this field in the years which followed. Two characteristics of nuclear submarines are noteworthy: their size and quietness. The *Nautilus* is 319 ft. (97 m) long and has a surface displacement of 3,764 tons (4,040 tons submerged), figures two or three times as big as the average run of early submarines. The latest American ballistic-missile submarines are reported to be 425 ft. (130 m) long and of 7,320 tons displacement (8,250 tons submerged). Quietness has been a preoccupation of submarine designers over the years since the vessels can be located when sub-

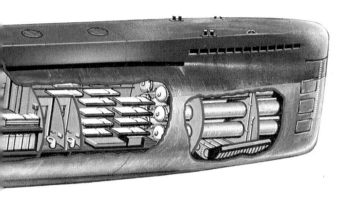

Royal Navy nuclear submarine Churchill.

merged by the noise they make. The increasing sophistication of passive detection devices and the strategic importance of the ballistic-missile submarines have combined to sharpen appreciation of the problem. Efforts to reduce noise have concentrated especially on propeller design and hull forms. It is interesting to note that the tear-drop hull shape which accords best with modern submarine performance is similar to that of Simon Lake's submarine *Protector*, developed in about 1920.

One name stands out in the history of nuclear power for ships: Hyman G. RICKOVER, who in 1947 was a captain in the U.S. Navy with wartime service in the electrical department of the Bureau of Ships. Building on prewar work in Columbia University and in the U.S. Naval Research Laboratory, he drove ahead in the face of bureaucratic resistance and gave his country a lead in the adoption of nuclear power for ships. Nuclear power has been used for propulsion in surface ships such as aircraft carriers, but it is mainly in submarine warfare and in the deployment of deterrent forces in the ocean depths that the great expense and enormous overheads of nuclear systems have been most readily justified. The capabilities of the new generation of submarines are such that it has proved difficult to develop a weapon system to match them. Ballistic-missile systems are highly sophisticated and of devastating effectiveness. When the *George Washington*, with its 16 Polaris missiles, was launched in 1959 it was the most powerful warship the world had ever seen. In the 1980s Polaris was replaced by the multiple-warhead Poseidon in the U.S. ballistic-missile submarine force, and now the new *Ohio*-class submarines are each being equipped with 24 Trident missiles. These new missiles have a range of over 4,000 miles (6,500 km) — twice the range of Polaris. In addition to long-range bombardment capabilities, the modern submarine can fire shorter-range weapons against ship and land targets or other submarines.

Modern materials and construction techniques, together with the increased power and efficient hull design of the nuclear submarines, give enhanced performance in depth as well as speed. World War I maximum diving depths were of the order of 200 ft. (61 m) and those of World War II had increased to 300-350 ft. (90-105 m). Today it has been made public that depths of about 500 ft. (150 m) have been reached, but it can be assumed that much greater depths have been attained by operational submarines of several nations.

Today the story of the submarine has reached a point where underwater speed exceeds that of most surface ships; the limits of endurance have become human rather than material; sizes range across and beyond the spectrum of 20th-century cruiser dimensions, while hitting power is incomparably enhanced, even in nonnuclear terms.

See also SUBMARINES and the chapter on *Warships and Sea Warfare*.

Warships and Sea Warfare

Ships designed purely as warships date back at least to the Minoan civilization of Crete, which was overthrown by the Mycenaeans some years before 1450 BC. But it is to the Phoenicians, a few centuries later, that we must look for the design and development of the war GALLEY, which was to become the standard warship type of the Mediterranean for the next 2,500 years. Its original and principal armament was a pointed ram or beak attached to the bow and designed to hole and sink enemy vessels. As the years passed new weapons were added to the war galley's armament: the *corvus*, a spiked boarding plank over which the troops carried on board could capture a ship by assault; the catapult, to hurl firebrands into an enemy ship; and the mangonel, which could bombard an enemy with heavy stones from a distance of 200 yd. (180 m). At the final stage of its development in the 17th century, the Mediterranean war galley was armed with cannon which could fire round shot to a range of 1,000 yd. (910 m), though it was not particularly accurate at that distance. (See also the chapter on *Oared Ships*.)

Beyond the Mediterranean in north European waters the warship was no more than the current design of trading ship, with soldiers embarked to do the fighting — a pattern which lasted until the 15th century. The Norse LONGSHIP, essentially designed for trade, was adapted for warlike purposes by adding a couple of strakes to the hull so that the crew of warriors had the extra height from which to launch their darts. At the battle of Sluys, fought in 1340 between an English fleet, commanded by King Edward III, and a French fleet, Edward's flagship was the COG *Thomas*, and most of the 200 ships of his fleet were cogs, manned principally by archers. The cog was the standard north European trading ship of the period,

Galley warfare in the early 16th century.

designed very full in the beam to carry the largest possible cargo, and it was this fullness which gave her the generic description of 'round ship.'

Gunpowder and the Gun

It was the introduction of gunpowder and the gun and their adaptation for use on board a ship that brought about in these northern waters the separation of warship and trading ship into distinct types. It took a long time for the gun to find a naval application; it was well over a century after its introduction on land that a ship first mounted a gun on board. Small hand guns were carried in ships very shortly after their original appearance on land (the first recorded instance is in the English cog *Christopher*, captured by the French in 1339), but this was virtually no more than a step forward from the archers of older days. These guns had little or no influence on the basic methods of warfare at sea, which remained hand-to-hand fighting. The vital change came when the big gun, the cannon, was mounted on board and enabled a ship to engage an enemy without first having to go alongside her to get within effective fighting range.

The difficulty with the cannon on board ship was where to mount it. The first warship to carry cannon was the English HENRY GRÂCE À DIEU, a big ship of 1,000 tons launched in 1514. Contemporary records give her a total of 21 guns, ranging from cannon firing a 66-lb. iron shot to falcons with a 3 lb. weight of shot. In addition she carried 230 light guns, but these were really no more than hand guns for the 349 soldiers who formed part of her war complement. We do not know for sure where in the ship the larger guns were mounted, though the famous picture by Volpe, now at Hampton Court in England, shows that two of them fired through gunports cut in the square stern. It is probable that the remaining 19 were mounted in the fore- and aftercastles and in the waist.

William of Normandy's longship Mora *(1066), from the Bayeux Tapestry.*

This was always the main difficulty which faced warship designers in these early days. The standard design of warship featured high fore- and aftercastles to command the low central waist, the point where the enemy would board the ship. The towering structures fore and aft provided natural platforms from which to fire downwards on the ship's attackers as they swarmed in across the waist. But guns were heavy; the cannon royal, the biggest ship's gun then made, weighed 7,000 lb. (3,180 kg), and mounting guns of this weight high up in the two castles made the ship unstable. It was obvious, even to these early 16th-century ship designers, that the heavier the gun, the lower down in the ship it needed to be mounted.

The answer to this problem came with the building of the English *Mary Rose*, reconstructed in 1536 from an earlier ship of the same name built in 1509. During her rebuilding she was given a gundeck below her upper deck, and the guns were fired through square ports cut in her side. The gunports were fitted with hinged lids. This design for mounting guns effectively overcame the danger of instability associated with the placing of heavy guns high up in the two castles; consequently it was almost immediately accepted as the standard pattern for the arming of warships throughout the western world. Only in the Mediterranean did the old design survive, for it was impossible to mount guns low down in a galley because of the rowers on their benches. In the galley all guns, even the heavy cannon, had to be mounted on the upper deck. A danger inherent in the new design of a lower gundeck and gunports cut in the ship's side was made evident in 1545 when the *Mary Rose* sank at Spithead, being swamped by the sea pouring in through her open ports as she was leaving harbor. It was obviously due to temporary carelessness on board, for the basic principle of square port and hinged lid proved sound enough throughout the succeeding centuries, though the *Mary Rose* was by no means the only sailing warship to be lost in this way.

The naval introduction of the big gun revolutionized sea warfare. In all the earlier warships fighting was done by soldiers carried on board, the sailors' duty being simply to navigate the ship to the scene of battle. There, the normal battle tactic was to try to weaken the enemy crew with a hail of arrows before taking the ship alongside for the soldiers to jump across to board the vessel. But with the introduction of the big gun, mounted to fire through gunports cut in the ship's side, the only way of fighting was to sail broadside on to an enemy's ship and pound him with cannon balls, hoping to disable him by dismounting his guns, decimating his crew, or shooting down his masts and yards so that he was forced to surrender. There was no longer any role for the soldiers on board, and so the sailor began to develop into the seaman, trained not only to sail the ship to the scene of battle but also to man the big guns. With ships sailing broadside-on

Dutch 16th-century warship.

to an enemy, there began to develop the battle tactic of ships in a fleet forming a close line ahead when going into battle, both for mutual support and because there was no other way in which the maximum weight of gunfire could be brought to bear against an enemy.

It took a hundred years for the line-ahead formation to evolve, largely because of the difficulty of controlling the individual ships in a fleet without an efficient signaling system. Gunpowder, the only known form of propellent until comparatively modern days, forms a thick black oily smoke when it is exploded, and ships firing at each other soon found themselves virtually on their own, even in their own fleet, simply because they could see no signals through the gunpowder smoke. Not that, in those early days, there were many signals to see. So until nearly the end of the 17th century naval battles, which may have begun in line-ahead formation, normally developed into disorganized melees, with individual ships fighting each other irrespective of the movements or wishes of their fleet commanders. But during the second half of the century the first naval signal books began to make their appearance, and national fleets began to be accompanied to sea by smaller ships whose only duty in battle was to lie behind the battle line clear of the smoke and repeat the admiral's signals so that they could be seen by the ships actually engaged in the fighting. It took a long time for the naval battle to emerge from the original 'free-for-all' into an ordered encounter with a fleet acting together as an efficient whole. It finally came about during the 18th century with the introduction of more sophisticated naval signal books and the increasing use of repeating ships in order to make the admiral's signals visible to all.

113

One of Matthew Baker's galleon designs from Fragments of Ancient Shipwrightry, *c. 1585. The 'low-charged' hull form revolutionized naval warfare; it probably evolved from a collaboration between Baker and John Hawkins.*

The Low-charged Ships

The next great step forward in warship hull design came about as a result of the loss of the English *Jesus of Lubeck*, captured by the Spanish at San Juan de Ulúa in 1568. John HAWKINS, commander of the English expedition, attributed the loss of the *Jesus of Lubeck* to the high castle built up over the ship's bows which, catching the wind, forced the ship down to leeward. Shortly after his return to England Hawkins was made treasurer of the Elizabethan navy and began to take an active part in naval ship design. In 1570 two small naval ships, the *Bull* and the *Tiger*, both of about 200 tons, came into the royal dockyards for rebuilding, and this gave Hawkins his chance to make his experiments. His idea was to test whether a ship could be made more weatherly, holding her course into the wind without sagging down to leeward, by building her to lie lower in the water and replacing the high castle over the stem with a lower structure placed further aft on the upper deck. The *Bull* and the *Tiger* were rebuilt to this design, with their high sides cut down and with a low beakhead and cutwater forward of the reduced forecastle. At the same time the length-to-beam ratio was increased from 2½ to 1 to 3 to 1, the height of the aftercastle reduced to improve the overall balance, and the shape of the stern altered from round to square.

How much of the new design was due to Hawkins and how much to the Elizabethan shipwright Matthew Baker is uncertain. Baker's treatise on shipbuilding is in the Pepysian Library at Magdalene College, Cambridge, England, and it contains several design drawings for Elizabethan warships, all with the new low-charged profile proposed by Hawkins. It seems most probable that the two men worked hand-in-hand, Hawkins explaining his general ideas and leaving it to the experienced shipwright to draw the plans and decide the measurements.

The new design had its first test in battle in 1588 during the campaign known as the Spanish Armada. King Philip of Spain had embarked on his 'Enterprise of England,' sending a large fleet into the English Channel to defeat the English fleet and to transport to England a Spanish army from the Netherlands. The Spanish warships were mainly CARRACKS, the high-charged trading ships adapted for war by giving them a gun armament and embarking soldiers on board. The Spanish fleet also included galleys, unsuited for rough northern waters. Most of the carracks were significantly larger ships than the new English low-charged warships, but their general design was still that of the ill-fated *Jesus of Lubeck*, with towering fore- and aftercastles. In the running battles up the English Channel the low-charged ships of the new design proved themselves not only faster through the water but also much more weatherly, so that they could run in, fire their broadsides, and tack away to safety almost before the Spanish ships could reply. The defeat of the Spanish fleet, the largest

National navies began to grow in size and develop in power with the opening up of the known world at the end of the 15th century, around the time the big gun made its first appearance at sea. The Spanish voyages to America and the Portuguese voyages to India opened the eyes of the other European nations to these new El Dorados of east and west, and they knew that if they were to win a share of these new riches they would have to fight for them. That meant the growth of ships, navies, and trained seamen, and it also meant a new impetus towards the design of more efficient ships. Although warships had been steadily growing larger throughout the past century, far outstripping the merchant ship in size, there had been no radical alteration in design beyond the introduction of gunports; in all essentials the warship was still no more than a large version of the merchant ship. Both warship and merchantman had the low central waist with the high overhanging castles forward and aft; both had the deep, round-bellied beam, designed for cargo in the merchant ship and for guns in the warship; and both were inefficient sailers, because of the large area of windage which their towering castles presented. Even the four masts of the larger warships failed to overcome the dismal sailing qualities inherent in these high-charged ships.

Launch of the English fireships against King Philip of Spain's Armada, 1588.

fleet of sailing ships the world had yet seen, proved beyond all doubt the superiority of Hawkins' new design. For want of a better word, the new ships were given the generic name of GALLEON; only in England, the country of its birth, was the new design of ship called a queen's or king's ship. Introduced in England during the decade 1570-80, the galleon design was adopted by all other European maritime nations over the next 20 to 30 years.

The changes in warship design over the next few years were more in the rig than in the shape of the hull. As masts grew higher with the stepping of a topgallant mast above the topmast, the four masts of the Elizabethan galleon — fore, main, mizzen, and bonaventure mizzen — were reduced to three by dropping the bonaventure mizzen. They were square-rigged on the fore- and mainmasts, with topgallant sails set above the topsails, and lateen-rigged on the mizzen. In the mid-17th century the lateen sail on the mizzen, always a difficult sail to handle when tacking into the wind, was replaced by a spritsail, introduced by the Dutch. By the end of that century triangular sails (jibs) set on the foremast, fore-topmast, and fore-topgallant mast stays took the place of the two inefficient spritsails set above and below the bowsprit. With the later addition of triangular staysails between the masts, royals set above the topgallants, and the substitution of a gaffsail for the spritsail on the mizzen, the sailing warship had now attained the final development of rig which was to hold sway throughout the remaining years of the age of sail.

Apart from the growth in size, Hawkins' galleon remained largely the SHIP OF THE LINE design throughout the world until the close of the sailing warship era. As navies grew in size and ubiquity with the growth of world trade, the need for maritime protection, and the many and varied problems of empire, other designs of warships made their appearance — FRIGATES (which came next below the ships of the line), SLOOPS, gun-BRIGS, CUTTERS, BOMB VESSELS, and the like — each designed for a particular task in the general pattern of developing naval war. So far as the principal fighting ship, the ship of the line, was concerned, the growth in size reflected the introduction of additional gundecks. By the 18th century the largest ships (apart from one or two Spanish monsters which were built with four) had three gundecks and mounted around 100 guns. Tonnages grew from an average of under 1,000 at the end of the 16th century (the 24 principal queen's ships in the English fleet during the Armada campaign averaged 490 tons each, with the *Triumph* as the largest at 1,100 tons) to an average figure of about 3,000 in the mid-19th century for a first-rate ship of the line. Ships were rated by the number of guns they carried: from first-rates, which had over 90 guns, down to sixth-rates, which carried 18 guns or less. Fourth-rates (50-38 guns) were forerunners of later frigates, while the

Longitudinal section of a first-rate warship, c.1680, showing positions of cannon.

first three rates formed the line of battle. Like the slightly smaller second-rates, also three-deckers with about 90 guns, a few first-rate ships of the line served in major fleets as flagships: the VICTORY, Nelson's flagship, was a 100-gun first-rate with a tonnage measurement of 2,162. The towering height of three-deckers gave them a certain advantage in action but they were not as seaworthy as the two-decked third-rates, which made up the major part of the battle line. Third-rates could carry between 64 and 80 guns, although those with only 64 were hardly strong enough for the line of battle. Of the 60 ships of the line at the Battle of Trafalgar (1805), 38 were the popular 74-gun third-rates.

The wooden ship of the line was immensely strong and powerful for her day. Massive oak or elm timbers were clothed with oak side planking to an overall thickness of 18 to 20 in. (46-51 cm), virtually impenetrable to the solid iron shot fired from cannon. Ship-borne armament ranged from 42-pounder cannon (the weight of the shot fired) down to 9-pounder guns, and although the maximum range of any gun was about 2,000 yd. (1,830 m), the preferred range for battle was what was known as 'half pistol shot,' or about 100 yd. (90 m). Even at that range a 42-lb. solid shot would not penetrate the thick sides of a ship, though it could cause the wood to splinter and the splinters to fly, killing and wounding.

Naval Tactics of the 18th Century

Yet with all her strength, the wooden warship had two weak points. The lesser of them was at the bow: shots fired into the ship from over her beakhead had only the thin forecastle doors to stop them causing havoc along the length of the upper deck. But the major weakness was the stern, wide and square, with little but the glass of the sternwalk windows to stop a well-directed broadside penetrating to the gundecks and causing immense slaughter among the gun crews. As these weak points came to the attention of the more intelligent admirals, they brought about a revolution in the tactics of naval warfare.

To a large extent the mounting of the guns on board dictated the pattern of naval battle. Ranged along the gundecks, they fired through the gunports cut in the ship's sides. Very little lateral training movement was possible, both because of the wooden carriages on which guns were mounted and the limitations in size of the gunports themselves, and therefore they were able to fire in virtually one direction only, directly abeam. This naturally dictated the line-ahead formations for battle, for only when ranged in this formation against an enemy in similar single line could the ships hope to hit each other with their heavy guns.

This line-ahead formation, allied to the rigidity of naval signals to which most commanders of fleets felt themselves bound, led to the almost complete sterility of battle which characterized the first three-quarters of the 18th century. Fleets would meet in battle, range themselves in parallel lines, and pound away at each other, firing their shots at the strongest parts of their opponent. Very rarely was any wooden warship sunk by gunfire throughout these years; about the only hope of success was to revert to the tactics of earlier centuries by sailing alongside an enemy ship, holding her with grappling line, and capturing her by boarding. It was either that, or shooting away her masts with a lucky shot so that she became incapable of movement and an easy prey to well-directed broadsides aimed at her weakest parts until she surrendered.

Towards the end of the century, with the help of new signal books and methods of signaling by which a fleet commander could express a wide range of orders, and by a more intellectual approach to the theory of battle, methods of breaking this sterility were found. Admirals and captains were encouraged to use their initiative in battle without being called to account for ignoring the strict letter of the signal book, providing, of course, that they were successful. It was discovered at the Battle of the Saints in 1782 that an enemy's fleet could be demoralized and his line of battle thrown into confusion by sailing through the gaps between his ships (a tactic known as breaking the line), and the individual squadrons of a fleet, and even individual ships, were encouraged to do so whenever the opportunity offered. It was a maneuver that called for courage and endurance in its early stages, for during the end-on approach to the opposing line the ship was open to the broadside fire of enemy ships without being able to bring her own guns to bear. But as she passed between the stern of one ship and the bows of the next in line, she was presented with two targets, each in turn the weakest part of every ship, at which to fire her port and starboard broadsides at point-blank range with negligible opposition. With the enemy line of battle broken and its cohesion destroyed by this new tactic, the subsequent battle could develop into ship-to-ship encoun-

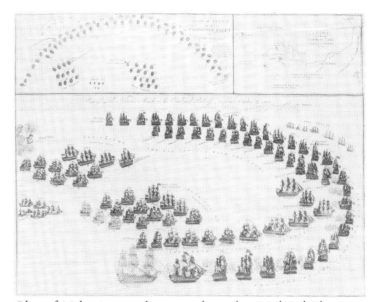

Plan of Nelson's two-column attack on the Combined Fleet at the Battle of Trafalgar (1805).

The Victory, *Nelson's famous flagship at Trafalgar.*

Victory *breaking through the enemy line.*

HMS Resolution, *a third-rate ship of the line, 1669.*

ters with much more chance of a decisive result. These were, in general, the preferred battle tactics of the Napoleonic and Revolutionary Wars of 1793-1815, the last great campaign in which sailing warships were engaged before a new breed of warship made her appearance.

The Marine Steam Engine

Right at the end of the 18th century marine steam engines were introduced. The first examples, in 1783 and 1786, were so inefficient that they can hardly be classed as effective propulsion units, but in March 1802 a small vessel with a 12-hp engine linked to a stern-mounted paddle wheel proved successful (see the chapter on *The History of Powered Ships*).

The first steam-driven armored warship was an American achievement — the DEMOLOGUS, built in 1813 by John FULTON. With a centerline paddle wheel she was 140 ft. (43 m) long. Her hull of 5 ft. (1.5 m) thick timber had external iron plating and her weapons were thirty 32-pounder guns. However, in its earliest development the marine steam engine was of little use to warships, except for auxiliary purposes to tow the sailing ships out of harbor when the wind was contrary, because the side paddle wheels, as yet the only method of converting steam-generated power to ship motion, were extremely vulnerable to gunfire. But with the introduction of the

screw propeller in 1836 by John ERICSSON and Pettit Smith, this disadvantage was removed and the steam-driven warship became a reality, posing many questions for the national authorities in charge of warship design and building. In 1843 the first propeller-driven warship, the 154-ton PRINCETON, was built in the United States just ahead of the British 888-ton sloop RATTLER. The British Admiralty was finally convinced of the screw propeller's merits by the celebrated tug-of-war between *Rattler* and the paddle-wheeler *Alecto* when the latter was towed at 2.5 knots stern first.

In many ways it was, for all the maritime nations, a painful transformation. It took some decades for the marine steam engine to develop from being merely a useful addition to the conventional sailing rig to the stage where its reliability and power enabled it to take over as the prime agent of warship propulsion. The introduction of the compound engine in the 1860s, and its development into the triple-expansion engine about 15 years later, coupled with new designs of boilers which increased the steam pressure from about the 25 lb./sq. in. (1.75 kg/cm^2) of the early days to 120 lb./sq. in. (8.4 kg/cm^2) in the 1870s, finally sealed the fate of the sailing warship. Although, in many instances, warships were still built with a full outfit of masts and sails, it was only as an insurance against engine breakdown and because of a reluctance on the part of many naval officers to break with tradition. After about 1850 none of the principal maritime nations of the world built a major warship without incorporating a steam engine, even though the ships they built still resembled the old vessels with their tall masts and yards and rows of guns mounted on the gundecks and fired through gunports cut in the ships' sides.

The Iron Warship

The next step forward in the development of the warship was the introduction of the iron hull. The first ship to demonstrate the possibility of using iron as a shipbuilding material was the AARON MANBY, which first went into service in 1820, but it was another 30 years before the experience of war and the development of a new type of naval gun persuaded the naval authorities that wood was no longer the best material for warships.

The introduction of the new Paixhans gun was a major factor. Explosive shells had been used for several years, but only for bombardment purposes, fired from mortars mounted in specially designed small ships and never used as a ship-to-ship weapon. The main battle weapon remained the cannon, firing a solid iron shot at point-blank range. In 1822, in a book called *Nouvelle Force Maritime et Artillerie*, a French artillery general, Henri-Joseph Paixhans, described a gun which he had designed, capable of firing a mortar bomb instead of a solid shot, and producing a flat trajectory instead of the normal parabolic arc of a bomb fired from a mortar. Such a trajectory had, of course, an important application in naval warfare. The gun was demonstrated in France in 1824 in a series of highly successful trials.

The Russians adopted the Paixhans gun for their navy and mounted it in their wooden-hulled ships. At the Battle of Sinope in the Black Sea in 1853, the Russian ships, armed with their new shells, set afire a fleet of Turkish ships which only had the normal naval gun firing solid shot, and burned them down to the waterline. This victory did not go unremarked by the other navies of the world, particularly in France, where the construction of a flotilla of floating batteries, wooden-hulled but protected by iron armor against the danger of fire from the new shell, was put in hand. During the Crimean War three of these armored floating batteries were used during the bombardment of Kinburn, anchoring within 1,000 yd. (910 m) of one of the Russian forts. They emerged after the bombardment undamaged, having fired their guns at the fort from a range at which any wooden warship would have been blown to bits.

There had been a number of experimental attempts with iron even before the Battle of Sinope and the Kinburn bombardment. In 1840 the British Admiralty built three small iron gunboats, each mounting two guns and fitted with paddle-wheel propulsion. A year or two later an iron frigate was built privately by John Laird at his Birkenhead shipyard and was offered to the British Admiralty. The Admiralty turned down the offer and the ship was sold instead to the Mexican navy. In 1846, again in Britain, three iron steam frigates were ordered, the BIRKENHEAD, *Magaera* and *Simoon*, but gunnery trials indicated that their iron would fracture when hit by solid shot, and the three ships were completed as troopships. Although it was by then apparent that an iron hull by itself was too vulnerable for warship use, the subsequent development of an additional iron armor cladding to absorb the explosion of a shell was not long in coming.

Small iron-hulled warships had also been built by the British East India Company to protect their Indian and Chinese trade monopolies. In 1839 the Company had commissioned John Laird to build iron-hulled ships of 600 tons, each armed with two 32-pounder pivot guns, a new form of mounting which, carried to its logical conclusion, was to have a profound effect on warship armament design in the future.

Nevertheless, in spite of these earlier experiments with iron as a warship building material, it still needed the Paixhans gun and the Kinburn bombardment finally to seal the fate of the wooden warship. Once again the Royal Navy was the first to react to these lessons, and in 1856 built the first iron-hulled armored warships: the floating batteries *Aetna, Erebus, Terror*, and *Thunderbolt*. They carried 16 muzzle-loading 68-pounder guns and their 200-hp

The British iron steam frigate Birkenhead, *1845.*

engines produced a speed of 5.5 knots, but the most significant feature of their design was the combination of armor with an iron hull.

These were, of course, even including the three 1,400-ton *Birkenhead*s, all small ships; they were perhaps no more than the first hesitant steps along the road of progress made by inherently conservative naval authorities. But it was appreciated that, with the use of iron as a new shipbuilding material, the limits on the size of ships which the use of wood had dictated were now being stretched to almost unbelievable dimensions. The maximum size of a wooden-hulled ship was something around 7,000 tons on a waterline length of about 340 ft. (100 m); the strength of oak could not by itself support anything larger. And even ships built up to this maximum size had proved to be unwieldy monsters, requiring immense crews to handle them and drawing so much water that they were useless for inshore work, such as the traditional naval strategy of close blockade of an enemy fleet. Moreover, they could barely support the immense masts and yards needed to drive them through the water. But there were no such limitations on the use of iron; its tensile strength in comparison with wood enabled designers to think in tens of thousands of tons where before they could only think in thousands. The stage was set for a great leap forward.

The French navy was the first to get started. Four 'IRONCLAD' frigates were ordered, three of them designed by Dupuy de Lôme, the great French naval architect, and the fourth by Audenet. Dupuy de Lôme's three, the GLOIRE, *Invincible*, and *Normandie* were wooden-hulled ships of 5,617 tons, the hulls plated with 4.5-in. (115-mm) iron to the level of the upper deck. Audenet's ship was the *Couronne* of 6,428 tons. She had an armored iron hull 4 in. (100 mm) thick, with a 4-in. (100-mm)

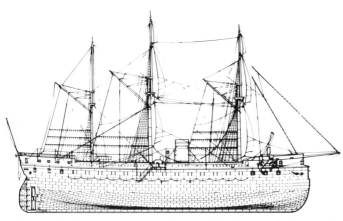

The ironclad Gloire (1859), designed by Dupuy de Lôme for the French navy.

teak backing, iron lattice work 1.33 in. (34 mm) thick, and a final internal teak skin of 11 in. (28 cm). This sandwich method of hull construction proved to be stronger and more resilient than that of Dupuy de Lôme's ships, which had a single internal skin of 26 in. (66 cm) of oak behind the outer iron plates. The first of the four to be launched was the *Gloire* in 1859, rigged initially as a BARKENTINE, remasted later with full square ship rig, and finally rerigged again as a BARK. She carried all her 36 guns on a single gundeck, a new design of breech-loading 66-pounders with rifled barrels which fired shells.

Britain went one better in the following year when the WARRIOR was launched. Her hull was of iron construction and her armor was of 4.5 in. (115 mm) iron with a teak backing 18 in. (46 cm) thick. It extended for 213 ft. (65 m), protecting the full length of the gundeck, and was

built to a height of 21 ft. (6.4 m) above the waterline and 6 ft. (1.8 m) below it. The two armor belts, one each side of the ship, were closed forward and aft with a 4.5-in. (115-mm) armored transverse bulkhead to form an armored citadel in which all her guns were mounted. She was armed with twenty-six 68-pounder muzzle-loaders and 14 breech-loaders, all firing shells. Her tonnage was 9,210, and although originally designated as an armored frigate, she was later reclassed as a third-class armored screw-battleship. The weakness of her design lay in her unarmored bow and stern, each projecting 85 ft. (26 m) beyond the armored citadel and consisting of the iron hull plating alone without any teak backing. Her engines gave her a speed of 15 knots, and in addition she carried a full sailing ship rig on three masts.

The *Warrior* is generally regarded as the world's first battleship in the modern sense of the term, though for the next 50 years all these new warships built on battleship lines were more generally known as IRONCLADS. These were years of experiment, development, and technological change in all branches of naval architecture and armament: from iron to steel, from shot to shell, from smooth bore to rifled bore, from muzzle-loading to breech-loading, from the fixed broadside gun mounting to the revolving turret, from reciprocating engine to turbine.

The Revolving Gun Turret

The 19th century was known as the century of the *Pax Britannica* because of Britain's overall naval supremacy at sea, and many of the major developments in the fields of shipbuilding and marine engineering came largely from Britain, with perhaps France leading the world in gun design. Another possible exception was the invention of the revolving gun turret which, perhaps more than any other innovation, was to revolutionize the practice and theory of naval war.

As has been seen, even in the new iron battleships of the 1860s and 1870s the mounting of guns had not progressed since the days of John Hawkins and Francis DRAKE. Although the guns themselves had been vastly improved, explosive shell replacing solid iron shot, and although the world's gunfounders had introduced the rifled gun barrel to prevent a shell tumbling over through the air after it was fired, the gun itself was still mounted either on a wooden carriage or on an iron slide and was still fired on the broadside through a square gunport cut in the ship's side. The carriage or slide was designed to allow the gun to be elevated or depressed through narrow limits, but there was still no way in which it could be trained laterally. The process of taking aim could only be effected by maneuvering the entire ship.

There was, as we have seen, one small answer to this problem in the pivot guns mounted in the East India Company's warships of 1839, but while this could be

The Warrior, *completed for the Royal Navy in 1860.*

done with small guns, it was impossible with the big ones used in the new iron battleships. These big guns weighed several tons, and the force of the recoil when they were fired would dismount them from their pivots. The answer to this problem was some method of making the gun mounting revolve, carrying the gun with it, so that the mounting could absorb the force of the recoil.

It is impossible to say which of two, or perhaps even three, men first devised the solution. The two most important names are Cowper Coles, a captain in the British navy, and John Ericsson, a Swedish engineer who had emigrated to the United States and become an American citizen in 1848. The other name associated with this development is that of Prince Albert, the consort of Queen Victoria, who is thought to have worked out the mechanical details and given them to Coles.

Coles' invention stemmed from an armed raft which he designed and constructed for coastal bombardment in the Sea of Azov during the Crimean War. The raft was 45 ft. (13.7 m) long and 15 ft. (4.6 m) wide, and it floated on 29 casks held together in a framework of spars. He called her the *Lady Nancy* and on the centerline he mounted a long 32-pounder gun. As the raft drew only 20 in. (50 cm) of water, she could be towed close inshore where her gun could do the maximum damage. At the bombardment of Taganrog, she fired her gun into the dockyard with great accuracy. Coles then designed a larger raft 150 ft. (46 m) long, armored, fitted with an engine and propeller, and mounting a 68-pounder gun on the centerline. The gun crew was protected with a fixed hemispherical shield of iron, with gunports pointing ahead and on either beam. The British Admiralty, to whom he offered the design, expressed no interest in the invention and the raft was never built. But the important innovation was the mounting of guns on the centerline instead of along each side, which was still standard practice in all warships. In 1859 Coles filed his first patent for a revolving turret.

A design which he submitted to the British Admiralty in the same year for a 9,200-ton 'cupola' ship was also ignored. 'Cupola' was Coles' description of what we now call a 'turret,' and his was based on the hemispherical armored shield which he had designed for his large raft, although now not fixed but made to revolve with the gun inside it. His design allowed for ten cupolas, or turrets, each of them mounting two of the largest naval guns. Eight of the turrets were to be placed on the ship's centerline, the remaining two on either side of a low forecastle, sited to provide axial fire covering an arc from dead ahead to the ship's quarter.

Although this particular 9,200-ton ship was never built, Coles' design for centerline guns mounted in a turret was accepted by the British Admiralty for a coast defense ship, *Prince Albert*, which was laid down in 1862. Her armament was four 9-in. guns, each in its own turret which

was trained to the desired bearing for firing by means of a rack and pinion gear operated on the main deck by men with handspikes. It was, of course, a crude method of operation, initially taking a crew of 18 men the best part of a minute to achieve one full revolution of the turret, but with the technological skill available in mid-19th century a mechanical means of training the turret was quickly found. Another drawback of this design was that none of the 18 men concerned, whether inside or outside the turret, could see or hear the ship's gunnery control officer and had no way of knowing where their target was. In many ways this was typical of the period; technological advance in engineering was always considered more important per se than its practical application.

While in Britain Cowper Coles was engaged in his revolving turret designs, John Ericsson was designing and building a small warship in the Brooklyn Navy Yard in the United States. Named MONITOR, she was designed for shallow-water operations against Confederate ships during the Civil War in America. She was a small iron vessel with no more than a few inches of seaboard, and her armament was two 11-in. Dahlgren guns in a revolving central turret protected with 9-in. (230-mm) armor. She was laid down in October 1861 and was completed the following February. Within a month of completion she was put into service. Her gun duel with the Confederate ship *Virginia* (ex-MERRIMACK) at Hampton Roads on March 9, 1862, is part of naval history, the world's first engagement between two armored ships. After six hours of firing at each other without inflicting any worthwhile damage, the two ships withdrew, never to meet again. The *Virginia* was scuttled when the Confederates were forced to abandon Norfolk, Virginia, and the *Monitor* foundered in a gale because her lack of freeboard made her unstable in anything beyond a flat calm.

The importance of the revolving gun turret in naval warfare can hardly be exaggerated. It arrived at almost the same moment as the final development of the rifled gun, which not only considerably increased the range at which

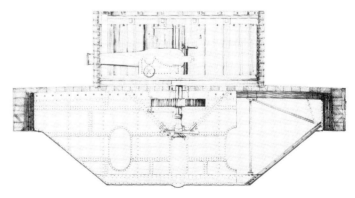

Transverse section of the ironclad Monitor, *built by the American John Ericsson in 1862.*

Floating batteries and mortar boats in action during the American Civil War in 1862.

the Austrian flagship *Erzherzog Ferdinand Maximilian* rammed and sank the Italian flagship *Re d'Italia*. That the *Re d'Italia* was lying dead in the water with a damaged rudder at the time and unable to get out of the way, and that in the many other attempts by Austrian ships to ram their Italian enemies all of them missed their target, was conveniently ignored by enthusiasts for the new weapon. Similar experiences in the American Civil War, where in the action at Mobile Bay ramming tactics had been singularly unsuccessful, were also ignored, even though the only damage caused by ramming in that action was a smashed-up bow in one of the would-be rammers.

Belief in the ram remained as a cardinal factor in naval tactical thought throughout the remainder of the 19th century. Every peacetime collision between warships during naval maneuvers (and there were several of them), in which one of the ships concerned sank, was hailed as a vindication of the ram. Belief in its all-conquering power reached its peak after the *Camperdown* accidentally rammed and sank the *Victoria* in 1893, during exercises in the Mediterranean. Both were comparatively modern British battleships, one flying the flag of the Commander in Chief of the Mediterranean Fleet and the other that of his second in command, and there was a heavy loss of life, including that of the Commander in Chief himself, when the *Victoria* went down. The majority opinion, expressed in the words of Lord Charles Beresford, an up-and-coming naval officer, was: 'In my opinion the ram is the most fatal weapon in naval warfare, more fatal even than the torpedo,' and his belief was closely echoed in other navies. And as the result, the major warships throughout the world were built with rams incorporated into their bows, both reducing their speed and making them singularly difficult to steer. This feature of warship design and construction continued until at last sanity prevailed at the beginning of the 20th century, when it was recognized that speed and maneuverability would enable any ship to avoid another intent on ramming, and that the range and power of the modern naval gun would blow would-be rammers out of the water long before they could come close enough to deal a lethal blow.

The Late 19th Century: a Period of Growth

The first fifty years of the ironclad warship era was in all countries largely a period of experiment, with continual changes in the design of armored hulls to accommodate the growth and development both of the marine engine and the naval gun and, in the end, the final elimination of masts and sails. Inevitably, warships had to be built larger to accommodate the more powerful engines and the banks of boilers needed to feed them with steam, and at the same time the armor they carried had to be applied more thickly to provide adequate protection from the shells fired by the bigger naval guns. This became something of a race be-

naval battles could be fought, but provided the shell fired from it with a predictable path, both to increase accuracy and ease of control. There were, however, few naval officers in any navy ready for such an advance or indeed capable of taking any advantage of it. They were still too close to the era of sail and smooth-bore, muzzle-loading guns to appreciate the potential of this immensely powerful new weapon which technical development had placed in their hands; it is hardly surprising that their ideas of sea warfare took some odd turns. Admiral Sir Charles Napier, who commanded the first British all-steam-driven fleet which was sent into the Baltic Sea during the Crimean War, had so little conception of how to use the new mobility which enabled him to maneuver ships irrespective of the wind direction, that his sole tactical idea for battle was to use steam power to drive his ships alongside those of the Russians for the crews to fight it out with cutlasses in true Nelsonian tradition. Admirals of other navies were equally unable to recognize the potentialities now offered by increased mobility and gun range.

The Iron Ram

One of the oddest of the new ideas engendered by the combination of the steam engine and the iron ship, and current at this time in naval tactical thought in all the maritime nations, was the use of the ram as a new and powerful naval weapon, a reversion to the days of galley warfare in the Mediterranean. Unlike wood, iron could be bent into any desired shape below the waterline; moreover, the steam engine produced the desired speed, formerly achieved by slave labor on the oars, to deliver the blow with sufficient force to make a hole in the side of an enemy ship. This new weapon was given a spurious certificate of excellence at the Battle of Lissa, fought in 1866 between the ironclad fleets of Austria and Italy, in which

tween guns and armor, each new battleship built being given a bigger gun and thicker armor than her predecessors. The largest naval guns produced during the closing years of the 19th century were the Italian 18.1-in. gun and the British 16.25-in. gun, and iron armor up to 24 in. (61 cm) thick was being used as protection. Shortly before the close of the century steel had been produced to take the place of iron, and methods of case-hardening it were invented, so that the original 24 in. (61 cm) of iron armor could be replaced with 12 in. (30 cm) of toughened steel to provide an equal degree of protection. During these years, the size of armored ships in all navies increased from the 9,210 tons of the *Warrior* of 1860 to an average of around 16,000 tons for the battleships being built at the end of the century.

Methods of construction, too, were changing. In 1876 the French completed the battleship *Rédoutable*, taking several steps ahead in this one design. Not only was she built with steel frames and steel armor, but the first moves towards controlling damage in battle were incorporated in her design. She was built with a double bottom and her internal hull space was divided into compartments designed to limit the amount of flooding in the event of being holed in battle.

Theories of naval warfare had also changed by the end of the 19th century. The gun duel between ships, in spite of current theories about the value of ramming, was still the prime weapon of naval battle as it had been since the days of sailing warships, but the range at which the duel was fought was increasing from the 'half pistol shot' of sailing ship days to around 6,000 yd. (5500 m) by 1900. Most navies carried out firing practices at about that range; some, notably the French and Italians, at ranges half as great again. But more efficient guns, and particularly the development of new and more efficient propellents in place of the traditional gunpowder, were already heralding battle ranges greatly in excess of that.

Tactical theory was changing too, to take account of the new weapons of naval warfare which were making their appearance as the 19th century drew to its close. Explosive mines had been used defensively by the Russians during the Crimean War, and the locomotive torpedo had been developed from its crude beginnings in 1865 into a weapon of account. By 1877, armed with a powerful explosive charge in its head, it was capable of a range of 1,000 yd. (900 m) at a speed of 7 knots. By the end of the century its explosive charge, its range, and its speed had been more than trebled and it had become a formidable weapon at sea. This, too, added to the complexities of naval warfare, for its use involved not only the design and building of special vessels to launch the new weapon but also the development of special craft to prevent these torpedo carriers from reaching a position where they could launch their torpedoes. Eventually, in 1893, these two special types were combined into a single vessel which not only fired the torpedoes at an enemy but also carried a gun armament powerful enough to drive off the similar ships of an enemy. They were known as torpedo-boat destroyers, and eventually DESTROYERS for short.

Yet another type of warship, the submarine, was added to navies at the start of the 20th century. The story of its long years of development is told in the preceding chapter on *The History of Powered Ships*, but by 1900 it not only had as its weapon the locomotive torpedo, but also, through the invention of the internal combustion engine, a combined means both of surface propulsion and recharging its electric batteries for submerged propulsion. In their early days submarines were not regarded in many of the world's navies as an offensive threat against the main battleship fleet but rather as a defensive weapon against an enemy who might approach too close to the homeland on bombardment or close-blockade operations, but their many successes in fleet exercises, and particularly their use in operations during the Russo-Japanese War of 1904-05, made it clear that their offensive capabilities could not be ignored.

By 1900 the world's principal navies were those of Russia, Italy, France, Britain, and the United States, with those of Japan and Germany increasing in importance. Basically, they all conformed approximately to the same pattern, with their main strength concentrated in the battleship fleet of heavily armed and armored ships approaching 20,000 tons each, of cruisers varying from about 12,000 tons in the armored variety to about 3,000 tons in the case of unarmored ships, and destroyers of around 700 to 800 tons. Submarines were, in general, not counted as a part of the fleet since they operated alone and not in company with other ships. Coal-burning boilers feeding triple-expansion steam engines gave their battleships a maximum speed of from 18 to 20 knots; they were armored along the sides over the vital machinery and armament areas with about 12 in. (305 mm) of case-hardened steel; and they carried a mixed battery of guns of which the largest was usually 12 in. The heaviest guns were mounted in power-operated revolving turrets, smaller guns were hand-operated, sometimes behind casemates, sometimes in the open. The heavier guns (12-in., 10-in., 8-in.) had maximum ranges of from 8,000 to 12,000 yd (7,300-11,000 m) and were normally used at a range of 10,000 yd (9,150 m). There was not a great deal to choose between the fighting qualities of the ships of any of the navies and, in theory, supremacy at sea was claimed by the navy which had the greatest number of ships and the shipbuilding capacity to keep ahead of all competitors. Theory could, however, be upset by the quality of the men who managed the ships and the skill of their commanders, and in this respect a smaller navy was not necessarily outclassed in battle by a larger one.

Coming of the Dreadnought

This balance of approximate national naval equality was upset in 1906 by Britain. Battleship design had reached something of a deadlock, with the mixed battery of guns of different sizes mounted in the best positions for producing the maximum density of fire on all bearings. A major drawback of carrying a mixed battery was that different sizes of shell needed to be taken on board, all requiring different magazines and different methods of handling to get them to the guns. A second difficulty was in differentiating between the different gun sizes in the fall of shot when correcting for range and deflection. A design was produced in Britain for a battleship to be armed with big guns all of the same caliber, not only to ease the problems of different shell sizes and handling methods but also to produce a greater weight of broadside fire at the maximum range. To add to the impact which her appearance would create among the world's other navies, she was to be fitted with new turbine engines in place of reciprocating engines. This would give her a speed in excess of any other battleship yet built. The ship was built in considerable secrecy and at record speed. She was launched only four months after she was laid down and completed eight months later, and was named DREADNOUGHT. She was armed with ten 12-in. guns in five turrets, 27 small 12-pounder guns as an antitorpedo boat armament, and her displacement was 17,900 tons. Her turbine engines gave her a speed of 21 knots, three knots faster than her immediate predecessors. This margin of speed, it was held, would enable her to overtake any enemy battleship and bring her within range of her massive main armament. Her sudden appearance on the naval capital ship scene made every other existing battleship in the world obsolete.

By 1906, the year of the *Dreadnought*, there were preliminary rumbles of war throughout Europe, fed by massive warship building programs among the nations concerned, and there began a growing concentration on preparedness for battle by means of extensive naval maneuvers and gunnery practices. The principle of the 'all-big-gun' battleship, exemplified in the *Dreadnought* herself, led to similar designs for all other navies, resulting in a new breed of battleship to which the generic name of *Dreadnought* was given. With the increase over the next six years in big gun size from 12 in. to 15 in., in battle ranges from 6,000 yd. (5,500 m) to 20,000 yd. (18,300 m), in displacement from 18,000 tons to over 27,000 tons, and in speed from 21 knots to 24 knots, the generic battleship name was altered from *Dreadnought* to *Superdreadnought*. It was this new type of battleship that fought the main fleet actions of the coming war.

The new ships, the new weapons, and the likely ranges at which future gun battles at sea would be fought, made necessary new theories of sea warfare. There was not a great deal of modern experience on which to build up new ideas of national naval strategy or of new naval tactics to match the ships and weapons which technology had now placed in the hands of sailors. The Sino-Japanese War of 1894-95 and the Russo-Japanese War of 1904-05 had both included battles between fleets of armored ships. In the first of them about the only lesson to be learned was that an efficient, well-led fleet held an advantage over an inefficient, poorly led fleet, even if the latter had the larger ships — a lesson which most navies had already recognized in any case. An equally obvious conclusion was that a reasonable margin of speed provided tactical flexibility, and that offensive tactics gave a better chance of victory than defensive tactics. Foreign naval observers of the conflict searched in vain for some more definite clues to the future conduct of naval warfare. In the second conflict the Battle of Port Arthur indicated the range of future battle. The Russian battleships opened fire at 20,000 yd. (18,300 m) and their first shells landed 200 yd. (180 m) beyond the Japanese ships; the Japanese flagship was hit by a 12-in. shell at a range of 14,000 yd. (12,800 m). In the Battle of Tsushima the Japanese victory was gained partly by the use of superior speed but mainly by the accuracy of their big guns. Both fleets were of pre-*Dreadnought* design with mixed batteries of 12-in., 8-in., and 6-in. guns and, in the words of an eye-witness, 'for all the respect they instill, 8-in. or 6-in. guns might just as well be pea-shooters.' This was a vindication of the theory of the all-big-gun capital ship, but in fact it came too late, for the design of the new *Dreadnought* had already been settled before the battle was fought and in no way reflected the Tsushima experience.

World War I

Europe went to war in 1914 with no very clear ideas on either side of how to use the formidable ships at their disposal. There was an understandable desire on the side of the nation with the greater fleet to search for the big battle at sea, and an equally understandable desire on the opposite side to avoid it. But on the occasion of the one and only big battle of the war, the Battle of Jutland, the overriding tactic by both sides was to avoid loss of the expensive ships in which the nations had invested so heavily, and during the battle all the admirals concerned turned their battle fleets or squadrons away from the battle line when they were seriously threatened.

Another painful lesson of the war was that the big armored cruiser, which had been further developed into the battle cruiser only a very few years before the outbreak of the war, was already an anachronism. In spite of a speed of up to 29 knots, achieved mainly by reducing the thickness and thus the weight of the protective armor, the battle cruiser could not take the force of a battleship's salvoes of heavy guns.

The Japanese battle cruiser Kongo, *completed in 1913.*

Yet another lesson which had become apparent by the end of the war was that the big naval gun was no longer the dominant weapon at sea. For centuries the gun had commanded the seas, whether in the form of cannon in the sailing warships or the long-range breech-loading 15-in. guns of the newest battleships, but World War I demonstrated that the torpedo and the mine were now supreme in naval warfare, even dictating the movement of fleets in a pitched gun battle. The torpedo had by 1914 been developed into a tremendously powerful weapon, carrying a 500-lb. charge of high explosive at a speed of 44 knots for 4,000 yd. (3,660 m) or at a speed of 28 knots for 10,000 yd. (9,140 m). A small internal gyroscope held it rigidly to its firing course so that it should not wander from its target. For a generation of naval officers brought up in the belief that gunnery was the supreme arbiter at sea, this lesson was too painful to be immediately absorbed.

There were other wartime experiences which were to have a profound effect on the design and development of new types of warship. An overriding and unexpected feature of the war had been the emergence of the submarine as a strategic weapon of supreme importance, leading not only to new and better designs of submarine but also to a new generation of warships designed both to hunt and

destroy submarines and to protect fleets and merchant ships from underwater attack. These new ships went under the generic title of escort vessels, modeled to some extent on the DESTROYER but without the destroyer's speed or armament of guns and torpedoes. Instead they carried depth charges which could be controlled by a hydrostatic valve to explode at the depth at which it was thought that the submarine would be. They were also equipped, after the war, with a supersonic underwater search beam which reflected an echo back to the escort vessel from the hull of a submerged submarine, to give the

British battle cruiser Inflexible, *which was lost at the Battle of Jutland in 1916.*

125

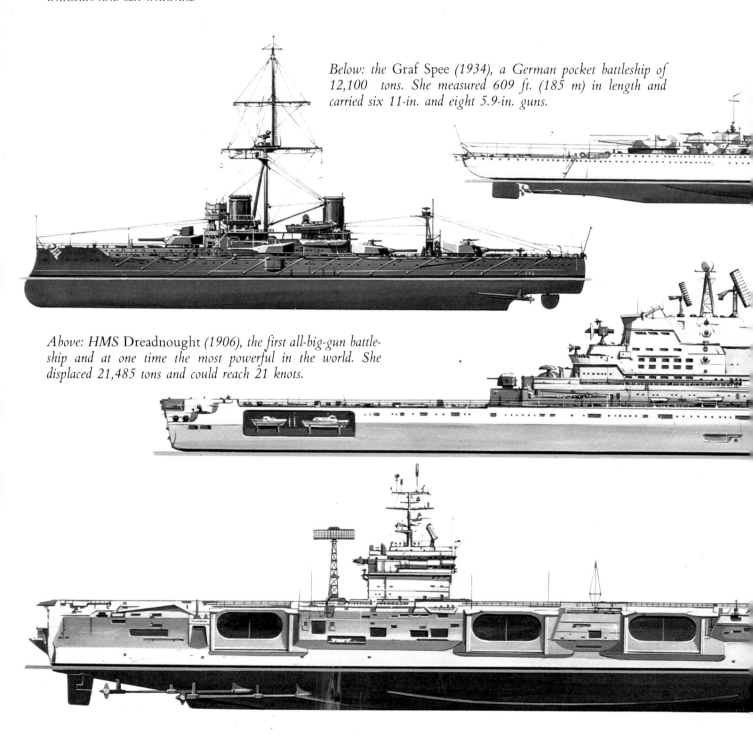

Below: the Graf Spee *(1934), a German pocket battleship of 12,100 tons. She measured 609 ft. (185 m) in length and carried six 11-in. and eight 5.9-in. guns.*

Above: HMS Dreadnought *(1906), the first all-big-gun battleship and at one time the most powerful in the world. She displaced 21,485 tons and could reach 21 knots.*

vessel the bearing along which to attack. These escort vessels were later developed in World War II into FRIGATES, CORVETTES, and SLOOPS which, together with aircraft, were to become the main weapons of antisubmarine warfare.

Another of the war's new weapons to have a profound influence on the development of the warship was the aeroplane. It had made its first impact on naval thought in 1911, when it had been successfully launched from platforms temporarily erected over the bows of warships, and in these early experiments it had been envisaged only as a means of distant reconnaisance rather than as a weapon in

its own right. In 1915, operating from merchant ships converted into temporary seaplane carriers, the first attack was made on a ship by a torpedo released from the air. Aircraft already had bombs for use as land weapons — bomb sights were still too inaccurate for a bomb aimer to hit a moving target like a ship — but with the torpedo they now had a maritime weapon as well. In the first year of World War I naval aircraft were all seaplanes, lifted into and out of the sea for take-off and recovery after landing, but before the end of the war aircraft had taken off and landed on a specially constructed flying deck, indicating the new type of naval ship about to be born.

Below: the Kiev *(1972), first of a class of Soviet antisubmarine cruisers. She measures 898 ft. (274 m) in length, 135 ft. (41.2 m) in the beam, and is of 38,000 tons. Her flight deck measures 620 ft. by 68 ft. (189 x 20.7 m). Her armament includes surface-to-surface missiles.*

Below: the USS Nimitz *(1972), the largest warship ever built. This nuclear-powered aircraft carrier has a displacement tonnage of 81,600 tons, measures 1,092 ft. by 134 ft. (332 × 40.8 m), and her flight deck is 252 ft. (76.8 m) wide. She carries 90 aircraft.*

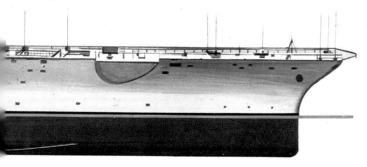

The Birth of the Aircraft Carrier

The first AIRCRAFT CARRIERS, as opposed to seaplane carriers, were conversions of existing warship hulls, mainly types which World War I had proved to have no place in a modern fleet. Being hybrids they were not particularly successful, generally being able to carry fewer aircraft than their hull size promised. But within three or four years true aircraft carriers were built, specially designed from the keel up with a full-length flying deck uncluttered by funnels and bridge, which were built out on the side to provide an unrestricted runway from stern to bow. In the United States they were colloquially known as 'flat-tops.'

They were, like all warships, virtually self-supporting, with below-deck hangars for stowage of their aircraft, workshops for their maintenance, bomb and torpedo stores, and special tanks for aviation fuel. They were armed, apart from their aircraft, with batteries of anti-aircraft guns, since it was believed that they would be prime targets for air attack during the war. Their complement of aircraft included fighters for fleet air cover in addition to bombers and torpedo-bombers. They were large ships, averaging around 25,000 tons at the beginning of World War II, although the United States and Japan had built them larger, the former with the 33,000-ton *Saratoga* and *Lexington* and the latter with the 36,000-ton *Akagi* and the 38,000-ton *Kaga*. A 25,000-ton aircraft carrier had, in Britain, a complement of about 65 aircraft, in Japan about 84, and in the United States about 100. The discrepancies in numbers reflected in part the British use of 3-in. (76-mm) armor for the carrier's flight deck and for the sides and ends of the aircraft hangars (those of other navies were generally unarmored), and, on the American side, a better technique in handling aircraft which enabled a proportion of their normal complement of aircraft to be stowed on deck whenever the hangars were full.

World War II

When warship building was resumed shortly before the outbreak of World War II after years of disarmament and standstill, the world's navies concentrated on battleships and aircraft carriers, with one eye on the past, as it were, and the other on the future. The decision to build new battleships, after the experiences of World War I, was curious, partly a sort of restatement of faith in the big gun as the dominant weapon in spite of all past evidence, and partly an attitude of 'if *they* are building battleships, *we* must build them too.' And they were built increasingly large. The first navy to set the pace was Italy when she laid down three 41,000-ton battleships, the *Vittorio Veneto* class, armed with nine 15-in. and twelve 6-in. guns, and capable of 30 knots. Britain and the United States, in an attempt to reinstate the limiting battleship

HMS Argus, *an early aircraft carrier of 1918.*

The pocket battleship Deutschland, *laid down in 1929.*

tonnage agreed in the Washington Treaty but generally ignored by Italy and Japan, built the *King George V* class (38,000 tons, ten 14-in. and sixteen 5.25-in. guns, 27 knots) and the *South Dakota* class (37,000 tons, nine 16-in. guns and twenty 5-in. guns, 28 knots) respectively. France, in reply to the Italian *Vittorio Veneto*, laid down the *Richelieu* (39,000 tons) and *Jean Bart* (43,000 tons), each armed with eight 15-in. and nine 6-in. guns and with a speed of 30 knots. Germany built the BISMARCK and *Tirpitz*, both 42,000 tons with eight 15-in. and twelve 5.9-in. guns, capable of 29 knots. Meanwhile, Japan was constructing two monster ships, the YAMATO and MUSASHI, both 65,000 tons, with nine 18.1-in. and twelve 6.1-in. guns, and a speed of 27 knots. The United States and Britain, finding themselves outbuilt in size by the other navies, replied to the general trend towards increased tonnage and armament with, in the United States, the *Iowa* class (46,000 tons, nine 16-in. and twenty 5-in. guns, 33 knots) and in Britain with the *Lion* class, which was in fact never built but was designed with a tonnage of 40,000, armed with nine 16-in. and sixteen 5.25-in. guns, and with a speed of 30 knots.

War experience in 1939-45 to some extent bore out the lesson of World War I, that the battleship was no longer the ultimate weapon at sea. Of the total 32 battleships lost during the war, only four were sunk by the gunfire of other battleships alone, and one of these was at anchor in harbor at the time of her loss. In two other cases battleships were present in conjunction with cruisers, destroyers, and aircraft. The others were sunk by submarine (three), aircraft (ten), or by scuttling themselves, usually after being mined or bombed by aircraft. Once again the dominant weapon of the war was the torpedo, whether launched by submarine, surface ship, or aircraft, with the aircraft bomb, in combination with the dive bomber, proving itself a new and potent weapon against ships. Early war experience in 1939 and 1940 indicated that the

age-old theories of the conduct of war at sea were changing fast. It showed that the surface warship was vulnerable to attack from the air, and that no surface fleet could operate at sea except under friendly air cover from fighter aircraft. The devastation that could be caused by seaborne aircraft was proved only too convincingly by the Japanese at Pearl Harbor on December 7th, 1941. This new fact of naval warfare enhanced the role of the aircraft carrier, both in attack on an enemy and in defense against his aircraft. As events developed, the carrier's role became even more decisive as the war progressed, whether in direct battle between fleets, as happened so frequently in the Pacific, or in crippling warships for subsequent destruction by surface forces, a feature of the Atlantic and Mediterranean fighting. In the Pacific campaign it was rare for the surface fleets of the United States and Japan to come within gun range of each other (the Battle of Leyte Gulf was one occasion when they did); it was more usual for the main fleet actions to be fought at a range of 100 to 200 miles (160-320 km), with carrier-borne aircraft launching the attacks with bombs and torpedoes and with carrier-borne fighters, in combination with ship-mounted anti-aircraft gunfire, providing a defense.

The submarine, in large measure, repeated the World War I experience, though by the end of World War II there were strong indications that its defensive role was beginning to outweigh its offensive one. The development of more sophisticated antisubmarine weapons and the introduction of new techniques of detection, particularly of sonar, radar, and high-frequency direction finding, made their destruction by surface-escort vessel easier, and similar facilities accompanied by specially designed depth charges mounted in aircraft increased the toll. New developments to enable submarines to use their surface engines when submerged and thus increase their underwater speed might have redressed the balance, but this advance arrived too late in the war to have any significant effect.

Another new feature of naval warfare was the use of assault landings on an enemy-held coast. They had of course been a feature of many past wars, using the boats normally carried on board a warship to land the soldiers, but in World War II, against a much more sophisticated and accurate defense, assault landings required specially designed craft to carry the assault force through the shallow coastal waters and land them and their weapons dryshod on the beach. The craft specially designed to perform this task had been pioneered by Japan between the two world wars for their operations against China, and it was this initial Japanese design, enlarged and refined by Britain and the United States during the war, that made possible the many large assault landings in Europe and in the Pacific which played so large a part in the ultimate victory.

The mine, too, was becoming a more important weapon, both in offense and defense. The moored impact mine, was reasonably easy to remove with a sweep, towed by minesweepers, which cut their mooring wires and released them to the surface where they could readily be destroyed. But a new generation of influence mines proved more difficult to handle. Magnetic mines, exploded by the residual magnetism in a ship when she passed over them, had been used by the British navy in World War I, but the fact appears to have largely been forgotten by the time of the outbreak of World War II 20 years later. After many initial losses an adequate countermeasure to the magnetic mine was developed by the degaussing of ships to remove their residual magnetism. Other types of influence mines, acoustic mines (exploded by the noise of a ship's propellers as she passed overhead), pressure mines (exploded by the difference in water pressure caused by the movement of a ship), and combinations of the two, were more difficult to counter, and some of the problems they raised were still unsolved when the war came to an end.

A major lesson of sea operations in World War II was the need to maintain fleets at sea for long periods without returning to base for replenishment and/or repair. This was particularly necessary in the Pacific where the immense distances from bases to the battle areas required fleets able to remain operational at sea for weeks at a time instead of the more usual periods of a few days. Even in the Atlantic, where the distances are not nearly so great, it was usually necessary to attach an oil tanker to the transatlantic convoys for the escorts to refuel at sea. On one important occasion a shortage of fuel in British warships, after prolonged steaming during the operations which ended with the sinking of the German battleship *Bismarck* in 1941, caused many anxieties as to whether the enemy could be brought to action before the British ships needed to return to their bases to refuel.

The answer to this particular problem pioneered by the U.S. Navy, was known during the war as the Fleet Train; today it is known as Afloat Support. During the war the Fleet Train was, in numbers of ships engaged, not far short in size of the fleet it was to support, remaining outside the battle area but within comfortable range of the fighting ships. It comprised oilers for refueling the warships at sea, store and replenishment ships to carry supplies of all forms of food, equipment, and ammunition needed to keep the warships in full fighting trim with contented crews throughout the longest operations. Today, with the benefit of 30 years of technological advance, such overall maintenance and replenishment can be provided with fewer ships, but the principle still remains and is still essential in modern naval warfare.

Modern Naval Warfare

At the end of World War II it was possible for the world's navies to take stock of its events, to analyze them in relation to the emerging patterns of modern warfare at

American battleships entering Lingayen Gulf in the Philippines for a bombardment attack, October 1944.

sea, and to plan the new warship designs which this evaluation demanded. Beyond the completion of battleships actually laid down in wartime and too advanced in construction to be scrapped on the stocks, no navy was prepared to design and construct new ones. The wartime lesson was, this time, too evident to be ignored. New designs of aircraft carriers, larger and more efficient than the wartime models, were built, for there was no denying their immense contribution to modern naval warfare. New submarine designs, incorporating the means of using surface engine propulsion when dived, were also added to the world's fleets, and the new antisubmarine vessels built carried the means of location and destruction evolved during the war and further developed after it. Only in landing craft for amphibious operations was something of a halt in development called, for during the closing days of the war a new weapon had made its appearance in the shape of the atomic bomb which, because of its immense destructive power, effectively ruled out any future assault landings on the scale of the major operations of World War II.

It was natural that, following the experience of World War II, the world's navies should adopt the aircraft carrier as the most important type of warship in a modern fleet. The aircraft had dominated naval tactics during that war, and in its postwar development, particularly with the introduction of the jet engine and vastly sophisticated electronic aids in new forms of detection and weapon guidance, it was to become an even more powerful influence in naval operations. The new carriers were designed to accommodate and service these new aircraft,

Aircraft carriers HMS Ark Royal *and USS* Forrestal.

The 3,500-ton Sheffield-class destroyer, HMS Birmingham.

themselves becoming the agents of a tremendous strike power.

But perhaps even more decisive in postwar naval terms than the new aircraft and their strike capabilities has been the development of nuclear power for ship propulsion and the shipborne missile. Nuclear power for propulsion owes its naval birth to Admiral RICKOVER of the U.S. Navy, and the signal 'underway on nuclear power,' sent by the American submarine NAUTILUS on January 17, 1955, heralded the start of a new age of naval experience and, indeed, naval problems. Although the building and upkeep of nuclear power plants is an extremely expensive operation, the fact that four modern navies, those of the United States, Britain, France, and the Soviet Union, have taken this step means that all major naval forces must also be considering their counter to this threat. Modern nuclear cores allow a range of action limited only by the resilience of ships' companies and the capacities of the stores and weapon magazines on board.

Nuclear propulsion has given the navies their first true submarine. The conventional submarines which operated during the two world wars of this century depended on periodic visits to the surface to recharge their batteries for further underwater navigation, and a submarine on the surface is at her most vulnerable to attack. With nuclear propulsion she no longer needs to surface and can remain submerged for the entire period she is at sea. Underwater speed, too, has been vastly increased by nuclear propulsion, with the Soviet *Alfa*-class submarines already capable of 40 knots. The American *Ohio*-class submarines can launch the latest Trident ballistic missiles to a range of over 4,000 nautical miles (7,400 km). Submarines can also fire shorter-range weapons against ship and land targets.

Surface ships fitted with nuclear propulsion can maintain high speeds indefinitely, limited only by the state of the sea. The American nuclear-propelled carriers of the *Nimitz* class, each carrying over 100 aircraft, many of them supersonic and missile-armed, probably represent today the ultimate in this type of development. But the pace of technical development does not slacken. A new type of ship has been built by the Soviet navy, a 30,000-ton nuclear-propelled battle cruiser carrying mis-

Guided-missile destroyers HMS Bristol *and HMS* Fife, *July 1973.*

siles, guns, and about six aircraft, possibly designed to escort a nuclear-propelled aircraft carrier.

Yet the smaller navies of the world, those which cannot face the economic pressures of nuclear propulsion, have also advanced with the times. An example of their new powers came on October 21, 1967, when a missile fired by an Egyptian ship sank an Israeli destroyer — the two ships not even being within sight of each other. Modern guided missiles, with ranges of from 500 to 700 nautical miles (930-1,300 km) and equipped with radar, infrared, and other forms of terminal guidance, have transformed all aspects of naval warfare. With such weapons, even the small, conventionally-powered ship has few limits to her powers of destruction.

The coming year may well see such conventional forms of ship propulsion as steam turbines, gas turbines, and diesel engines replaced by other machines that do not rely on fossil fuels — for example, fuel cells and hydrogen engines. But there can be little doubt, even with such advances, that nuclear power at sea will survive. Missiles there certainly will be. New possibilities of long-range bombardment have been created by submarine-launched intercontinental ballistic missiles such as Polaris, Poseidon, and now Trident. Each Trident missile carries eight separately targetable nuclear warheads with a range of from 4,000 to 6,000 nautical miles (7,400-1,100 km) — double the range of Polaris. For use against other ships there are missiles resembling small aircraft, such as the Soviet Styx, and others looking like rockets, for example the French Exocet. Antiaircraft missiles are of great importance and come in various sizes intended for different ranges, such as the British Seadart for long range and Seawolf for close range. The American Asroc is a rocket-launched missile which parachutes a homing torpedo into the sea at the end of its trajectory, while the Subroc is a rocket fired from the torpedo tube of a submarine, which then comes to the surface and travels the remainder of its journey in the air.

As always, throughout naval history, tomorrow's warship is the concern of today's designers and engineers. There can be little doubt that, whatever her final shape, she will be fast, deadly, and well served both by satellite reconnaissance and improved communications. Perhaps one final question remains. With the present pace of development, with the large and growing costs of ship building, of nuclear installations, of yet more sophisticated weapon systems, computerization, and electronics, how long can the world's nations continue to face the economic consequences of continued naval development?

Extreme left: British nuclear-powered submarine Revenge, *which is armed with 16 Polaris missiles with a range of 2,500 nautical miles (4,630 km).*
Center: An Oberon-class patrol submarine, HMS Osiris, *leaving Faslane in Scotland.*
Left: Seacat missile drill on board assault ship HMS Intrepid. *Seacat is used as a close-range antiaircraft missile.*

Navigation

The word navigation comes from the Latin *navis*, a ship, and *agere*, to drive. Today the term navigation can be applied not only to ships, but to aircraft and in some cases to land vehicles as well, although here the discussion will be concerned primarily with marine navigation. Navigation embraces the whole art of accurately fixing the position of a craft, and of directing it safely and expeditiously from one point to another.

Although the navigational aids now available, including highly advanced radar and satellite systems, have removed many of the uncertainties surrounding early sea voyages, the questions asked by the modern navigator are much the same as those posed by his ancient counterpart: Where am I? What direction must I take in order to reach my destination safely? How long is my voyage likely to take me? To a great extent it is the new-found accuracy of the answers to these questions that reveals the enormous chasm bridged by 20th-century technology.

The Birth of Navigation

Our knowledge of the early development of navigation centers upon the Mediterranean, an island sea with no tides, shoals, or significant current, and one which, surrounded as it was by trading civilizations, offered the ideal area for the emergence of maritime skills. The birth of navigation runs parallel with the building of boats large enough for the transportation of goods, some time around 3500 BC. At first navigation was entirely coastal, relying on visual contact with the shore and the recognition of landmarks to give the master of a ship an idea of the position and course of his vessel. Before knowledge of celestial navigation became widespread, ships would sail by day and anchor by night, to avoid losing sight of the shore.

The first artificial navigational aid, which developed in the 2nd millennium BC, was the sounding rod for measuring the depth of water. A subsequent and natural development for measuring deeper water was a line with a weight attached to its lower end, an aid used by Posidonius in the 2nd century BC to measure depths of 6,000 ft. (1,800 m). Another very early navigational aid was the wind rose, an early type of compass without a magnetic needle, which had eight points named for the eight principal winds. Seafarers must therefore have been able to tell the winds apart, by recognition of their temperature, moisture content, strength, or some other characteristic, or by association with the heavenly bodies, in order to use the wind rose effectively.

It is well established that the Phoenicians relied to a great extent on celestial navigation. The ancient Greek poet Aratus describes how the Phoenicians used the constellation Ursa Minor: 'By her guidance, the men of Sidon steer the straightest course.' Ursa Minor contains the Pole star, which never varies more than 2½° from true North, and which, through its importance as a navigational aid,

Compass rose, c. 1770.

has become known as the seaman's star. This ability to steer by the stars, coupled with the development of the wind rose, allowed the Phoenicians to travel by night as well as by day in their long trading voyages. The farthest points reached by their expeditions can only be surmised from the evidence available, but it is believed that they sailed west as far as the Azores, and on trading missions for tin, as far north as the Shetland Islands.

There seems to have been very little development in navigational instruments or techniques over the next few centuries. Yet the Greeks too were a nation of seafarers, venturing beyond the confines of their familiar Mediterranean waters on hazardous voyages of discovery. In 320 BC, for example, the Greek navigator PYTHEAS embarked from Massilia and sailed around the western coasts of Spain and France, over to Britain and perhaps Thule (now identified most probably as the Orkney Islands rather than Iceland or Greenland). Pytheas' knowledge of astronomy and mathematics enabled him to compute, within an accuracy of a few miles, the correct latitude of Massilia, and he was also the first Greek to notice the influence of the moon on tides.

It must have been the knowledge and experience gained on voyages such as this which enabled the Greek mathematicians and astronomers of the 3rd century BC, such as

Timosthenes and Eratosthenes, to compile their maps. Timosthenes' map is of interest for its use of coordinates of latitude and longitude for indicating position, and Eratosthenes, in his map of the then known world, also employed vertical and horizontal lines, giving distance in *stadia* (1 Roman mile = 8 stadia) north and west of zero lines in the Atlantic and Indian Oceans.

In the 1st century AD Marinus of Tyre produced the first charts for seamen. He too employed meridians and parallels, though equally spaced and based on the primary meridian and parallel of Rhodes. But the greatest Greek cartographer of all was Ptolemy, who worked in Alexandria in the 2nd century AD. He was probably the first to devise a map projection in which a portion of the earth's curved surface could be transferred to the flat surface of a map. In his first projection he employed meridians every 10° coming together at the pole, the point of contact of the cone providing a curved parallel through Rhodes while two similar parallels passed through the farthest known southerly and northerly points. In his second, more refined projection he gave a curvature to all meridians except the central one, and also to the parallels.

The Romans showed little active interest in mapping the world, and after the fall of Rome in AD 476, Ptolemy's maps were lost for nearly a millennium. The Arabs fell heir to Greek science, and it is interesting to note that it was principally Arab cartographers and Jewish astronomers who staffed Prince Henry of Portugal's famous school of navigation in the 15th century

From the 8th to the 10th century a quite separate seafaring tradition was reaching its zenith in northern waters. This was a culture founded upon a love of the sea and a reliance on maritime trade, but which degenerated into a series of barbaric plundering forays. The Vikings left in their sagas records of their many voyages and proof of their natural ability to steer a course by the stars. It is clear that they made regular voyages to Iceland, Greenland, and to the shores of Britain and France, and in AD 1001, according to Norse sagas, they traveled across the Atlantic to reach Vinland, reputedly Newfoundland.

It is just conceivable they may have used a primitive compass, although it is impossible to establish exactly when and where the compass first emerged. The magnetic property of the lodestone was appreciated in ancient times in places as far apart as China and Scandinavia. An 11th-century work refers to the use of the compass at sea, as does an Arab work of AD 1220. The primitive compass took the form of a piece of a lodestone or magnetized piece of iron attached to a piece of floating wood. This would be checked against the Pole star and the north end of the lodestone marked. This was later refined in the 13th century to a pivoting needle in a glass-topped box, more suitable for seaboard conditions, and later still a compass card was incorporated into the design.

Mariner's compass, 1719.

Cartography and Navigational Instruments in the Renaissance

It was in the 13th century, when the more accurate form of magnetic compass was being introduced, that a new kind of chart first made its appearance. This was the sheepskin or goatskin manuscript chart known as a portulan. Portulans were mainly of the Mediterranean, although some extended into the Atlantic or even covered the entire then-known world. The oldest portulan in existence, dated c. 1275, was found in Pisa and has become known as the Carta Pisani. The portulan chart probably originated in Venice and Genoa, was further developed by the Catalan chartmakers, and reached its peak of perfection in Portugal and Spain in the 16th century.

Portulans generally included a large number of compass roses and loxodromic (rhumb) lines to show the mariner the correct heading between various points. These charts were drawn from compass bearings, imperfect latitude sights, and estimates of distance run. The errors that were the natural result were of relatively little consequence when confined to the Mediterranean. However, extrapolated over transatlantic distances small errors became much more significant. Portulans made no allowance for magnetic variation or for the curvature of the earth, as the mapmakers made the parallels of latitude equidistant. However, it was the inability to determine longitude that most adversely affected their accuracy.

One of the earliest methods of finding longitude at sea was by lunar observation, referring to astronomical tables to translate celestial sightings. The first significant set of tables, known as the Alphonsine tables, was published in Spain in 1252. These were later improved upon by German astronomers of the 15th century and proved of enormous value to the Portuguese navigators sent out to discover routes to India and China in the 15th and early 16th centuries. The discovery made in Constantinople in 1400 of Ptolemy's long-forgotten works and maps gave a further impetus to the Age of Discovery. Portugal began to

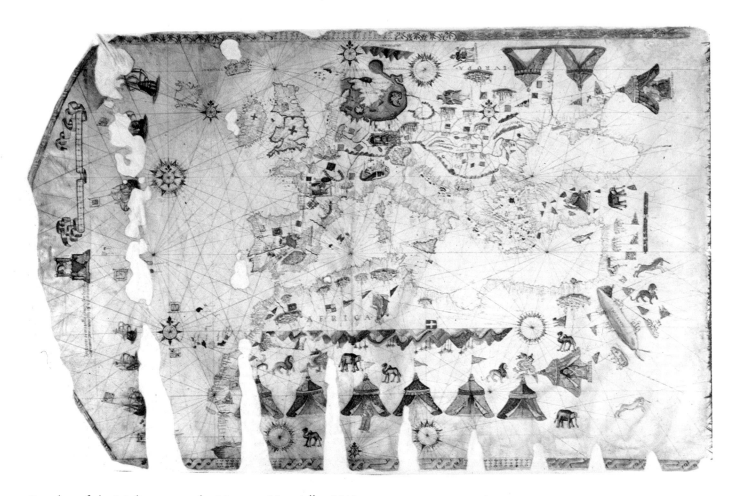

Portulan of the Mediterranean, by Vesconte Maggiollo, 1548.

take the lead in navigation and chartmaking, spurred on initially by the development of more seaworthy vessels, such as the Portuguese CARAVEL, and by the enthusiasm and patronage of Prince Henry, who set up an observatory and school of navigation in 1420.

The voyages undertaken by such men as Vasco da GAMA and Christopher COLUMBUS revealed the inaccuracies of the charts then available, and the possible consequences of relying solely on them. When Christopher Columbus set sail from the port of Palos in 1492, in an attempt to discover the riches of the east by sailing west, what he found were outlying islands of the American continent. Columbus' only chart was a copy of the conical projection first drawn by Ptolemy in AD 150. Of course, the Americas found no place on his chart; he had been encouraged to make his voyage in the first place by an estimate of the earth's size that placed Japan only 2,400 nautical miles (4,500 km) west of the Canaries — a quarter of the real distance between the two points.

Even if charts proved unreliable, there were a great number of navigational instruments introduced in the 15th and 16th centuries as ships ventured out on long voyages to unknown destinations. The majority of these aids

were for measuring the altitude of celestial bodies, in order to find a latitude bearing. The first of these instruments was the seaman's quadrant, which was employed by Portuguese navigators in the second half of the 15th century for measuring the altitude of the Pole star. The quadrant had the shape of a quarter circle and was held in the vertical plane with the arc downward, a plumb bob and line hanging from the right angle and across the arc. The arc was originally marked only with names of rele-

Quadrant, 1600.

Mariner's astrolabe, c. 1585.

to find its altitude was overcome by the backstaff, or Davis' quadrant, invented by the English explorer John DAVIS at the end of the 16th century. The backstaff bore a resemblance to the cross staff, but relied on the shadow cast by the movable arm rather than on direct sighting. Davis also invented a more complex backstaff, which was modified by Elton in 1732, so that a sighting could be taken whether the horizon could be seen or not.

All these instruments relied on the observer being able to sight celestial objects. However, before the advent of such technologically advanced systems as hyperbolic navigation, there would, in any long voyage, be times when because of storm or cloud the navigator would be unable to see sun, moon, or stars. The only way he could find his position would be by dead reckoning. This system is based on the premise that starting from a known point, the navigator can deduce his subsequent position if he knows for how long, at what speed, and in what direction he has been traveling. The expression 'dead reckoning' is a contraction of deduced reckoning. In the 15th and 16th centuries the speed was estimated with the help of a log, the direction with a compass, and elapsed time with a sandglass. The information was then recorded on a traverse board marked with the points of the compass, by means of wooden pegs inserted into the board.

The first widely used log was the log and line, described in print in 1574. A quadrant of flat wood, weighted to float vertically, was attached by three cords to a marked

vant ports and headlands, each marking being at the appropriate angle for the corresponding latitude. The mariner would sail north or south until he reached the latitude of his destination and then sail east or west as required, a method known as 'latitude sailing.'

The successor to the quadrant was the seaman's astrolabe, which was apparently introduced at the end of the 15th century. It, too, depended on a plumb line and was, like the quadrant, only really suited for calm sea conditions. In its simple form it consisted of a graduated circular disk with a movable sighting device. In 1530 there emerged yet another instrument for taking the altitude of celestial bodies — the cross staff — which was based on the principle of the ancient Arab *kamal*. This instrument was constructed of a long wooden shaft, the staff, with a movable crosspiece set at right angles to it. Holding one end of it to his eye, the navigator slid the cross along until the horizon was in line with the lower end of the cross and the celestial object with the upper end. The staff was marked with a graduated scale on which the position of the crosspiece gave the altitude of the celestial object being observed.

The disadvantage of having to look directly into the sun

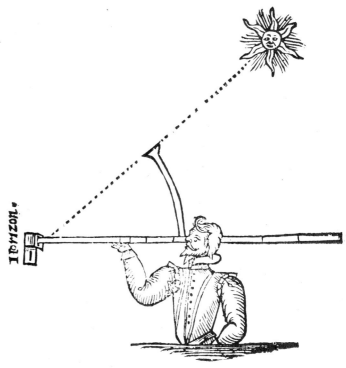

Illustration of an early backstaff, from John Davis' The Seamans Secrets *(1594).*

Davis' quadrant, invented at the end of the 16th century.

reproducing the curved surface of the earth on a flat piece of paper in such a way that distances could be accurately measured and courses laid off on it. Mercator's system of projection was to assume the earth to be surrounded at the equator by a cylinder of paper, the axis of the cylinder being parallel to that of the earth from pole to pole. Onto this cylinder Mercator projected the shape of the land-masses and oceans, as then known, using the earth's center as that of projection. Obviously, as the poles were approached the distortion increased, but as most navigation took place within the temperate zones this was not of great consequence. Both the parallels of latitude and meridians of longitude emerged as straight lines, though the rectangles thus formed grew more elongated in the higher latitudes and it was not possible to include a universal scale of distance, unless the area covered was small. Despite this, the advantage of being able to lay off a course between any two points as a straight line of constant com-

line. It was thrown overboard periodically, and after the ship had sailed a defined time interval the line that had run out was measured. The line was marked by knots, and the timing was taken by means of a 28-second sandglass. Contemporary with the log and line was the Dutchman's log. This consisted of two lines marked on the ship's side and a piece of wood thrown into the water. The time taken to pass from one line to the other was used to estimate the speed. However, for purposes of dead reckoning neither the log nor the compass was particularly accurate, and neither took account of sideways drift due to wind or current. Improvements were to come, but at this early stage, before the invention of the chronometer, dead reckoning could be only an imprecise navigational aid.

Perhaps the greatest contribution to the development of navigation during the 16th century was that made by the Flemish instrument-maker Gerhard Kremer, better known as Mercator, who in 1569 published his famous map of the world based on a system of projection still in use today. The problem which faced all cartographers of the age was, as previously outlined, that of faithfully

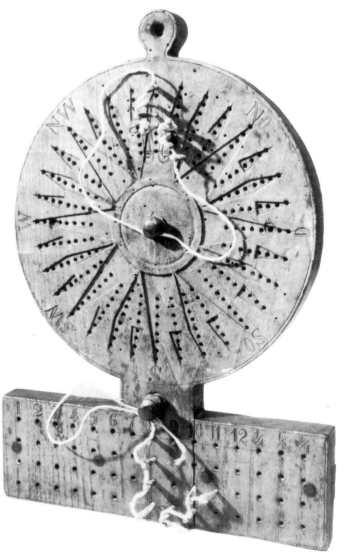

Traverse board of a type used in the 16th and 17th centuries.

pass bearing which cut all meridians at a constant angle outweighed all the disadvantages. Mercator took the 'linea noctialis,' or equator, as the zero line from which to reckon latitude in both directions towards the poles, but until the last decade of the 19th century, when the meridian of Greenwich gained universal acceptance as the zero line from which longitude should be measured, there was no general agreement on which meridian should be chosen for this purpose.

The Search for Longitude

The main problem which beset navigators during the age of exploration and for some centuries following was that of finding longitude. The lunar distance method, which was the generally accepted procedure prior to the invention of the chronometer, was imprecise and depended on the mariner's skill and willingness to compute from complex mathematical tables, such as the Alphonsine tables of 1252. The publication in 1614 of John Napier's table of logarithms shortened the work involved in reckoning by this method, but it demanded a certain amount of mathematical expertise, which was at that time often beyond the capabilities of the average navigator.

Recognition of the need for a more accurate means of determining longitude was prompt in coming. Many nations offered subtantial prizes for a solution to the problem, and England's Royal Observatory at Greenwich was established by Charles II in 1675 'so as to find out the so much desired longitude of places for perfecting the art of navigation.' In 1714 the British government offered a prize of £20,000 to the person who could find an accurate and practical method of determining longitude, and the Board of Longitude was set up specifically to consider the applications.

The introduction of lunar prediction tables by Tobias Mayer in 1755 attempted to give the navigator a more accurate method of measuring longitude by lunar observation. By using the table an observer taking a lunar distance in another part of the world would know the time at Greenwich and be able to compare it with his local time. This, and the publication in 1776 of the first Nautical Almanac, which gave the distance of fixed stars from the moon at specific times for each day of the year, made lunar observation a far more reliable method for calculating longitude, but a method still far too complex for the majority of seafarers at that period.

In 1730 the octant was invented independently in America and England by Thomas Godfrey and John Hadley respectively. Both submitted their designs to the Royal Society, but Hadley produced an improved design in 1734 and his octant generally adopted. Hadley's octant measured angles up to 90° using the reflection principle, which doubled the degree of altitude that could be measured by the simple quadrant. The other great

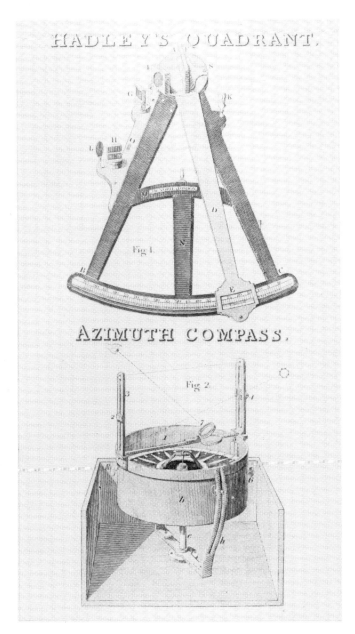

The frontispiece to J.W. Norie's A new and complete epitome of practical navigation *(1828). It shows Hadley's quadrant (which was in fact an octant) and an azimuth compass.*

advantage of this instrument was that it could bring the image of the celestial body in line with the horizon and enable a more accurate reading to be taken. Because of its accuracy, cheapness, and ease of handling, the octant proved an extremely popular navigational instrument and was still in use at the beginning of the 20th century as a means of measuring the altitude of heavenly bodies.

The accuracy obtainable with the octant made possible, on occasion, the use of the lunar distance method of finding longitude. This method had of course been known for some time, but an instrument capable of achieving

Reflecting circle, c. 1800.

sufficient accuracy for its implementation had not been available. The 90° scale of the octant proved too limited for taking lunar distances in general, and so a complete circle, capable of measuring up to 360°, was made by John Bird in the 1750s. Bird's reflecting circle was efficient but very heavy and inconvenient for use at sea. The compromise between the circle and octant was the sextant, an instrument modeled on the octant but with a 120° scale. Although the sextant made possible the use of the lunar distance method of finding longitude, before the invention of the chronometer the system was far from precise and still demanded a degree of skill which most seamen of that period did not possess. Today, however, the modern sextant, a precision instrument much improved from the 18th-century prototype, is used in conjunction with a chronometer and Nautical Almanac to determine both latitude and longitude and so 'fix' the ship's position with a high degree of accuracy.

It had become clear to many different bodies engaged in establishing a means of finding the longitude of a ship at sea that the solution would be a horological one, dependent on the production of an accurate timekeeper which could withstand not only the motion of a ship but also the changes in temperature likely to be encountered during an ocean passage. In 1735 a Yorkshire clockmaker named John HARRISON produced his first chronometer, Harrison 1, or H1. His fourth attempt, H4, finally won him the Board of Longitude prize in 1765, but only after Captain James COOK had taken a copy of the chronometer on his second voyage of exploration to the Pacific and had reported very favorably on its performance. In fact, after circumnavigating the world, Cook calculated his longitude with an error of only 8 miles (12.87 km). Harrison's chronometer was, however, too costly to be immediately adopted for general use at sea.

In 1766 Pierre Leroy improved on Harrison's design and produced a marine timekeeper with a mechanism embodying in rudimentary form all the essential features of the modern chronometer. By 1825 production techniques had allowed the chronometer to be made cheaply enough to be issued to all Royal Navy ships. With the proven efficiency of the chronometer, the lunar distance method of finding longitude soon fell into disuse.

In 1843 Thomas Sumner, an American merchant ship captain, discovered that by comparing an astronomical sight with one taken earlier, both latitude and longitude could be found at the same time. With this method allowance had to be made for the passage of the ship between the two sightings. This technique is known as position line navigation; in 1875 it was rounded out by the development of the altitude difference or 'intercept' concept of Marcq St. Hilaire, a French naval officer.

Refinement of Instruments in the 19th Century

The 19th century saw further refinements and improvements in the navigational aids already in existence, and a determined effort to overcome the difficulties associated with them. The log, for example, which was used to mea-

John Harrison's first chronometer, 1735.

sure a ship's speed, had been halted in its development by the problem of friction. Henry de Saumarez had made an instrument which consisted of a towed rotator. This was tested early in the 18th century, but the weight of the rotator itself produced so much friction that the readings were valueless. Many further attempts were made, but none overcame the friction problem until Richard Gower and Edward Massey devised solutions that were accurate, but which entailed the hauling in of the log to take a reading. It was not until 1884 that progress in engineering enabled Thomas Walker to patent his successful Cherub log. This met the demands for accuracy and reliability in a log consisting of a towed rotator, the revolutions of which were recorded on a dial on the taffrail to which the log line was attached.

Most modern ships have bottom logs, protruding from the bottom of the hull. One type takes the form of the Pitot tube and is a device for measuring the flow velocity of water. Another type is the electromagnetic log, which employs an electromagnet and a pair of electrodes projecting beneath the hull. Movement of the water relative to the magnetic field creates a varying potential difference (depending on speed) across the electrodes. When very great accuracy of measurement of distance run is required, as, for example, in minelaying, minesweeping, and surveying, a ship can be fitted with taut-wire measuring gear. This is a drum carrying 140 miles (225 km) of fine wire. In use, the ship takes her departure from a position in which an accurate land fix can be obtained. The wire, weighted at one end, is then released and the amount of

wire paid out, denoting distance run, is recorded on a dial attached to the drum. Allowance must be made for the fact that, due to tidal streams or currents, the wire may not be laid out in a straight line.

Magnetic variation and the deviation of the compass needle had been appreciated since the 15th century. One solution to this problem was the development of azimuth compasses, which, however, required two operators, one to align the sight and another to read off the bearing. The first major step forward took place in 1812, when a prism was fitted to the compass sight, allowing an operator to align the sight and take the reading at the same time. Azimuth compasses were eventually superseded by the azimuth ring, which could be simply fitted over the top of the standard compass and rotated around it. Today the amount of magnetic variation is recorded on every chart, and the azimuth ring is therefore largely obsolete, at least in its original purpose.

With the introduction of iron-hulled ships in the mid-19th century, it was discovered that the iron used in a ship's construction could affect the accuracy of a magnetic compass carried on board. Consequently groups such as the Liverpool Compass Committee of 1855 were formed to investigate the positioning of compasses in iron ships and to try to find a solution. Through the work of the Astronomer Royal Sir George Airy and the navigator and explorer Matthew Flinders a means was found of neutralizing the ship's magnetism with pieces of soft iron (known as Flinders' bars) and permanent magnets attached to the binnacle housing the compass, and it was

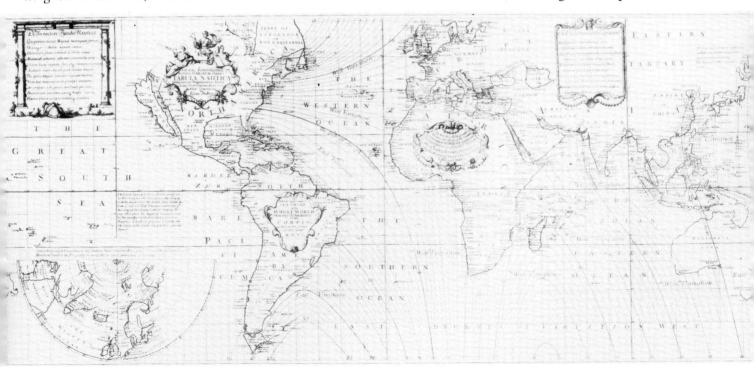

Halley's chart of 1700, showing magnetic variation throughout the world.

A compass binnacle with compensating spheres, Flinders' bar, and vertical magnets (inside the binnacle), to correct the effect of the ship's own magnetism on the compass it houses.

Smythies in 1856, but it was never developed. It was not until 1906, with the gyroscopic compass of Anschütz-Kaempfe, that this concept became a practical reality. Adopted in capital ships of the Royal Navy in 1911, the Anschütz was replaced in 1913 by the newly emerging and superior Sperry gyroscopic compass, invented by the American scientist Dr. Elmer Sperry. By the end of World War I Sperry was supplying the entire British fleet. A rival design by the British scientist S.G. Brown appeared on the market in 1916, and because of its lightness compared with the Sperry type, it proved suitable for use in aircraft. The most important feature of the gyrocompass is that it always points to true north, and since it does not rely on magnetism it is unaffected by variation and deviation. The gyroscope wheel is surrounded by a case with a compass card that always remains horizontal. This is achieved because the gyroscope's axis is made to precess at the rate necessary to keep step with the rotation of the earth. The value of the gyroscopic compass is not restricted solely to its directonal uses; it can be employed to operate repeater compasses in different parts of the ship, to act as a course recorder, and most important of all, to serve as an automatic pilot.

this solution that was recommended by the Liverpool Compass Committee. In 1876 Sir William Thomson (later Lord Kelvin) produced a new binnacle design to house the magnets, compensating spheres, and Flinders' bar used to correct the deviation.

The 20th Century

The 20th century has brought about a revolution in navigational instruments. The harnessing of electricity has brought with it the development of instruments capable of a degree of accuracy never known before. Ships can now not only fix their own position but can plot the position and course of other ships.

The Gyroscopic Compass

The properties of the gyroscope had long been known, but until this century the necessary technology was not available to use the gyroscope in the field of navigation. The first gyroscopic compass to be patented was that of J.

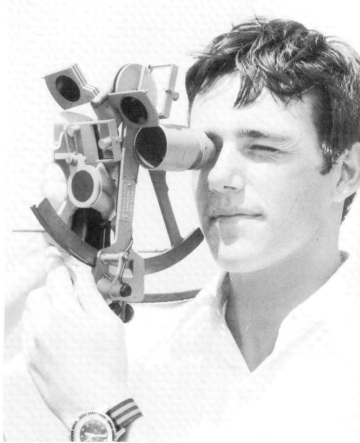

Taking an altitude with the aid of a modern sextant.

Royal Navy officer taking a compass bearing.

Radio Direction Finding

The major navigational advances of the age have been concerned with radio direction finding, developed at the beginning of this century as a means of helping ships fix position in poor visibility. Before and during World War I a position-fixing system using wireless telegraphy was in operation. Initially shore stations were set up to take bearings of a ship's radio transmissions and from these plot her position, which would then be transmitted back to the ship. Even though most shore stations were capable of doing this, the method proved of little use during the war, for breaking radio silence spelled danger. A second system circumvented this problem by the use of directional apparatus fitted to the ship herself. By establishing the direction of the radio transmissions made by shore stations, the ship could fix a position without breaking radio silence. Experiments in the English Channel in 1924 with this type of apparatus proved successful, and most ships today have direction-finding loops fitted.

In the period between the two world wars the Germans developed a rotating long-range radio beacon called Sonne. It worked by transmitting a continuous rotating beam that made a distinctive note as it passed through true north. The ship or aircraft navigator used a stopwatch to measure the amount of time between the north note and the minimum amount of reception indicated on his receiver. This time was converted into a direction and laid off on a normal ship's chart. By taking two or more bearings a position could be found. This system was ideal over relatively short distances but suffered from distortion by the ionosphere when used over long distances.

Radar was developed more or less simultaneously in the 1930s by Britain, France, and Germany. Known as RDF (Radio Direction Finding) in the UK, the American term

RADAR (RAdio Detection and Ranging) was later generally adopted. In radar, objects are detected by sending out ultrahigh-frequency radio waves which, if they strike anything, are reflected back. The echoes, or reflections, are analyzed and the object's direction, range, and even velocity can be ascertained. Radar is used as a maneuvering aid, for collision avoidance, position-fixing in coastal navigation, and as a long-range indicator of approaching shipping, icebergs, and weather conditions. A radar set operating with a rotating aerial will produce a picture on a Plan Position Indicator (PPI) of every object in view above the horizon. Conventional radio direction finding before the advent of radar required at least two intersecting beams if range as well as direction was to be obtained. With radar, on the other hand, the direction and range of objects in the air as well as on land and sea can be detected by a single transmitter/receiver. Radar first went to sea in 1936 in a British and in a German warship, then in 1937 in the French liner *Normandie*, but none of these early sets proved reliable. In 1940 the British invention of the magnetron enabled sets using wavelengths of under 10 cm to be constructed. By 1943 this had been reduced to 1.9 cm, which made possible the detection and ranging of an object as small as a U-boat's periscope.

The present radar set has changed little in principle from its prototype. Modern technology has, however, provided more advanced techniques for plotting positions of other ships. As well as showing either true or relative displays of shipping around the user, modern radar display units can show the positions of individual ships at three previous instances. Modern sets are linked to computers designed to give visual and audio warning of ships whose estimated courses will bring them within a distance unacceptable to the user.

Hyperbolic Navigation

World War II also led to the development, in both the United States and Britain, of several hyperbolic fixing systems, all originally designed to assist bombers in finding their targets but now equally important for shipping. Its principles can be best explained by imagining a man listening to the sound of two explosions, A and B, occurring simultaneously. If the listener is exactly midway between A and B, then the sound waves from the two explosions will reach him at the same time. If he is closer to A than he is to B, then he will naturally hear the explosion A before that of B. By timing the rate at which the sound waves reach the listener and plotting where the two sets of waves intersect, a position can be found. The hyperbolae are formed by joining the points of intersection of the two sets of waves. Hyperbolic radio transmission systems use sets of transmitters called chains. The chains consist of a master transmitter with slave transmitters

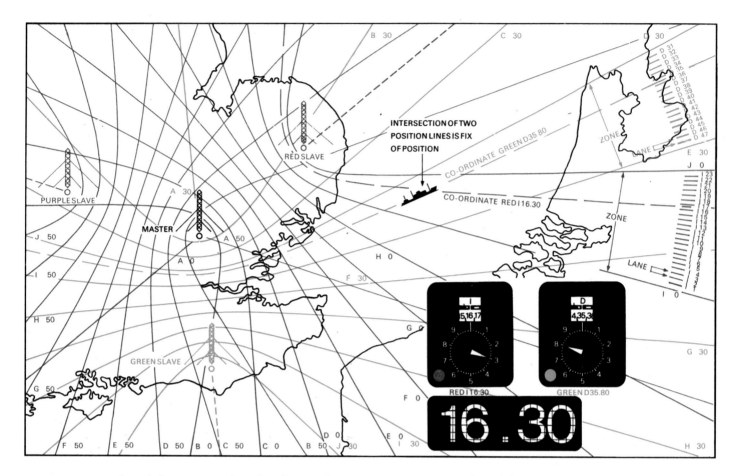

Decca Navigator hyperbolic system. The red and green decometer readings give a fix of the ship's position.

electronically linked to it. The master and the slaves in most chains transmit radio waves simultaneously. The accuracy of any one system depends on the frequency used for the transmissions, and this in turn dictates the range. The higher the frequency, the greater the accuracy, but the shorter the effective range.

The first hyperbolic system was Gee, introduced by the British in 1940 and originally developed so that Allied bombers could accurately find their positions. It had a maximum range of some 300 miles (480 km), with an accuracy of within 5 miles (8 km) at its limits. In Gee, the chains consisted of three radio beacons which transmitted simultaneously, but on different frequencies. The United States developed a similar system over the North Atlantic called Loran. During the next few years these aircraft systems were developed for use by ships; the Decca Navigator system (QM) was successfully used for the first time in the Allied invasion of Europe in June 1944.

The Decca Navigator hyperbolic system operates on a lattice system using continuous wave transmission. The chains are made up of a master and three slave transmitters, the slaves being set around the master at distances of 50-100 nautical miles (93-185 km). The slaves are phase-locked to the master and make up three pairs which each

produce their own hyperbolae. Hyperbolic lines are printed on the charts in three colors, each color denoting one of the three pairs. The receiver displays its information numerically on decometers, the numbers indicating which hyperbola or 'lane' is being identified and allowing the navigator to plot his position manually on the chart. There is also a marine automatic plotter which can be used to provide a pictorial history of the courses steered, using a variety of small computers. The effective range of this system is a little over 200 nautical miles (370 km), and the accuracy can vary from one-quarter of a nautical mile during the day to 4 nautical miles (7.4 km) at night.

A new French-developed worldwide hyperbolic system called Omega has recently come into operation. It employs eight stations, in different parts of the world, by means of which a ship anywhere between latitudes 75°N and 75°S can obtain her position. The results so far give an accuracy of about one-tenth of the distance between the hyperbolae.

The useful distance at which Loran can be used extends to about 800 nautical miles (1,480 km) by day and 1,400 nautical miles (2,590 km) by night, when sky-wave signals are available. Gee is usable only to a distance about twice that to the horizon.

Satellite Systems

Another innovation of recent decades has been the development of navigation by satellite. In 1957 the first satellite was launched by the Soviet Union, and not long after specialized satellites were being launched into space purely as navigational aids. Trials began in 1959, but it was not until 1967 that they became generally available. There are three types of satellite navigation systems: the first is Transit; the second system involves synchronous satellites normally used for communications; the third is called Navstar/GPS and is not yet fully operational.

The Transit system was introduced in 1964 by the U.S. Navy for use by its nuclear submarines. The system involves five satellites which are in polar orbit. To use the system a ship must be equipped with a special receiver, a computer, and a printer. The receiver picks up the satellite's call sign, reads the parameters of its orbit and a time signal on two frequencies transmitted by each satellite every two minutes. The change in the frequencies due to the movement of the satellite produces a doppler effect directly proportional to the change in distance between the satellite and the receiver. With this information from two or more satellites the computer is able to calculate the ship's position. The average time a satellite is accessible is about 20 minutes, and in theory ten doppler counts can be made within this time, though in practice only five to eight are used. With the ship on a steady course and speed, the system has an accuracy of the order of 820 ft. (250 m), but it is very expensive to operate. It is more suitable for work demanding great accuracy, such as the siting of oil rigs and the laying of submarine cables.

The second satellite system, the Synchronous (Stationary) system, involves the ship transmitting an interrogation signal to two satellites of known position and then timing their responses. Satellites are used that are in orbit above the earth's equator and traveling in the same direction that the earth is spinning, so that they appear to be stationary overhead.

The most recently developed satellite system, Navstar/GPS, was started in 1977 with the launching of six satellites by the U.S. Air Force and Navy. It is hoped to provide worldwide coverage, using 24 satellites, by 1983. Working on the hyperbolic principle, using radio transmission from four satellites at a time, the system should provide considerable accuracy in position fixing.

Inertial Navigation

Another postwar development of considerable importance is that of the Ship's Inertial Navigational System (SINS). SINS is a dead reckoning system par excellence. It was developed by the U.S. Navy for its nuclear-powered submarines, which to retain secrecy of movement cannot ascend at frequent intervals to periscope level. These submarines are therefore virtually isolated from radio and celestial navigation systems. SINS is a fully self-contained system, requiring no receiving or transmitting apparatus and thus involving no signals that might be detectable by hostile forces.

The system consists essentially of accelerometers, gyroscopes, and a computer. Two accelerometers are set up with their axes mutually perpendicular. They sense and measure changes of speed in any direction and are coupled to three gyroscopes, which provide an independent frame of reference. The measurements of the accelerometers, which can eliminate changes of acceleration caused by pitching, rolling, and the like, as opposed to changes in speed and course, are fed into the computer, which calculates the actual path of the submarine from a known starting point and records it. The computer may also be programed with the desired course so that it can act as an automatic pilot. Inertial navigation is thus a sophisticated form of dead reckoning, the traditional procedure of estimating position from speed and direction, and it was used by the NAUTILUS in her historic voyage under the North Pole in 1958. This system produces errors of less than a mile after a week's continuous cruising, but a submarine on a prolonged submerged mission normally still ascends to periscope level from time to time to check position by radio or celestial navigation.

The cost of an inertial navigation assembly is high, and its use is at present confined to nuclear-powered submarines and certain selected warships, but it is the most revolutionary piece of equipment so far made available to the navigator. A brochure issued by the British Admiralty Compass Department describes it as '. . . a navigational milestone of the stature of Harrison's chronometer, the sextant, or Kelvin's compass.'

Alongside inertial navigation is another method of navigation also particularly suited to submarines. This is to monitor the contours of the seabed beneath the vessel, an increasingly practical proposition with the development of sophisticated echo sounders and detailed charts of the ocean floor.

In spite of the spectacular advances made in recent years with the development of radio aids to navigation, the end is certainly not in sight. Apart from a general improvement in reliability and performance of existing systems, an entirely new approach, called integrated navigation, is being tested. The idea is to link exact but discontinuous navigation systems, such as Transit, with continuous ones, such as Omega and Loran, which need more or less frequent recalibration. By integrating, with the help of a computer, the results obtained from the radio-navigational sensors currently available, it is possible to obtain a continuous 'optimization' of the ship's position. Studies along these lines are being pursued by NATO, France, the Netherlands, and the United States, and the results so far obtained are most promising.

Diving and Salvage

The practice of diving for commercial and military purposes was recorded many centuries before the beginning of the Christian era. Thucydides reported that divers were used to remove the wooden barriers erected in the harbor mouth during the siege of Syracuse in 413 BC; Livy mentions the employment of divers in the reign of Perseus to recover treasure from sunken ships; and the ancient sea rules known as the Rhodian Law laid down the scales of payment for divers engaged in salvage.

Since early diving was largely unassisted, without recourse to any mechanical aids, the diver relied solely on the volume and power of his lungs to sustain himself. Normally the maximum time that can be spent underwater by an unassisted diver is of the order of two minutes at a depth of about 6 fathoms (10-11 m). In some parts of the world where unassisted commercial diving still survives, in the pearl fisheries of Sri Lanka for example, greater depths have been recorded. But any unassisted dive at a depth greater than about 30 ft. (9 m) causes great pressure on the diver's lungs and eardrums and is extremely hazardous. To achieve any greater depth a means had to be found to increase the diver's air supply and to protect him in some way from the pressure.

Assisted Diving

Perhaps the earliest form of assisted diving was a method employing metal tubes to enable the diver to draw air from the surface of the water. Aristotle mentions a system based on this simple principle; in another work he describes a metal vessel which was lowered down to a diver — some form of diving bell. This dates the origins of assisted diving to at least the 4th century BC. However, the real beginning of assisted diving had to await the introduction of the air-filled diving bell, the diving helmet, diving dress, and diving (aqua) lung.

The Diving Bell

The principle of the diving bell is the containment of air in an inverted, open-bottomed vessel. As the vessel is lowered into the sea, the air inside it is compressed relative to the depth of water reached. If air is then pumped into the container at a pressure equal to that of the water around it, the container will remain full of air and a diver inside it will be able to breathe and work at that depth, either inside the container, if it is positioned exactly, or in the near vicinity, using it as a means of replenishing the air in his lungs when he can no longer hold his breath.

The invention of the diving bell is sometimes attributed to Roger Bacon in the mid-13th century, though without much firm evidence. In 1538 John Taisnier demonstrated the principle in a successful experiment at Toledo in Spain, when two Greek divers were lowered to the seabed in an inverted 'kettle' — a demonstration watched by the Emperor Charles V and a large crowd of spectators. There

were other similar experiments from time to time, but the first really successful diving bell was that invented in 1717 by Dr. Edmund Halley, at the time Secretary of the Royal Society of England. It was constructed of wood in the form of a truncated cone, 3 ft. (0.9 m) in diameter at the top, 4 ft. 6 in. (1.4 m) at the bottom, and nearly 9 ft. (2.7 m) high. To give it the required weight to sink to the bottom and to keep it vertical, it was sheathed with lead, and to provide light a glass lens was let into the dome. Foul air escaped from the bell through a tap, and a continuous supply of new air was provided by an ingenious alternating system of two barrels lined with lead, each with top and bottom bungholes and connected to the bell with leather hoses from the top bungholes. The pressure of the water through the bottom bunghole forced the air it contained into the diving bell, and as one barrel was emptied and raised to the surface, the other one was lowered.

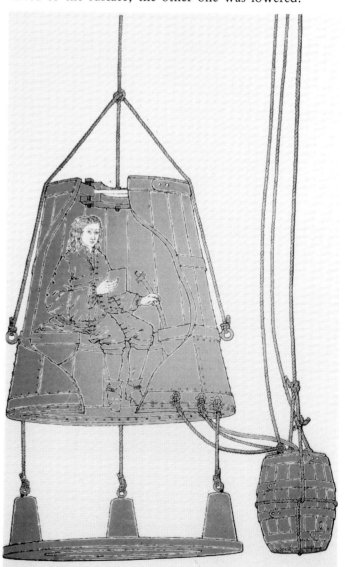

Halley's diving bell.

In 1778 the English engineer John Smeaton improved on Halley's system of air replenishment by substituting an air pump for the more cumbersome weighted barrels. Smeaton's diving bell was used for repairing the foundations of Hexham Bridge in Durham, and ten years later he refined the design for use in the construction of Ramsgate Harbor. This later bell, made of cast iron and weighing 2.5 tons, was heavy enough to sink under its own weight. It was rectangular instead of conical in shape, with a height of 4 ft. 6 in. (1.4 m) and a width of 3 ft. (0.9 m), which gave sufficient room for two men to work in it side by side, air being supplied by a pump in the support boat on the surface.

The next major improvement was made by John Rennie, a civil engineer who specialized in harbor and canal works. In 1813 Rennie designed a cast-iron diving bell 6 ft. (1.8 m) high and 4 ft. 6 in. (1.4 m) wide, weighing 5 tons. Six glass eyes in the top admitted light, and air was supplied through a valve in the top of the bell by a pump using a 2.5-in. (62-mm) hose. The interior was equipped with seats, chains, and tool racks.

The largest diving bells used in recent history were constructed for building the new Dover Harbor in the early 1900s. Four of them, each weighing 35 tons and measuring 17 ft. by 10 ft. (5 m × 3 m), were employed simultaneously to lay concrete foundations for the breakwater at a depth of 70 ft. (21 m). All were lit by electricity and connected by telephone to the surface.

Diving bells, though they were used extensively throughout the 19th century, had many obvious limitations, mainly in restricting the area in which the diver could work at his job. Improvements in the dress of the assisted diver, which allowed him to work at increasing depths, were soon to make the diving bell obsolete.

The Diving Helmet and Diving Dress

The earliest description of a diving helmet is contained in *De Re Militari*, written in 1511 by Vegetius, and an illustration shows a diver with a tight-fitting helmet, to which is connected a leather pipe with a bell-shaped mouth supported above the surface by an air-filled bladder. As apparently no means was provided of expelling the foul air from the helmet after exhalation, it is certain that the idea would not have worked in practice.

The Italian physicist G.A. Borelli was the first man to realize that air supplied to a diving helmet would need to be pumped down under pressure, and in 1679 he designed a watertight diving helmet using air forced down by means of a bellows. In 1715 the Englishman John Lethbridge invented a watertight leather suit which completely enclosed the diver, yet allowed for movement of arms and legs. The suit held enough air to sustain a diver for 30 minutes and became very popular for salvage work.

The next step forward came in 1797 when the German

Divers working on the seabed, 1750.

inventor C.H. Kleingert produced a diving dress which begins to resemble the modern design. It too consisted of a leather suit, but had a large domed cylinder with a glass window fitted over the head and shoulders and reaching down to the hips, with two armholes to allow for movement. The cylinder was fixed to the dress so that it was both watertight and airtight, and lead weights were hooked onto the cylinder to take the diver down to the bottom. A retrograde step in this design was that air was supplied through a pipe attached to a floating bladder, but a considerable advance on previous designs was the addition of a similarly designed pipe for the removal of the exhaled air. The end of the air-intake pipe was held by the diver in his teeth, and the expansion of his chest as he inhaled forced the foul air out through the second pipe. In order to ascend to the surface the diver simply unhooked the lead weight which held him down.

Ingenuity was the keynote of John Deane's idea for a

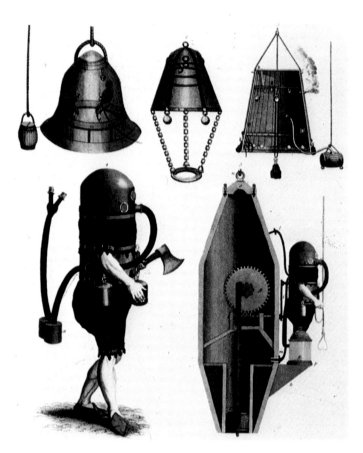

with the horses, and suggested that the dress could be adapted to enable men to work underwater. His first diving dress, known as an 'open' dress, consisted of a metal helmet and breastplate attached to a loose, watertight jacket underneath which the diver wore a combination suit. The innovatory feature of Siebe's helmet was a spring-loaded air-inlet valve, so that the diver enjoyed a constant stream of fresh air pumped from the surface which escaped between the jacket and the combination suit, carrying with it the air exhaled by the diver. The pressure at which the air was supplied prevented water from entering the jacket from below.

The great disadvantage of this 'open' dress was that if the diver stumbled and fell, the dress rapidly filled with water and there was therefore a high risk of drowning. This danger was overcome in Siebe's 'closed' dress of 1830 which was completely watertight and remained full of air whatever the diver's position. The removal of foul air was achieved through an air-regulating valve in the

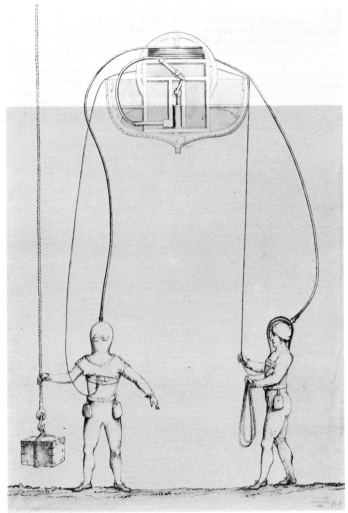

In this apparatus of 1811 an air pump has replaced the more cumbersome weighted barrels as the method of air replenishment.

diving dress about 1820. A few years earlier, in order to rescue some horses from a burning stable, Deane had utilized the helmet from a suit of armor and fixed it to a pipe from an old waterpump. Air pumped through the pipe enabled Deane to breathe while he was surrounded by dense smoke. Later he rigged up the same helmet with a glass window and then attached a watertight dress to it. It proved unsuitable, however, when he entered the sea, since the pressure of the pumped air turned him upside down. To overcome this setback Deane weighted the shoes with lead, which provided reasonable stability. In 1832, in collaboration with his brother Charles, he produced an improved diving apparatus which included a watertight rubber dress and a helmet large enough for the diver to turn his head. It was fitted with three glasses to admit light and a flexible rubber tube through which air was pumped from the surface. In this dress a diver could walk on the seabed, wield a hatchet, and remain submerged for about an hour. This was the dress worn by divers engaged in the salvage of the *Royal George*, which had overturned at Spithead in 1782.

However, the true father of the modern diving dress was Augustus Siebe, a contemporary of John Deane. In 1820 Siebe met Charles Deane, who was working on the invention of a fireman's suit after his brother's exploit

Closed diving helmet, 1839.

helmet. The diver descended with the aid of weights attached to his suit and boots.

The Siebe 'closed' dress of 1830 remained in its essentials the standard diving dress until well into the 20th century. It was operational up to depths of about 200 ft. (60 m) and it opened a new era in the history of diving, particularly in dock and pier construction, underwater repair work, and salvage. Before the introduction of the modern deep-diving techniques, armored articulated shells were used to reach depths greater than 200 ft. (60 m). When the P & O liner *Egypt* sank off Ushant in 1922, she lay on the bottom in 65 fathoms (390 ft. or 119 m) of water, well below the maximum depth at which divers wearing the standard diving helmet and rubber dress could operate. Since she was known to be carrying about five tons of gold and ten tons of silver when she went down, attempts were soon made to reach her. The recovery was organized by the Italian firm of Sorima, their divers working from the specially equipped salvage ship *Artiglio*. They used armored shells designed by the German firm of Neufeldt and Kuhnke, fitted with articulated joints to permit a small amount of movement. Because of the strength of the armored suit or shell, air does not have to be supplied to it under pressure, and the diver inside works at the ordinary atmospheric pressure. The air inside the suit is used many times over; the diver wears a mask covering nose and mouth and connected to a chamber containing caustic soda or caustic potash. As the diver breathes out,

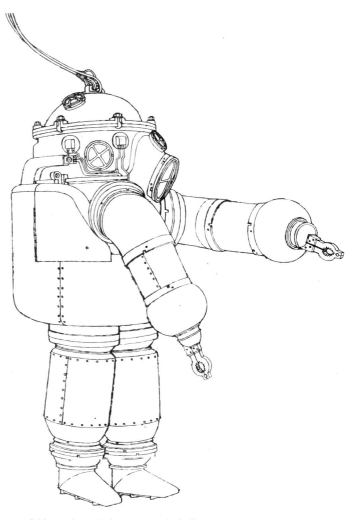

Neufeldt and Kuhnke armored shell, 1923.

the exhaled air passes through the caustic soda which removes the carbonic acid or carbon dioxide, and oxygen is then released from bottles within the armored shell to provide a constant supply of pure air. And because the diver inside is breathing air at normal pressure, there is no danger of decompression sickness when he ascends. The principal limitation of such a suit is that it lacks mobility, for although arms and legs are jointed, the need to ensure that the joints remain watertight under very heavy water pressure severely limits the amount of movement the diver can make. Nor can he use his hands; all he is able to do is to manipulate a pair of pincers extending through the arms of the armored suit through watertight ball joints. In spite of these limitations, the Italian divers did finally recover all the bullion from the sunken *Egypt*.

Free Diving

Although the Siebe diving dress was remarkably efficient, it was still dependent on air pumped from the surface through hosepipes. As the 20th century advanced with its progressive technological demands, what was needed was a diving apparatus incorporating its own supply of air and completely free from the inhibiting umbilical cord and air-lines attached to a parent ship or mother pontoon on the surface. Before the advent of the aqualung, the free diver wore the normal dress of metal helmet and rubber suit but, instead of the connecting airhose, carried on his back cylinders of oxygen compressed to a pressure of 120 atmospheres. As he exhaled through a canister of caustic soda, the carbon dioxide in the exhausted air was absorbed and oxygen released from the bottles on his back reconstituted clean air suitable for re-breathing.

Self-contained Diving

Although French technicians were working on the principle of the aqualung as long ago as 1872, the invention of the 'self-contained underwater breathing apparatus' (scuba) is attributed to Captain Jacques COUSTEAU and Emile Gagnan in 1943. It consists of three small bottles of highly compressed air secured to the back of the diver and connected to a demand regulator which automatically supplies air at the correct pressure according to the diver's depth. The diver draws air through a mouthpiece which is connected by two tubes to the regulator and air bottles. The diver's nose and eyes are enclosed in a rubber mask fitted with a glass front, and the diving dress is completed with rubber flippers. The safe depth to which a free diver wearing the aqualung can operate is about 180 ft. (55 m).

On the surface a diver can inflate his lungs with some 6 liters of air, but during diving water pressure gradually compresses the air until, by about 100 ft. (30 m) down, the volume is reduced to around 1.5 liters. If the diver continues his descent he risks permanent lung damage and probably death. This simple effect of increasing pressure on the volume of gas, summarized in Boyle's Law (the volume of a given mass of gas at a constant temperature varies with the pressure exerted upon it), sets a natural limit to unaided diving. To descend deeper the diver must be supplied with air at the same pressure as his surroundings, the ambient sea pressure, thus keeping changes in lung volume the same as on the surface.

The early solution of providing the diver with a helmet receiving air pumped down from the surface and the excess air escaping through the headgear persisted with comparatively few modifications until modern times. The self-contained diving apparatus came much later. Because there were no tell-tale bubbles of escaping air, closed-circuit oxygen scuba equipment, containing an inhalation and an exhalation bag, was used by frogmen in World War II for clandestine military missions.

But, open or closed, there are more limits to diving than Boyle's Law. One of the more alarming discoveries was that oxygen becomes toxic at the comparatively low pressure of two atmospheres or 33 ft. (10 m) down from

Diving with an aqualung is safe down to about 180 ft. (55 m).

the surface, a fact which nearly cost Cousteau his life during experiments with oxygen-fed apparatus. Oxygen is not the only atmospheric gas to become dangerous. Nitrogen induces a form of narcotic trance somewhat akin to alcoholic intoxication, and at 300 ft. (91.5 m) down a diver might become so exhilarated that he would gladly tear off his mask, with fatal results, a narcosis which Cousteau has called 'rapture of the deep.'

Mixed-gas Scuba

In the last few years the science of diving has accelerated from practical engineering to high technology, and the specification for the latest closed-circuit deep-diving pack, using a mixture of oxygen and helium instead of the normal air mixture of oxygen and nitrogen, provides for a maximum operating depth of 273 fathoms (1,640 ft. or 500 m). This backpack has been designed specifically for commercial diving operations. It is a self-contained apparatus and will operate for a working period of up to six hours without the need for any external gas supply, except where this is required to meet the appropriate diving regulations for emergency purposes (in many offshore waters an umbilical supply fulfills this requirement).

The self-contained pack can be used for both shallow-

of such possible faults as low or high oxygen partial pressure, discrepancy between outputs of the two oxygen sensors, low bottle pressure, or low battery voltage. Electrical signals generated within the backpack can be used to operate illuminated displays to give visual information and warning to both supervisor and diver.

Decompression Sickness

Air is mainly a mixture of oxygen and nitrogen, and at the normal atmospheric pressure our blood can absorb both the oxygen which the body uses up and the nitrogen which lies inert in the body tissues. When a diver underwater receives this mixture at a pressure equal to the depth of water in which he is working, he still has no difficulty in breathing it in the normal fashion. It is only when he rises again to the surface, and the pressure of the air he breathes is released, that difficulties occur.

These difficulties are caused because the nitrogen which has been breathed in under pressure forms bubbles when the pressure is suddenly reduced. The bubbles act as airlocks, blocking the blood supply to various tissues, causing muscle and joint pain and sometimes, if no remedial action is taken, death or brain damage. This is known as decompression sickness, or the 'bends.'

Divers using a mixed-gas backpack of oxygen and helium can work at depths of 1,000 ft. (350 m) or more.

water and deep-water diving. Its major advantage is in saturation diving where, compared with open-circuit systems, it uses less gas. This appreciably reduces both gas costs and the logistics problem of shipping and storage of large quantities of breathing gas. The pack can be used with a diving helmet, bandmask, or mouthpiece, to meet the specific needs of an operator. Two flexible hoses connect the pack to whichever of these is used. Where an umbilical emergency supply is used, it is connected directly to a manually operated valve on the diver's helmet or bandmask.

The gas exhaled by the diver passes through a scrubber to remove the carbon dioxide. It then passes into a counterlung past a galvanic sensor which gives an electrical output proportional to the partial pressure of the oxygen. This signal is fed into an electric controller which regulates the opening of a solenoid valve to admit oxygen into the gas, thereby maintaining the oxygen pressure at a predetermined level. Electrical power is supplied by a battery.

Valves operated by movement of the counterlung either admit diluting gas into the system or vent gas to equalize the internal and external pressures. A second sensor provides a continuous digital display of oxygen partial pressure on the diver's display unit. The pressure switches operate at a preset gauge pressure to give warning of low bottle pressure. An audible warning located in the pack operates to alert the diver and supervisor to the existence

Royal Navy submersible compression chamber for lowering divers onto the seabed for research work.

The necessary remedial action is relatively simple. If a diver has come up too quickly and the nitrogen in his tissues has formed bubbles, he can be put under pressure again, which will force the nitrogen back into solution. If the pressure is now gradually reduced at a rate which enables the body tissues to rid themselves of the nitrogen without bubble formation, the danger is eliminated.

There are two ways in which this gradual decompression can be achieved, the first method being to arrange that the diver makes his ascent in stages, with pauses for various periods of time at various depths. During the first decade of the 20th century, a scale of times and depths was worked out by Dr. J.B.S. Haldane. For example, if a diver has worked for 15 minutes at a depth of 20 fathoms (120 ft. or 36 m) he must pause during his ascent at 5, 3.5, and 1.5 fathoms and must take not less than 17 minutes over his ascent. If he has been working at this depth for more than 90 minutes, he must pause at 8.5, 6.5, 5, 3.5, and 1.5 fathoms and take at least 163 minutes over his ascent.

The second, and easier, method of decompression is to put the diver into a decompression chamber during his ascent. The chamber acts much as a diving bell when it is in the water and the diver enters it through a hatch in the bottom with the pressure inside the chamber equal to the pressure of water at that depth. When he is inside, the diver closes the hatch and the chamber is hoisted to the surface with the pressure inside maintained at its initial level. The diver remains in the chamber with the pressure in the chamber being gradually reduced to correspond with the ascent stages at which he should have paused on his way up.

The maximum depth at which the normal air mixture of oxygen and nitrogen can be used is about 45 fathoms (270 ft. or 82 m), but by using a mixture of oxygen and helium much greater depths can be reached. The lightness of this mixture makes breathing easier and it acts as a passive carrier for oxygen. Even with this mixture, the risk of decompression sickness remains. With an oxygen and helium mixture there is in theory no depth limit for deep diving, the only limit being the decompression time which, at great depths, is considerable. As an example, a diver who has worked for five minutes at a depth of 100 fathoms (600 ft. or 182 m) requires a decompression time of 5 hours and 38 minutes before the risk of decompression sickness is eliminated.

Saturation Diving

In recent years experimental projects have been carried out to examine the resources of the seabed and, of equal importance, the effects of a prolonged deep-sea environment on man. In 1968, for example, the U.S. Navy in its Sealab III project sent five 8-man teams down to a depth of 600 ft. (180 m), where they spent 12 days on the ocean floor. The aquanauts lived in a pressurized capsule and made daily excursions out onto the seabed of the continental shelf to carry out physiological testing, marine biology, geology studies, sonic work, and evaluation of thermal protection. The American Tektite and French Conshelf projects carried out similar experiments.

This type of prolonged diving is known as saturation diving; the diver is under pressure so long that his body tissues absorb their full capacity of inert gas and become saturated. Once this stage has been reached no more gas can be dissolved and additional time spent underwater

Decompression chamber to prevent decompression sickness.

The American underwater habitat, Tektite.

does not increase the time needed for decompression on surfacing. A saturated diver generally requires 24 hours of decompression for every 100 ft. (30 m) of depth at which he was saturated. One interesting aspect of saturation diving is that once divers have reached the full saturation point, they can make excursion dives to greater depths, almost as if they were making a dive from the surface.

To reach extreme depths of 1,000 ft. (300 m) or more, men must be protected from the pressure of the sea by strong-walled containers. Special capsules and submarine-like submersible vehicles such as the bathysphere, COUSTEAU's diving saucer, and the BATHYSCAPHE are employed. At such depths, the men remain within the pressurized submersible and therefore these deep diving systems are strictly speaking submarine operations.

Salvage

In addition to giving man the means of discovering more about the underwater world, diving, whether assisted, unassisted, free, or self-contained, is the prime means of salvage (and marine archeology). In its original meaning salvage entailed the rescue or saving of a ship in danger and also the proportion of the value of the ship or cargo allocated to the salvors for their work. But today it more often means the physical recovery of a sunken ship or her contents, or the underwater repair of damaged vessels or other marine engineering operations.

This has been achieved in many ways. One of the first methods was to send down watertight barrels to be packed into the ship's holds by divers, the operation to be completed when the barrels were in place by introducing air pressure until the ship's negative buoyancy was reversed and she rose to the surface. A similar idea was to use a device of rubberized canvas bags lashed to the sunken ship's side which could then be inflated by air pumped from the surface, again reversing the negative buoyancy. Another way to restore buoyancy, when conditions on board the sunken ship allow, is to use divers to patch any external hull damage and arrange compartmental inlets and outlets so that the water in whole compartments of the ship can be blown out by high-pressure air.

In general, however, most modern salvage is achieved by the use of pontoons or heavy hydraulic lifts, or by a combination of both. A pontoon, also known as a camel, is a watertight cylinder provided with inlet and escape valves for the admittance and ejection of water, and with hawsepipes through which cables can be passed for securing to sunken vessels. The camels are initially filled with water to give them negative buoyancy so that they can be easily positioned underwater. When they are in position above or alongside the wreck, the water is blown out to give them positive buoyancy. Camels can be used in two ways. In the first, lifting action is regulated by the tide.

A bathyscaphe, used for exploring the ocean depths.

Camels with a combined buoyancy superior to that of the deadweight of the ship are positioned over the wreck, to which cables are attached by divers, and the slack is drawn as tight as possible at low tide. As the tide rises, the camels lift the wreck from the bottom and the whole rig is then towed into shallower water until the ship grounds. The slack of the cables is again taken up at the next low tide, and the whole process is repeated until the ship is sufficiently high and dry at low tide for repairs to be made.

If there is insufficient rise and fall of tide for this method of salvage, an alternative method is adopted. The camels are either sunk and attached to the sides of the wreck, or the ship is held in a cradle of cables passed under her hull by divers and slung between half-submerged camels. The water held in the camels is then expelled by air pumps in the salvage vessels, and the wreck is raised from the seabed to be towed away. A more manageable way for salvors to see what they are doing is to use lifting lighters instead of camels. These lighters, with their tanks full of water, are attached to the sunken wreck by divers and when the tanks are pumped out at low tide they lift the wreck, having the advantage of a double lift as the tide rises to high. A more modern and controllable way of lifting, when extreme care is required owing to the age or frailty of the wreck, is to draw up the cradle under the wreck by hydraulic power and take the wreck in, either in suspension or supported by a buoyant platform.

Modern Soviet salvage ships of improved design specifically intended for submarine rescue are provided with a specially high stern which extends out over the water for rescue maneuvers with a 600-ton lift. Of some 5,000 tons full-load displacement, with a length of over 410 ft. (125 m) and a wide beam of 53 ft. (16 m), they are equipped with several other lifting points and also have rescue bells and observation chambers. The world's first ships designed specifically for submarine rescue, the new U.S. salvage ships with a displacement of 3,500 tons full load have twin catamaran hulls each 251 ft. (76.5 m) long and 26 ft. (8 m) wide. As the well between is 34 ft. (10 m) across, they have an overall beam of 86 ft. (26 m). They are equipped with a deep diving system to support con-

Salvage pontoon for lifting sunken or capsized ships.

ventional or saturation divers operating at depths of up to 142 fathoms (850 ft. or 259 m). The system comprises two decompression chambers, two personal transfer capsules to transport divers between the ship and ocean floor, and associated controls, winches, cables, and gas supplies and fittings for helium-oxygen diving.

Marine Archeology

Marine archeology is a relatively new science which owes its existence to improved diving techniques. Ancient ship objects and cargoes can tell us a great deal about the past and its material culture. The oceans conceal, but they also preserve. The great growth in recent years of free or self-contained diving has resulted in a great volume of archeological treasure recovered from sunken ships or from the seabed. They range from the small artefacts picked up during casual dives to whole ships of a distant age. A Carthaginian trireme sunk off Marsala during the first Punic war of the 3rd century BC is one of the major marine archeological treasures laid bare by divers and carefully brought ashore, bit by bit, for permanent preservation. A more recent example, representing a major salvage operation, is the bringing back to her original home port of Bristol, England, of the steamer GREAT BRITAIN, the greatest ship in the world when she was built in 1843, and in 1970 towed for more than 7,600 miles (12,200 km) on a salvage pontoon to reach her final destination.

Among the most remarkable diving and salvage operations in the field of marine archeology in recent years is the discovery and raising of the 17th-century Swedish warship VASA. She was built in the naval dockyard at Stockholm and overturned and sank at the start of her maiden voyage in 1628. She was a galleon of 1,300 tons, six decks, and carried 64 guns. Attempts to raise her during the 17th century were not successful, and over the intervening years all traces of her were lost. Relocated in 1956, she was successfully salvaged in 1961. The *Vasa* had sunk into the mud up to the level of her original waterline, but instead of being destroyed above that level, as would normally have been the case, she had survived not only intact to her upper deck but still strong enough to be raised whole, pumped out, and then floated into a modern dock specifically prepared to receive her. All the usual complications of undersea excavation were thus obviated, although the mud trough from which she was lifted had to be searched for carvings and other fittings which had come adrift from the hull. Some 16,000 artefacts, including 700 wooden sculptures and several of the skeleton corpses complete with hats, purses, and shoes, were recovered from the ship, which is now preserved at the Vasa Museum in Stockholm, the only surviving example of the complete hull of a 17th-century fighting ship.

An even older warship which is in the process of being recovered from the sea is the English *Mary Rose*, a 'high-charged' ship of 700 tons which sank off Portsmouth in 1545 while leaving harbor to engage the French fleet. But, unlike the *Vasa*, the *Mary Rose* will not render up a complete hull. She lies heeled on her starboard side and the upper (port) side has been eroded away to well below the waterline. Three-quarters of the hull lies preserved in the mud and sections of three decks are still intact in the waist of the ship. So, when she comes up and is put on display, she will present something like a cutaway drawing showing the construction, weapons, stowage and naval methods in the days of Henry VIII.

The Sea as a World Resource

The world's oceans and seas cover more than seven-tenths of the earth's surface. Although mankind is terrestrial, the oceans have played an enormous role in human history — originally as a source of food, then as a medium for transportation (allowing trade and communication between peoples, migration, discovery, and of course conquest), and more recently as a source of valuable mineral resources. Without the oceans' rich resources of food, much of the world's population would face starvation. Without the sea as a means of travel and communication, world trade on today's scale, with all its significance for human welfare and living standards, would be impossible. Without the resources of oil and natural gas lying under the seabed, the energy crisis of the late 20th century would have assumed even greater proportions. Yet despite the sea's inestimable value to man, its complex ecological balance is threatened by man-made pollution.

Until about the middle of the 19th century, when serious study of the oceans became an accepted science, man's exploitation of the sea's riches was largely haphazard. Today, research continues on an unprecedented scale into means of extending that exploitation.

Fishing

No one can know when the taking of fish from the sea for food was first begun, but it must have been at around the time man first ventured out to sea in his crude craft. And sea-fishing must have developed quite quickly into a recognized way of life in those early days, for the bones of deep-sea fish have been found during an archeological excavation of a stone-age site near Stavanger in Norway. This argues that there was organized fishing in the Atlantic Ocean long before Peter, the fisherman of Galilee, arrived in Rome and the outline of a fish became the symbol of Christianity. Whether these deep-sea fish were caught by line fishing with bone hooks or by some sort of net or basket towed along the floor of the ocean has not yet been discovered.

Early Fishing Methods

The use of nets for taking fish certainly dates back a great many centuries. The gospels give us a vivid picture of the method of casting nets nearly two thousand years ago. We know that in the early days of the Hanseatic League, during the 13th century, a fishing port in Holland was noted for making nets longer than those used by any other fishermen. They were almost certainly seine nets, since the fish to be caught in those waters were pelagic, mainly herring, about to make their huge migration from the Baltic to the North Sea. Until the development of the trawl net, bottom-lying fish such as cod or halibut were normally caught by line. The usual method employed so-called trawl lines — long lines, buoyed at each end, with shorter lines carried at intervals of about 4 ft. (1.2 m)

along their length, each with a baited hook. This was the method used by the schooners from the Massachusetts ports fishing for cod on the Grand Banks off Newfoundland in the 17th century. It was soon adopted by fishermen in the other great cod fisheries. Lobsters and crabs were caught in pots made of osier, almost identical to those used today.

The success of sea and ocean fishing in those early days depended almost entirely on local knowledge of the best fishing areas. John CABOT, during his return to England in 1497 from the voyage in which he discovered Newfoundland, sailed across what we now know as the Grand Banks and he records that his crew caught huge quantities of cod merely by lowering baskets into the sea and hauling them up on board.

Surface fish, such as herring, pilchard, and mackerel, which gathered together for their annual spawning in vast shoals in well-defined areas, provided a rich harvest for seine and ring netters. So huge were the shoals that there was no danger of overfishing and consequent depletion of stocks in those days, when fishing methods were relatively unsophisticated and demand was still modest. Not for centuries was the fierce competition caused by today's factory fishing methods to arise.

Influence of Oceanography on Fishing

It was the American naval officer, Matthew Fontaine MAURY, who began to open the eyes of the world to the new science of oceanography. In its widest sense it embraces every aspect of the world's oceans — flora and fauna, prevailing winds and currents, the nature of the ocean bottom, the breeding habits and migrations of mammals and fish, and the depth, salinity, density, and average temperature of water. Knowledge of the oceans and their natural inhabitants is built up from the vast accumulation of information collected from ship's logs and the observations of research vessels. Maury's plans and methods were accepted by international congresses in 1853 and 1873. The actual start of oceanography as a precise science is generally held to be the voyage of the *Challenger* in 1872-76, made at the instigation of the Royal Society in London. Following the work of Maury and the *Challenger*, the International Council for the Study of the Sea, sponsored by Norway, Sweden, Denmark, Great Britain, Finland, Russia, Holland, Belgium, and Germany was set up in 1901 with its headquarters in Copenhagen and a central laboratory in Oslo. Its initial objective was a study of the North Sea fisheries, but this limited goal was quickly overtaken by the need to study the natural phenomena of all the world's oceans.

This birth of world interest in oceanography coincided approximately with the 19th-century leap into industrial expansion, which was accompanied by a constant population explosion. Fish was a cheap food and still plentiful in the seas and oceans, and fishing therefore grew into big business. For the remainder of the 19th century there was no form of international regulation of fishing; the seas remained free for all to take as much fish as they could catch by whatever means they wished. By the beginning of the 20th century, as a result of this lack of control, some areas were becoming fished out, partly because of the growing demands of a hungry world, partly because of the development of more efficient fishing vessels and fishing gear, and partly because the oceanographers were now able to indicate the most prolific breeding grounds of fish and the likely directions of their subsequent migrations. The importance of national fishing industries as a source of food and the danger of allowing completely unregulated fishing to continue were recognized early in the 20th century, and at international conventions nations agreed to preserve the supply of fish by such measures as national quotas in certain types of fish, closed seasons during breeding, and minimum sizes of mesh so that immature fish caught in nets could escape and live to breed.

Trawling: Deep-water Fishing

The trawl was developed during the 19th-century expansion of fishing as a faster and more efficient means of catching bottom-lying fish than the trawl lines with their rows of baited hooks. It originated in about mid-century in the Scottish fishing port of Aberdeen in the form of the beam trawl. All trawls are flattened conical nets, open at the wide end and closed at the narrow; in the beam trawl, the mouth of the net is held open with a heavy wooden beam mounted on metal runners so that it can slide along the seabed. Beam trawls were generally associated with sailing trawlers and the smaller sort of fishing vessels such as SMACKS; the more powerful steam trawlers which began to come into use in the 1890s coincided with the invention of the otter trawl, which has no heavy beam, the mouth of the net being held open by otter boards, or 'doors' in fishing language. This is achieved by the pressure of the water acting on the flat surfaces of the otter boards as the trawl is towed, forcing them outwards to stretch the

mouth of the net. Not being limited by the length of a beam, and being towed by the greater power of a steam trawler, an otter trawl could be made much larger than a beam trawl and consequently could catch more fish. It was also a more efficient trawl: the upper lip of the opening, known as the headline, is forced up into an arch by the pressure of the water, giving the trawl a wide opening to catch the fish swimming near the bottom as well as the bottom fish themselves. The height of this arch can be as much as 15 ft. (4.5 m) above the seabed, with the distance between the otter boards, one at each end of the mouth of the trawl, being about 60 ft. (18 m), giving a much wider mouth than is possible with a beam trawl.

Until the development of the stern trawler, the trawl was hauled in over the side of the ship in order to keep the net away from the propeller. This meant that the trawl had to be hoisted and the fish emptied into the trawler's fishwells before another trawl could be shot. In the modern stern trawler, the trawl is hauled in up the stern (in much the same way as a whale is hauled up a stern ramp onto the flensing deck of a whale factory ship), and a second trawl can be shot while the first is being brought on board. Modern long-distance trawlers are built to a tonnage of about 2,500-3,000, as compared with 400-500 tons at the start of the century, and the diesel engine has taken the place of the steam engine. Most of them carry their own refrigerating plant to preserve the catches so that they can remain on the fishing grounds for long periods. By altering the length of the towing warps, it is possible to tow a trawl at intermediate depths to catch fish which may be swimming well above the bottom. To determine the actual location of fish and the depth at which they are swimming, all trawlers today are fitted with sonar gear.

A more modern development which has been introduced in Soviet trawlers is somewhat akin to a vacuum scoop; the seawater from the bottom and all its contents is sucked up on board and discharged over grids which retain the fish while the water returns to the sea. This method is condemned by most conservationists since it

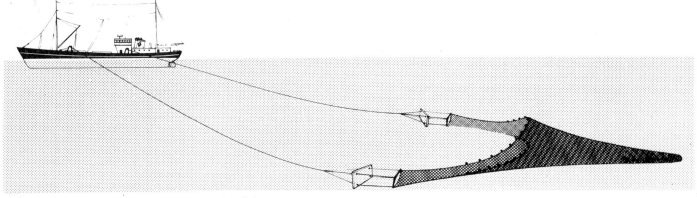

Otter trawl, used for catching bottom-lying fish.

Modern Soviet trawler.

virtually sweeps whole areas clean of fish, removing in a single operation the fish of all species, immature as well as fully grown.

Surface Fishing

One method of catching surface fish today is by using drift nets, which consist of a long line of netting (sometimes nearly a mile long), with its top edge buoyed with cork or plastic spheres so that it remains on the surface. The nets are laid across the expected path of advance of pelagic fish and hang vertically downwards to a depth of around 30 ft. (9 m), the fishing vessel (known as a drifter) securing herself to them at the leeward end of the line. Fish attempt to swim through the mesh and are caught by their gills. The nets are known as drift nets, and the craft involved as drifters, because unlike trawls they involve no towing and merely drift with the current. As the long line of nets is hauled on board, the fish are shaken out into the drifter's fishwell, gutted, and stowed in ice.

Another method of catching surface fish is by means of ring netting. A shoal of fish is located, either by the diving of sea birds or by the fish themselves leaping out of the water. Sometimes an experienced skipper can find a shoal by the smell of the sea, particularly mackerel. A net with a draw rope through the bottom edge is laid around the shoal and gradually drawn tight, compressing the fish into a dense mass. The draw rope is then hauled in, closing the

Drift nets and fishing boats at Peterhead Harbor in Scotland.

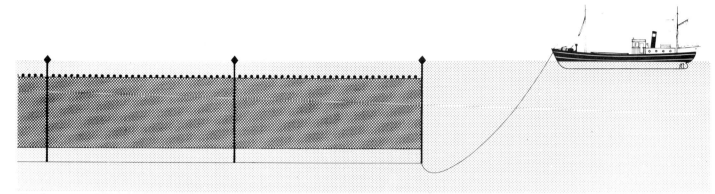

Drift net, used for catching surface fish.

net beneath the fish and preventing any from escaping below the ring. In many areas, particularly in the Mediterranean, ring netting is carried out at night: the fish are attracted together by electric arc lights mounted in small boats which, when they have collected a following of fish, converge on their parent vessel drawing the fish in with them. The ring net is passed around the fish, the bottom closed by the draw rope, and the catch brought on board.

International Fishing Limits

For many centuries a generally accepted law of fishery held that the catching of fish within the territorial waters of a nation was reserved to the citizens of that nation, but that on the high seas outside territorial waters a common right to catch fish existed for people of any nation. There were some agreed exceptions, particularly in the case of oyster fisheries and the taking of lobsters, crabs, mussels, and cockles, where fishing rights were reserved exclusively for certain individuals. On occasions this general law was modified by agreement between nations with regard to certain areas, or by custom in cases of ancient right of fishery. Restrictions were also imposed in some areas on the taking of certain types of fish, and on fishing or hunting in the breeding season of whales, seals, etc.

In recent years, however, the validity of this traditional law of fishery has been brought into question, partly by the lack of international agreement on the limits of territorial waters (the old territorial limit of 3 miles (4.8 km) has been abrogated by most maritime nations, though without any new internationally agreed limit) and partly

British frigate and minesweeper with Bulgarian trawler Flamingo, *which they arrested for breaching fishing regulations.*

by national declarations of reserved fishing waters, in some cases to a distance of 200 miles (322 km) from the coastline. In Europe there is a generally accepted 12-mile (19-km) limit of territorial waters, reached by the European Fishery Limits Convention of 1964 and based on a consensus which emerged from the United Nations Law of the Sea Conference of a year or two earlier, but it has not yet been fully accepted as a part of international law. The United States has traditionally had a 3-mile (4.8-km) territorial water limit, but in recent years large-scale factory fishing by ships from the Soviet Union and some European nations has led to increased demands for a much wider restricted zone.

The desire of a nation to extend and safeguard its territorial waters is based on a realization that the sea as a source of food may diminish. There are already ominous signs of decreased fish stocks, resulting from improvements in fishing technology, particularly in oceanographic research into the movements and habits of fish, the development of sonar to pinpoint the location of fish, the advent of the stern trawler, which provides virtually continuous operation of a trawl on the fishing grounds, and the building of large trawlers of up to about 3,000 tons equipped with refrigerating machinery to preserve the catch so that they may remain operational for longer periods. These developments have hugely increased catches of fish to the extent that large areas of sea are in danger of being fished out. As yet, no solution to this problem has been agreed.

Whaling

Whale catching was certainly practiced in neolithic times, although at that time it probably involved no more than driving shoals of the smaller cetaceans, such as dolphins and porpoises, into confined waters and slaughtering them. This method is still used in some parts of the world — for example, in Newfoundland, the Faeroe Islands, the Azores, and the Solomon Islands. It is known that Basque fishermen hunted the larger species of cetaceans in European waters as early as the 10th century, their chief prey being the Atlantic right whale (*Balaena glasialis*). The whales were normally caught from small boats with a harping iron, towed to the shore, and cut up; the animal's tongue was apparently a much-prized delicacy. By the 16th century these Basque whalers established another whaling field off the Newfoundland Banks, in time to replace the Bay of Biscay field when it began to decline in the 17th century.

The discovery of Spitsbergen by William BARENTS in 1596, and his report of a multitude of whales in its waters, brought the Basque fishermen north to open an Arctic whaling field. The English Muscovy Company, engaging Basque harpooners to teach the English their art, fitted out the first English whaling voyage in 1610, and by virtue of its Letters Patent giving it a monopoly of trade with Russia, claimed exclusive rights to this new whaling field. It was challenged by various other whaling interests, particularly Dutch, Danish, and Biscayan, and when the civil war broke out in England the Dutch established themselves as the main exploiters of this Arctic field. The whalers used during this period were ships of about 200 tons, which was fairly large for those days, manned by a crew of about 50 men. The whales were chased in small boats known as pinnaces or shallops, harpooned with a harping iron, and then lanced in the underbelly to weaken them through loss of blood. The captured whale was towed to the mother ship, laid across the stern, and the blubber peeled off with a hook operated by a crane or capstan. This was then taken ashore and boiled, or 'tryed out,' in large vats. Each nation engaged in whaling had its own harbor in Spitsbergen where the oil was tryed out and spare whaling gear kept. The Dutch whaling port, widely known as 'Blubbertown,' was the village of Smeerenburg and was the center for over 1,000 Dutch whalers. By 1663 it had become so rich through its whaling industry that it boasted several shops, a church, and a bakehouse.

The Spitsbergen field began to decline through overfishing early in the 18th century, but a search of Arctic waters in the area of the Davis Strait discovered large numbers of whales in the neighborhood of Disko Island. German and Dutch whalers were the first to establish themselves there, but by the middle of the century British whalers were there in force with many seaports, particularly London, Hull, and Whitby, regularly sending out whaling expeditions. These British expeditions were en-

16th-century engraving of North American Indians whaling.

The Hull whaleship William Lee *in the Arctic, c. 1831.*

Illustration of 1814 depicting whalebone scrapers at work.

couraged by bounties paid to the skippers of whalers who agreed to sign on five supernumerary hands, known as 'green men,' for each voyage, the main purpose being to build up a pool of men with experience of the hardships of an Arctic voyage for future explorations in the area.

While this new Arctic whaling field was being exploited by European whalers, the British colonies in North America were developing their own field, which in 1712 became known as the Southern Whale Fishery. The prey here was the sperm whale, or Cachalot (*Physeter catodon*), whose oil was considered much superior to that of right whales. By the mid-18th century this Southern Fishery had extended southwards as far as the coast of Brazil, and in spite of occasional interruptions caused by the American War of Independence (1775-83) and the Napoleonic Wars (1793-1815), continued to push south-wards and westwards until by 1820 American whalers had penetrated to all parts of the Pacific and Indian Oceans. By 1840 they had sailed through the Bering Strait into the Arctic Ocean, west of northern Canada, where a large colony of right whales was discovered. The rich whaling in this area was brought to an end by a major di-saster in 1871, when almost the entire fleet of American whalers in the North Pacific was caught in the Arctic ice and crushed. Japan, too, had been a major whaling coun-try in the Pacific from very early days.

All this killing of whales around the world was carried out by harpoons launched by hand from small boats, and the basic limitations of this crude weapon ensured that the species were not endangered by overkilling. But the devel-opment of the harpoon gun by the Norwegian Sven Foyn during the 1860s, and the introduction of steam-powered whaling ships during the 1890s, increased the rate of kill-ing by a considerable factor, and the demand for whale

products engendered by World War I led to such an onslaught that whale stocks began to decline. Whaling intensified during the interwar years, particularly with the introduction during the 1920s of whale factory ships and their attendant fleets of small whalecatchers which could operate over large areas of ocean. These factory ships, act-ing independently of shore bases which could have kept a check on the number of whales killed, concentrated mainly in the Antarctic and made huge inroads into the whale population in those waters.

It became evident during the 1930s that some restric-tion on the killing of whales was necessary if the whale was to survive, and in 1937 an international agreement set limits to the duration of the whaling season and also agreed minimum sizes below which whales were not to be killed. When these restrictions proved insufficient to pre-serve whale stocks from still further decline, the Inter-national Whaling Commission was set up in 1947 to give scientific advice to the whaling industry and to attempt to regulate fishing on a world basis. The attempts to control the catching of whales have met with little success, and the blue whale (*Balaenoptera musculus*), the largest and commercially most valuable whale, has been hunted almost to extinction. The smaller fin and sei whales are also sadly in decline. More recently, quotas for whale kill-ing have been agreed, though the numbers for each species are still thought by conservationists to be too large, and the killing of fin and sei whales has been prohibited except in one or two specified areas. The International Whaling Commission, however, is mainly an advisory body and its recommendations, while influential, do not have the force of international law. For this reason it cannot effectively safeguard the whale's survival.

In recent years demands for the protection of whales

have been given extra weight by a strong awakening of public concern for the fate of these animals, and a more promising line of attack against the extinction of the whale population than the international quotas is perhaps to be found in national bans on imports of whale products. The main use of whalemeat, for example, is in the production of pet foods, and both Britain and the United States have banned its import for this purpose, with some other nations agreeing to follow their lead. The success of these controls could perhaps put enough economic pressure on the whaling industry to curtail killing sufficiently to ensure the survival of all types of cetaceans.

Today the Antarctic whaling ground, which only four or five decades ago supplied more than three-quarters of the world's catch of whales, is in decline, and only two countries, Japan and the Soviet Union, now send annual whaling expeditions into these southern waters. The major whaling field has now moved to the North Pacific, where the United States, the Soviet Union, and Japan share the quota of permissible killings. There is a small local field in Icelandic waters which the fishermen of that island reserve to themselves, and no doubt the occasional whale is still killed or driven into shallow waters for slaughter by small island communities who have practiced this method of whale catching for centuries.

Sealing

Like the whaling industry, with which it once had close links, sealing has been an activity of man from the earliest days. Seals were killed for their blubber, meat, and skins, and some peoples, such as the Eskimos, still depend largely on seals for their food, clothing, and fuel. The seals of major commercial importance belong to the three families of the suborder *Pinnipedia*: the eared seal (*Otariidae*), the walrus (*Odobaenidae*), and the earless seal (*Phocidae*). Walrus are found only in the Arctic, but the other two families are widely distributed in the world's oceans, and are sometimes found even in inland waters.

Sealing in the North Atlantic is based on two species of seal, the harp or Greenland seal (*Phoca groenlandica*) which breeds in spring in the pack ice of the White Sea, the waters around Jan Mayen Island, and the Newfoundland coast, and the hood seal (*Cystophora cristata*), which is found off the eastern coast of Greenland, the Davis Strait, and in Newfoundland waters. The main harp sealing grounds were developed during the 18th century when whaling off Greenland became unprofitable, the Norwegians taking the biggest share. Hood seals were first taken by shore parties advancing upon them over the ice off the Newfoundland coast. In the early 19th century it was the custom of Scottish whalers to hunt seal off Newfoundland before proceeding north to the main Arctic whaling grounds. Today, the nations which hunt the North Atlantic seals are Canada, Norway, Denmark on behalf of

Catcher delivering sperm whales to slipway.

Greenland, and the Soviet Union. The control of seal hunting in the Atlantic is in the hands of the International Commission for the Northwest Atlantic Fisheries.

The commercially attractive seals in the North Pacific are those belonging to the family of eared seals, particularly the northern fur seals of the *Callorhinas* species. They are valuable because, unlike the earless seals, they have a permanent undercoat of short, soft fur which is much sought after by furriers and dressmakers. Their main breeding areas are the Pribilof Islands and Komandorskie

Walrus hunting in the Indies in the 16th century.

Islands in the Bering Sea and the Kurile Islands in the Sea of Okhotsk. This ground was discovered by Vitus Bering during his voyage of exploration in those waters in 1741, and his reports of huge colonies of seals attracted a host of seal hunters and resulted in so huge a slaughter, both on the seals' breeding grounds and during their migrations at sea, that the colonies were approaching annihilation by the end of the 19th century. To prevent this disaster an international convention was held in Washington in 1911, attended by Britain, Japan, Russia, and the United States, which resulted in an agreement regulating hunting. So stringent was this agreement that the northern fur seal has become commercially the most valuable seal in the world because so few are allowed to be taken annually.

Sealing in the southern hemisphere began when American sealers, pushing southwards in their search for commercially worthwhile colonies, reached the Falkland Islands and rounded Cape Horn into the south Pacific during the 18th century. British sealers joined them in the search a few years later. Fishing, if that is the correct word, was centered mainly on the fur seals of the *Aretocephalus* species and the elephant seals of the *Mirounga* species, the former for their skins of fur, the latter for their oil. James COOK's discovery in 1775 of South Georgia, with its immense colonies of fur seals, unleashed a rush of sealers into the southern Atlantic with results as savage as those which had followed the earlier North Pacific discoveries of Vitus Bering. The virtual extinction of the South Georgia colonies within a few years forced the sealers to explore still further southwards, and in 1819 William Smith, a British sealing captain, discovered the South Shetland Islands, which had even richer colonies than those of South Georgia. Once again this new discovery started a rush of sealers to the area, mainly from Argentina, Britain, and the United States, and only ten years later, in 1829, it was reported that not a single fur seal remained alive in the South Shetlands. The same sad fate attended the other colonies of fur seals in the southern Pacific and Indian Oceans. With the virtual extinction of the fur seal trade in southern waters, the sealers turned to the elephant seals, killing so many for their oil that by 1870 even that trade had become completely unprofitable because of the lack of numbers.

Gradually, as a result of a long period of rigid protection by intergovernmental agreement, the stocks of both fur seals and elephant seals in these southern waters are recovering. As yet the growth in numbers has not yet reached such commercially attractive proportions as to rival the North Pacific sealing grounds, but if the present tight protection continues this may well occur within a few years. When this happens, however, it is probable that international control of national quotas will succeed in protecting the seal population against such holocausts as happened in the past.

Unlike whales, seals feed on fish, and there is always a conflict between sea fishermen, whose livelihood depends on their catches of fish, and those who wish to see seal colonies increase through natural and unhindered breeding. A fully grown seal will catch and eat daily a considerable quantity of fish, and it has been calculated that in coastal waters where seal colonies are active they may eat four times as much fish as are caught by modern fishing methods. This has led to policies of annual culling of seal pups designed, in the interests of local fisheries, to maintain local seal populations but not to allow an increase in numbers to a point where the fish stocks are threatened. These policies, however, are being challenged by a growing number of conservationists who object to the killing of seal pups on humanitarian as well as ecological grounds. It is perhaps unfortunate for the pups of harp seals that, within hours of their birth, they produce a downy skin much prized for its soft, cream-colored fur, which changes color and is lost after a few days of life. It is perhaps this commercial aspect of the culling, entailing the killing of pups so soon after birth, which arouses so much repugnance among so many people. It has been estimated that as many as 150,000 harp seal pups are culled annually, most of them by clubbing to death on the ice off the Newfoundland and Greenland coasts and in the Davis Strait. Attempts to bring this annual cull to an end on humanitarian grounds by banning of imports of harp seal products have been supported by the United States, France, and Italy, and other nations are being pressed to follow suit. The fur of the pups is used in dressmaking and in the manufacture of trinkets such as paperweights and car keyrings, while the oil of the seals is used for making chocolate and margarine.

The Search for Oil

The wealth of the world's oceans does not reside exclusively in the fish and mammals which inhabit them. Marine flora, in the form of seaweed, is a valuable agricultural fertilizer and is also used in the manufacture of washing powders and detergents. But in recent years man's greatest interest has been in the seabed and what lies beneath it, particularly fossil fuels, where there is an obvious limit to shore-based reserves. Increasing world demand for energy has made exploitation of oilfields which lie beneath the sea a project of major importance, and technology has developed ways of overcoming most of the technical difficulties of extracting this increasingly valuable fuel from considerable depths.

Potential oil-bearing rock formations below the seabed are discovered in the normal way by seismic survey; trial boreholes to test for the presence of oil are then drilled through the rock by floating exploration rigs held firmly in position with heavy cables and anchors. The maximum depth of water in which drilling for oil is at present car-

Semi-submersible pipe-laying barge, Semac 1, *433 ft. (132 m) long and operational even in heavy weather conditions.*

ried out varies according to local sea conditions, up to about 1,000 ft. (300 m) in normally calm waters such as the Persian Gulf and about 650 ft. (200 m) in more hostile areas such as the North Sea. These depths are imposed by the limitations of the fixed production platforms which need to be erected above the underwater oilfields before extraction can be begun. The maximum depth of water in which drilling is possible does not limit the depth to which drills can be driven through the rock below the seabed, and many oil wells at sea are drilled to a depth of 15,000 ft. (4,570 m) or more before the oil deposit is finally reached.

Once the presence of oil in commercial quantities is confirmed by exploratory drills, a fixed production platform is anchored above the site of the field. This is a very large structure, made of steel or concrete, standing up to 700 ft. (215 m) or more in height, with 400 ft. (120 m) or so of it under water in the shape of giant legs anchoring the platform in position. The great positional accuracy required to anchor the platform exactly over the field is normally achieved by means of a navigational fix from orbiting satellites, the most accurate form of navigational measurement yet evolved. The main purpose of the production platform is to drill the actual production wells needed to exploit the field, perhaps as many as 40 of them, some traveling vertically downwards, others curving away from the platform, some to bring up the oil, others to send down water and gas to lighten the oil, pressure the reservoir, and get the whole operation flowing.

The extraction of oil from fields beneath the seabed is a nonstop business, for once the oil starts to flow the immense amount of capital invested in the venture necessitates continuous production if the cost is to be justified. So the production platform has to become something resembling a small town, with the drilling crews, engineers, and the rest of the workforce living on the platform during the tour of duty, which is usually about 28 days on duty followed by 28 days off ashore; helicopters are used as ferries to bring relief crews out to the platform and take crews off duty back to the shore. Production platforms fulfill their own energy requirements, using the gas which every oilfield produces in quantity.

There are two ways in which the oil can be transported once it reaches the production platform from the wells. In the case of major fields, or of several small fields concentrated in a reasonably small area, it is pumped through a system of steel pipes laid on the seabed from the platform to an oil terminal ashore. The lengths of pipe are welded together by divers as they are laid. The other method is to pump the oil to a terminal buoy where it is loaded into tankers which take it to the refinery.

A new development in this offshore search for oil is the tethered platform system to replace the hugely expensive fixed platform, with its limitations on the depth of water in which drilling can take place. It has been claimed that, using a buoyant platform anchored to the seabed with steel tubes or wire tethers, the maximum drilling depths can be trebled, even in hostile sea areas where storms and high winds make conditions difficult. One advantage of this development is that it can be installed and maintained without divers; another is that the deeper the water, the more economic it becomes in comparison with a fixed platform because it is quicker to construct and install and so produces a faster return on the initial investment; and a third advantage is that the cost of construction, consider-

ably less than that of a fixed platform, will allow the commercial exploitation of much smaller oilfields.

Other Sources of Energy

Natural gas is also found in vast quantities in fields under the seabed and is exploited in much the same way as oil. The wells are drilled in the same way and the gas taken to terminals ashore through similar networks of pipes laid on the seabed from field to terminal.

All fossil fuels are finite, and sooner or later the earth's reserves of all of them will become exhausted, including those under the seabed. At present, however, there are still large areas of relatively shallow waters which remain to be explored for possible oil deposits, and no doubt there will be new discoveries which an energy-hungry world will require to be exploited. Yet even allowing for these possible new discoveries, the present rate of world consumption is such that eventual exhaustion of the oil reserves is inevitable.

Oil and gas, however, are not the only sources of energy provided by the sea. All forms of natural movement can be converted into usable energy, and the sea is in perpetual motion. The regular, worldwide rise and fall of the tide can be translated into energy, particularly when a barrage is used to accentuate the speed of the movement. Wave motion is another form of sea movement which can be harnessed to generate energy. Several studies into these possible energy sources are in progress, and although as yet they are largely uneconomic in terms of capital investment and energy production, a growth in the world demand for energy may combine with a scarcity of traditional energy resources to make them commercially viable at some future date.

The 250,000-ton tanker Esso Demetia at an oil terminal.

Oil production platform in the North Sea.

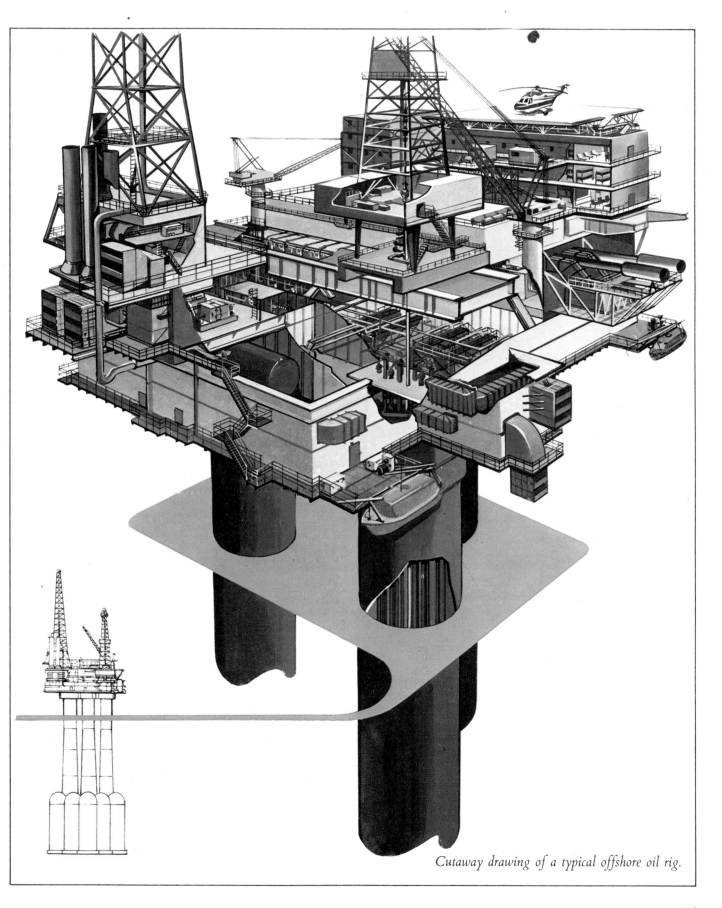

Cutaway drawing of a typical offshore oil rig.

Mineral Resources

The sea has other mineral riches as well as oil, some held in solution in seawater and others on and under the seabed. Manganese, which in certain areas lies on the seabed in the form of small nodules, is one of the most important. As with the conversion of tidal and wave movements into energy, exploitation of these minerals is still largely uneconomic, and there is an added difficulty in the lack of any international agreement on the ownership of these resources, which lie largely in waters beyond the continental shelves of the maritime nations. In a perfect world such mineral wealth as resides in the oceans would be shared between all nations, whether maritime or not and irrespective of technical know-how, but unhappily the world today does not work in this way. National rivalries are still strong enough to prevent unilateral exploitation in international waters. Because of the economic difficulties, the question of possible mining and seabed exploitation is at the present time somewhat academic; there is still a great amount of oceanographical research to be done on the seabed before we can be certain that worthwhile exploitation is possible.

Pollution of the Seas

A matter of far greater long-term importance than the extraction of oil and gas from below the seabed, the problematical exploitation of other mineral deposits, or even the conversion of sea movement into energy, is the growing menace of sea pollution. Even a small upset in the ecological balance of marine life, whether of microorganisms, weed, fish, or mammals, can have far-reaching consequences for future generations. The combination of world population growth and industrial growth compounds the risk of serious pollution, whether through untreated sewage, oil spillage, industrial waste, or even the greater use of the sea to serve the needs of an expanding humanity. All these sources of pollution can affect one or more of the living elements of the sea and thus put others at risk by upsetting the delicate and complex balance which maintains them all.

Sewage and Industrial Waste

There has, of course, always been pollution of the sea through untreated human sewage, but until relatively recently the sea was always able to accept the flow of sewage and break it down without any harm. Today's problem results from the great population growth of the last three or four decades, with the concomitant increase in sewage. Most of the industrially developed countries have installed, or are installing, treatment plants to process sewage before it is discharged into the sea, but many other countries bordering the sea are unable to afford the expense of prior treatment and still discharge raw sewage at a rate greater than the sea can accommodate. The area most at risk from this source of pollution is probably the Mediterranean, which has large populations along its shores and no appreciable tides to disperse the sewage.

Sewage, however, is perhaps the least of the pollution menaces which threaten the seas; more dangerous is industrial waste, much of which is extremely toxic. Regulations controlling the discharge of such waste have been established only comparatively recently, and these are issued only on a national, and not an international, scale. A large amount of industrial development is, naturally enough, concentrated in and around the major ports of the world, which become particularly vulnerable to uncontrolled waste disposal. Where waste is poisonous, the effect on sea life, particularly fish life in all its forms, is devastating. The effects can also spread to humans, as, for example, in the notorious outbreak of mercury poisoning at Minamata Bay, Japan, where hundreds of people died or suffered irreversible brain damage between 1953 and 1958 as a result of eating fish which had absorbed a mercury compound from industrial effluent in the sea.

Equally menacing are marine accidents involving ships loaded with dangerous chemicals; one such ship sank recently after a collision in the southern Adriatic and lay on the bottom with her cargo of lethal chemicals carried in thin steel drums for more than three years before the danger was fully appreciated and the drums recovered from her holds by divers. But for every ship with such a cargo which sinks in waters shallow enough for divers to reach her, there are others lying at a depth below the diving limit. Sooner or later the steel of the drums must rust away and release the contents. Another source of pollution, though one that is not confined to the sea, has arisen from the invention and use of nonbiodegradable plastics. These materials, which do not decay and rot in the natural way, are so widely used as packaging materials that significant amounts find their way into coastal waters, not necessarily contaminating them but sometimes strangling the natural growth of weed and occasionally of fish.

Oil Pollution

Moving up the pollution scale, one of the biggest problems today stems from the carriage of oil across the seas in tankers and the production of oil from fields below the seabed. Huge quantities of oil are transported by sea and by submarine pipeline. Oil kills seaweed, fish (particularly shellfish), and seabirds; a big spill can do an immense amount of damage over a large area for a very long time. Notorious disasters were caused by the tanker TORREY CANYON, which in 1967 ran aground on rocks off the Scilly Islands and leaked 90,000 tons of oil which the tide carried to the southern coast of England; the *Amoco Cadiz*, which in 1978 broke in two after drifting ashore and spilled 200,000 tons of oil along the Brittany coast; and the *Eleni V*, which was involved in a collision in the

North Sea, also in 1978, and lost her cargo of heavy crude oil before she was towed away and sunk. These are the most dramatic of many similar incidents involving oil tankers, but the ecological havoc they caused provides a grim reminder of the extent of sea pollution which a single accident to a large oil tanker can produce. It is not the damage to coastline and beaches which such spillages can create, spectacular as that always is, that provides most cause for alarm. This sort of damage is relatively short-term and can often be cleaned up mechanically. The main damage is at sea and, even when the oil is treated chemically so that it sinks to the bottom, it produces a long-term hazard to all forms of sea life, often requiring years to dissipate its effects fully.

The pressures under which oil is forced up from subter-ranean fields can on occasion build up to such an extent that the well undergoes a blowout. When this occurs in an oil well on land it is a relatively easy matter to stop the flow by capping the well and sealing the outflow. When it occurs at sea the operation is much more difficult and lengthy, and there are usually enormous spillages before the damaged well can be sealed. This has happened in the North Sea where a well in the Norwegian Ekofisk oilfield blew out in 1977, producing an immense oil slick covering many square miles; similarly in the Gulf of Mexico in 1979, where the spillage amounted to over a million gallons of crude oil a day lasting over many weeks, much of it drifting ashore onto the United States coast. Such disasters may be rare, but when they occur the resultant oil pollution is always on a massive scale.

The sinking of the supertanker Torrey Canyon *in 1967.*

Methods of Pollution Control

Other causes of oil pollution are mechanical leakages from laden tankers and the practice of washing out the oil tanks after their contents have been discharged. This can be controlled to a large extent by a system of heavy fines for such offenses committed within national waters, though when an oil slick is discovered at sea it is not always easy to find the culprit and to bring him to justice. Another method, introduced after the *Amoco Cadiz* disaster, is for national shipping authorities to require oil tankers to use routes farther away from the coastline than those used by other traffic, on the grounds that oil spillages in the open sea are less dangerous ecologically than spillages in coastal waters. The Intergovernmental Maritime Consultative Organization (IMCO), an advisory body for the international control of shipping, has established traffic separation rules for shipping in congested waters which have been accepted internationally; these go some way towards meeting the oil-tanker problem, but it does not yet require ships carrying dangerous cargoes — crude oil, liquid natural gas, chemicals, etc. — to identify themselves before they enter the separation zones. As a start, shipowners have been invited to do so in the zones around the English Channel, but many of them are resisting the invitation on the grounds that some of their cargoes may be commercially secret and that to reveal them could prejudice their ultimate sale values. Such are some of the difficulties which beset attempts to control the free flow of shipping as it approaches national waters: a conflict between commercial enterprise and ecological danger, sometimes exacerbated by the difficulties of securing any form of worldwide acceptance of new sea traffic rules which can be backed by the force of international law. We may hope that, if other large oil spillages should occur (and it seems almost certain that they will), the time will come when the dangers of large and long-term pollution will outweigh the interests of commercial profit, and a more stringent control of dangerous cargoes will be adopted.

Radiation

Another possible cause of pollution of the sea, and potentially the most dangerous of all, is radiation. It could arise from two main sources: through leakage into the sea of contaminated cooling water from nuclear power stations and from the dumping of nuclear waste at sea. These possible sources are, however, very carefully monitored by every nation with a nuclear capability, and the risk of contamination of the sea appears to be very small at the moment. Another possible source of radioactive contamination can come from the fallout of test explosions in the air, but most such tests are now carried out deep underground, France being the only nuclear nation to continue testing above ground.

Radiation from any source which finds its way into the sea will contaminate all marine life in the affected area and is easily transferable to humans through fish which are caught in that area and subsequently eaten. Since most of the radioactive material which can cause pollution has a half-life of several hundreds of years or more, the danger is a very real one. Control of this danger lies in strict and continuous monitoring and the use of automatic safety measures which ensure a complete shutdown in the event of any radioactive leak. In the past some waste products of nuclear processing have been dumped in sealed containers in deep water in the oceans, but fortunately this means of waste disposal is no longer being used. In general, although the possibility of nuclear contamination of the seas at levels harmful to fish and mammals is a highly emotive one, it is unlikely to become a potent danger unless the present systems of strict monitoring and automatic shutdown in emergencies are relaxed.

Fire is another major hazard for tankers. In 1970 the Liberian tanker Pacific Glory *ran aground and caught fire off the Isle of Wight after a collision.*

Famous Ships
in History

Aaron Manby The world's first iron steamship, launched in 1822. An iron-hulled pleasure boat had been built in England as early as 1777, and an iron-hulled barge in 1787, but both elicited mistrust and ridicule. In Scotland, Thomas Wilson constructed the coastal sailing vessel *Vulcan* in 1818. But iron was still far from being accepted as a suitable material for ships in the 1820s, and *Aaron Manby* was an important pioneer. She was a small vessel of 116 tons; her engine was designed by the Scottish steamboat pioneer, Henry BELL. She was built with ¼-in. (6.35-mm) iron plates shaped at Aaron Manby's ironworks in Staffordshire, in the industrial midlands of England. The sections were transported to Rotherhithe on the Thames below London, where she was assembled. The inside of the hull was given an insulating timber lining. This was intended to protect the cargo, but it was at least as important in reassuring passengers. The ship was completed on April 20, 1822, and after trials she crossed the English Channel and steamed up the Seine to arrive in Paris on June 10. She achieved speeds of between 8 and 9 knots. After a brief period crossing between France and England, she was purchased by French owners and put into service on the Seine between Paris and Le Havre. She was broken up in 1855.

Admiral Graf von Spee See GRAF SPEE.

Admiral Popov Circular Russian warship, built on the Black Sea in 1875 to a design by Vice Admiral Popov. She displaced 3,533 tons and was 101 ft. (30.8 m) in diameter. Her unusual shape had been chosen in order to provide a steady platform, which would neither pitch nor roll, for her two 11.8-in. guns mounted amidships. The *Admiral Popov* was powered by eight engines driving six propellers, and she featured two huge funnels.

A second vessel, the *Novgorod*, was built to the same design a short time later; the two ships were familiarly known as 'popoffkas.' A considerable disadvantage was their low freeboard, which meant they were awash in the slightest sea and suffered bad pounding. It was also found that on river duties, while they were manageable against the current, they

The *Novgorod, built to a design by Vice Admiral Popov.*

went totally out of control going downstream and rotated helplessly. The Czar, however, was so impressed with the *Admiral Popov*'s stability in rough seas that he ordered an imperial yacht to be built on the same principles. This was the highly successful 3,900-ton *Livadia*, completed in Scotland in 1880. Above her nearly circular underwater hull was a conventional yacht's superstructure; she had three engines powering three large propellers to give her a speed of 17 knots.

Alabama The most successful Confederate commerce raider of the Civil War, built in Britain in 1861-62 and commanded by Raphael SEMMES. The

Alabama was a composite-built, 1,016-ton SCHOONER with an auxiliary steam engine and hoisting screw. While she was under construction at Birkenhead the British government, as a neutral in the Civil War, issued a detention order on her. However, delays ensued and before the order could be enforced, she put out to sea secretly, eluded the Federal frigate *Tuscaloosa*, and was fitted out in the Azores, with guns brought from Liverpool by British ships.

The *Alabama* was commissioned on August 24, 1862, and during her 22 months of cruising took some 80 Union ships as prizes, doing damage estimated at $6 million. She was finally sunk by the

The Confederate commerce raider *Alabama*.

Union ship *Kearsarge* off Cherbourg on June 19, 1864. The issue of British responsibility for the Union vessels destroyed by the *Alabama* and other British-built Confederate cruisers became a sore point in Anglo-American relations. The so-called Alabama Claims were finally settled by arbitration in 1872, with Britain compensating the United States for the direct damage done by the *Alabama, Shenandoah*, and *Florida*.

Alecto   See RATTLER AND ALECTO.

America   American SCHOONER which has given its name to the America's Cup, the world's foremost series of yacht races. The *America* was a vessel of 170 tons, built in New York in 1851 for John Stevens of the New York Yacht Club. On August 12, 1851, she finished first against 15 competing English yachts in a race around the Isle of Wight off the south coast of England. The cup presented to the winner by the Royal Yacht Squadron became known as the 'America's Cup' and remains in the hands of the New York Yacht Club to this day.

The *America* was rebuilt in England in 1858. During the Civil War she was a Confederate blockade-runner before being scuttled and then raised and commissioned in the Federal navy. She was reconverted into a yacht in 1870 and participated in occasional races for several more decades.

Ann McKim   American sailing ship, developed from the fast BALTIMORE CLIPPERs and considered by some to be the ancestor of the true CLIPPERs. Built in 1832-33 by Kennard and Williamson of Baltimore, she was a full-rigged ship of 649 tons, and measured 143 ft. (43.5 m) in length and 31 ft. (9.4 m) in the beam. She was built for Isaac McKim, a wealthy Baltimore merchant, and was probably the first ship in which an attempt was made to give a sizable trading vessel the lines of a small craft built for speed alone. Although she proved very fast, shipowners were not unduly impressed, since her capacity, though larger than that of the Baltimore clippers on which she was modeled, was still relatively modest. After a period in the China trade she was sold to Howland & Aspinwall of New York in 1837. She

ended her days under the Chilean flag and was broken up at Valparaiso in 1852. Her design was not copied, but shippers and designers were encouraged to experiment with finer lines for merchant ships, a process which led to the building of the first true clipper, RAINBOW, in 1845.

Archimedes   The world's first sizable seagoing vessel driven by a screw propeller. She was built at Millwall on the Thames for the Ship Propeller Company, and launched in November 1838. Her designer was the English inventor Francis Pettit Smith, who had taken out a patent on a marine propeller three years earlier. Smith had already built a 10-ton vessel which achieved considerable success, and the *Archimedes* was built to test his invention on a larger vessel. She was a three-masted topsail schooner of 237 tons, 106 ft. (32.3 m) in length and 22 ft. (6.7 m) in the beam. Her screw, 5 ft. 9 in. (1.75 m) in diameter, was turned by a 90-hp steam engine and propelled her at speeds of up to 10 knots. She demonstrated the effectiveness of screw propulsion by steaming around Great Britain and across to Portugal. Her performance so impressed the engineer I.K. BRUNEL that he chartered her for 6 months in 1840 to examine her novel means of propulsion. The result was the adoption of screw propulsion for the GREAT BRITAIN, already under construction as a paddle steamer. *Archimedes*, however, ended her days as a sailing vessel trading between Australia and South America.

Ariel   British tea CLIPPER built by

Robert Steele of Greenock, Scotland, in 1865. Considered by many to be the finest of all the China tea clippers, she was a composite ship with teak and rock-elm hull planking. Of 852 tons, she was 197 ft. (60 m) long and 34 ft. (10.4 m) in the beam. She was commanded throughout her life by John Keay, one of the most celebrated and resourceful of all clipper captains. She often sailed for hours on end at 16 knots, achieved a best day's sailing of 340 nautical miles (630 km), and between October 1866 and January 1867 she made the fastest-ever outward passage to China against the monsoon — 80 days between pilots. Like most British clippers, she excelled in light winds. In a strong gale, which would have driven a large American clipper along at top speed, *Ariel* and most other British clippers would be forced to reduce sail drastically or to heave to.

Ariel was one of the participants in the most famous of all the tea-clipper races. Nine ships were to compete, but in the event four failed to finish loading in time, and the five left in the race were *Ariel*, TAEPING, *Serica, Fiery Cross*, and *Taitsin. Fiery Cross* was the first to leave Foochow early in the morning of May 29, 1866. *Ariel* followed at 10:30 am, *Serica* and *Taeping* at 10:50. *Taitsin* sailed late the next day. *Fiery Cross* was the first to round the Cape of Good Hope, after 46 days, followed by *Ariel* (46 days), *Taeping* (47 days), *Serica* (50 days), and *Taitsin* (54 days). *Fiery Cross* held her position to the equator, but thereafter *Ariel* took the lead. On September 5 she was closely followed by *Taeping* as the

Taeping *and* Ariel *in the famous tea-clipper race of 1866.*

The 542,400-ton oil tanker Batillus, *launched in 1976.*

two ships raced up the English Channel at some 15 knots. Off Deal, in southeast England, *Ariel* was just 10 minutes ahead of *Taeping*, but since *Taeping* had left Foochow 20 minutes later, hers was the best time. *Ariel*, *Taeping*, and *Serica*, all ships built by Robert Steele, completed the run to London in 99 days, while *Fiery Cross* and *Taitsin* took 101 days, an astonishingly close finish to a 16,000-nautical mile (29,650-km) race.

Ariel continued in the China trade until 1871. In 1872 she left London for Sydney, and was never seen again.

Batillus Giant oil tanker, with her sister ship *Bellamya* the largest ship ever built. She was constructed at St. Nazaire, France, and entered service with Shell in July 1976. Of 542,400 tons deadweight, she measures 1,312 ft. (400 m) in length and 207 ft. (63 m) in the beam, with a draft of 93 ft. (28.5 m). Her two steam turbines provide a total output of 64,800 hp and give her a service speed of 17 knots. She is manned by a complement of 44. Her sister ship *Bellamya* joined the Shell fleet in December 1976. Japanese

shipbuilders have had plans for tankers of 700,000 tons, and a 1,000,000-tonner has been suggested. These super-giants would be articulated to ride more safely over the waves. But with world concern today about tanker safety and pollution it seems likely that *Batillus* and *Bellamya* will remain the largest ships afloat for some time to come.

Beagle The 240-ton surveying SLOOP of the Royal Navy on which Charles Darwin served as naturalist on a famous five-year voyage around the world. The *Beagle* was commanded by Captain Robert Fitzroy, who was instructed to survey the southern coasts of South America, visit certain Pacific islands, and establish a chain of chronometric stations. Darwin was just 22, with little scientific training or experience, when he took up the unpaid post of official naturalist on the voyage. The *Beagle* left Devonport, England, on December 27, 1831, on an expedition that lasted nearly five years. It was a voyage that Darwin called 'by far the most important event of my life,' and one which provided him

with the observations that were to be the basis for his theory of evolution. Darwin's *Voyage of the Beagle* (1839) is a work of great scientific importance as well as a classic of travel literature.

Bessemer Experimental steamship of 1875 possessing a swinging saloon or passenger cabin. She was the brainchild of Sir Henry Bessemer, better known as the inventor of the revolutionary process for producing inexpensive steel. Bessemer's wealth enabled him to experiment with a novel if impractical way of improving passenger comfort in rough seas. The saloon was pivoted on a longitudinal beam, and hydraulic machinery was fitted to swing the saloon so that it could be kept horizontal no matter how much the ship rolled. To reduce pitching, the ship was designed with long low decks at bow and stern instead of the usual raised decks. This reduced buoyancy at the ends, thereby minimizing the normal tendency of a ship to rise up over waves. Built for service across the English Channel, *Bessemer* was double-ended, with a steam engine and pair of paddle wheels both forward and aft of the saloon. The swinging passenger cabin was controlled by an engineer on the floor of the saloon, who gauged the extent of each roll and corrected it. The ship made several crossings, but due to faults in the hydraulic equipment and the inability of the engineer to produce counteracting movements quickly enough, the *Bessemer* was a failure. With the swinging saloon removed, *Bessemer* was converted to a freighter, only to be overwhelmed in a gale.

Birkenhead British troopship of 1,400 tons whose sinking was one of the greatest tragedies at sea of the 19th century. The *Birkenhead* was a steam frigate built in 1845, and the first iron-hulled ship of the Royal Navy. She was found unsuitable as a warship because her iron plates could not withstand solid shot, and she was converted into a troop carrier.

On January 7, 1852, she left Cork for South Africa with 494 officers and men, a crew of 130, and 56 women and children. In February the vessel arrived at Capetown, disembarked sick men, and took on stores and additional horses. She then set sail for Port Elizabeth, and in the early hours of the morning of February 26 she struck an uncharted rock — now known as Birkenhead Rock — in Walkers Bay, 50 miles (80 km) east of Capetown. The captain ordered the boats lowered and the engines stopped. The vessel struck the rock again, flooding the engine room. The rush of water through the first hole filled the forward lower troop decks, and the men sleeping there were drowned. The surviving soldiers were drawn up on deck and squads were detailed to operate the pumps and launch the eight boats. The *Birkenhead* broke her back, and the mast and funnel fell onto the crowded deck, killing and wounding more men and smashing a number of the boats. The horses were cut free to allow them to swim ashore but they were soon attacked by sharks. Finally three boats filled with the women and children were launched. The troops had formed up on deck in disciplined columns. With the officers at their head, only three men broke ranks, the remainder going down with the ship, sacrificing their lives to enable the women and children to be got off safely. Of the ship's total company, numbering 638, only 193 were saved.

The experimental steamship Bessemer, *1875.*

The Bessemer's *saloon, designed for maximum passenger comfort.*

Bismarck German battleship of World War II, whose pursuit and sinking by the Royal Navy was one of the most famous naval actions of the war. The keel of the *Bismarck* was laid down in 1935, in violation of the Treaty of Versailles, and she was followed a year later by her sister ship *Tirpitz*. The *Bismarck* was launched in 1939. She displaced 50,900 tons under full load and was 823 ft. (251 m) in length, mounting eight 15-in. guns.

She set out to attack Allied trade in the North Atlantic in May 1941, but her departure was discovered, and ships of the British Home Fleet were ordered out in pursuit. On May 24 the *Bismarck* destroyed Britain's largest warship, the *Hood*, but suffered a hit from the *Prince of Wales* that reduced her fuel supply. Hunted by more than 40 British warships she headed for the coast of France.

On May 26 she was hit by torpedoes from aircraft belonging to the carrier *Ark Royal* and her steering gear was jammed. The following day she was brought to

The Bismarck, *launched in 1939.*

171

action by the *King George V* and *Rodney* and finished off by three torpedoes from the cruiser *Dorsetshire*. Only 110 survivors were picked up.

Bonhomme Richard The warship commanded by John Paul JONES in which he defeated the *Serapis* in one of the most famous engagements in American naval history. The *Bonhomme Richard* was a French East Indiaman, originally the *Duc de Duras*, built in 1766 and carrying 42 guns. She was purchased for Jones by the French government, refitted, and given her new name in tribute to Benjamin Franklin's 'Poor Richard.' On September 23, 1779, she met the British frigate *Serapis*, commanded by Richard Pearson, off Flamborough Head in northeast England. The convoy Pearson was escorting escaped as the *Serapis* engaged the *Bonhomme Richard*, while the accompanying *Countess of Scarborough* brought to battle the French frigate *Pallas*. The *Bonhomme Richard* and *Serapis* fought muzzle to muzzle in the moonlight for three hours. Only two of *Bonhomme Richard*'s guns were still in operation when fire aboard the *Serapis* forced Pearson to surrender. Jones later commented that never before had there been a naval battle 'so bloody, so severe and so lasting.' The loss of life was so great that neither Jones nor Pearson ever issued a full list of casualties. The *Bonhomme Richard* was so badly damaged that she sank two days later, after Jones had transferred his crew to the *Serapis*.

Bounty Royal Navy transport commanded by William BLIGH, scene of a famous mutiny on April 28, 1789. The *Bounty* was built at Hull in 1784 as the 220-ton merchant ship *Bethia*. She was converted into an armed transport and sent out to Tahiti in 1788 to transplant young breadfruit trees to the West Indies. The mutiny of acting lieutenant Fletcher Christian and a majority of the crew of 45 near Tonga on the return voyage has traditionally been ascribed to Bligh's brutality, but the allure of life in Tahiti also played a part. Bligh and 18 men loyal to him were put in the ship's boat; they eventually reached Timor after a 48-day voyage. The *Bounty* returned to Tahiti. The next year Christian, eight mutineers, and 18 Tahitians, sailed her to lonely Pitcairn Island, where she was

The Bremen, *holder of the Blue Riband 1929-1935.*

beached and burned. The mutineers who had stayed on Tahiti were captured by men from the Royal Navy frigate *Pandora*, which had been sent out by the Admiralty after Bligh's return to England.

Bremen Transatlantic passenger LINER operated by North German Lloyd of Bremen, launched on August 16, 1928. The *Bremen* was the fastest liner of the early 1930s and marked Germany's reappearance in the prestige transatlantic trade. She plied between Bremerhaven, Southampton, Cherbourg, and New York, carrying up to 2,224 passengers and a crew of 960. Of 51,656 tons gross, she was 938 ft. (287 m) long and 102 ft. (31 m) in the beam, with a draft of 34 ft. (10.3 m). Her geared turbine engines developed 135,000 hp and turned four screws, giving her a cruising speed of 26.25 knots.

On her maiden voyage in 1929 she set new records for the transatlantic crossing in both directions. The outward passage to New York was made in 4 days, 14 hours, 42 minutes. In 1933 she achieved an average of 28.51 knots across the Atlantic. She held the Blue Riband until 1935. *Bremen* and her slightly smaller sister ship *Europa* were the first large liners built with bulbous bows, a feature that improved speed and buoyancy and reduced pitching. Above the bulbous underwater section the bow was given a pronounced rake, another novel feature. *Bremen* had two funnels and a total of 11 decks, four of them in the superstructure. She was also notable for carrying a catapult-launched seaplane.

At the outbreak of World War II she was in New York, but successfully escaped from the United States, evaded the British fleet, and returned safely to her home port after sailing a northerly course that brought her to shelter for several weeks at the Russian port of Murmansk. She was destroyed by fire after an air raid early in 1941; German sources attributed her loss to criminal sabotage.

Castalia Experimental twin-hulled paddle steamer which entered service in 1875. She was designed as a passenger ferry on the frequently stormy route across the English Channel between Dover and Calais. Like her equally novel contemporary the BESSEMER, she was built to minimize rolling and pitching in order to improve passenger comfort.

The 1,533-ton *Castalia* was constructed for the Channel Steamship Company by the Thames Ironworks and Shipbuilding Company, and measured 290 ft. (88.4 m) in length. Each hull was 17 ft. (5.2 m) in the beam, and with a 26-ft. (7.9-m) gap between them the overall beam was 60 ft. (18.3 m). The hulls of modern twin-hulled craft are usually each built in the shape of a small ship, but those of *Castalia* resembled two separate halves of a single hull cut down the middle. The two paddle wheels, each 21 ft. (6.4 m) in diameter, were positioned side by side between the halves. A contemporary report stated that her maximum roll in weather conditions encountered in the Channel was 5°, compared to 14-15° for conventional packets, while pitching was down to little more than 3°.

The twin-hulled paddle steamer Castalia, *launched in 1875.*

Castalia was popular with passengers, but her design did not prove a success. It was found that the space between the hulls became choked with a churning mass of water that damaged the paddles and reduced their efficiency drastically. She was withdrawn from service after a short time, and was later converted into a permanently moored isolation hospital. Despite her failure, the Channel Steamship Company ordered a second and larger twin-hulled ship, the 1,820-ton *Calais-Douvres*, with more powerful engines and two ship-shaped hulls. She suffered from the same drawbacks as *Castalia* and, like her, was withdrawn after a short working life and converted into a hospital ship.

Challenge Famous clipper built by William A. Webb of New York and launched in 1851. For a short time the biggest sailing ship afloat, she was of 2,000 tons and measured 230 ft. 6 in. (70.2 m) in length and 43 ft. (13.2 m) in the beam. Her mainmast was 97 ft. (29.6 m) high and, including topmasts and skysail poles, it extended to an overall height of 160 ft. (49 m). The mainyard

The Challenge, *1851.*

was 90 ft. (27.4 m) long and, with studding sail booms, stretched a total of 160 ft. (48.8 m). Her full suit of sails had an area of 115,020 sq. ft. (10,685 m²). The first American sailing ship to be braced with iron, and the first with three decks, she was luxuriously appointed. Her two cabin decks included six ornately decorated staterooms. She had a crew of 34. Designed with an unusually sharp bow, she was expected to be the fastest clipper afloat. However, she created an extremely large bow wave that slowed her down significantly.

On her maiden voyage from New York to San Francisco in July 1851, her captain Robert H. Waterman, a seaman with an unrivaled record for speed in the trade, was offered a $10,000 bonus if he could complete the trip in 90 days. *Challenge*'s best day's run was only 336 nautical miles (622 km), and the voyage took 108 days. This was in part due to an ill-assorted crew and to the time of year, unsuitable for fast passages. She was also 'over-hatted' and twice dismasted. Although later captains produced improved performances, *Challenge* did not live up to her designer's expectations. She continued in the China trade until 1861, when she was renamed *Golden City* and based at Hong Kong. In 1866 she was purchased by British owners and sailed in the Bombay and Java trades. Finally, in 1876, she was wrecked off Ushant, France.

Champion of the Seas One of the famous series of four CLIPPERs built by Donald MCKAY in 1853-54 for the Black Ball Line of Liverpool. On her maiden voyage to Melbourne in 1854, running before a gale in the Indian Ocean, she sailed 465 nautical miles (861 km) in 24 hours, an average of 19.97 knots. This is the longest day's run ever logged by a sailing ship. Of 2,722 tons, *Champion of the Seas* measured 296 ft. (82 m) in length and 45 ft. (13.7 m) in the beam.

Charlotte Dundas Pioneer Scottish steamboat of 1802, one of the first commercial applications of steam propulsion to navigation. She was built for Lord Dundas, a governor of Scotland's Forth and Clyde Canal, and was named for his daughter. Intended to demonstrate the possibility of using steam power instead of horses to tow barges on the canal, she was constructed under the direction of William Symington. Symington built an improved double-acting steam engine of the type developed by James Watt. In place of the crude systems of chains and ratchets used by earlier pioneers such as John FITCH, Symington used a connecting rod and crank to convert the engine's reciprocating motion into the rotary action needed to turn the paddle wheel. The craft was initially designed with side paddles, but to reduce the danger that her wash might erode the canal banks, a stern wheel was fitted instead. She was 56 ft. (17 m) long and 18 ft. (5.5 m) in the beam. Her 12-hp single-cylinder engine enabled her on her first voyage to pull two 70-ton barges 20 miles (32 km) in 6 hours against a strong wind. Despite her practical success, she was soon taken out of service because of fears that the canal banks might fall in. On Lord Dundas' death the project was abandoned.

Chesapeake One of the original six frigates of the U.S. Navy, authorized in 1794. She carried 36 guns and, under the command of James BARRON, was at the center of the 'Chesapeake Affair' of 1807. The ship had only just left Hampton Roads on June 22 when the British frigate *Leopard* stopped her and demanded the right to search her for British deserters among the crew. Barron refused, and the *Leopard* opened fire. The *Chesapeake*'s decks were littered with stores and she was unready for action; the *Leopard* sailed away with alleged deserters, including two U.S. citizens. The *Chesapeake*, slightly damaged, returned to Hampton Roads and Barron was court-martialed.

On June 1, 1813, short of officers and with an inexperienced crew, the *Chesapeake* sailed out of Boston Harbor to engage the British frigate *Shannon*. In an action lasting less than 15 minutes the *Chesapeake*'s commander James Lawrence was killed — his dying words were 'Don't give up the ship!' The *Chesapeake* was reduced to a shambles with 146 men killed or wounded, and she was taken as a prize to England.

Clermont The world's first commercially successful steamboat, built by Robert FULTON in 1807. Launched at Paulus Hook near New York, she was a flat-bottomed wooden vessel of some 100 tons and measured 133 ft. (40 m) in length and 18 ft. (5.5 m) in the beam. Fulton equipped his craft with a British engine built by Boulton and Watt of Birmingham. It was a single-cylinder modified beam engine, with the beams placed beside the base of the engine to ensure a low center of gravity. Fulton himself designed the transmission gear, which followed the example set by William Symington in his CHARLOTTE DUNDAS. The engine turned two side paddles 15 ft. (4.6 m) in diameter, each carrying eight floats.

On August 17, 1807, she began her famous voyage up the Hudson to Albany and back, a total distance of some 240 miles (390 km), which she accomplished in 63 hours. Regular, profitable passenger services to Albany began in September; the ship eventually acquired three large cabins containing more than 50 berths and provisions for serving meals. She was finally withdrawn from service

Henry Bell's Comet *of 1812.*

in 1814. She was variously known as *The Steamboat, The North River Steamboat, The North River, The North River Steamboat of Clermont,* and *Clermont.*

Comet The first steamboat to operate a regular passenger service in Europe. Designed by the engineer Henry BELL and built at Port Glasgow, Scotland, in 1812, she was a small wooden craft displacing 21.5 tons and measuring 45 ft. (13.7 m) in length and 11 ft. (3.5 m) in the beam. Her single-cylinder modified beam engine turned a pair of side paddles. The engine was designed by Bell and built by John Robertson; it is preserved today in London's Science Museum.

Comet was completed on August 15, 1812, and was put into service on the Clyde between Glasgow, Greenock, and Helensburgh. Her average speed was more than 6 knots. In 1819, after lengthening *Comet* by just over 20 ft. (6 m) and fitting a new engine, Bell extended her run to Oban and Fort William in the Western Highlands. On December 13, 1820, she was driven ashore in a storm and wrecked.

Connector An unusual hinged ship built for the Jointed Ship Company of London, one of the most ingenious vessels of the mid-19th century, but one which ultimately proved a failure. *Connector* was essentially a development of the barge train used on inland waterways, which consisted of a number of individual craft (a tug and several barges). *Connector*, however, was

designed as a complete ship, but one which possessed hinged or articulated joints that allowed her to be split up into three parts. The aftermost section was equipped with a steam engine and screw propeller. The officers' accommodation was in this section, while the crew's quarters were in the bow unit. Each section was fitted with a mast and sails, so that it could make its way independently to its final destination. *Connector* was built to carry coal, and the design allowed the powered section to drop off or attach units without the time-consuming process of entering port to load or discharge cargo. According to a contemporary report, the process of uncoupling required no more than the movement of one lever on deck and took only a few seconds. The design also produced a ship that would not break its back in a fore-and-aft pitching sea despite its exceptional length. However, sideways rolling would have easily torn the sections apart, however strong the hinges, and *Connector* was in fact never tried at sea because this fatal flaw was quickly realized.

Constellation The first of the U.S. Navy's original six frigates to go to sea (in June 1798). She was given her name by President Washington in commemoration of the 'new constellation' of stars on the U.S. flag. Her most famous exploits took place under the command of Captain Thomas Truxtun during the undeclared naval war with France. On February 9, 1799, she captured the

French frigate *Insurgente*; a year later she defeated another French ship, the *Vengeance*.

The *Constellation* had a long career and several rebuilds. She served against Confederate commerce raiders during the Civil War and was used for a period as a naval training ship. In 1940 she was brought back into full commission as a flagship of the U.S. Atlantic Fleet during World War II; she was the longest-serving ship in the U.S. Navy. The *Constellation* was designated a National Historic Landmark in 1955 and is permanently moored at Baltimore, where she was originally built.

Constitution The most famous ship in American naval history, nicknamed 'Old Ironsides.' She was built as one of the original six frigates of the U.S. Navy and launched at Boston on October 21, 1797. She carried from 44 to 50 or more guns and was 204 ft. (62.1 m) in length and 43 ft. (13.1 m) in the beam.

The *Constitution* served in the undeclared naval war against France of 1798. During the war against the Barbary pirates of Tripoli, she was the flagship of Commodore Edward Preble. Under the command of Isaac HULL the *Constitution* met the British frigate *Guerrière* on August 19, 1812, in the first major naval engagement of the War of 1812. After a close and hard-fought battle lasting 30 minutes the *Guerrière* was dismasted and surrendered. It was in this battle that her apparent imperviousness to British shot led the crew to give the *Constitution* the famous nickname 'Old Ironsides.' On December 19, 1812, commanded by William BAINBRIDGE, she defeated the British frigate *Java* off the coast of Brazil, and on February 20, 1815, with Charles Stewart commanding, she overcame the British frigate *Cyane* and sloop *Levant* in a four-hour battle.

The *Constitution* was condemned as unseaworthy, but Oliver Wendell Holmes' famous poem *Old Ironsides* (1830) stirred up public feeling and saved her from being broken up. She was rebuilt in 1833 and again in 1877, and was for a period a training ship before being berthed at Boston Navy Yard in 1897. An Act of Congress in 1925 authorized her restoration by public subscription; on completion she visited 90 ports before returning to Boston in 1934, where she is now on permanent exhibition.

Cutty Sark The most famous of all the British CLIPPERS and the only survivor of her type. Her name comes from the poem *Tam O'Shanter* by Robert Burns, and refers to the short shirt or shift worn by the young witch Nannie. The witch on the ship's figurehead is shown reaching for the tail of Tam's horse. Built at Dumbarton, Scotland, in 1869, the *Cutty Sark* was small compared to her American counterparts. Of 963 tons gross, she measured 212 ft. (64.7 m) in length (280 ft. or 85.3 m overall) and 36 ft. (10.9 m) in the beam. Her mainmast was 145 ft. (44.2 m) tall, and her sail area amounted to 32,000 sq. ft. (3,000 m²). Built to rival the almost equally famous THERMOPYLAE, she was, like her, a composite ship. Her iron frame was planked with rock elm and teak, and her bottom was protected by copper sheathing. She had two full decks, together with raised forecastle and quarterdeck and two deckhouses. She was sailed in her original rig by a crew of 35. With a very sharp bow, a full midships section, and fine lines at the stern, she handled exceptionally well and was potentially very fast. She was designed for the China tea trade but made only eight voyages on the run, under a competent but uninspired captain. Her rig was then reduced, and, with a smaller crew, she entered the Australian wool trade, in which she attained her best runs.

In 1895 she was sold to Portuguese owners and renamed *Ferreira*. She worked as a TRAMP ship until 1922. After being dismasted in a storm in 1916, she was rerigged as a BARKENTINE. In 1922 an English sea captain bought her for £6,000 and restored her clipper rig. After a period as a sail training ship she was installed in a specially built dry dock at Greenwich in 1954. Her restoration was completed in 1957, and she was opened to the public as a monument to the great age of sail.

Demologus The first steam-powered warship, designed by Robert FULTON and completed at New York in 1815. The 38-ton vessel was of an unusual design, with a single paddle wheel in a well in the middle of the ship, which resembled a catamaran with its two hulls. To one side was the boiler, to the other the engine. The ship's sides were extremely thick and she was equipped with 30 guns designed to fire red-hot shot heated in the boiler fires. Fulton also intended to fit another of his inventions, a cannon which fired shells underwater, but this was probably never in fact carried out. *Demologus* was never intended as a seagoing vessel, and her top speed was less than 7 knots. She would, however, have been a formidable opponent for any enemy sailing ship in the approaches to New York Harbor. She was completed after the War of 1812 had ended and was never tried in action. Renamed the *Fulton*, she survived until 1830.

Devastation British battleship, the first to rely entirely on steam propulsion. Designed in 1869, the *Devastation* displaced 9,330 tons and was known as a 'mastless' ship. She was 285 ft. (86.9 m) long and armed with two twin turrets with 12-in. guns, one forward and one aft, and was essentially a larger and far more seaworthy counterpart of the American MONITOR, but possessing twin screws and enormous coal supplies. *Devastation* was not completed until 1873, and her sister ship *Thunderer* only in 1877, evidence of how little importance was placed on their revolutionary design. *Thunderer* did, however, mark another significant advance: she was the first ship of the Royal Navy equipped with hydraulic loading for her guns.

Discovery Name given to a number of ships used on voyages of exploration and discovery. **(1)** The ship that sailed

HMS Devastation.

under Charles Clerke on Captain James COOK's third and last voyage of discovery. She was originally a Whitby COLLIER, and was acquired by the Royal Navy in 1775. *Discovery* set off for the Pacific with Cook's own vessel, the RESOLUTION, in July 1776. Both ships had been poorly refitted, and their masts and spars in particular were unsatisfactory on the voyage. After Cook's death in February 1779, Captain Clerke took command of the expedition, but when he died in August, command reverted to Lieutenant Gore of the *Resolution*. Both ships returned to England in October 1780, and *Discovery* was sold out of service in 1781. Like Cook's ENDEAVOUR, *Discovery* was a cat, with the same advantages of a low waist and large cargo-carrying capacity. She was 87 ft. 6 in. (29.7 m) long and 27 ft. 6 in. (8.4 m) in the beam, of 299 tons builder's measurement. She carried eight guns.

(2) The ship in which Henry HUDSON sailed on his fourth and last voyage of exploration (1610).

(3) The converted collier used by George Vancouver on his circumnavigation of the globe (1791-95).

(4) The polar research vessel commanded by Captain R. F. SCOTT on his first expedition to Antarctica (1901-04).

Dreadnought The world's first 'all-big-gun' battleship, superior in speed and armament to any warship afloat when she was launched in 1906, and the model for all subsequent battleships of the world's navies. The *Dreadnought* displaced 21,485 tons under full load and was armed with ten 12-in. guns in five twin turrets, three of them on the centerline. Her maximum speed of 21 knots exceeded that of any other battleship and was the result of her steam turbine propulsion, which she was the first large warship to adopt.

The decision to construct a warship carrying only guns of the largest caliber stemmed from revolutionary new improvements in the range and accuracy of naval gunnery in the first years of the 20th century. A special committee of the British Admiralty was created to decide on future warships for the Royal Navy, and the result was the *Dreadnought*, ardently championed by First Sea Lord Sir John FISHER. Only 14 months elapsed

between the laying of her keel and her commissioning. The appearance of the *Dreadnought* overturned the building programs of the world's navies, rendering all existing battleships obsolete and giving Britain a headstart in what developed into the 'dreadnought race' with Germany. The *Dreadnought* herself, after giving her name to a new class of battleship, rapidly became outperformed by her successors. She did, however, serve in World War I, ramming and sinking the German submarine *U-29* in 1915. She was finally sold for breaking up in 1920.

Emden German light cruiser, during her spectacular but brief career the most successful surface commerce raider of World War I. The 3,600-ton *Emden* was completed in 1909 and mounted 4.1-in. guns. At the outbreak of World War I she was detached from the German East Asiatic Squadron and began operations in the Indian Ocean, where she was responsible for capturing or sinking more than 20 merchant ships amounting to over 100,000 tons. Among her most spectacular exploits were the shelling of oil installations at Madras and the sinking of a

HMS Dreadnought, *prototype of all other pre-World War II battleships.*

Russian light cruiser and French destroyer in Penang Harbor. Marine insurance markets were in chaos, and troop movements from Australia and New Zealand disrupted. On November 9, 1914, the *Emden* was taken by surprise off the Cocos Islands by the Australian cruiser *Sydney*. The German ship was shattered by the *Sydney*'s 6-in. guns and beached as a wreck. A number of the *Emden*'s crew had already gone ashore on Direction Island to attack a cable station; they escaped in a captured schooner and eventually made their way to Constantinople via Arabia, after an epic journey of seven months.

Endeavour The ship used by James COOK on his first voyage of exploration to the Pacific (1768-71). The *Endeavour* was built in northeast England and was originally a COLLIER named the *Earl of Pembroke*. She was a cat (that is, she had a bluff bow without a beakhead, a deep waist, and a canoe stern), and was typical of the strongly built ships used to carry coal down the east coast of England until well into the 19th century. She was of 366 tons and was armed with between six and ten 4-pounder carriage guns and twelve small swivel guns.

The *Endeavour* was specially purchased on Cook's recommendation; he had served his apprenticeship on Whitby colliers and knew their suitability for his expedition. Her large holds enabled her to carry large quantities of stores, and her deep waist was well adapted for hydrographic surveys involving a large amount of boatwork with frequent transfers of equipment. The *Endeavour* was bought into service with the Royal Navy in March 1768 and set sail for the Pacific, with Cook in command, on August 25, 1768. She was nearly lost on Australia's Great Barrier Reef, but was beached and repaired. She was sold out of service on March 7, 1775.

Enterprise The world's first nuclear-powered aircraft carrier, and the world's largest warship when she was launched on September 24, 1960. She displaces 75,700 tons (89,600 tons under full load) and is 1,102 ft. (336 m) in length and 133 ft. (40.5 m) in the beam. Proposals for a nuclear-powered carrier were first discussed as early as 1950, and once the problem of designing a power plant for

The wreck of the Emden, *November 1914.*

so large a vessel was overcome, construction from the laying of the keel to launch took only 31 months.

The *Enterprise* is powered by eight pressurized-water-cooled reactors; her four steam turbines generate 280,000 hp and give her a cruising speed of 35 knots. Without any need for the fuel bunkers and ducts for the elimination of fuel gases that occupy so much space in conventional carriers, she is able to carry 84 aircraft (compared to 70 for carriers of the *Forrestal* class). Some 2,400 men are needed for the operation of the aircraft, in addition to a crew of 3,100. Her present set of reactor cores will enable her to

operate for 10 to 13 years without refueling, another advantage over conventionally powered carriers.

Flying Cloud American CLIPPER built by Donald MCKAY in 1851, one of the most handsome of all sailing ships and renowned for her historic maiden voyage from New York to San Francisco in 89 days, 21 hours, a record for a sailing ship that has never been beaten. Until 1851 the time had stood at 120 days. During that famous voyage the *Flying Cloud* achieved a remarkable day's sailing of 374 nautical miles (693 km). She was of 1,793 tons, measured 225 ft. (68.5 m) in

The nuclear-powered aircraft carrier USS Enterprise.

length and 40 ft. (12 m) in the beam. Her mainmast was 88 ft. (27 m) tall, and her mainyard 82 ft. (25 m) in length. After sailing for some years on voyages to California and China, she was sold to British owners and used on the Australian route. She ended her days in the Canadian lumber trade and was destroyed by fire in 1873.

Forrestal The first new aircraft carrier to be built after the end of World War II and the first specifically designed to operate jet aircraft. The *Forrestal* was the initial ship in a class of carriers that includes the *Saratoga, Ranger,* and *Independence.* She was launched on December 11, 1954, and displaces 59,060 tons (75,900 tons under full load). Her length is 1,086 ft. (331 m), her beam 129 ft. (39.3 m), and the width of her flight deck is 252 ft. (76.8 m). Early in her planning she was redesigned to incorporate the British-developed angled flight deck (a feature of all subsequent carriers) and steam catapults (she possesses four, as do all built since her day). She was also the first U.S. Navy carrier built with an enclosed bow for greater seaworthiness; her flight deck is heavily armored. Four turbines generating 260,000 hp give her a top speed of 33 knots; 2,150 men are needed for the operation of her 70 aircraft, and the crew numbers 2,790. The *Forrestal* is scheduled to undergo a modernization program that will extend her service life to the end of the century.

Fram Polar exploration vessel specially built for the Norwegian explorer Fridtjof NANSEN. The first ship designed to withstand being frozen into the polar pack ice, she had a specially reinforced hull with a semicircular hull section so that she would be lifted up by the pressure of the ice instead of being crushed by it. *Fram* was a three-masted, 402-ton SCHOONER with an auxiliary engine. She possessed two watertight bulkheads and carried eight boats, two of which were large enough to carry her small crew with ample provisions.

She sailed from Norway in June 1893 with Otto Sverdrup as captain, Nansen, and ten others on board. She was frozen into the pack ice off Siberia on September 22, 1893, and drifted in the ice for 35 months, emerging near Spitsbergen in August 1896. She was later used by

The liner France, *over 1,000 ft. (300 m) long from bow to stern.*

Sverdrup in an expedition to northwest Greenland and adjacent islands between 1898 and 1902. In 1910 Roald AMUNDSEN sailed in her to Antarctica, on an expedition that was the first to reach the South Pole, and on the *Fram*'s return to Norway she was preserved near Oslo as a national monument.

France **(1)** The name of two steel-hulled, five-masted BARKS, the largest sailing ships of their day. The first was built in 1890 by Henderson & Son of Glasgow for the French shipping line of A.D. Bordes. With a tonnage of 3,874 (5,900 tons deadweight), she measured 361 ft. (110 m) in length, 49 ft. (14.8 m) in the beam, and had two steel decks and a double bottom. She was built for the South American nitrate trade and was equipped with steam winches for cargo handling. She was a fast ship, reaching Rio de Janeiro in 32 days on her maiden voyage, and on one occasion making the passage between France and Chile in 63 days. She sank off South America in 1901 after being disabled in hurricane-force winds.

(2) The second bark, usually known as *France II,* was launched at Bordeaux, France, in 1911. The largest sailing ship ever constructed, she was of 5,806 tons (8,000 tons deadweight) and measured 419 ft. (127.7 m) in length and 56 ft. (17 m) in the beam. She was equipped with an electricity generator, radio, and auxiliary engine turning twin screws, and was designed for the nickel and iron trade from New Caledonia in the southwest Pacific. In fact, she carried a variety of

cargoes, including coal and wool. In July 1922 she set sail from New Caledonia loaded with iron ore, but before the voyage her auxiliary engine had been removed, and on a windless day she drifted helplessly onto a coral reef. Rather than bear the cost of her refloating and repairs her owners decided to sell her for scrap.

(3) The longest passenger LINER ever built, and when she entered service the third largest in terms of tonnage. Launched at St. Nazaire, France, on May 11, 1960, she carried 2,044 passengers, a crew of 1,171, and was the last great liner to be built purely for the transatlantic trade. Her gross tonnage was 66,348, and she was 1,035 ft. (315.5 m) in length and 111 ft. (33.8 m) in the beam, with a draft of 34 ft. (10.4 m). Her four steam turbines developed a total of 160,000 hp, turning four screws to give her a top speed during trials of 35.21 knots. Her normal cruising speed was 31 knots. She had two sets of fin stabilizers, 11 decks, and a light aluminum superstructure. Her two funnels were immediately recognizable by their small 'wings,' added to divert the smoke away from the deck. Designed as the prestige flagship of the Compagnie Générale Transatlantique, *France* ran at an increasingly large loss, covered by government subsidies. She was withdrawn from service in 1974 and five years later was sold to Norwegian owners to be refitted as a Caribbean cruise ship under the new name *Norway.*

Gipsy Moth IV The specially built 53-ft. (16.1-m) KETCH in which Sir

Francis CHICHESTER made his famous single-handed voyage around the world. *Gipsy Moth IV* left Plymouth on August 27, 1966; Chichester's goal was to reach Sydney in under 100 days. The self-steering gear broke in heavy gales, but Chichester was still able to arrive in Australia in the remarkably fast time of 107 days, covering a distance of 14,100 miles (22,690 km). Leaving Sydney on January 29, 1967, Chichester sailed around Cape Horn and returned to Plymouth on May 28, after a voyage of 119 days. He had sailed 15,517 miles (24,967 km) on this second stage of his circumnavigation, at that time the greatest distance covered by a small sailing vessel between two ports. Chichester proceeded in the *Gipsy Moth IV* up the Thames to Greenwich, where he was knighted with Sir Francis Drake's sword. The *Gipsy Moth IV* is now preserved on exhibition at Greenwich next to the CUTTY SARK.

Gloire The world's first seagoing IRONCLAD warship, designed by Stanislas Dupuy de Lôme and launched in 1859. She displaced 5,617 tons and, because she carried her 36 rifled guns on one deck, was officially known as a steam frigate. Her length was 252 ft. (76.8 m) and her beam 55 ft. (16.7 m). Like all warships of the period she carried a full rig of sails. The *Gloire* was the first notable result of the French policy of naval expansion in the aftermath of the Crimean War. Experiments with rifled guns led the French to conclude that armor was necessary for their new warships, and the *Gloire* was the first of a series of ironclads begun in March 1858. The sides of her oak hull were protected by iron armor up to 4.7 in. (119 mm) thick. The British reply to the *Gloire* was the WARRIOR (1861), an ironclad with an iron hull that can claim to be the direct ancestor of the modern battleship.

Glückauf The first true oil TANKER, operated by the German-American Petroleum Company and launched at Newcastle, England, in June 1886. Of some 3,020 tons deadweight (compared to today's giants of over 500,000 tons), she was 300 ft. (91.5 m) long and 37 ft. (11.3 m) in the beam. Her speed was about 10 knots. Oil had simply been transported in barrels before the appearance of the *Glückauf*; she was the first oceangoing

Gloire, the first ironclad warship, 1859.

tanker to transport oil in bulk in her hull. As in modern tankers, her engines and accommodation were positioned well aft, allowing the main part of the hull to form a set of unobstructed oil tanks isolated from the machinery and crew. The pioneering example set by *Glückauf* was not widely followed until after World War I. Instead, during this transition period, oil was generally carried in converted dry cargo ships fitted with large cylindrical drums in the holds. *Glückauf* continued in service until stranded on Fire Island near New York in 1893.

Gneisenau See SCHARNHORST AND GNEISENAU.

Goeben German battle cruiser famous for her role in bringing Turkey into World War I. The *Goeben* displaced 22,640 tons and mounted ten 11-in. guns; her crew numbered 1,107 men. At the outbreak of the war in 1914 she was in the Mediterranean in company with the light cruiser *Breslau*. After bombarding the coast of Algeria to disrupt troop movement to France, the *Goeben* and the *Breslau* eluded a British squadron off Sicily and arrived at Constantinople on August 10. The two ships were presented to the Turks to take the place of two modern battleships being built in British shipyards but taken over by the Royal Navy the previous week. They kept their German crews, and a German admiral was appointed to head the Turkish navy. Turkish reluctance to enter the

war continued, however. It was finally overcome only when the *Goeben* and other ships of the Turkish fleet, under German command, shelled Russian Black Sea ports on October 29-30, 1914. The Allies responded by declaring war. For the following four years the *Goeben* remained based at Constantinople. Towards the end of the war she was mined in the Dardanelles, and while grounded was hit by two bombs from British aircraft, the first major warship to be subjected to attack from the air. After the war the *Goeben*, renamed the *Yawuz*, remained in Turkish service and was sold for breaking up only in 1973.

Golden Hind Flagship of Sir Francis DRAKE's famous round-the-world voyage of 1577-80. She was built as the *Pelican*; her name was changed to *Golden Hind* in the Straits of Magellan in September 1578, to honor Drake's patron Sir Christopher Hatton, whose crest was a golden hind. She was the only one of Drake's five ships to complete the circumnavigation, and Drake was knighted on her quarterdeck at Deptford Dockyard on April 4, 1581.

The *Golden Hind* was put on permanent exhibition at Deptford and survived, patched and repatched, well into the next century. Her ultimate fate is unknown, though she was most probably dismantled because of her poor condition, and no accurate description of her has survived. It is known that she had 18 guns and was of 100 tons, but the *Golden Hind* now on display at San Francisco, which

The Graf Spee *being scuttled in 1939.*

sailed there from Greenwich in 1977, is not a copy of any specific Elizabethan ship, though she accurately portrays their general appearance.

Graf Spee German POCKET BATTLESHIP of 12,100 tons, best known of three such ships built as heavily armed commerce raiders in the early 1930s. Titled in full the *Admiral Graf von Spee*, she carried six 11-in. guns in two triple turrets, together with eight 5.9-in. guns. Her diesel engines of 56,800 hp gave her exceptional range and endurance; maximum speed was 26-28 knots. In the opening months of World War II the *Graf Spee*, commanded by Captain Hans Langsdorff, began a cruise in southern waters that claimed nine ships, totaling 50,000 tons. On December 13, 1939, in what has become known as the Battle of the River Plate, she was engaged by three British cruisers, *Ajax, Achilles,* and *Exeter*, which had been sent out to hunt her. She escaped serious damage and put into the neutral port of Montevideo, where she received permission to stay four days for repairs. Langsdorff believed, erroneously, that a far superior British force had assembled to await him when he put to sea. On December 17 the *Graf Spee* sailed out of Montevideo as far as the 3-mile limit, where she was scuttled, to the astonishment of all observers. Captain Langsdorff committed suicide a few days later by shooting himself.

Great Britain The first large iron-hulled ship and the first screw-propelled vessel to cross the Atlantic. The *Great Britain* was the second steamship designed by the British engineer Isambard Kingdom BRUNEL and was by a wide margin the largest ship of her day. She was built by William Patterson of Bristol, and floated out of dry dock on July 19, 1843. With a gross tonnage of 3,270, she measured 322 ft. (98.1 m) in length and 50 ft. (15.3 m) in the beam. She had cabin accommodation for 360 passengers.

In her construction Brunel pioneered the use of transverse watertight bulkheads for safety, and the hull was of an unprecedented strength. Her four-cylinder, 1,500-hp steam engine gave her a speed of 11 knots on trials, later improved when her original six-bladed propeller was replaced by one of four blades. She was also equipped with six masts, her sail area totaling 15,300 sq. ft. (1,420 m²).

On her first transatlantic voyage in August 1845 she carried 600 tons of freight and 60 first-class passengers; the time from Liverpool to New York was just under 15 days. After a year of successful voyages across the Atlantic she ran aground off the Irish coast, where she remained for 11 months in conditions that would have smashed any other ship of the time to pieces. Once refloated and repaired, she spent nearly 30 years carrying passengers, sometimes as many as 600, to Australia. In 1866, disabled by a storm off Cape Horn, she was beached in the Falkland Islands. In 1970 she was towed back on a floating platform to her original dock at Bristol to be restored and opened to the public.

Great Eastern Ill-fated giant steamship, the third and last designed by Isambard Kingdom BRUNEL. She was built by Scott Russell & Co. of Millwall on the Thames, and was launched on January 31, 1858. With a gross tonnage of 18,914, and measuring 692 ft. (211 m) in

Brunel's last ship, the Great Eastern *of 1858.*

length and 83 ft. (25 m) in the beam, she was for over 40 years the world's largest ship. She was by any standard immensely strong and, with transverse watertight bulkheads and a cellular double bottom, very safe. The only ship ever built with screw, paddles, and sails, she was still, however, underpowered. She had a four-cylinder oscillating steam engine of 3,410 hp turning 56-ft. (17-m) paddle wheels, a four-cylinder horizontal direct-acting steam engine of 4,890 hp turning a 24-ft. (7.3-m) four-bladed screw propeller, and six masts carrying a total of 58,500 sq. ft. (5,435 m²) of sail. Her top speed was 15 knots, and she was remarkably maneuverable. She was designed to carry 4,000 passengers (or 10,000 as a troopship), 6,000 tons of freight, and 12,200 tons of coal — enough to take her to Australia without refueling en route.

A magnificent ship in conception, she was dogged by ill luck and suffered from misuse. Her launching took three months, bankrupted her builders, and hastened Brunel's death, and instead of making the intended voyages to India, Australia, and the east, she was put into service on the North Atlantic. She ran at a loss and was sold at auction in 1864 for only £25,000 and spent the remainder of her working life as a cable layer. She was responsible for laying the first successful transatlantic cable in 1866 and went on to weave a web of cables from France to America and from Bombay to Aden and up the Red Sea. On this last occasion she left England with the enormous displacement of 32,724 tons and a draft of 34 ft. 6 in. (10.5 m). The *Great Eastern* spent her last years as a showboat at Liverpool before being broken up in 1888.

Great Republic The largest wooden sailing ship ever built, a four-masted BARK built by Donald MCKAY at Boston and launched in 1853, some 20 years before the four-masted bark rig entered general use. Originally a 4,555-ton ship, she was 335 ft. (102 m) long and 53 ft. (16.2 m) in the beam. She was constructed with four decks, and her wooden hull was strengthened with diagonal iron braces. She was the first ship to have a steam donkey engine to sway the yards and work the pumps.

When completed, she was towed to New York, but before her maiden voyage she was severely damaged by fire.

The Great Republic, *built by McKay in 1853.*

She was rebuilt with three decks, a tonnage of 3,357, and a reduced sail plan, but she remained the world's largest wooden sailing vessel and proved a fast ship. On her maiden voyage she made the passage from New York to Liverpool in 19 days. During her working life she traded between New York and California, and between England and South America. She was also chartered as a troopship by the French government during the Crimean War, and by the North during the American Civil War. Towards the end of her career she was sold to a Liverpool shipping company and renamed *Denmark*. She sank in 1872.

Great Western First steamship built to make regular crossings of the Atlantic. The *Great Western* was a wooden paddle steamer, the largest of her day and the first vessel designed by the great British engineer Isambard Kingdom BRUNEL. She was built to extend across the Atlantic the services of the Great Western Railway, which had its western terminus at Bristol. Constructed by the shipbuilder William Patterson of Bristol, she was floated out of dry dock on July 19, 1837. She was of 1,340 tons gross and measured 236 ft. (71.9 m) in length and 35 ft. (10.7 m) in the beam (58 ft. or 17 m over the paddle boxes). Her 50-hp side-

Brunel's Great Western, *completed in 1838 for the transatlantic passage.*

lever steam engine turned side paddles 28 ft. 9 in. (8.76 m) in diameter. She was also equipped with four gaff-rigged masts and was capable of carrying 148 passengers in a luxury unparalleled in her day.

During her fitting out on the Thames it became clear that the race was on with the rival British and American Steam Navigation Company to provide the first regular steamship service across the North Atlantic. The rival company chartered the Irish packet steamer SIRIUS, which set out from Cork in Ireland on April 4, 1838. *Great Western* left four days later, but arrived in New York only four hours after *Sirius*. Her voyage took 15 days, 5 hours, at an average speed of 8.8 knots, and she arrived with some 25 percent of her fuel in reserve, thus finally establishing that steamships, if properly designed, could carry fuel sufficient for long voyages. *Great Western* spent eight years in transatlantic service, during which she made 67 effortless crossings and brought her time down to 12 days, 6 hours. The next 10 years of her working life were spent on voyages between Southampton and the West Indies. She was finally broken up in 1856-57.

Havock The world's first DESTROYER, built by the English shipbuilder Alfred Yarrow for the Royal Navy in 1892-93. The *Havock* and her sister ship the *Hornet*, together with the *Daring* and *Decoy* built by Thornycroft, were the result of an order from Sir John FISHER of the British Admiralty for a new type of ship that could counter the threat of the high-speed TORPEDO BOAT. The *Havock* was the first of these new and successful 'torpedo-boat destroyers.' Displacing 260 tons, capable of 26.7 knots, and armed with three torpedo tubes and four guns, she proved more than a match for any existing torpedo boat. She was 180 ft. (54.8 m) long and 18 ft. 6 in. (5.6 m) in the beam and was equipped with a conventional locomotive-type boiler. The *Hornet* and the Thornycroft ships used the new and much more efficient water-tube boiler; the *Hornet* was the fastest ship of her day with a maximum speed of 28 knots.

Henry Grâce à Dieu The greatest warship of Henry VIII's navy, and one of the largest CARRACKS of her day. The

The world's first torpedo-boat destroyer, HMS Havock.

Great Harry, as she was familiarly known, displaced at least 1,000 tons and carried four masts. She was launched in 1514, rebuilt in 1540, and represented Henry VIII's principal contribution to the creation of England's navy. She featured 21 heavy bronze cannon, an important innovation for her day, and also carried some 230 smaller weapons of a wide variety of types. Her crew numbered about 700. The *Great Harry* was accidentally destroyed by fire at Woolwich in 1553. There is a contemporary illustration of the ship in the Anthony Roll, now preserved at Magdalene College, Cambridge, England.

Kaiser Wilhelm der Grosse The first large German transatlantic liner, operated by North German Lloyd of Bremen, and the world's largest and fastest liner when she was launched on May 4, 1897. She carried 2,070 passengers and a crew of 488. Her gross tonnage was 14,349 and she was 656 ft. (199.5 m) long and 66 ft. (20.1 m) in the beam. On her maiden voyage in September 1897 she made the crossing from Southampton, England, to New York in 5 days, 22 hours, and 5 minutes, at an average speed of 21.35 knots. This was improved on a later voyage of 1898 to 22.35 knots and she became Germany's first holder of the Blue Riband, keeping that honor until it was won by another express liner from the same yard, *Deutschland*, in July 1900.

The Henry Grâce à Dieu, *as illustrated in the Anthony Roll, Cambridge.*

Kaiser Wilhelm der Grosse had four funnels and a hull subdivided by 16 watertight bulkheads. She was one of the first ships equipped with radio. In 1913 she was altered to carry third-class and steerage passengers only, and the following year was refitted as an armed merchant cruiser. She was sunk off the coast of West Africa on August 27, 1914, by the British cruiser *Highflyer*.

Karteria The first steam warship to attack and sink other vessels. *Karteria (Perseverance)* was a ship of the Greek navy in the war of independence against Turkey. She was the first of several paddle steamers ordered, at the instigation of Lord COCHRANE, from a British shipyard, but she was the only one to enter action, due to delays in construction and shortage of fuels. A small, flat-bottomed steamer with eight guns, *Karteria* was put under the command of a half-pay British naval officer, Frank Hastings, in 1827, and proceeded to strike terror into Turkish ships wherever she could find them. Her engine was unreliable and she was very slow, even by the standards of the day, but the red-hot cannon balls heated in her boiler fires were deadly weapons against wooden ships. A number of small Turkish and Egyptian vessels were set ablaze and sunk by the *Karteria*.

Kiev First of a new class of ships of the Soviet navy, officially termed 'antisubmarine cruisers' but closely resembling aircraft carriers in appearance, with an angled, through flight deck but very heavy armament forward. The 38,000-ton *Kiev* (launched in 1972) and her sister ship the *Minsk* (launched three years later) represent an important new departure in Soviet naval policy as the first postwar Soviet ships with flat decks. They point to a new and more significant role for the Soviet navy in international affairs. Their predecessors, the *Moskva*-class antisubmarine cruisers, were equipped with a flight deck aft for helicopters; the *Kiev* and *Minsk* were built to operate the new Yakovlev 36 *Forger* VTOL aircraft as well as a fleet of large *Hormone* advanced antisubmarine helicopters.

The *Kiev* is 898 ft. (274 m) in length and 135 ft. (41.2 m) in the beam; the flight deck is 620 ft. (189 m) long and 68 ft. (20.7 m) wide. Capable of 32 knots

Model of Thor Heyerdahl's Kon-Tiki *raft.*

and possessing a cruising range of 13,000 miles (21,000 km), the *Kiev* carries a crew of 1,800 with 13 aircraft and 30 helicopters; a heavy missile armament features surface-to-surface missiles and numerous surface-to-air weapons. Two further ships of the *Kiev* class are reported to be under construction.

Kon-Tiki The first craft built by Thor HEYERDAHL in his efforts to prove his theory that peoples of the ancient world were capable of making great transoceanic migrations. *Kon-Tiki*, built to test whether the Incas of Peru could have settled in Polynesia, was named for the legendary Inca sun king. She was a 45 ft. by 18 ft. (13.7 m × 5.5 m) raft made of balsa logs lashed together. She carried a small deckhouse for the crew of six and had a single small square sail. Her design was derived from the rafts still used as fishing platforms by the Indians. Heyerdahl and his five companions sailed some 4,300 miles (6,900 km) in 101 days from Callao in Peru to Raroia in the Tuamotu Islands, where they arrived on August 7, 1947. The raft itself is now preserved at the Kon-Tiki Museum at Oslo in Norway.

Lenin Soviet icebreaker, the world's first nuclear-powered surface ship to enter service. She was launched at Leningrad in December 1957 and commissioned in September 1959. Displacing 15,300 tons, she is 440 ft. (134 m) long and 90 ft. (27.6 m) in the beam. Her three screws are turned by steam turbines with an output of 39,200 hp; steam is generated by three independent nuclear reactors, one of which is normally held in reserve. With a top speed in open water of 19.7 knots, she can clear a passage 100 ft. (30.5 m) wide through 8-ft. (2.4-m) pack ice at a steady 3 to 4 knots. Refueling is necessary only once a year, a feature of particular importance for this type of ship.

Reports have been received of considerable trouble with the *Lenin*'s reactors, initially of a type principally intended for submarines, and it seems that late in 1979 the decision was taken to scrap her. Even larger nuclear-powered vessels, the *Arktika* and *Sibir*, have now taken her place as the pride of the large Soviet fleet of icebreakers.

Lightning (1) The world's first TORPEDO BOAT, equipped to launch the

183

The clipper ship Lightning.

The Lusitania, *sunk by a German submarine in 1915.*

new self-propelled torpedo invented by Robert Whitehead. The product of the Thames shipbuilder John Thornycroft, who had specialized in fast steam launches and spar-torpedo boats for foreign navies, *Lightning* was built for the Royal Navy in 1876 and became its *Torpedo Boat No. 1*. She displaced 34 tons, was 75 ft. (22.9 m) long, and was capable of the impressive speed of 19 knots from an engine of 477 hp. In 1879 she was reequipped to carry a revolving torpedo tube at her bow, capable of launching torpedoes while the ship was steaming at speed. Her success led the British Admiralty to place orders for 12 more vessels, and other navies soon followed suit.

(2) Celebrated American CLIPPER, one of four built by Donald MCKAY in 1853-54 for the Black Ball Line of Liverpool, England. Her sister ships were CHAMPION OF THE SEAS, *Donald McKay*, and *James Baines*; the four were among the fastest sailing ships ever built. Of 1,468 tons, *Lightning* measured 244 ft. (74.4 m) in length and 44 ft. (13.4 m) in the beam. She carried an enormous spread of 117,000 sq. ft. (10,869 m²) of sail. Her three masts had overall heights from deck to truck of 151 ft. (46 m), 164 ft. (50 m), and 115 ft. (35 m). She had two full decks, with four large staterooms and a sumptuous 86-ft. (26-m) main saloon between decks. A large deckhouse amidships contained a further six staterooms, and forecastle and poop decks provided accommodation for crew and officers.

Lightning was an extreme clipper, and

her bows were claimed to be more hollow than those of any other ship. She was certainly very fast. Her maiden voyage from Boston to Liverpool included 24-hour runs of 306, 312, 328, and 436 nautical miles (567, 578, 607, and 807 km). Her first voyage from Liverpool to Melbourne was made in 77 days, and the return passage took just 64 days, a record never beaten. With the exception of a brief period carrying out troops to quell the Indian mutiny of 1857, she spent her working life in the Australian emigrant trade. She was destroyed by fire in 1869 at Victoria, Australia.

Long Beach The world's first nuclear-powered surface warship, and the first to have a guided-missile main battery. The *Long Beach* was the first ship designed as a CRUISER for the U.S. Navy since the end of World War II. She was launched at Quincy, Massachusetts, on July 14, 1959, and was commissioned on September 9, 1961. Displacing 14,200 tons (17,100 tons under full load), she measures 721 ft. (219.8 m) in length and 73 ft. (22.3 m) in the beam. Her two reactors give her a speed of 30 knots from turbines generating 80,000 hp. The principal armament of the *Long Beach* includes two Terrier twin missile launchers forward and a Talos twin missile launcher aft; after being in operation for nearly 20 years her entire missile system is now scheduled for modernization at a cost in excess of $250 million.

Lusitania British transatlantic passenger liner sunk by a German submarine on

May 7, 1915, in one of the most serious strategic blunders made by the German navy in World War I. The *Lusitania* was a Cunard liner built by John Brown and Company at Clydebank, Scotland. She was launched in 1906, shortly before her sister ship MAURETANIA. On her maiden voyage in September 1907 she took the Blue Riband from the German liner *Kaiser Wilhelm II*, averaging 23.825 knots for the two crossings.

After the outbreak of World War I she continued sailing between Liverpool and New York. She left New York on her last voyage on May 1, 1915, carrying 1,959 passengers and crew and a cargo that included 5,000 cases of ammunition and a small quantity of other munitions. The German embassy in the United States had warned intending passengers that a war zone existed around the British Isles and that all vessels flying the British flag were subject to attack. Approaching the Irish coast on May 7, and neglecting to take antisubmarine precautions, she was struck without warning by two torpedoes from the German submarine *U-20*. She sank in only 20 minutes, and 1,198 lives were lost including those of 124 Americans. A wave of indignation swept the United States, and a declaration of war was widely expected. It did not come. Further attacks on unarmed passenger liners followed before the United States extracted a pledge from Germany to cease its unrestricted submarine warfare. The German concession had been made only upon the threat of severing diplomatic relations. When Germany resumed unrestricted submarine warfare against all merchant shipping early in 1917, American entry into World War I soon followed.

Maine American battleship whose explosion and sinking in Havana Harbor in 1898 helped precipitate the Spanish-American War. The *Maine* was a second-class battleship of 6,682 tons, commissioned in 1895 and manned by 354 officers and crew. On January 24, 1898, she was dispatched from Key West under Captain C.D. Sigsbee to protect American lives and property in riot-torn Havana. At 9:40 pm on February 15, she was at anchor 500 yards (460 m) off the Arsenal in Havana Harbor when two explosions were heard, the first a dull thud, followed by one much more powerful. Parts of the *Maine* were thrown 200 ft. (60 m) into the air and the entire harbor was illuminated; 258 seamen and 2 officers were killed or died soon afterwards.

Separate investigations by Spanish and American authorities came to contradictory conclusions. The Spanish report pointed to an accidental internal explosion as the cause, possibly spontaneous combustion in the coal bunkers. An American court of inquiry attributed the sinking to an external explosion by a mine or a torpedo, which set off the forward magazine. News of the disaster aroused widespread indignation throughout the United States. The American public placed the responsibility for the explosion firmly on Spain, and newspapers coined the slogan 'Remember the *Maine*, to hell with Spain.' Little more than two months after the *Maine*'s destruction the United States and Spain were at war.

In 1911 part of the Maine's hull was raised. A new American inquiry was held and confirmed the verdict of its predecessor but some European experts remained convinced that an internal explosion had taken place. The mystery of the *Maine*'s sinking has never been solved.

Manhattan The largest ship and the first commercial vessel to navigate the Northwest Passage in an experimental voyage to establish the best way of transporting oil from Alaska's North Slope. The *Manhattan* was an Esso tanker of 151,000 tons, refitted as an icebreaker to undertake her voyage. She was cut into four sections to speed her conversion and was fitted with an enormous spoon-shaped icebreaking bow, a steel belt at the waterline, modern inertial navigation equipment, and a helicopter pad at the stern. The specially strengthened propellers and rudders were encased in ice shields.

She sailed from Chester, Pennsylvania, on August 24, 1969, reached Thule in Greenland on September 4, and with her accompanying icebreakers arrived at Prudhoe Bay, Alaska, on September 19. After tests, she returned home, again through the Northwest Passage, arriving in New York on November 12. A Canadian icebreaker had to be called out to free her in McClure Strait on her outward voyage, and on her return her side plating was severely damaged. The experiment was therefore risky as well as expensive, and the Canadian government, not officially informed of the venture, expressed concern about ecological damage in the event of an oil spill. Strict conditions for any further voyages were laid down, and their economic viability was in any case questionable; the oil companies chose instead to build a pipeline to the ice-free Pacific coast of Alaska.

Mary Celeste American sailing ship found abandoned in perfect condition in the Atlantic in 1872; still one of the great mysteries of the sea. The *Mary Celeste* was a 280-ton brig-schooner, built in 1861 and registered under the United States flag in 1868. On November 5, 1872, she sailed from New York for Italy carrying a cargo of 1,700 barrels of crude alcohol. She was next seen on December 5 by the Nova Scotian brigantine *Dei Gratia*, about 600 miles (965 km) west of Gibraltar. The captain of the *Dei Gratia* could see the other vessel was in distress, but on moving closer he found no helmsman and no crew on deck. Men were sent across to the *Mary Celeste*, and they found her completely seaworthy, but deserted. The ship had obviously been abandoned hurriedly. Her boat had gone, as had the captain's chronometer, sextant, and most of the official papers. The log book still remaining on board had been entered up to November 24, and a slate showed observations for 8 am on the following day. Contrary to popular legend, there were no half-eaten meals on the table and no signs of violence.

Seamen from the *Dei Gratia* sailed the *Mary Celeste* to Gibraltar, and a new crew took her on to her destination, Genoa, where it was discovered that nine barrels of the cargo had leaked. Fear that fire or an explosion was about to occur could therefore have led those on board to take to a boat. Bad weather reported in the area for November 25 could have prevented them from reboarding (there were signs that the rope from the boat to the *Mary Celeste*'s stern had parted), and the captain, his wife and child, and the crew simply vanished in the small boat. Another possible explanation suggests that a waterspout, forcing a surge of water up the pump well, led the captain to think that his ship was sinking fast and had to be abandoned. It seems unlikely that the mystery will ever be finally solved. The *Mary Celeste* herself, after going through the hands of 17 subsequent owners, was deliberately wrecked off Haiti 13 years later by an owner anxious for insurance money.

Mauretania One of the most successful of all the great Cunard LINERS, holder of the Blue Riband of the North Atlantic for 20 years. She was built by Swan Hunter & Wigham Richardson at Wallsend-on-Tyne in the north of England, and was launched on September 20, 1906. She and her ill-fated sister ship LUSITANIA plied between Liverpool and New York, and were the first major liners fitted with steam turbines.

Mauretania carried 2,335 passengers and a crew of 812. She had a gross tonnage of 37,938, was 790 ft. (240 m) long, 88 ft. (27 m) in the beam, and had a draft of 25 ft. (7.6 m). Her four direct-coupled turbines produced a total output of 68,000 hp and drove four screws. She carried over 6,000 tons of coal and consumed 1,000 tons a day. On her maiden voyage in November 1907 she made the crossing in 5 days, 5 hours, and 10 minutes at an average of 22.21 knots. On her return voyage she set a new record of 23.69 knots. Her speed actually increased over the years. In September 1909 she made the westward passage in 4 days, 10 hours, and 51 minutes at an average of 26.06 knots, taking the Blue Riband from *Lusitania*. She lost the Blue Riband to BREMEN in July 1929, but in the following month she broke her own record with an average speed for the crossing of 27.22 knots, and in 1933, already 27 years old, she maintained a speed of 32 knots for over three hours. During World War I she served as a troopship and as a hospital ship, and after the war, when she was given a major refit, her boilers were converted to oil firing. From 1931 until she was scrapped in 1935 she sailed as a cruise ship.

Mayflower   The ship that carried the Pilgrim Fathers to Plymouth, Massachussetts, in 1620. With Christopher Jones in command, she sailed from Southampton on August 15, 1620, together with the *Speedwell*, which had brought some of the company from Holland. The tiny *Speedwell* was forced to turn back twice because of unseaworthiness, and *Mayflower* eventually set out alone from Plymouth, England, on September 16 with some of *Speedwell*'s passengers in addition to her own. It was intended that she should sail to Virginia Colony, where territory had been granted to the prospective settlers, but she was forced off course by storms and eventually reached what is now Provincetown on Cape Cod on November 21. The famous Mayflower Compact was signed on board that day. She landed her 102 passengers at Plymouth on December 26 and returned to England the following April. Her subsequent history is not known.

No contemporary drawing or plan of the *Mayflower* has survived, but she was probably about 90 ft. (27 m) long and of 180 tons. The *Mayflower II*, which sailed across the Atlantic in 53 days in 1957, is representative of the general appearance of ships of the period, rather than of any particular vessel.

The Mayflower, *1620.*

Merrimack   Confederate IRONCLAD warship famous for her inconclusive duel with the MONITOR at Hampton Roads on March 9, 1862. The *Merrimack* was originally a wooden-hulled steam frigate 275 ft. (83.2 m) in length and displacing 4,650 tons. When Union Forces abandoned the Norfolk Navy Yard in April 1861 she was scuttled. The Confederates raised her, rechristened her the *Virginia* and built a sloping wooden penthouse or casemate over her entire deck. This was covered with iron armor plates 4 in. (100 mm) thick. She was equipped with 10 guns and an iron ram. At Hampton Roads on March 8, 1862, the *Merrimack* attacked a Union blockading force, ramming and sinking the *Cumberland* and destroying the *Congress*. That night the *Monitor* arrived at Hampton Roads, and the following day the two ships engaged in a close-range battle which lasted more than four hours. Neither ship suffered serious damage and the *Merrimack* withdrew to Norfolk. She appeared at Hampton Roads the following month but did not engage again in battle. When the Confederates evacuated Norfolk on May 11, 1862, she was burned and scuttled.

Mikasa   Japanese battleship, flagship of Admiral TOGO in the victory over the Russian fleet at the Battle of Tsushima Strait (May 27-28, 1905). The new Japanese navy had been almost entirely equipped with foreign-built ships, mostly British; the *Mikasa* was one of them. She was built by the British firm of Vickers and was launched in 1902. *Mikasa* was one of the classics of battleship design of the years immediately preceding the appearance of the DREADNOUGHT. She displaced 15,200 tons and carried four 12-in. and sixteen 6-in. guns; her top speed was 18.5 knots. In September 1905 she sank as the result of a magazine explosion but was raised and put back into service. She was finally retired in the 1920s, but kept afloat as a national memorial at Yokosuka dockyard. She survived American air strikes in World War II to be preserved, set in concrete, as a permanent memorial to Japan's greatest admiral.

Missouri   U.S. battleship, scene of the Japanese surrender in Tokyo Bay on September 2, 1945. The *Missouri* was commissioned on June 11, 1944, as the last of

four battleships of the *Iowa* class. Except for the Japanese YAMATO AND MUSASHI, the *Missouri* and her sister ships *Iowa*, *New Jersey*, and *Wisconsin* were the largest and most powerful battleships ever built. Displacing 58,000 tons under full load, and carrying nine 16-in. guns in triple turrets, *Missouri* was still capable of 33 knots from her 212,000-hp turbines. Her length was 887 ft. (270 m) and beam 108 ft. (33 m); she carried 2,365 officers and crew. Her guns were capable of hurling 2,700-lb. (1,225-kg) projectiles up to 23 miles (39 km) with great accuracy.

The *Missouri* saw action in the Pacific in the last year of World War II; she and her sister ships performed shore bombardment duties during the Korean War. The *New Jersey* was brought out of retirement for service off Vietnam in 1968-69. Decommissioned since the 1950s, the *Missouri* is in mothballs at Puget Sound Naval Shipyard.

Monitor   The 'cheesebox on a raft' whose inconclusive duel with the Confederate MERRIMACK on March 9, 1862, was the world's first battle between ironclad warships. The *Monitor* was hurriedly built to a design by John ERICSSON and towed out of New York Harbor on March 6. Two days later she appeared at Hampton Roads. On a flat iron hull almost awash in the water, she mounted a single revolving turret carrying two 11-in. guns. She displaced 978 tons and was 172 ft. (52.5 m) long. Twice on the passage from New York she nearly sank, and she finally foundered under tow off Cape Hatteras on December 31, 1862.

Musashi   See YAMATO AND MUSASHI.

Nautilus   U.S. SUBMARINE, the world's first nuclear-powered vessel, launched in January 1954. The brainchild of Hyman RICKOVER of the U.S. Navy, she was named after the pioneering craft built a century and a half earlier by Robert FULTON and after the submarine of Jules Verne's science fiction classic. When the *Nautilus* first put to sea under nuclear power on January 17, 1955, the submarine truly came of age: at last a vessel had been built capable of operating deep beneath the sea's surface for a period of duty limited only by the crew's endurance and provisioning. A vivid demonstration of her capabilities was made be-

Above: The Merrimack *ramming the* Cumberland, *March 1862.*
Right: The sinking of the Monitor, *1862.*

tween August 1 and 5, 1958, when she sailed beneath the polar ice cap from Point Barrow, Alaska, to the Greenland Sea. During this voyage, at 11:15 pm on August 3, she became the first vessel to reach the North Pole.

The *Nautilus* is 319 ft. (97 m) long and displaces 3,764 tons on the surface, 4,040 tons submerged. She has a complement of 105 men and is armed with six torpedo tubes. Her submerged speed is in excess of 20 knots, and she can dive to a depth of 720 ft. (220 m). The *Nautilus* is approaching the end of her active career but will be preserved as a permanent memorial at Annapolis.

Nemesis The first iron warship, a small paddle steamer designed and constructed by the Birkenhead shipbuilder John Laird for the British East India Company. The 660-ton *Nemesis* was launched in 1839; armed with two swivel guns, themselves an innovation, she was the first of a class of similar ships for the company. Considerable interest was taken in her voyage out to India because of her iron structure, which stood up to the voyage well despite the fact that she drew only 5 ft. (1.5 m) of water. *Nemesis* demonstrated her worth in 1841-42 during the Opium War, when she had little difficulty in sinking numerous Chinese war junks off Canton.

Nimitz First of a new class of U.S. nuclear-powered AIRCRAFT CARRIERS (including the *Dwight David Eisenhower* and *Carl Vinson*), which are the largest warships ever built. The *Nimitz* was launched on May 13, 1972, and displaces 81,600 tons (91,487 tons under full load). Her length is 1,092 ft. (332 m) and beam 134 ft. (40.8 m); the width of the flight deck is 252 ft. (76.8 m). Powered by two nuclear reactors (in contrast to the eight of the ENTERPRISE), she is capable of speeds in excess of 30 knots from four steam turbines generating 280,000 hp. Her reactor cores have an estimated life of 13 years, enabling her to sail about 1,000,000 miles (1,600,000 km) before refueling. The *Nimitz*'s crew of 3,300 is supplemented by an additional 3,000 men for the operation of her 90 aircraft. The *Nimitz* took $1.8 billion to build; each of her two sister ships have cost over $2 billion, and the construction of any further giant carriers is the subject of considerable debate. Many naval strategists recommend instead the building of 'medium-size,' conventionally powered carriers of 50,000 tons displacement.

Normandie The world's first passenger LINER to exceed 1,000 ft. (305 m) in length, and the largest and fastest transatlantic liner of the mid-1930s. She was built for the Compagnie Générale Transatlantique, and launched at St. Nazaire on October 29, 1932. Sailing between Le Havre and New York, she was the pride of the French merchant marine and carried on her 11 decks 1,972 passengers and a crew of 1,345. She had a gross tonnage of 83,432 and was 1,029 ft. (313.6 m) long and 118 ft. (36 m) in the beam, with a draft of 37 ft. (11.2 m). She was unusual in having turbo-electric propulsion, and her four screws gave her a cruising speed of over 29 knots. Her boilers consumed fuel oil at the rate of 1,200 tons a day.

On her maiden voyage in May 1935 the *Normandie* crossed the Atlantic in 4 days, 3 hours, and 2 minutes at an average of 29.98 knots, and returned at an average of 30.31 knots. In 1937 she was fitted with four-bladed screws and took the Blue Riband with a crossing of 3 days, 22 hours, and 7 minutes at an average of 31.20 knots. One of the reasons for her outstanding performance was the unusual design of her hull, with great height, a very full midship section, and extremely fine lines at bow and stern. Fuel consumption at 29 knots was no greater than that of the much smaller liner *Ile de France* at 23.5 knots. Less than two weeks after America's entry into World War II the *Normandie*, which was anchored at New York, was taken over by the U.S. Maritime Commission and renamed *Lafayette*. While undergoing conversion to a troopship, she caught fire and capsized in New York Harbor on February 9, 1942. She was finally scrapped in 1946.

The Normandie, *the largest transatlantic liner built before World War II.*

Potemkin Russian battleship of the Black Sea Fleet, famed for the mutiny that took place aboard her on June 25, 1905. The *Potemkin*, or more properly the *Kniaz Potemkin Tavrichevsky*, was commissioned in 1904 and was one of the most modern ships of the Russian navy. She displaced 12,548 tons, and her two heavy turrets, one forward and one aft, carried four 12-in. guns. The disastrous course of the Russo-Japanese War had sparked off a revolution in Russia, and the mutiny was one of its most dramatic events. The crew eventually scuttled the *Potemkin* in Rumanian waters. She was raised and renamed *Panteleimon* on her return to the Imperial Navy. She fought in World War I with her original name restored.

Preussen The largest full-rigged ship ever built, and the only one to carry five masts. *Preussen* belonged to the famous P-Line, which operated from Hamburg, Germany. She was launched in 1902, was of 5,548 tons (8,000 tons deadweight), and measured 433 ft. (131.9 m) in length (482 ft. or 146.9 m overall including the jib boom) and 54 ft. (16.5 m) in the beam. The leading four masts were identical, each being of steel and 3 ft. (0.9 m) in diameter, with an overall height of 227 ft. (69.2 m). The 100-ft. (30.5-m) mainyards each weighed 6.5 tons, and her total sail area was 60,000 sq. ft. (5,574 m²). She had a crew of only 48, for in those last years of sail every economy possible had to be made. In terms of tons of cargo carried per crew member, she was nearly six times as efficient as the sleek clipper CUTTY SARK, for example, which needed a crew of 35

to transport some 1,000 tons.

Preussen was built of steel and was very full-hulled; with her straight sides and horizontal deck she resembled a floating crate in cross section, but the hull was very streamlined. She was equipped with two small steam engines to power cargo-handling winches and weigh anchor; power was also sometimes used to turn the wheel, an operation which could otherwise require eight or more men. The ingenious deck winches for the rigging were turned by hand.

Although a very large ship to maneuver, *Preussen* sailed well and could maintain 16 to 17 knots for hours on end. Financially, however, she was not a success; it proved virtually impossible to find 8,000 tons of economic cargo. She made a total of 14 voyages but only sailed fully laden twice. Her life was short: on November 6, 1910, she collided with a steamship off Beachy Head in the English Channel. Partly disabled, she made for Dover, but was wrecked in a storm. The

The five-masted Preussen, *1902.*

subsequent inquiry placed blame for the collision firmly on the steamer, which had attempted to pass in front of *Preussen*, underestimating her speed and breaking the rule that steam must give way to sail.

Pyroscaphe One of the earliest paddle steamboats, *Pyroscaphe* was built by the Marquis Claude de Jouffroy d'Abbans at Lyons, France, in 1783. De Jouffroy had experimented as early as 1778 with a boat propelled by 'duck-foot' paddles and powered by a single-acting steam engine. His 182-ton *Pyroscaphe* had a far more efficient engine that turned a pair of side paddle wheels through a double-acting ratchet mechanism. The 150-ft. (46-m) craft made its way up the River Saône for 15 minutes before the engine broke down. De Jouffroy ran his vessel intermittently during the next 16 months but aroused little interest.

Queen Elizabeth The largest passenger LINER ever built, launched at John Brown and Company's shipyard at Clydebank, Scotland, in September 1938. The 83,673-ton *Queen Elizabeth* was 1,031 ft. (314.2 m) long and 119 ft. (6.3 m) in the beam, and was designed to carry 2,288 passengers and a crew of 1,296. Her four turbines produced 181,700 hp and gave her a cruising speed of 28.5 knots. Her fitting out was overtaken by the outbreak of World War II, and she left Britain secretly to join her Cunard sister ship *Queen Mary*, arriving unheralded at New York on March 7, 1940. The two vessels were refitted as troopships (*Mary* in Australia, *Elizabeth* in Singapore) with an initial capacity of 8,200. On her voyages across the Atlantic between 1943 and 1945 she carried as many as 15,000 troops at a time; by the end of the war the two ships had transported a total of 1,243,538 troops between them.

After war service *Queen Elizabeth* was fitted out as a luxury liner and left Southampton on her first commercial transatlantic voyage on October 16, 1946. In 1969 she was sold for conversion to a floating hotel and exhibition center at Port Everglades, Florida. Two years later she was sold again, but before her refitting was completed she was set on fire and sank in Hong Kong Harbor on January 9, 1972.

The Cunard liner Queen Elizabeth, *launched in 1938.*

Queen Elizabeth 2 (QE 2) The only great luxury passenger liner still in transatlantic service, built by Upper Clyde Shipbuilders at Clydebank, Scotland, and launched on September 20, 1967. She was designed to be a far more versatile ship than the earlier Cunard Queens, capable of holiday cruising as well as maintaining regular transatlantic services. She consumes only half as much fuel as the earlier *Queen Elizabeth* and her lightweight aluminum superstructure gives her a draft shallow enough to berth at a wide range of ports. Passenger accommodation plans vary; she was initially designed to carry 2,025 passengers in two classes on the North Atlantic run and 1,400 in one class on cruises, with a crew of 920.

The gross tonnage of the *QE 2* is 65,863. She is 963 ft. (293.5 m) in length, 105 ft. (32 m) in the beam and has a maximum draft of 32 ft. 6 in. (9.9 m). Her steam turbines produce 110,000 hp, turn two six-bladed screws, and give her a service speed of 28.5 knots. On trials she attained a top speed of 32.46 knots. She has 13 decks, a hull subdivided into 15 watertight compartments, bow thrusters, and two sets of fin stabilizers capable of damping a 20° roll to only 3°. Her open deck space covers 6,000 sq. yd. (5,000 m²) and is the greatest of any passenger ship; her public rooms include the Double Room, the largest room afloat.

Queen Mary The fastest transatlantic liner for some 15 years, built by John Brown and Company at Clydebank, Scotland, and launched on September 26, 1934. She carried 2,139 passengers and a crew of 1,101. Her gross tonnage was 80,774, and she was 1,019 ft. (310.6 m) long and 119 ft. (36.2 m) in the beam, with a draft of 39 ft. (11.8 m). Her turbines developed 162,176 hp and drove four screws. On trials she reputedly attained 33 knots; her normal service speed was 28.5 knots. Her maiden voyage to New York in May 1936 took 4 days, 27 minutes. Later in the year she improved her record to 3 days, 23 hours, and 57 minutes, averaging 30.63 knots and taking the Blue Riband from NORMANDIE. The French ship soon achieved an even faster crossing, but the *Queen Mary* recaptured the honor in

1938, completing her voyage in 3 days, 20 hours, and 42 minutes at an average of 31.69 knots, a record unbeaten until the maiden voyage of the UNITED STATES.

During World War II the *Queen Mary* served as a troopship, returning to the commercial Atlantic run on July 1, 1947, refitted and newly equipped with radar. She left Southampton on her last voyage on October 31, 1967, and is now anchored at Long Beach, California, as a floating Museum of the Sea.

Ra Papyrus-reed boat built by the Norwegian anthropologist and adventurer Thor HEYERDAHL. The design of the

The Queen Mary *(1938), Cunard Line's flagship before the* Queen Elizabeth.

13-ton *Ra*, named for the ancient Egyptian sun god, was based on boats portrayed in ancient wall paintings. She was constructed in the shadow of the pyramids from papyrus reeds gathered in Ethiopia (papyrus no longer grows in Egypt itself). She measured some 45 ft. (14 m) in length, and featured a distinctive high prow and stern. Heyerdahl's aim was to prove that the Egyptians could have crossed the Atlantic; he believed that the Maya and Inca civilizations of the New World bore resemblances to ancient Egypt that could not be merely coincidental.

Manned by an international crew, the *Ra* left Safi in Morocco in May 1969 and met with a series of disasters; the steering oar broke, the mast fractured, and eventually the boat became waterlogged and had to be abandoned only 600 miles (960 km) from a landfall in the West Indies. The following year Heyerdahl made a second attempt with a similar boat, the *Ra II*, built by four Bolivian Indians from the shores of Lake Titicaca, where reed boats are still in use. The new boat was a success, and Heyerdahl and his crew made the crossing from Morocco to Bridgetown, Barbados, without incident.

Rainbow American sailing ship, generally considered the first true CLIPPER. Designed by John Willis Griffith of New York and built at a cost of $22,500, she was launched in 1845. Griffith designed her with a raked-forward stempost and flared bow, a streamlined rounded stern, long hollow lines for the underwater body, and the greatest breadth further aft than was usual. His views aroused much opposition, his critics arguing that he had turned the bow outside in and defied the laws of nature. The *Rainbow*, however, proved an outstanding success in the China trade. She was of 1,043 tons and measured 159 ft. (48.5 m) in length and 31 ft. (9.5 m) in the beam. On her maiden voyage she broke all records with a round trip from New York to China and back in 6 months and 14 days, including two weeks in port at Canton. In 1848, on her fifth voyage, she was lost en route from New York to Valparaiso; she probably sank in the stormy seas off Cape Horn.

Rattler and Alecto Two Royal Navy frigates of 880 tons, famous for their participation in tests that conclusively demonstrated the superiority of the screw propeller over the paddle wheel. The ships were virtually identical and were powered by similar steam engines of 220 hp, but the *Alecto* was fitted with a pair of side paddles, and the *Rattler* with a screw propeller. In March 1845, the *Rattler* easily beat the *Alecto* in a race over 100 miles (160 km). On April 3 the two vessels were secured stern-to-stern, and in a remarkable tug-of-war with both ships steaming full ahead the *Rattler* pulled her rival backwards at a speed of 2.8 knots. The greater speed and power available from a screw propeller was dramatically demonstrated for all to see, and the adoption of screw propulsion for Royal Navy ships followed rapidly.

Resolution Flagship of Captain James COOK on his second and third voyages of exploration. She was a vessel of 562 tons, a cat-built collier originally called the *Marquis of Granby* and launched in 1770 at Whitby in northeast England. She was purchased by the Royal Navy shortly after she was built and was renamed the *Drake*. In December 1771 she received the new name *Resolution* and set sail under Cook's command on July 13, 1772. Aboard her for tests went a copy of John HARRISON's famous chronometer. She returned to Portsmouth on July 29, 1775, having circumnavigated the globe from east to west. She was poorly refitted before leaving Plymouth on Cook's final and ill-fated voyage on July 12, 1776. Repairs to her masts and spars were made at Nootka Sound and Hawaii, and it was after she had sprung her foremast and put back into Hawaii in February 1779 that Cook was killed. She was brought home via Canton and the Cape of Good Hope in October 1780.

The following year the *Resolution* was converted into an armed transport; her career in the Royal Navy was ended a few years later when she was captured in eastern waters by a French squadron commanded by Suffren de Saint Tropez.

Revenge Flagship of Sir Francis DRAKE in the battle against the Spanish Armada, and perhaps most celebrated for her final, gallant action against overwhelming odds under the command of Sir Richard GRENVILLE. The *Revenge* was a vessel of some 440 tons, mounting 34 guns. She was launched at Deptford in 1577. After service against the Armada in 1588 she was commanded by Drake in an abortive expedition against Lisbon (1589) and by Sir Martin FROBISHER in an attempt to capture the Spanish treasure fleet (1590).

In 1591 she became the flagship of Sir Richard Grenville, second-in-command of a squadron sent to intercept the homeward-bound Spanish treasure fleet. On August 31, off Flores in the Azores, the *Revenge* found herself cut off from the rest of her squadron in the face of more than 50 Spanish warships. Grenville tried fruitlessly to break through the Spanish lines, and after a heroic but hopeless 15-hour battle against 15 Spanish vessels carrying 5,000 men, the 190-man *Revenge* finally surrendered with Grenville mortally wounded. Five days later the badly battered *Revenge* sank in a storm with the loss of the entire Spanish crew put aboard her.

Royal Sovereign Name of a number of famous vessels of the Royal Navy. **(1)** The first of these was a handsome and lavishly decorated three-masted sailing ship, considered the prototype of the 100-gun three-decker SHIP OF THE LINE. The largest (1,500 tons) and most impressive warship of her day, she was designed by Phineas Pett and launched in 1637 under the name *Sovereign of the Seas*. Under the name *Sovereign* she took part in the First Anglo-Dutch War; after the Restoration she came to be known as the *Royal Sovereign* and saw action against the Dutch as the flagship of Prince Rupert and Admiral Lord Torrington. She was finally burned at Chatham in 1696.

(2) A revolutionary wooden-hulled ironclad turret ship of 5,080 tons, designed by Cowper Coles and completed in 1864. She was originally a 131-gun three-decker, but was rebuilt and equipped with four turrets carrying five 10.5-in. guns. She was followed within a few years by the *Prince Albert*, a sister ship with an iron hull. The two were built as coastal defense vessels and made little impact at the time, but with their multiple turrets on the centerline they prefigured in many ways the modern warship.

(3) The battleship *Royal Sovereign*, completed in May 1892, was the first of a

The ship of the line Royal Sovereign (launched as Sovereign of the Seas), 1637.

Replica of Columbus' Santa Maria, *moored at Barcelona, Spain.*

powerful new class of ships that set a pattern for the building of battleships until the appearance of the DREADNOUGHT. With her high freeboard and twin 13.5-in. guns mounted on barbettes at either end, she displayed a handsome profile, displacing 15,585 tons under full load. She was the first ship to carry steel armor and could attain the remarkable speed of 18 knots.

Santa Maria Flagship of Christopher COLUMBUS on his first voyage to the New World. Columbus himself described the *Santa Maria* as a NAO, a very general and imprecise term which gives us little firm evidence of what she was like. It seems likely she was about 80 to 90 tons, with a length of some 80 ft. (24.4 m), possibly more, and draft of 6 ft. (1.8 m). No building plans have survived, but she probably had a *caravela redonda* rig with the addition of a small main-topsail and a spritsail. *Santa Maria* sailed on August 3, 1492, with a crew of 40, in company with the slightly smaller caravels *Pinta* and *Niña*. *Santa Maria* was wrecked on a coral reef in Caracol Bay, Haiti, at midnight on Christmas Day, and her timbers were used to build a fort at a settlement that Columbus christened Navidad.

Savannah (1) Three-masted, full-rigged sailing ship fitted with an auxiliary steam engine and detachable paddle wheels, commonly, but mistakenly, considered the first steamship to cross the Atlantic. During her 27-day passage from Savannah, Georgia, to Liverpool (May 24-June 20, 1819), her 90-hp engine was in fact in use for only 85 hours; the first ships to cross the Atlantic entirely under steam were the SIRIUS and GREAT WESTERN (1838). The *Savannah* was built by Francis Fickett at New York and was of some 380 tons. She measured 98 ft. 6 in. (30 m) in length and 25 ft. 9 in. (7.8 m) in the beam. Her engine was later removed and she spent the rest of her short life sailing between New York and Savannah. She was wrecked in a storm in November 1821.

(2) The world's first nuclear-powered merchant ship, sponsored jointly by the U.S. Atomic Energy Commission and the Federal Maritime Commission, built by New York Shipbuilding Corporation at Camden, and launched on July 21, 1959. Of 12,220 gross tons, she was 595 ft. (181.5 m) long, and 78 ft. (23.8 m) in the beam. She carried 60 passengers, 9,400 tons of cargo, and a crew of 110. One fueling of her nuclear reactor provided energy for 16,000 hours at full power (for which a conventional ship would have used some 90,000 tons of oil). Steam generated by the reactor powered a turbine with an output of 22,000 hp. Service speed was more than 20 knots. The *Savannah* was built to show

the uses of nuclear power for merchant shipping, and during the 1960s she made a series of demonstration cruises. Although a technical success, her high cost of operation meant she could not compete on equal terms with conventional freighters and she has been laid up. With the exception of the experimental nuclear ships *Otto Hahn* (West Germany) and *Mutsu* (Japan), her pioneering example has not yet been followed.

Scharnhorst and Gneisenau The name of two pairs of sister ships of the German navy: two armored cruisers sunk in the opening months of World War I, and two battle cruisers of World War II.

(1) The armored cruisers *Scharnhorst* and *Gneisenau* were ships of 11,600 tons, the

191

largest vessels of the German East Asiatic Squadron under the command of Maximilian Graf von Spee. On November 1, 1914, in company with smaller ships of the squadron, the *Scharnhorst* and *Gneisenau* engaged a British force commanded by Sir Christopher Cradock off Coronel on the coast of Chile. The two largest British vessels, the cruisers *Good Hope* and *Monmouth*, were both destroyed and Cradock and their entire crews lost. On December 8, the *Scharnhorst* and *Gneisenau* were sunk off the Falkland Islands by a superior British force that included the battle cruisers *Invincible* and *Inflexible*. Spee and the entire crew of the *Scharnhorst* lost their lives; only 187 men were rescued from the *Gneisenau*.

(2) The battle cruisers *Scharnhorst* and *Gneisenau* displaced 31,000 tons and entered service shortly before the outbreak of World War II. They were involved in covering the invasion of Norway in 1940 and sank the British aircraft carrier *Glorious*, although both were soon laid up with torpedo damage. In January 1941 they broke out into the Atlantic and inflicted heavy damage on merchant shipping. After 11 months in harbor at the French port of Brest, subjected to continual air attacks, they made a daring passage up the English Channel and through the Straits of Dover in February 1942. When they had almost reached their destination both vessels ran into a minefield in the North Sea. Docked for repairs at Kiel, the *Gneisenau* never again saw action; she was finally scuttled at Gdynia in March 1945. The *Scharnhorst* was repaired and sent to northern Norway. On December 26, 1943, under the command of Rear Admiral Erich Bey, she was sunk by a large British force that included the battleship *Duke of York* in what became known as the Battle of North Cape. Only 36 of her crew of 2,000 survived. With the destruction of the *Scharnhorst*, one of the last surface threats to Allied shipping on northern sea routes was removed.

Selandia The world's first oceangoing motor ship, built at Copenhagen in 1912 for the Danish East Asiatic Company. Of 7,400 tons deadweight (4,694 gross), she measured 370 ft. (112.8 m) in length and 53 ft. (16.2 m) in the beam. She had two eight-cylinder four-stroke diesel engines

the 11,600-ton armored cruiser Scharnhorst *(1910).*

The Gneisenau *(1906), sister ship of the* Scharnhorst.

which developed a total of 2,450 hp and drove twin screws. Her cruising speed was 11 knots. She had no funnel; exhaust gases were discharged through one of her masts. Despite much skepticism, she proved outstandingly reliable, until 1936 working the very long passage between Copenhagen and Bangkok. Thereafter she was successively renamed *Norseman* (in Norwegian ownership) and *Tornador* (under the Finnish flag), before finally being wrecked off the coast of Japan in 1942.

Sirius The first vessel to cross the Atlantic under continuous steam power. She left Cork, in Ireland, on April 4, 1838, with 40 passengers on board, and

arrived off New York on April 22, after a voyage made at an average of 6.7 knots. She was built in 1837 at Leith, in Scotland, for service on the short passage between England and Ireland. She was thus a relatively small ship, with inadequate space for the coal needed for a transatlantic voyage. According to a popular account, her coal actually ran out, and furniture, paneling, spare yards, and a mast were burned to keep steam up. She had been chartered for the voyage by the British and American Steam Navigation Company, which was anxious to make an Atlantic crossing under steam before Isambard Kingdom BRUNEL's ship GREAT WESTERN could leave port. *Sirius* just succeeded. A few hours after she docked

Brunel's *Great Western* arrived in New York after a crossing of 15 days from Bristol with 200 tons of coal to spare.

Sirius' two-cylinder side-lever engine developed 320 hp. She was one of the first ships equipped with a surface condenser, which meant the boilers could be operated with fresh water. Of 703 tons gross, she measured 208 ft. (63.4 m) in length and 26 ft. (7.8 m) in the beam. She made one further Atlantic crossing before returning to service on the Irish Sea. She was wrecked in 1847.

Taeping   One of the finest of all British tea clippers, built by Robert Steele at Greenock, Scotland, in 1863. She was a composite-built ship of 767 tons gross and measured 184 ft. (56 m) in length and 31 ft. (9.4 m) in the beam. *Taeping* was built at Steele's yard alongside the *Serica*, a clipper of similar dimensions. These two vessels, together with the Steele-built ARIEL and two other ships, participated in a famous race from Foochow to England in 1866, carrying the first of the season's tea crop. *Taeping*, *Ariel*, and *Serica* all arrived in the Thames on the same tide in record time, after a voyage of 16,000 nautical miles (29,630 km). *Taeping* was wrecked in September 1871 in the China Sea, at the beginning of a voyage to New York.

Thermopylae   One of the last and most famous of the British tea clippers, a composite-built ship constructed by Walter Hood at Aberdeen, Scotland, and launched in August 1868. Of 991 tons, she measured 212 ft. (64.6 m) in length, and 36 ft. (11 m) in the beam. With an 80-ft. (24.4-m) mainyard, her sail plan was designed for width rather than height, and she was reputedly able to 'ghost' along at 7 knots in a wind too light to blow out a candle.

Thermopylae was built for the China tea trade, sailing on the outward passage with a mixed cargo for Australia. Her owners claimed her to be the fastest sailing ship in the world, and on her maiden voyage she beat an earlier record held by the American-built clipper *James Baines* by sailing from London to Melbourne in 63 days. Her best day's run during the voyage was 326 nautical miles (604 km). On the return passage from China she took part in a race with TAEPING, ARIEL, *Sir Lancelot* and other clippers, complet-

ing the voyage in 91 days and being beaten only by *Sir Lancelot* (89 days).

In 1882 *Thermopylae* entered the Australian wool trade, in which her fastest passage from London to Sydney was 75 days (1887), compared to the 71 days of her great rival the CUTTY SARK. In 1890 she was sold to Canadian owners; rerigged as a BARK she was still capable of 16 knots. In 1895 she was bought by the Portuguese navy and renamed *Pedro Nuñes*. She served as a training ship until 1907, when she was used as a target for torpedo practice and sunk.

Thomas W. Lawson   The ship possessing more masts than any other vessel in the final years of the age of sail, an enormous seven-masted SCHOONER, the only one of her type ever built. Constructed at Quincy, Mass., for the Coastwise Transportation Company in 1902, she was a ship of 5,218 gross tons and measured 375 ft. (114.5 m) in length and 50 ft. (15.2 m) in the beam. Each of her masts was some 195 ft. (59.4 m) tall, and made up of a lower mast of steel and a topmast of Oregon pine. Her total sail area was an impressive 40,000 sq. ft. (3,700 m²), yet she required a crew of only 16. Her fore-and-aft rigging was simple to manage, and she was equipped with two steam winches to hoist, lower, and trim the sails.

The *Thomas W. Lawson* was built of steel, with three full-length steel decks, and her hull was fitted with bilge keels to improve her stability by providing a better grip on the water. She was built for the coastal trade, for which her rig was in theory well-suited, but she proved difficult to handle. Until 1906 she sailed between Texas and Philadelphia, but the following year she was chartered to carry oil across the Atlantic, a voyage ill-suited to the best of schooners, and one which proved disastrous. Riding out a storm at anchor off the Scilly Isles, she capsized on December 13, 1907; only one member of the crew survived.

Titanic   British transatlantic passenger liner which sank on her maiden voyage in one of the greatest of disasters at sea. With her sister ship, the *Olympic*, she was the world's largest passenger ship at the time she set out on her ill-fated voyage. The *Titanic* was operated by the White Star Line, built by Harland and

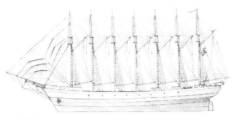

T.W. Lawson, a seven-masted schooner.

Wolff of Belfast, and launched on May 31, 1911. A ship of 46,328 tons, she was 883 ft. (269 m) long, 92 ft. 6 in. (28.2 m) in the beam, and had a draft of 34 ft. 6 in. (10.5 m). She had two four-cylinder triple-expansion steam engines each of 15,000 hp, and one steam turbine (on the center shaft) of 16,000 hp. Her three screws drove her at a service speed of 22 knots. Designed for unequaled luxury and comfort, and intended to be the rival of the smaller but faster Cunarders LUSITANIA and MAURETANIA, she could carry 2,603 passengers and a crew of 892. She was announced as the safest liner afloat, and was claimed to be unsinkable. She was, in fact, a very safe ship, with a double bottom and a hull which was divided into 16 watertight compartments.

She set out on her maiden voyage to New York amid great acclaim on April 10, 1912, carrying 1,316 passengers and 885 crew members. Four days out, and some 95 miles (153 km) south of the Grand Banks of Newfoundland, she was steaming at 22 knots in clear weather when she struck an iceberg. The time was 11:40 pm on April 14. The impact ripped a 300-ft. (91.5-m) gash in her hull low on the starboard side, puncturing six watertight compartments. There had been no lifeboat drill, and in any event the lifeboats aboard could only hold 1,178 people. There was also an initial lack of urgency on the passengers' part; they did not believe the ship could sink, and consequently 1,589 passengers and crew lost their lives when the ship sank.

In the ensuing inquiry neither the actions of the captain nor the design of his ship was blamed for the unprecedented disaster. However, several important steps were taken. Ships were required to follow a more southerly course and reduce speed in the vicinity of ice; lifeboat drill was made compulsory, with sufficient lifeboats carried to accommodate everyone on board, and an international ice patrol was established.

The Titanic, *which sank on her maiden voyage in 1912.*

Torrey Canyon Giant oil TANKER whose wreck off the southwest coast of England led to the first great oil pollution disaster at sea. The 118,285-ton *Torrey Canyon* ran aground on the Seven Stones Reef between the Scilly Isles and Land's End at 9 am on March 18, 1967. Bound for the Welsh oil terminal of Milford Haven with 117,000 tons of Kuwaiti crude, she was proceeding at about 17 knots when she grounded. By evening a fleet of Royal Navy ships, soon joined by commercial vessels, was involved in a continuous spraying operation to disperse the oil slick. A salvage crew put aboard the first day estimated that 30,000 tons of oil had already escaped from ruptured tanks. Salvage operations got underway in poor weather, and some progress was made. However, on March 26 high seas and strong winds broke the ship's back, releasing yet more oil. The next day, it was decided that the possibility of salvaging the ship was negligible, and after removing the *Seven Stones* lightship the Royal Navy and R.A.F. bombed the wreck to set the oil on fire. In all, over 100 miles (160 km) of the Cornish coastline suffered serious pollution, as did a similar length of the north coast of Brittany.

Trent British mail steamer stopped on the high seas by a U.S. warship during the Civil War in an incident that nearly led to war between the United States and Britain. The Federal warship *San Jacinto*, commanded by Captain Charles WILKES and ordered to search for the Confederate commerce raider *Sumter*, stopped the *Trent* in the Bahama Channel off Cuba on November 8, 1861. Acting without orders, Wilkes had the Confederate envoys to Britain and France, James Mason and John Slidell, forcibly removed. They were taken to Boston and interned at Fort Warren. Wilkes' action won wide popular acclaim in the North, but British opinion was outraged and release of the envoys was demanded. It seemed that Britain would not only recognize the Confederacy, but actually enter the war against the North. The incident was finally resolved through diplomatic channels, and in January 1862 Mason and Slidell were released.

Turbinia The world's first vessel powered by steam turbines, built by the Parsons Marine Steam Turbine Company at Wallsend in northeast England in 1894. She was a small ship of only 44.5 tons, 100 ft. (30.8 m) long and 9 ft. (2.7 m) in the beam. She was built specifically to demonstrate the capabilities of Charles Parsons' epoch-making invention, and had three turbines each turning a shaft carrying three screw propellers. At the Diamond Jubilee Naval Review at Spithead in 1897 she astounded onlookers by

seeming to appear from nowhere and racing among the rows of anchored ships of the world's navies at the unprecedented speed of 34.5 knots. Following her success, marine steam turbines began to be widely adopted in the next decade.

United States The largest American passenger ship ever built, the fastest transatlantic liner of all time and the first large vessel with a light aluminum-alloy superstructure. She was operated by the United States Lines of New York, and built at Newport News, Virginia. She was launched, or rather floated out of building dock, on June 23, 1951, and entered service a year later. Although she was designed for the transatlantic passenger trade, she was built to U.S. Navy specifications that would allow her, if necessary, to be converted into a troop ship capable of carrying 14,000 men, and she was thus eligible for a sizable government subsidy.

The 53,329-ton *United States* was 990 ft. (301.7 m) long and 101 ft. 6 in. (30.9 m) in the beam, with a draft of 36 ft. (11 m). Her four steam turbines developed a total of 240,000 hp, turned four screws, and gave her the unprecedented top speed of 41.75 knots. On her maiden transatlantic voyage in July 1952, she made the eastbound crossing in 3 days, 10 hours, and 40 minutes, at an average speed of 35.59 knots, returning at an average of 34.51 knots. She thus took the Blue Riband from the Cunarder QUEEN MARY by a margin of almost 4 knots, and her record was never beaten. She had two funnels with 'wings' to carry smoke and smuts away, 12 decks, and a hull subdivided into watertight compartments to the standard of a warship. She carried 2,008 passengers and 1,093 crew. Like the other large liners of her day, her operation became increasingly uneconomic and she was therefore withdrawn from service in 1969.

Vasa Swedish warship of 64 guns, launched at Stockholm in 1627 and famous today for having been raised to the surface and put on display more than three centuries after sinking in a squall. The *Vasa* (or *Wasa*) carried her guns on two decks and displaced 1,279 tons. She was about 170 ft. (52 m) in length and 38 ft. (11.5 m) in the beam. On August 10, 1628, she had barely set out on her

Turbinia, *built by Charles Parsons.*

The remains of the Vasa *at Stockholm.*

Augustus Keppel at the second Battle of
Ushant (July 27, 1778), and later of Rear
Admiral Richard Kempenfelt and
Admiral Lord Howe. But the most dis-
tinguished period in her career was as
Nelson's flagship (1803-05). Her years of
active service ended in 1835, and she
became the port admiral's ship at Ports-

maiden voyage when she was hit by a
sudden squall. Water rushed in through
her lower gunports and she sank rapidly.
The hull of the *Vasa* was rediscovered in
1956, buried in mud on the seabed in 110
ft. (33.5 m) of water. Five years later, on
April 24, 1961, she was raised to the surface in a remarkable state of preservation.
After careful treatment to prevent her
from disintegrating on contact with the
air, she was put on permanent exhibition
at the Vasa Museum in Stockholm, the
only complete hull of a 17th-century
warship surviving today.

Victory Most famous ship in the history of the Royal Navy, flagship of
Admiral Lord NELSON at the Battle of
Trafalgar (October 21, 1805). The
Victory was a 100-gun first-rate SHIP OF
THE LINE, a three-decker displacing 2,162
tons. She was the largest British warship
of her day, 186 ft. (56.7 m) on the gun
deck and 52 ft. (15.8 m) in the beam, and
she was the work of Sir Thomas Slade,
probably the greatest warship designer of
the age. Begun at Chatham in 1759, she
stood with her frames seasoning for several years before she was completed and
launched on May 7, 1765. She was not
actually put into service until 1778, and
her prolonged building time meant she
was unusually sound in her timbers.

The *Victory* was the flagship of Admiral

The Victory, *Nelson's flagship, now preserved at Portsmouth, England.*

mouth. She remained afloat at her permanent moorings until 1922, when she was rebuilt to her Trafalgar appearance and dry-docked at Portsmouth Dockyard. There she remains as a memorial at Britain's premier naval port.

Volturno Emigrant and cargo steamer lost in the mid-Atlantic in Octoer 1913. She was on a voyage from Rotterdam to New York, with 650 passengers and crew, when on October 9 smoke was seen coming from number one hatch and the crew prepared to tackle the fire. The vessel was carrying dangerous chemicals and highly combustible materials, and an explosion took place that wrecked the forward half of the ship and jammed the steering and engine-room telegraph. An SOS was sent giving the ship's position, and the Cunard liner *Carmania* hurried to assist, while relaying the distress call. Eight steamships were soon on the scene, although they could do nothing due to high winds and rough seas. Before the arrival of the *Carmania*, and under the threat of a further explosion, the *Volturno*'s boats were swung out and six of them launched. Four capsized immediately and two were lost sight of and never seen again. The following day a tanker spread oil on the heavy seas and 521 passengers and crew were rescued by boats from the surrounding vessels. The *Volturno*'s loss led to regulations prohibiting passenger ships from transporting dangerous cargoes.

Waratah A passenger cargo liner of the Blue Anchor Line whose mysterious disappearance remains one of the most puzzling examples of a ship lost at sea without a trace. The *Waratah* was a vessel of 9,339 tons, built in 1908 for service on the England-Australia route via the Cape of Good Hope. On her first voyage the captain noted that the vessel was rather tender in a beam sea, and it was thought inadvisable to move the ship in dock without ballast. On July 25, 1909, she called into Durban on her second homeward voyage, leaving the next day for Capetown with 211 people on board. While in Durban one passenger left the ship saying he considered her unseaworthy due to her pronounced roll. She was expected in Capetown on July 29, and when she became overdue the delay was put down to bad weather. On July

The Warrior, 1861.

31 and August 1 four ships were sent out to look for the *Waratah*, but they returned having found no trace of her. Two further searches by specially chartered vessels went on for over six months but failed to discover any evidence of the liner's fate. No wreckage was ever found, and no bodies were washed ashore. She was finally posted missing on December 15, 1909.

Warrior British iron-hulled IRONCLAD warship, the first of her kind, and the ancestor of the modern battleship. She was laid down at Blackwall on the Thames below London in 1859 and completed two years later; she was intended to meet the challenge posed by France's GLOIRE (1859), the world's first ironclad, but a smaller and less powerful wooden-hulled ship. The *Warrior* displaced 9,210 tons and was 380 ft. (115.8 m) in length, larger than any other warship then afloat. Her speed was 14.35 knots, but she still carried a full set of masts and sails. With a complement of 707 officers and men, she mounted 40 guns on a single gundeck protected by 4.5-in. (115-mm) armor. The *Warrior* and her sister ship *Black Prince*, completed in 1862, were the only British ironclads with clipper bows, and were called the

'black snakes of the channel' because of their long sleek black hulls. The hull of *Warrior* has unexpectedly survived, doing service as an oil-loading pier at Pembroke in Wales. In 1979 her restoration to her original appearance was begun.

Yamato and Musashi The largest battleships ever built, each displacing 72,800 tons under full load. The two sister ships were laid down in 1937 and completed in 1941-42 under great secrecy. They were 865 ft. (263.6 m) in length and had a complement of 2,500 men. Their nine 18.1-in. guns in three triple turrets had a range of 27 miles (43.5 km). The *Yamato* and *Musashi* were designed for action against other battleships, but neither in fact fired her big guns against an enemy ship. They were both sunk by bombs and torpedoes dropped by carrier-borne aircraft — the *Musashi* on October 24, 1944, during the Battle of Leyte Gulf, and the *Yamato*, taking part in a desperate suicide sortie without air cover, on April 7, 1945, off Okinawa. Two more sister ships were never completed, and a third, *Shinano*, was hastily converted into an aircraft carrier, only to be sunk by a submarine attack on her first voyage, before she was fully completed.

Complete Guide to Ship and Boat Types

Aircraft carrier In the years immediately before World War I both the United States and Britain experimented in equipping warships to operate aircraft. In November 1910 the American pilot Eugene Ely took off from a specially built platform on the deck of the cruiser *Birmingham*; two months later he landed and then flew off again from the similarly equipped *Pennsylvania*. By 1913 British experiments led to the fitting out of an old cruiser, the *Hermes*, as a seaplane carrier. Aircraft were hoisted over the side by crane. During the war several ships of the Royal Navy were turned into seaplane carriers and some were given catapults or short decks from which planes could take off. A light battle cruiser, the *Furious*, was completed with a deck of this type forward. She carried landplanes, originally intended to ditch at the end of a sortie, but it was inevitable that they would attempt landing back on the deck. Thus the true aircraft carrier began to evolve. In 1918 the *Conte Rosso*, an uncompleted passenger liner, was equipped with a flight deck running the length of the vessel and was renamed the *Argus*. No superstructure protruded above the flush deck. In 1920 she was followed by the *Eagle*, a converted battleship built to accommodate the first 'island' superstructure on one side of the flight deck. In 1921 the first aircraft carrier designed as such from the keel up, the *Hermes*, was launched. The United States and Japan followed suit; the *Langley*, a converted collier, and the *Hosho* were both commissioned in 1922.

At the outset of World War II the aircraft carrier was still an untried warship. The experience of the war soon proved, however, that it was the most important surface ship in a fleet, of even greater importance than the BATTLESHIP. In the Far East the Japanese navy used carrier-borne aircraft to immense effect in its sweep across the Pacific. The carriers of the U.S. Navy had not been at Pearl Harbor when the Japanese attacked; they proved indispensable in halting the enemy advance. The two great battles that checked the Japanese offensive in 1942, Midway and the Coral Sea, were engagements in which the surface fleets did not even sight each other. By the end of the war the United States and Britain were operating great carrier task forces to overwhelm Japanese opposition. The

The Royal Navy's aircraft carrier Ark Royal.

aircraft carrier had become the principal fighting ship of the world's navies.

In the Atlantic the role of the carrier was less dramatic, though of critical importance. Escort carriers converted from merchant hulls played an important role in the defeat of the U-boat. In addition, oil tankers or grain ships, still capable of carrying their original cargo, were fitted with a flight deck to carry a handful of antisubmarine aircraft and became known as merchant aircraft carriers (Macships).

After 1945 wartime experience, combined with the needs of new jet aircraft, resulted in far larger and more sophisticated ships. The U.S. *Midway*-class carriers, completed at the close of the war, displaced 45,000 tons and featured an armored flight deck, an innovation adopted from the British example. Steam catapults and an angled flight deck appeared on the new carriers of the *Forrestal* class, which displaced over 60,000 tons. They were followed by the 75,000-ton nuclear-powered *Enterprise* and by the NIMITZ and her sister ships: carriers displacing over 91,000 tons under full load, capable of sailing 13 years before refueling, and costing more than $2 billion each.

At the same time several navies have developed specially built helicopter cruisers. In the 1960s the Soviet Union

moved into the field with the two large *Moskva*-class helicopter cruisers, classed as large antisubmarine ships and armed with a comprehensive array of missiles. These have now been followed by the KIEV and *Minsk*, which have full-length flight decks and operate vertical-takeoff aircraft as well as helicopters. Britain has designed the new *Invincible* class of light carriers to operate Sea Harrier VTOL aircraft, and the United States is considering building medium-sized carriers of 50,000 tons for a variety of missions.

Air-cushion vehicle A vehicle that rides on a layer or cushion of air. The idea of such a vehicle was first discussed more than 100 years ago, but the problem of how to contain the cushion of air remained a stumbling block until 1955, when the Englishman Sir Christopher Cockerell patented the design of the hovercraft. This new amphibious vehicle featured a flexible skirt that held the cushion in place despite unevenness of the surface over which it traveled. The first flight by a full-scale ACV (the *SR.N1*) came four years later. Since then, hovercraft have gone into service on several short sea crossings, the most important of which is across the English Channel, where a fleet of *SR.N4* car- and passenger-ferries operates regularly.

The hovercraft's cushion of air is main-

An SR.N4 *hovercraft on the English Channel crossing.*

tained by massive lift fans or blowers. Four aircraft-type propellers, 20 ft. (6 m) across and mounted on pylons, push the *SR.N4* forward at speeds in excess of 60 knots. Since it 'flies' above the surface of the water it is provided with controls and stabilizing surfaces similar to those on airplanes — vertical tail fins with hinged rudders at the rear.

A more boat-like variant of the air-cushion vehicle is known as the surface-effect ship (SES). It has rigid sidewalls that penetrate deep into the water to provide stability for high-speed flight, with flexible skirts fore and aft. The SES is purely a marine craft and can be powered by conventional screw propellers or by water jets. Two 100-ton prototypes of what will be a 3,000-ton helicopter-carrying and missile-armed SES are undergoing tests by the U.S. Navy. They have achieved speeds of nearly 90 knots. The use of hovercraft as amphibious landing craft is also being evaluated by several of the world's navies.

Baltimore clipper Fast sailing ship built in Baltimore and elsewhere along Chesapeake Bay in the late 18th and early 19th centuries. Baltimore clippers are more correctly known as clipper schooners; the word clipper in this context simply means a fast sailing ship. They had a slim and streamlined V-shaped underwater section, were steeply raked at bow and stern, and sliced through the water far faster than the traditional 'fat-cheeked' ships of the past. Long and low, with a flush deck devoid of any superstructure and curving gracefully up fore and aft, the vessels measured some 90 ft. (27.4 m) long and 24 ft. (7.3 m) in the beam. They were rigged as topsail schooners, with two tall raking masts and two jibs. Although well-built, usually of oak and pine, their design necessarily sacrificed robustness and cargo capacity to speed. They were built as fast trading vessels but became famous, or on occasion infamous, as privateers, blockade runners, and even slave ships. During the War of 1812 their speed and maneuverability enabled them to wreak havoc on British convoys while evading attack from the more ponderous men-of-war.

Barge **(1)** At one time any small cargo-carrying sailing vessel, but in modern usage a barge is a flat-bottomed boat designed to carry cargo on inland waterways. Those transporting heavy goods on great European rivers such as the Rhine and Volga are extremely large and have their own engines, covered holds, and crew accommodation. Barges used on many American rivers and lakes are also of considerable size, but they have

neither engine nor accommodation. These straight-sided craft may be lashed together in a compact mass and pushed from behind by specially developed pusher tugs. Or they may be joined end to end in line and towed or pushed. Over 20 barges with a combined load of 60,000 tons or more may be linked in a single 'tow.' Barges with no engines are known as dumb barges. Small dumb barges for carrying cargo between ship and shore are an essential part of the equipment of any port and are generally known as LIGHTERS.

The size of a barge depends of course on the character of waterway it has to negotiate: the depth and width; the sharpness of the bends; and the speed of the current. Draft is normally between 5 and 10 ft. (1.5-3 m), and average dimensions are about 175 ft. by 25 ft. (53 m × 7.5 m). However, where conditions allow, 300-ft. (90-m) barges carrying over 3,000 tons are not uncommon.

(2) Flat-bottomed sailing vessel particularly characteristic of the Thames and southeast England. They were once the familiar workhorses of inland and coastal waters, but now are much declined in number. They usually carry a huge sprit-sail, jib, and jib-headed topsail. The mast is stepped in a lutchet for easy lowering when negotiating bridges, and instead of a keel there are huge, winch-operated lee-boards. A few Thames barges still survive as pleasure craft.

(3) Royal or state barges, richly ornamented, propelled by rowers, and used for ceremonial occasions. During the 17th century their use spread to guilds and livery companies, and to national East India companies whenever an occasion demanded a show of wealth or splendor. The age of steam saw the demise of these barges, though they were used on occasion in the early 1800s.

Bark, barkentine Sailing vessels with three or more masts and a combination of square and fore-and-aft sails. The bark (or barque) differs from the full-rigged ship in carrying only fore-and-aft sails on the aftermost mast. The principal and lowest sail on the aftermast is a spanker or gaff; above this are set an upper spanker and a triangular gaff-topsail. On a four-masted bark the masts are fore, main, mizzen, and jigger; on a five-master they are fore, main, middle, miz-

A Finnish three-masted bark.

zen, and jigger. The barkentine (or bar-quentine) is square-rigged only on the foremast, with gaffsails and gaff-topsails on the two or more remaining masts. Barkentines were built with as many as six masts (fore, main, mizzen, jigger, driver, and spanker).

Originally employed only on smaller craft, both rigs became popular on very large vessels at the end of the 19th century, at a time when competition from steam forced the owners of sailing ships to cut their costs to a minimum. The fore-and-aft sails of the bark and barkentine were easier to handle than square sails, and therefore both types needed smaller crews than did full-rigged ships. Many of the latter were in fact converted to bark rigs for this reason. Two of the largest sailing ships ever built, the FRANCE and *France II*, were five-masted steel barks. The handful of barks that survive are used as training ships or as floating museum ships.

Bathyscaphe Self-propelled diving vessel designed by the Swiss scientist Auguste Piccard for deep-sea observation. The prototype, *F.R.N.S.I.,* made its first unmanned dive in 1948. Driven forward at a speed of 2 knots by three electrically operated propellers, the bathyscaphe operates on much the same principle as an airship. Its small steel observation cabin, strong enough to withstand the enormous pressures at the seabed, and accommodating a crew of

three, is suspended below a large cylindrical float or tank filled with gasoline (which is lighter than water) to provide buoyancy. Air-filled ballast tanks keep the bathyscaphe afloat on the surface; to submerge the vessel, these tanks are filled with water. To decrease the speed of descent, or to ascend, ballast in the form of metal pellets is released.

In 1960 the bathyscaphe *Trieste*, the third bathyscaphe designed by Piccard, descended to a depth of 35,800 ft. (10,900 m) — over twice the record depth previously achieved by a submersible. In 1972 *Trieste II* carried out the deepest-ever salvage operation, at a depth of 16,500 ft. (5,030 m).

Battleship The battleship succeeded the old line-of-battle ship (see SHIP OF THE LINE) as the major fighting vessel, or capital ship, of the world's navies. Even after the introduction of side armor (see IRONCLAD), the battleship retained all the characteristics of the sailing warship: masts, sails, and broadside guns. The first battleships to rely entirely on steam propulsion were DEVASTATION and *Thunderer*. These British vessels of the 1870s were the first mastless oceangoing turret ships; one turret was mounted forward and one aft. This arrangement of the ship's heavy guns was little followed until the entry into service of the powerful ROYAL SOVEREIGN class ships. Previously, most capital ships had been built in ones and twos; this class, however,

consisted of a group of seven identical ships. With their high freeboard and large twin guns mounted on top of barbettes at either end of the vessel, these impressive ships set a recognizable and quickly copied pattern for the building of battleships until the DREADNOUGHT appeared in 1906.

By the beginning of the 20th century developments in explosives, guns, and training in gunnery made it possible to extend dramatically the range of a battleship's largest guns. The conventional mixed armament of four large guns supplemented by many smaller guns of calibers between 3 and 9.2 in. made an increasingly unsatisfactory combination. To concentrate fire on an enemy at extreme range it would be far more effective to produce an all-big-gun ship. The result was the hasty building of the *Dreadnought*, with its five twin 12-in. turrets, and, equally revolutionary, with turbines instead of reciprocating engines to increase both speed and reliability. The U.S. Navy was working on the design of a ship with four twin turrets, which improved on the *Dreadnought*'s layout by mounting all the turrets on the centerline and superimposing the second and third over the first and fourth. The *South Carolina*s were not to be completed for several years, but their layout was to become standard for battleships. It was adopted, for example, in the *Queen Elizabeth* class of 1914, which with a speed of 25 knots, displacement of

The American bathyscaphe Trieste, *designed by Auguste Piccard.*

The Thunderer, *a British battleship completed in 1877.*

33,000 tons, and eight 15-in. guns, represented a definitive form of the battleship.

World War II brought the battleship to the peak of its development; it also demonstrated its obsolescence. Sizes rose to 58,000 tons in the U.S. *Iowa* class, which had a speed of 35 knots and armament of nine 16-in guns, and to an all-time record of 63,000 tons in the YAMATO and *Musashi*, which carried nine 18.1-in. guns. The battleship saw far more action in World War II than it had in World War I, but the effectiveness of carrier-borne aircraft soon marked its end as the capital ship of the world's navies. The *New Jersey*, sister ship of the *Missouri*, was the last battleship to see action when she was temporarily brought out of mothballs in 1967-68 for shore bombardment of Vietnam.

Bergantina Small auxiliary craft of the Mediterranean in use from the 14th to the 16th century. Propelled either by a lateen sail or by oarsmen, bergantinas were lightly built, broad-beamed, and of very shallow draft. They were particularly useful on inland or sheltered coastal waters and, like the English PINNACE, they were often carried, dismantled, on board larger ships during voyages of exploration and discovery.

Bireme A GALLEY with two banks of oars, one of the principal warships of the Mediterranean from ancient times until well into the 17th century. The first galleys with two banks of oars were built by the Phoenicians, and using these as their model the Greeks developed their own biremes of lighter construction at the beginning of the 6th century BC. In the 5th century BC a three-banked galley, the TRIREME, was developed and the Romans later used both types for warfare.

Biremes carried as many as three to four rowers on each oar, the two banks of oars being positioned on different levels. Although the rowers provided the main motive power, a square sail was also used on long voyages when the wind served. The principal weapon of the bireme was a metal ram or beak projecting at or below the waterline. To withstand the force of the enemy's ramming, the bireme had a strong keel, but was of light overall construction to give her the speed necessary for galley warfare. Above the rowers ran a longitudinal bridge manned by archers and stone slingers. In the last centuries of their history galleys carried guns mounted in the bows.

Blackwall frigate Type of medium-speed full-rigged merchant sailing ship originating in the 1830s at Blackwall on the River Thames just below London. In design and performance these ships occupied a position roughly midway between the lumbering EAST INDIAMEN they replaced and the sleek CLIPPERS that eventually supplanted them. The end of the East India Company's monopoly of trade in 1833 opened the sea route to the east to all vessels, and the Blackwall frigates were built to provide faster passenger and freight services, principally between England and India. They were termed frigates, or said to be frigate-built, because they outclassed the ponderous East India 'tea wagons' in much the same way as the naval frigates outperformed the massive ships of the line.

The first Blackwall frigate, the 818-ton *Seringapatam* of 1837, measured 148 ft. 6 in. by 36 ft. 6 in. (45.26 m × 11.13 m) and broke all records by sailing from London to Bombay in 85 days. Her successors, like the 1,400-ton *Monarch* of 1844, which measured 180 ft. by 40 ft. (54.86 × 12.19 m), were sleeker vessels and had an increased length-to-beam ratio of 4½ to 1. Some Blackwall frigates built in the 1850s and 1860s with length-to-beam ratios of around 6 to 1 were almost as slender and fast as the medium clippers that were being built.

Blackwall frigates dominated the trade route to and from India until the opening of the Suez Canal in 1869. They survived for a while in the Australian wool trade but by the time the last Blackwall frigate was launched in 1869, they were already

The Macquarie, *a Blackwall frigate.*

being supplanted by the faster clippers and the more predictable steamships.

Bomb vessel A sailing ship armed with one or two large mortars and moored in position for high-angle fire against stationary targets such as shore installations and fleets at anchor. The French were the first to use such ships in their attack against the pirate port of Algiers in the 1680s.

In the early 18th century these vessels were usually built as KETCHes, although the term bomb ketch is often incorrectly used for craft of this type after the 1750s since they tended to be three-masted. The development of the revolving turret in the mid-19th century allowed a ship to train her guns irrespective of her course, and so the bomb vessel as a specific warship type disappeared. The role of the bomb vessel was taken over during World War I, and to a lesser extent during World War II, by MONITORs, and these in turn were made obsolete by the development of guided missiles.

Brig Until the 18th century, brig and BRIGANTINE were the same ship, the term brig being used merely as an abbreviation. Then a differentiation occurred in the rigging, and the word brig came to describe a ship carrying square sails on both masts and an additional gaffsail on the mainmast.

Brigs were widely used in the navies of Europe during the 18th century, and armed with up to 18 guns, became known as 'gun brigs.' They were also fitted out as privateers and used in the American War of 1812 against British shipping. Because they were so economic to operate, brigs were commonly used throughout the age of sail as coastal and short-sea merchantmen (see COLLIER). They survived into the 20th century as naval training ships.

Brigantine In the early 16th century the name brigantine was used to describe a small, open, galley-type craft with sails and oars, popular among pirates and sea brigands, hence the name. The trading brigantine of the 17th and 18th centuries was a very different vessel; a true sailing ship, square-rigged on the foremast like the brig but fore-and-aft rigged on the mainmast, with a gaff-mainsail and topsail. She was used both in the Mediterranean and in northern waters and, like the brig, proved popular for short and coastal trading voyages.

Bulk carrier Large 20th-century ship specially designed to transport vast amounts of a specific cargo. Originally the cargo carried was almost exclusively mineral, but bulk carriers now handle

such diverse goods as sugar, grain, wine, ore, chemicals, liquefied natural gas, bitumen, and oil (see TANKER).

Many bulk cargoes present special handling problems and require highly specialized ships. One of the most sophisticated of these vessels is the LNG (liquefied natural gas) ship. The cargo tanks are made of a special aluminum alloy and are heavily insulated, usually with a combination of balsa wood faced with plywood and fiberglass. The insulation serves two purposes: it prevents the LNG, which is at a temperature of $-258°F$ ($-161°C$), from absorbing an undue amount of heat from the atmosphere; it also protects the ship's hull, since steel at very low temperature becomes as brittle as glass. The LNG ship costs approximately twice as much as an oil tanker of the same size.

Bulk ore carriers present very different problems. Ore is an exceptionally heavy freight, and if it is loaded low in the hull the ship's overall center of gravity is affected. The ship becomes what is called 'stiff,' with a disinclination to roll and pitch which puts enormous stresses on the hull. Accordingly, a specialized ore carrier usually has centerline cargo holds raised 9 to 12 ft. (2.7-3.6 m) above the keel and flanked by side tanks filled with water ballast.

The great disadvantages of such specialized ships is that they make their return journey in ballast, carrying no cargo. To eliminate this waste, multipurpose bulk carriers have been developed, and though more costly to build, ultimately prove more economic vessels. Some are very large, in the range of 100,000 to 150,000 tons deadweight. Among them are OBO (ore-bulk-oil) ships, specially built to carry heavy dry bulk cargoes or oil. Many other multipurpose ships are more modest in size, a typical example being the series of multipurpose bulk- and general-cargo carriers of 32,200 tons deadweight built in the late 1970s by Mitsubishi Heavy Industries at Nagasaki, Japan. They have exceptionally large stern ramps for roll-on roll-off (RoRo) loading and discharge, a hoistable car deck, fixed ramps between decks, a deck crane capable of lifting 40 tons, and diesel engines developing 30,150 shp. More specialized bulk carriers include the LASH SHIP, SEABEE, CONTAINER SHIPS, and tankers.

Model of a merchant brig with studding sails set, c. 1840.

Liquefied natural gas carrier built in 1974.

Cable ship Oceangoing ship used for laying, inspecting, and repairing submarine telegraph and telephone cables. One of the earliest ships employed for this purpose was Brunel's GREAT EASTERN, which laid the first successful transatlantic cable. Modern cable ships carry up to 1,800 miles (2,800 km) of cable in giant drum-like holds. The cable may be coiled into the holds manually, but in the latest vessels it is packed in large pan-like containers resembling reels of magnetic tape. The cable is paid out over guides and rollers (sheaves) at stern and bow respectively. The sheaves, together with a large unobstructed area of working deck space forward and a deeply curved stern, give cable ships their distinctive appearance.

Cable ships usually range from 5,000 to 9,000 tons gross and are often equipped with diesel-electric propulsion. Accurate positioning and delicate maneuvers are produced by bow thrusters and variable-pitch (and sometimes shrouded variable-thrust) propellers. Navigational equipment includes sonar, radar, electronic position-fixing aids such as Decca Navigator and Loran, a submerged log, and optical rangefinders.

Caique (1) Term loosely applied to a wide variety of small vessels of the eastern Mediterranean. The original caique was a lateen-rigged coastal craft. (2) A light one- or two-oared Turkish boat; caique was also the name given to the Sultan's ceremonial barge.

Canoe Light, shallow-draft boat pointed at both ends and normally propelled by paddles. The canoe is one of the oldest of all boats. In its most primitive forms it is constructed by burning or cutting out a tree trunk to make a dugout, or by covering a wooden framework with skin or bark. The basic design is remarkably versatile. Early canoes were used primarily on calm inland waters, yet large twin-hulled canoes known as TAINUS were sailed enormous distances out into the Pacific by the Polynesians over 1,000 years ago. Adapted to very different conditions are the North American Indian birchbark canoes and Eskimo KAYAKS. They are so light they can easily be picked up and carried.

Modern canoes do not usually exceed 20 to 30 ft. (6-9 m) in length. They can be made of a variety of lightweight materials including molded plywood, canvas on a wooden frame, and glass-reinforced plastic (fiberglass).

Caravel Small or medium-sized sailing ship with a round bow and square stern which originated in the Mediterranean in the 14th century. The caravel evolved from the small, lateen-rigged, carvel-built coastal and fishing craft common in the Mediterranean from the 9th century. She developed into a two- or three-masted ship with a shallow draft and a rudder which hung in the center of the square stern. Lacking the towering and overhanging superstructure of the larger CARRACK, the caravel was well adapted to coastal work in contrary winds. As trade and the demand for shipping grew, the size of the caravel increased, and beyond a certain point the lateen rig became impractical, especially in stormy conditions on the open sea when the long lateen yard was very difficult to handle. Accordingly, a new type emerged, the *caravela redonda*, with square sails on fore- and mainmasts and a lateen sail on the mizzen. The original all-lateen craft became known as the *caravela latina*.

The caravela redonda was the craft used by the Portuguese navigators on their voyages of exploration. COLUMBUS in his first voyage across the Atlantic set out with caravels of both types, but finding the caravela latina rig unsuited to Atlantic conditions he had the *Niña* rerigged in the Canary Islands as a caravela redonda.

Carrack Large sailing merchantman and warship of the 14th to 17th century, developed by Spain and combining the square rig of northern Europe with the carvel-built hull typical of the Mediterra-

The bow of the cable ship Alert.

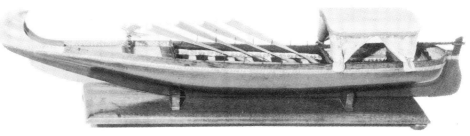

Model of a Turkish caique.

Mediterranean carrack, c. 1490.

nean. The carrack was originally two-masted, but as she grew in tonnage she took on a third mast and, like the contemporary caravela redonda, set square sails on fore- and mainmasts and a lateen sail on the mizzen. Occasionally, a second lateen-rigged aftermast, the bon-aventure mizzen, was carried. A small additional sail, the spritsail, was added beneath the bowsprit.

Carracks were large, beamy, robustly-built ships with very high fore- and after-castles which made them unhandy when sailing on a wind. By the end of the 15th century the carrack had grown immense-ly in size, up to a tonnage of 1,200 in the larger vessels. One or two were built up to 2,000 tons, but these were freaks and not very successful. With the growth in tonnage, the masts were lengthened to carry topsails and the superstructure accordingly increased in height. This was particularly true of carracks used for war-fare, which developed into ungainly and top-heavy floating fortresses. The invention of the gunport made it possible to bring the center of gravity down to a more seaworthy level, by moving the heavy guns from the castles into the hull. But the carrack remained a slow and cumbersome vessel, and during the 17th century she began to be superseded by the sleeker GALLEON which was a much

more weatherly ship because the tower-ing forecastle, so marked a feature of the carrack, was removed.

Catamaran The word catamaran comes from the Tamil language of South India and literally means 'tied logs.'

(1) It can describe a variety of primitive rafts, floats, and balance boards. A fine example is the flying-fish catamaran or *Kola Maram* of India's Coromandel coast. This consists of seven or nine logs tied together, with upward curving planks at the bow, and a pair of fore-and-aft sails similar to lugsails.

(2) A modern twin-hulled sailing yacht, very light and of shallow draft because of her broad beam. She can carry more sail than a monohull and can therefore attain remarkable speeds, but her hull and rig-ging are subject to considerable strain and in high winds the risk of capsizing is great.

Cigar ship Experimental spindle-shaped steamship pioneered by the American railroad engineers Ross and Walter Winans between 1858 and 1866. Disregarding traditional ship designs, the Winans Brothers did away with sails, keel, superstructure, deck, and — in the usual sense — bow and stern. The expec-tation was that a spindle-shaped craft would slip through the waves instead of riding over them, and that with no flat deck and no buoyancy or 'body' at bow

and stern, the ship would be unaffected by heavy seas.

The fourth and largest cigar ship, the *Ross Winans*, was built on the Thames near London in 1866. Some 256 ft. (78 m) in length and 16 ft. (5 m) in diameter, she had a low superstructure extending roughly half the length of the ship and two paddles, one at each end. Like her predecessors, the *Ross Winans* proved remarkably steady in a rough sea, but the paddles threw up so much spray that the deck was unusable and the helmsman's view ahead negligible. The narrow hull diameter allowed only very limited accommodation and, most serious of all, the basic design had no inherent stability. The hull needed permanent ballast to keep it upright, and if a roll had devel-oped in heavy seas, the ship could all too easily have turned over. *Ross Winans* made a few coastal voyages, but she was never anything more than an expensive novelty. Her original cost was £60,000 and she was sold to a breaker for £210.

Clipper A very fast full-rigged sailing ship of the 19th century. The clipper is probably the most handsome and best-remembered ship in the entire history of sail. The hull, five or six times as long as it was broad, had a steeply raked and pointed bow and an overhanging counter stern. The three tall raked masts carried a mass of huge sails on wide yards. Unlike previous large merchantmen,

The remarkable cigar ship Ross Winans, 1866.

whose tubby rounded bows lifted them over the waves, the concave hull section at bow and stern allowed the clipper to slice through waves like a wedge. The word clipper had long been used for any fast sailing ship, and the BALTIMORE CLIPPERS of the beginning of the 19th century already possessed many characteristics of the later true clippers. The ANN MCKIM of 1832 combined these fine lines with a square rig, and by 1845, when the RAINBOW was built in New York, the age of the clipper had arrived.

There is no precise definition of the various clipper types: extreme, sharp, medium, and half clipper. Extreme clippers were the ones with the slenderest lines. The LIGHTNING, for example, measured 244 ft. by 44 ft. (74.4 m × 13.4 m), with a depth of just 23 ft. (7 m) and a registered tonnage of 1,468. CHALLENGE was shorter (230 ft. 6 in. or 70.26 m) and marginally narrower, but considerably deeper (27 ft. 6 in. or 8.38 m) and more capacious (2,000 registered tons). She was thus significantly less sharp, and was considered a medium clipper.

Donald MCKAY of Boston was the most famous of all the clipper builders. His *Lightning* set a record of 436 nautical miles (807 km) in a day, which was unsurpassed for many years, while his FLYING CLOUD, probably the fastest American clipper of all, twice sailed from New York to San Francisco around Cape Horn in 89 days, a record that was never beaten. British clippers were smaller than their American rivals. They were often sturdier, being for the most part composite ships with wooden planking on an iron frame (American clippers were wooden throughout). Two of the most famous, CUTTY SARK and THERMOPYLAE, had unequaled records for speed. *Cutty Sark* had a length-to-beam ratio of nearly 6 to 1 compared to *Lightning*'s 5½ to 1.

The clipper excelled in trades which demanded the greatest possible speed. These included opium smuggling, carrying prospectors to the Californian and Australian gold rushes of the mid-19th century, and competing in the China tea trade, for which the clippers were most famous. The latter was opened to ships of all nations by the repeal of the British Navigation Acts in 1849, and developed into a race to return first with the new season's tea. With the opening in 1869 of both the Suez Canal and the first railroad across the United States, the clipper's brief era of glory was over. They continued to operate under reduced sail and crew in the Australian wool trade, but before long their place was taken by larger and more economical barks, and by steamships.

Coaster Small cargo ship that trades from one port to another along a coast. The coaster acts as an extension of a country's internal transportation system and relieves pressure on harbor facilities by taking cargoes directly off oceangoing vessels for distribution to small ports unable to accommodate large ships. Coasters are in effect small versions of large FREIGHTERS, and like them they appear in many forms, from general-cargo carriers to bulk ships. Typical cargoes include oil, grain, coal (see COLLIER), fertilizers, and even containers. Normally in the range of 300 to 1,500 tons gross, coasters often have a distinctive appearance, with a high bow for negotiating rough seas, a low freeboard amidships, and a raised superstructure (and funnel) at the stern. The diesel engine is fitted aft. Coasters carry their own cargo-handling gear and have a shallow draft for navigating inland waterways and reaching upriver ports.

Cog North European square-rigged merchant ship of the 13th, 14th, and 15th centuries. The founding of the Hanseatic League in 1241 brought about a sharp rise both in maritime trade and in shipbuilding and resulted in the development of the Hansa cog, which had smoother lines than contemporaneous Mediterranean vessels, with overlapping clinker planking on its high sides and deck beams projecting through the hull.

The contemporaneous English cog was unlike the Hansa cog in that she did not have a straight stem and long keel; her stem was curved and joined the keel further aft. She had three castles at bow, stern, and masthead and, although used principally as a merchant ship, she was also used for warfare if the need arose. However, by the 14th century the design of the cog had become virtually standardized. Her length-to-beam ratio was only about 2 or 2½ to 1, and she had evolved three masts with square sails on the fore and main and lateen on the mizzen. She had a rounded bow and stern and a high aftercastle. The cog drew a lot of draft but her large stowage capacity and fairly high speed made her the major merchant ship of the age.

Collier Coastal and short-sea merchantman used for transporting coal. Sailing ships such as BRIGS were used until the mid-19th century for this purpose and could carry 300 to 400 tons of coal. One of the sturdiest of all collier brigs was the cat, and this was the ship chosen by Captain COOK for his three famous voyages of discovery.

In the mid-19th century, with the advent of marine steam power and the growth of industry relying on coal, there developed a need for coal depots abroad at which oceangoing steamships could refuel. Consequently a larger capacity steam collier was introduced which could transport some 6,000 tons of coal. The continued importance of coal to world economy safeguarded the future of the collier, although the advent of oil and diesel as the main fuel for ships marked the end of the steam-driven collier.

Modern colliers are diesel-powered and carry from 7,000 to 60,000 tons of coal in bulk. They generally have a single deck with three to five holds and unusually large hatches with high hatch coamings. No cargo-handling gear is carried; the coal is loaded by gravity and discharged by dockside grab cranes. Self-trimming colliers have U-shaped holds in which the coal naturally settles evenly. Most colliers, like other COASTERS, have a high bow and raised forecastle, with engines and a raised superstructure aft.

Container ship Oceangoing merchant ship designed to transport a unit load of standard-sized containers 8 ft. (2.4 m) square in cross section and 20 or 40 ft. (6.1 or 12.2 m) long. The hull is divided into cells that are easily accessible through large hatches in the weather deck. With the hatches closed further layers of containers are loaded on deck, the number of layers depending on their weight and on the size and stability of the ship. The hull shape is designed to prevent water splashing up onto the upper deck and containers. Loading and discharge take place at special berths equipped with giant traveling gantry cranes; the two processes can in fact go on at the same time. To keep the ship on

A container ship, a cost-effective way of transporting general cargo.

an even keel during loading and discharge, water ballast is pumped from one side of the ship to the other to compensate for each container added or removed. Container ships are usually in the range of 25,000 to 50,000 tons deadweight; a 30,000-ton ship can carry about 1,300 20-ft. (6.1-m) containers.

Whereas a general-cargo ship can spend as much as 75 percent of its life in port in discharging and loading cargo, a modern container ship can be turned around in 36 hours or less; on the same run the time spent in port falls to as little as 20 percent. This enables the vessel to make three times as many voyages in a given period. To a great extent the prepackaging of goods in containers has brought the benefit of the bulk carrier to the transport of general cargo. Specialized types of container ships include the LASH SHIP and the SEABEE, which carry floating containers or lighters, and RORO SHIPS, which may carry containers on trailers.

Coracle Primitive Celtic boat made of a wicker frame traditionally covered with hides, now more often with tarred calico or canvas. Although some are circular, the usual shape is rectangular with round corners. Coracles (or curraghs) are still to be found on inland and inshore waters of Wales and Ireland where they are used principally for fishing. The smallest are light enough to be easily picked up and carried, but larger seagoing craft were also once built, such as those in which Irish invaders crossed to mainland Britain. According to legend, the Irish monk St. Brendan sailed to the 'Land of Promise,' later claimed to be America, in a large coracle. That a voyage of such length could be successfully undertaken in such a simple and primitive vessel was demonstrated in 1977, when Tim Severin sailed from Ireland to Newfoundland in a reconstruction of an ancient coracle. His craft was 36 ft. (11 m) in length, and the journey took 50 days.

Corvette Corvette is a French word that was used in the 17th and 18th centuries to describe a flush-deck warship next in size to the FRIGATE, carrying from 14 to 26 guns, and usually ship-rigged on all three masts. Called 'sloops of war' in the U.S. Navy, corvettes were smaller versions of the frigate, performing much the same miscellaneous duties. Early in the 19th century the Royal Navy began to adopt the term corvette and for a time in the 1870s used it to describe the steam warship which replaced the steam frigate and which later became known as a cruiser. The name then fell out of use until World War II, when it was revived by the Royal Navy to describe lightly armed and highly maneuverable antisub-marine escorts, adapted from a commercial whale-catcher design. These were the famous *Flower*-class corvettes, intended originally for coastal service, but which bore much of the brunt of the Battle of the Atlantic. They were highly successful, and by the end of the war more than 150 corvettes of various classes had been built in Britain and Canada. Several European navies still employ the name for ships that might otherwise be called small frigates. Today such vessels often carry guided-missile armament for anti-submarine warfare.

Cruiser In the 18th century a cruiser was any warship, such as a frigate, on detached service. It was not until the last quarter of the 19th century that the term was used to describe a specific type of ship: a large oceangoing vessel less powerful than a battleship and generally faster. The difference between the smallest type of cruiser and the SLOOP was often difficult to define as vessels originally classed as steam frigates or CORVETTES fell into the cruiser category.

Several lines of cruiser development can be distinguished in the years before World War I. At the end of the Civil War the United States was building a large commerce raider, the *Wampanoag*, which caused the Royal Navy to reply by building the *Inconstant*. These larger but unprotected ships were the forerunners of both the protected cruiser, with an armored deck but no side armor, and the armored cruiser, which had both. They were faster and larger than the battleships of the day, with a slightly less powerful armament and much less protection. Their development culminated in the battle cruiser, whose armament was of the same type as the battleship DREADNOUGHT. The *Invincible*, which was the first battle cruiser, appeared at the same time as the *Dreadnought*, but had much thinner armor in order to attain higher speeds. Battle cruisers inevitably suffered heavy casualties in World War I, when their original scouting role was exceeded. The Germans had wisely built their own models as fast BATTLESHIPS with heavy protection, and in the end the battle cruiser as a type became virtually indistinguishable from the battleship. The Royal Navy's *Hood*, for example, which was built as a battle cruiser during World War I, was actually completed with armor similar to that of the battleships of the day, though she remained classed as a battle cruiser.

Another line of cruiser development extends through smaller vessels intended for trade defense and miscellaneous duties. These were generally armed with guns of 6-in. caliber or less. The majority of British cruisers prior to 1914 belonged to this class, which was widely used on

overseas stations. Their evolution can be said to have terminated with the British pre-1914 *Town* class. Another class of cruisers stemmed from attempts to build small, fast torpedo cruisers to accompany the fleet. The light cruiser resulted, and in 1914 the finest examples were probably the British *Arethusa*s, developed for combat reconnaissance in the North Sea. The Washington Naval Treaty of 1922 placed restrictions on cruiser building, and the result was that several navies all produced so-called treaty cruisers — heavy cruisers with 8-in. guns and a theoretical displacement of 10,000 tons. By the late 1930s large numbers of light cruisers with 6-in. guns were also being built and Germany, Japan, and the United States were constructing very large heavy cruisers of up to 17,000 tons standard displacement.

Since 1945 few vessels classed as cruisers have been built. In many ways the larger frigates and guided-missile DESTROYERS fill the role of the cruiser, and the U.S. Navy recently took the step of reclassifying most of its guided-missile destroyers as cruisers in recognition of this fact. Old cruisers have been rebuilt by several navies to carry helicopters (Britain's *Tiger* class is an example), and the U.S. fleet of 28 cruisers, all guided-missile ships, includes nine nuclear-powered vessels, including LONG BEACH (the world's first nuclear surface warship).

Cutter Name applied to a variety of small vessels (1) The sailing cutter was a small, single-masted ship with gaff-mainsail on a boom, two or occasionally three foresails set on a very long bowsprit, and one or two yards carrying square topsails. From the mid-18th century, when the rig was first introduced, these fast and maneuverable craft were popular with smugglers and revenue forces alike; they were also used as auxiliaries to large warships. When employed as pilot craft, cutters generally had a simpler rig comprising a gaff-mainsail and two foresails. (2) A type of naval utility boat, originally clinker-built and propelled by oars or lugsails, which was carried aboard larger ships. (3) Modern powered coastguard, police, or pilot boat performing tasks similar to those of the original sailing cutter. (4) A sailing yacht, normally bermuda-rigged, though some older craft are gaff-rigged with a jib-headed topsail.

Destroyer The destroyer originated in the 1890s as an answer to the menace of the TORPEDO BOAT, and rapidly became the most versatile of all modern warships. As early as 1886 the British Admiralty had attempted to produce a vessel capable of chasing and sinking torpedo boats, but these first torpedo-boat catchers were not fast enough. In 1893 Admiral Sir John FISHER placed orders for a still faster craft, known as a torpedo-boat destroyer, later shortened to destroyer. The two great specialist torpedo-boat firms, Thornycroft and Yarrow, each built a pair of these new vessels. The HAVOCK and the *Hornet*, built by Yarrow, and the *Daring* and the *Decoy*, produced by Thornycroft, rapidly proved a success. Armed with three torpedo-tubes and four guns, and capable of 27 knots, they were more than a match for any torpedo boat.

In World War I the destroyer came into its own as an antisubmarine weapon. From May 1917 onward, destroyer-escorted convoys cut shipping losses dramatically, and during World War II an entire class of vessels, the destroyer-escorts, were built in large numbers. The size of the destroyer also increased sharply.

By 1945 the conventional gun- and torpedo-armed destroyer had reached virtually the end of its development; within a

The first British battle cruiser Invincible, *launched in 1907.*

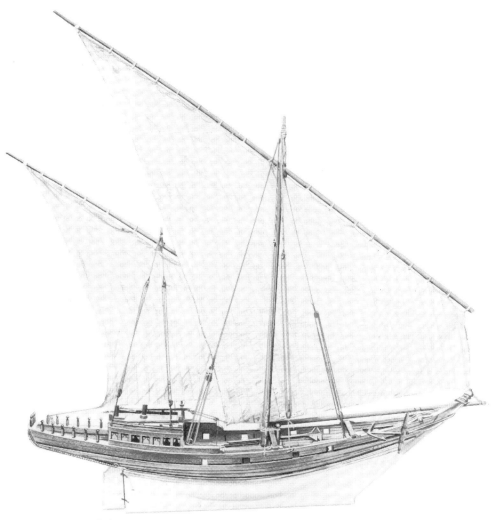

A two-masted, lateen-rigged dhow.

decade it was being replaced in many of its roles by the FRIGATE. In recent years, however, the deficiencies of the frigate in speed and weaponry have become apparent, and the U.S. Navy, for example, now has some 40 guided-missile destroyers and is building new *Spruance*-class vessels of 7,800 tons for antisubmarine duties as part of its carrier task force.

Dhow Traditional Arab trading vessel of about 200 tons with one or two masts carrying lateen sails. The word is now used in a very general way to refer to various diesel-engined boats as well as to a range of sailing vessels. The latter include the two-masted *baghla* (now extinct) and *sambuk*, both notable for their built-up and often ornately decorated poops. Smaller Arab craft sometimes termed dhow include the *zarook*, a fast, two-masted, shallow-draft craft with an unusually long raking bow and a pointed stern well adapted for sailing in heavy

surf; and the *badan*, a single-masted vessel with a straight bow, and, like the zarook, popular with smugglers.

Dory Small, flat-bottomed fishing boat, usually carried stacked in piles, called nests, aboard schooners and used for line fishing on Newfoundland's Grand Banks.

Dredger Vessel designed for underwater excavation; particularly for deepening canals, docks, harbors, and approach channels, and for constructing dams, breakwaters, etc.

Dredgers work on a variety of principles. The suction dredger trails a large-bore pipe along the seabed through which a mixture of solids and water is sucked. The spoil, most often a mixture of sand and mud, may be pumped into hoppers in the dredger and either taken out to sea and dumped, or pumped ashore for land reclamation. Alternative-

ly, the dredger may carry a long horizontal boom through which the spoil is pumped and ejected well clear of the channel being excavated. Suction dredgers are self-propelled seagoing vessels, often similar in general appearance to COASTERS, with bridge and engines aft and a high bow. The space between bridge and forecastle is filled with the suction-pipe hoisting equipment and gear for discharging the spoil.

The bucket or ladder dredger carries an endless chain of buckets on an angled frame known as a ladder. With the ladder lowered to the bottom, the buckets descend on the ladder's underside through an open well in the hull, dig into the mud, and return on its upper side to dump their contents either into the dredger itself, or into a barge. Bucket dredgers can work at depths of up to 70 ft. (21 m). Some are self-propelled, with engines and bridge aft, and the remainder of the ship occupied by the ladder and its gear. Others are towed into position by tugs, and can achieve limited movement by hauling on their mooring cables.

The dipper dredger is a barge-mounted power shovel. Closely related to it is the grab or clamshell dredger, fitted with one or more cranes each carrying a single bucket or grab. The grab is lowered to the bottom, where through gravity and its biting action it collects a load of spoil, raises it, and dumps it on board or into a waiting barge. The grab dredger has the great advantage of being able to work at considerable depths, and in harbor and dock dredging it can reach awkward corners which the bucket dredger cannot negotiate. It is, however, relatively slow in action. Both dipper and grab dredgers are often anchored to the bottom by means of stakes called spuds.

Dromon (1) Greek galley built for speed; a larger version of the BIREME. Built to a length of 150 ft. (46 m), the dromon generally pulled 50 oars a side in two banks and was armed with catapults and fighting towers. (2) Large Mediterranean vessel in use from the 9th to the 15th century. The name was used to describe any very large ship propelled by oars which set a large square sail on a single mast. Dromons were used for trade and also for carrying troops in wartime, including the Christian armies which fought in the Crusades.

DynaShip Revolutionary new design for an automated and computerized sailing ship, the work of the German engineer Wilhelm Prölss and now under development by the DynaShip Corporation of California. With fuel prices high and likely to increase, the DynaShip reverts to the use of the wind as a source of motive power. The designers of this 20th-century sailing ship have utilized to the full all the recent developments in computer technology and weather forecasting. Aerodynamic and test-tank experiments suggest that the DynaShip may be as much as 60 percent more efficient than the clippers of the 19th century. The traditional mass of rigging has been completely eliminated, cutting down aerodynamic drag significantly and allowing an uncluttered deck with easy access to the cargo hatches. The ship's six hollow masts carry 30 small square sails, with a total area of 17,000 sq. ft. (1,600 m²). This can be compared, for example, to the five-masted, full-rigged PREUSSEN, which also had 30 square sails, but an overall sail area of 60,000 sq. ft. (5,600 m²). *Preussen* was the largest square-rigged ship ever built. She carried a load of some 8,000 tons, was capable of up to 18 knots, and required a crew of 48. The first DynaShip is planned to load 25,000 tons and to sail at up to 20 knots, with a crew of only 26.

The DynaShip's sails are designed to be stored inside the hollow masts and unfurled along the yards as required. The process is controlled at the touch of a button from the computerized bridge, as is the rotation of the masts to trim the sails to the wind. The best setting will be calculated by an on-board computer, and the entire process will take a mere 20 seconds. A 1,000-hp diesel engine provides all the power necessary for regulating the sails and can be used when the ship is becalmed or for maneuvering the vessel into port.

East Indiaman Three-masted, square-rigged sailing ship engaged in trade between Europe and the east from the 17th to the early 19th century. Sometimes called tea wagons, East Indiamen were broad, round-bowed, and slow, with a top speed of about 8 knots. As much symbols of national pride as working merchantmen, they were the most magnificent ships of their period, with

The East Indiaman Bengal.

elaborate external carvings and luxuriously appointed accommodation for officers and passengers. They were heavily armed, a necessary protection against pirates and ships of rival companies. By the second half of the 18th century they differed from men-of-war in having the waist, the area between quarterdeck and forecastle, decked over to form a continuous flush upper deck, on which the guns were carried. The lower deck had a row of painted ports to imitate a genuine warship. In the final stage of development, in about 1815, a typical East Indiaman carried some 1,200 tons of cargo, was 165 ft. (50 m) long, 42 ft. (13 m) in the beam, and about 17 ft. (5 m) deep in the hold.

With the withdrawal of the British East India Company's monopoly of trade to India and China, the East Indiaman's place was taken by the faster BLACKWALL FRIGATE and then by the CLIPPER.

Felucca Small, Mediterranean open boat used for general work on coastal and inland waters. Smaller feluccas are propelled by oars alone, but larger craft have one or two masts carrying lateen sails, with the occasional addition of a small jib or mizzen. The two-masted Spanish felucca had a long overhanging stern and a raised stempost. The two-masted Nile felucca, still in wide use, is longer and may be double-ended or have an upward-curving bow and a flat stern.

Fembøring Traditional Norwegian coastal fishing craft. Clinker-built, broad, and double-ended, the fembøring measures about 50 ft. (15 m) in length and 12 ft. (3.5 m) in the beam. The upward-curving lines at bow and stern are reminiscent of the ancient Viking LONGSHIP. The fembøring is steered by a stern rudder and propelled by a square or lug mainsail and a small square topsail.

Ferry Vessel used to carry passengers, goods, or vehicles across relatively short stretches of water. Most ferries are self-powered, although on very short crossings cable-hauled craft are sometimes used. Ferries range from flat-bottomed rafts or barges to sophisticated high-speed AIR-CUSHION VEHICLES and HYDROFOIL craft. Early ferryboats were rowed, poled, or towed across stretches of water. Modern ferryboats today are usually between 100 and 400 ft. (30-120 m) in length, and are often fitted with propellers and rudders at both ends to save turning around on a short crossing. Bow thrusters may be fitted to assist maneuvering at slow speeds. Double-ended types normally have navigation bridges at both ends. Vehicle ferries are designed to dock end-on to a slipway, and if not double-ended are sometimes fitted with a turntable that rotates the

Drive-on, rear-loading cargo ferry, used for short-sea crossings.

entire load through 180° so that vehicles do not have to reverse off the ship.

Train ferries, with railroad tracks laid along the decks, are normally considerably larger. They are used to link the rail network of Britain and western Europe, and to provide a service between Denmark's principal islands and Sweden and Germany. Some Danish train ferries are well over 400 ft. (120 m) long, and one has four tracks across its breadth, giving a total track length of 1,350 ft. (510 m). In North America train ferries were once extremely common, especially on the Great Lakes. One of the earliest, operated by the Buffalo and Lake Huron Railroad, was opened in 1835, and as late as 1962 there were still ten train ferries operating on Lake Michigan. Today, however, such crossings are more commonly made by roll-on roll-off (RORO) road-vehicle ferries which are more flexible in operation; elsewhere bridges have been built to avoid the delays so often associated with ferries.

In recent years the British have pioneered the use of air-cushion vehicles operating high-speed ferry services. Most notable are the giant hovercraft that cross the English Channel at speeds of up to 65 knots, carrying as many as 610 passengers. Hydrofoils have also proved their value in providing smooth and rapid pas-

senger and vehicle services.

Fireship In the days of wooden ships fire was one of the greatest menaces, and fireships, filled with combustibles, set ablaze, and sent down on the enemy, were a dreadful if double-edged weapon. They were usually sailed down by a small crew towing a boat, in which the crew escaped after grappling the victim.

Fireships were used in the battle of the Spanish Armada (1588), in the three Anglo-Dutch wars of the 17th century, and at Basque Roads (1809).

Fluyt Small, three-masted, Dutch sailing ship evolved at the end of the 16th century and used for trade in North European waters. Fluyts were square-rigged on the fore- and mainmasts, lateen-rigged on the mizzen, with upper and lower spritsails set on the bowsprit. As they never carried any type of topgallants they were easier to handle and needed much smaller crews than ships of similar size built by other nations. These ships were long in relation to their beam, with an exceptionally rounded stern and a remarkably narrow deck. This last feature was probably a ruse to avoid or minimize taxation, since tax at that time was calculated according to the beam on the main deck.

Frigate The name frigate derives from the Spanish *fregata*: a small oared sailing ship. In the 17th century it came to refer to any fine-lined ship built for speed, including small battleships. A number of galley-frigates were built to operate under oars as well as sail; the private man-of-war *Adventure Galley*, commanded by Captain Kidd, was such a ship.

In the early 18th century the term 'frigate-built' could still refer to three-masted merchantmen as well as warships, but by the second quarter of the century the true sailing frigate was making its appearance. This was a ship carrying at first between 28 and 36 guns, filling a gap between the small two-deckers and the 20- and 24-gun ships that had hitherto borne the brunt of scouting and escort duties. These frigates carried most of their guns on one continuous gundeck, with some additional armament on the quarterdeck and often on the forecastle. They were too small for the line of battle, but soon became the principal warship for other tasks such as scouting for the fleet, escorting convoys, and serving on detached duty.

In the second half of the 18th century larger and more powerful frigates were designed. The French built 40-gun vessels, and by the end of the century first Sweden and then the United States began to build very large frigates as powerful as the smaller line-of-battle ships, and which outperformed old two-decker 44s and 50s. The 'six original frigates' authorized by Congress in 1794 formed the foundation of the U.S. Navy, and two of these ships, the 38-gun CONSTELLATION and 44-gun CONSTITUTION, are still afloat today. The Royal Navy produced similar vessels by cutting down line-of-battle ships to a single gundeck, creating a ship known as a *razee*. The success of the American ships against smaller British frigates in the War of 1812, together with advances in constructional techniques, resulted in 50-and even 60-gun frigates. These were two-deckers, since the old quarterdeck and forecastle had been joined to form a continuous upper, or spar, deck. Throughout the remaining years of the age of sail, frigates continued to play an important role. The term gradually gave way to 'CRUISER,' but even the first British ironclad, the WARRIOR, was described as a frigate because she had only

The Leander-*class frigate* Andromeda.

one continuous gundeck.

In 1942 the name was revived to describe the Royal Navy's new twin-screw escort vessels of the *River* class, intended for long-range antisubmarine duties in the North Atlantic. The design closely resembled that of earlier escort sloops, but the new name was widely adopted by other navies, and by the end of the war it was being used for a variety of vessels earlier described as corvettes, destroyer escorts, and sloops.

Since World War II the frigate as a type of warship has grown in number and expanded in its range of duties, now threatening to displace the DESTROYER as the vessel next in size to the cruiser, and already the most common type of warship in most navies. Their size has continued to grow, with such notable designs as the Canadian *St. Laurent* class and the British *Amazon*s and *Leander*s. Until the advent of the new *Oliver Hazard Perry* class, now under construction, the U.S. Navy's frigates were all intended primarily for antisubmarine duties. The large nuclear-powered, guided-missile ships such as the *Bainbridge* were built as frigates, but since 1975 they have been classed as cruisers.

Galleass The galleass was a hybrid, a vessel that combined the sails of the GALLEON with the oars of the GALLEY. As in the smaller galley, the heaviest guns were mounted forward, though lighter weapons could be placed along the sides above the rowers. The galleass probably evolved from the large merchant galleys first used by Venice and other Italian states in the late Middle Ages. The fighting galleass appears to have been developed in Venice, and indeed a handful of Venetian galleasses distinguished themselves at the great victory of Lepanto (1571). This success was mainly due to their greater size and power compared to the Turkish galleys. Galleasses were very slow under oars because of their size and weight, and with their inefficient lateen rigs they compared badly with conventional sailing warships.

Galleon Large sailing ship introduced at the end of the 16th century which marked a major revolution in naval architecture. The 'high-charged' CARRACK and other ships of the day that the galleon was to replace all featured a very high forecastle, bulging out over the stem. This tended to catch the wind, forcing the ship to leeward and making it hard to maneuver. The Elizabethan seaman Sir John HAWKINS, who is credited with devising the new ship design, realized the deficiencies of contemporary ship types and replaced the forecastle with a much lower structure aft, producing a long low beakhead reminiscent of the galley. He lowered the aftercastle and the sides of the ship to make her lie lower in the water, and replaced the traditional round stern with a square-ended one. This new low-charged design produced long lean ships that were faster and sailed closer to the wind, and which distinguished themselves against the cumbersome and top-heavy Spanish carracks of the Armada. The new design was eventually adopted by all the navies of Europe and set a pattern for men-of-war that was to remain standard up until the end of the age of sail.

Galley The oared galley was the principal warship of the Mediterranean from ancient times into the 17th century. The galleys of classical times (see BIREME and TRIREME) were intended primarily for ramming, although catapults and

balingers were also used by the Romans as a longer-range means of attack. Instead of an underwater ram, later galleys had a projection above water from the bows known as a beak. From the early 16th century guns were mounted in the bows of galleys and rapidly became their chief weapon. They could fire only directly ahead and were thus aimed by aligning the galley with its target. These might be supplemented by smaller guns along the sides and by very small guns mounted on swivels. The basic design hardly altered from the late 16th to the end of the 18th century. During this period the development of the sailing warship was gradually making the galley obsolete in northwest Europe and in the Mediterranean. The galley was an unstable vessel, unsuited for rough sea conditions, and so it was abandoned in the northern waters but lingered on for a while in the calmer conditions of the Mediterranean.

In a curious and later chapter of its history the galley was introduced into the Baltic in the early 18th century, and for 100 years continued to play a large part in the wars among the shallows and islands of that sea.

The basic layout of the Mediterranean galley during its final period included a fighting platform placed forward on two levels, guns on the lowest level, and swivel guns and soldiers on the higher platform. The vessel was commanded and steered from another platform at the stern, and the rest of the craft was occupied by the rowers. In Greek and Roman times slaves were used to man the oars; later some navies used paid volunteers or criminals and prisoners. The galley, in this final stage of development, had triangular lateen sails on two or three masts, which were lowered when going into action.

Great Lakes Ship Cargo ship specially developed to carry raw materials and manufactured goods on the Great Lakes of North America. Varying in internal design according to the type of goods carried (most commonly bulk cargoes of grain, iron ore, or coal), the ship has a distinctive appearance with machinery, funnel, and a low superstructure aft, and a higher superstructure at the bow containing the navigating bridge. The long clear deck area is unimpeded by cargo-handling gear since the ports of call all have well-equipped berths. The latest ships have deadweight tonnages of over 50,000 and lengths of up to 1,000 ft. (300 m).

Gunboat Shallow-draft, lightly armed vessel used along coasts and rivers where larger warships cannot venture. The idea of mounting a single heavy gun in a small open boat dates back to Tudor times, when Henry VIII's navy included a number of row-barges of this type. Until the 1770s, however, such vessels were most characteristic of the Mediterranean. Later, the Swedes produced a series of new and unusual designs for use in the Baltic, and in the upheavals of the Revolutionary and Napoleonic Wars a number of nations turned to the development of gunboats. The British introduced designs for use against possible French invasion, and the Danes used similar vessels with great success against British convoys. As President, Thomas Jefferson tried to base the defense of the United States entirely on small gunboats and thus eliminate the need for a seagoing navy. All these boats depended mainly on oars for propulsion, though they could use sail as well, and they usually had one heavy gun on the bow.

At the end of the 18th century the British and French were also building bigger shallow-draft vessels for coastal use. These gun brigs or gun vessels, as they were known, were sailing vessels with guns mounted along the sides, as well as in the bows; they were the ancestors of the gunboats developed in the Crimean War to carry three or more heavy guns on a small, steam-powered hull for shore bombardment. After the war these vessels were found to be very useful for colonial policing duties and the design was further developed, the larger types being classed as gun vessels.

It was not until the latter part of the 19th century that very shallow-draft screw, sternwheel, and paddle vessels were specially designed as river gunboats. Armored vessels of this type fought on the Mississippi during the American Civil War, but the true river gunboat was developed mainly for use on the rivers of colonial possessions and in China, where the U.S. and Royal Navies maintained regular patrols on the Yangtze. Larger vessels, sometimes called river monitors, fought on the

Danube in World War I.

Motor gunboats were developed during World War II on torpedo boat hulls to combat the high-speed German E-boats. The Russians at the same time developed armored motorboats with tank turrets for use on inland waters. By the end of the war several navies had built fleets of gunboats, mainly for use against enemy shipping, and capable of 40 knots from two or three 12-cylinder gasoline engines. Since the war motor gunboats and motor torpedo boats have both given way to all-purpose fast patrol boats, some of them HYDROFOILS, powered by gas turbine engines.

The traditional small gunboat reappeared, however, in a new guise in the Vietnam War. The U.S. Navy patrolled the coast of South Vietnam with a fleet of more than 100 'Swift' type inshore patrol craft. Fiberglass-hulled river patrol boats, together with armored troop carriers and turreted command boats undertook amphibious operations in the Mekong Delta.

Hovercraft A machine that rides over the surface of water or land on a layer of air. Sir Christopher Cockerell created the first practical design for what he called the hovercraft in 1950; since then these versatile craft have found many uses throughout the world. See AIR-CUSHION VEHICLE.

Hoy General term for a variety of small coastal sailing vessels of northern Europe. They were normally gaff- or lug-rigged open boats used for carrying passengers.

Hulk (1) European sailing merchantman falling approximately between the COG and CARRACK in period and development. They were large, full-hulled, and round-ended craft of up to about 400 tons. (2) The hull of an old ship moored in port and used for storage, temporary accommodation, or at one time, as a prison.

Hydrofoil An extremely fast vessel equipped with underwater planes or foils that operate like an airplane's wings and lift the ship's hull out of the water at high speed. When stationary, and at low speeds, a hydrofoil remains in the water like a boat, but as it gathers speed the fins provide enough lift to raise the hull

clear. Since their frictional resistance is so low, hydrofoils travel faster than normal watercraft; speeds of around 60 knots are common while experimental hydrofoils have reached 80 knots.

The first hydrofoil was developed in Italy by Enrico Forlanini in the first decade of the 20th century and used a system of ladder-like foils, each step on the ladder providing a separate lifting surface. The innovation of surface-piercing foils, which lift the vessel's hull high out of the water and so reduce drag and increase speed, came later in 1927 and was a German development. It was not until 1956 that the first commercial hydrofoil came into service between Sicily and mainland Italy and proved an immense success.

The fastest, smoothest, and most sophisticated hydrofoils have three fully submerged foils. They are comparatively uninfluenced by waves and give a perfectly smooth ride over choppy water provided that the height of the waves does not exceed the length of the struts. However, such foils need adjustable control surfaces to balance the craft — a complex process that is performed by an electronic sensor which measures the height of the oncoming waves, a computer which calculates the necessary settings for the foils, and a control mechanism that actually adjusts the foils.

Hydrofoils employ high-speed propellers, water jets, and even air propellers for propulsion, and they are powered by gas turbines or high-speed internal combustion engines. The hulls are usually constructed of high strength-to-weight materials such as glass-reinforced plastic (GRP). Because they are so fast and maneuverable, hydrofoils are widely used as high-speed ferryboats and for naval purposes. Many modern navies employ them as fast patrol boats, while in the United States and Canada they are being developed for antisubmarine warfare and for minesweeping applications.

Icebreaker Ship designed to maintain or clear a channel through ice in high latitudes and polar regions in order to keep ports and important shipping routes open. Icebreakers are unusually broad since the path cleared must be wide enough for conventional ships to pass through. They have a strengthened hull to withstand battering from the ice and

Hydrofoil used as a high-speed ferryboat.

are normally fitted with an additional band of plating at the waterline about 1 to 2 in. (25-50 mm) thick. The bow is cut away below the waterline, so that when the ship steams forward into ice she rides up on top, breaking the ice by sheer weight rather than impact. The midship section of the hull is rounded or wedge-shaped, so that pressure from the ice on the sides helps the ship to ride up. Forward trimming tanks can be pumped full of water to increase weight and crushing power at the bow, and water pumped between side trimming tanks gives the entire ship a rocking motion that helps to break ice. The screw or screws are protected by ice fins, and an 'ice knife' may be fitted at the stern to clear the water when moving astern. A normal icebreaker can steam steadily through ice up to about 3 ft. (1 m) thick; polar craft are capable of breaking ice up to 20 ft. (6 m) in thickness. Probably the largest fleet of icebreakers is maintained by the Soviet Union; the nuclear-powered LENIN was built as its flagship. Certain conventional vessels are strengthened for navigation in ice, notably small survey ships. An interesting large-scale experiment was the modification of the American tanker MANHATTAN to cope with the ice floes of the Northwest Pas-

sage. More successful are the ice-strengthened freighters used in the Soviet Arctic region.

Ironclad Early name for a warship whose vulnerable areas were protected by a covering (cladding) of iron armor. The first ironclad vessels were French and British floating batteries employed against Russian fortifications in the Crimean War. These were simply armored gun platforms that were towed into position, and they scored a considerable success. The first seagoing ironclad warship was built in 1859. This was the French GLOIRE, a wooden ship protected along the sides by iron plating 4.7 in. (119 mm) thick. She was soon followed by the first all-iron warship, the British WARRIOR. The first battle between ironclads was the confrontation between MONITOR and *Virginia*, ex-MERRIMACK, in the American Civil War. The term ironclad continued to be used to describe large iron and steel warships until gradually superseded by the term BATTLESHIP towards the end of the 19th century.

Jacht Small Dutch or Scandinavian sailing craft designed primarily for pleasure sailing on inland waters. It most commonly had a single mast, a gaff- or lug-mainsail, and one foresail. The jacht was the forerunner of the CUTTER, and of course, the YACHT.

Jangada Traditional log-built Brazilian sailing raft of very ancient origin. It consists essentially of five lightweight logs pinned together, with a drop keel amidship and a single mast carrying a fore-and-aft sail that bears similarities to both gaffsail and spritsail. Larger versions have a deckhouse aft, made of reeds or thatch.

Junk Fore-and-aft rigged Chinese sailing ship of ancient origin still in use today. The junk has a flat bottom, high

The Soviet nuclear-powered icebreaker Arktika, *of 25,000 tons.*

stern, forward-thrusting bows, and from one to five masts each carrying a single lugsail of unusual construction. The sails are made of matting and are stiffened laterally by bamboo battens that run the full width of the sail. The panels of sail between each batten are held to the mast individually by collars, and each panel has its own sheet; it is therefore possible to control the sail's shape very precisely, and to hold it firm throughout its height and width when sailing close to the wind. Junks are in fact often considered the most aerodynamically efficient of all rigs employed on large oceangoing sailing ships. Another advantage of the battened panel construction is that reefing is simplified. When the halyard is lowered the sail folds up panel by panel; the stronger the wind the more panels are lowered and reefed in.

The junk was probably the first ship to be equipped with a central stern rudder. This was usually mounted in a watertight slot that extended right through the deck just forward of the stern, so that it could be raised and lowered. Generally of large proportions, it doubled as a drop keel since the junk had no integral keel.

The junk probably originated as a square raft made by joining two dugout canoes with planking, with a box-like superstructure forming the hold. With the addition of a wedge-shaped bow, and internal bulkheads to strengthen the hull and subdivide it into watertight compartments, the junk was the largest, strongest, and most seaworthy sailing ship of ancient times. The largest junks traded regularly throughout the western Pacific, and voyages as far as Madagascar were made by imperial fleets. There were numerous different types of small Chinese junks, including the aptly named floating packing crate, the Yellow River junk. In contrast, Japan had only one standard type of junk, which bore little resemblance to its Chinese counterpart. It was overbeamy, heavy, and inefficiently rigged. In fact, it bore a striking similarity to the round grain ships of ancient Rome, with an artemon-like sail at the bow and a single square sail on the mainmast.

Kayak A long, narrow, partly enclosed one-man boat used by Eskimos for hunting and fishing, and propelled with a double paddle. Consisting of a

Eskimo kayak from Greenland.

wood or whalebone framework covered with sealskin, it weighs only about 60 lb. (27 kg) and is self-righting. Like other CANOE-type boats, modern versions of the kayak have been made of fiberglass and other materials for sport and recreation. A larger open craft, the UMIAK can carry an entire family and its possessions.

Keel An early version of the modern LIGHTER, the keel was a flat-bottomed craft used to ferry coal to and from COLLIERS. It had a single mast and was equipped with leeboards.

Ketch Two-masted coastal trading and fishing vessel similar to a YAWL, but with a larger mizzen and the mizzenmast stepped forward of the rudder-head. Evolved in England in the mid-17th century, ketches were originally square-rigged. They were widely employed in the navies of northern Europe as small supply ships and BOMB VESSELS. In this latter use one or two massive mortars were mounted in the clear deck space for-

ward of the mainmast. During the 19th century the ketch acquired a fore-and-aft rig and remained a widely used coastal trader, TRAWLER, and a PACKET. It has now become a popular yachting vessel.

Knorr Scandinavian merchant ship, an ancestor of the COG. Essentially a broader and more capacious version of the Viking LONGSHIP, the knorr shared the latter's clinker construction, double-ended shape, and single mast setting a square sail. The rig was like that of the longship; it had a special spar to hold the leading edge of the sail taut when heading into the wind. Knorrs excavated from Roskilde Fjord in Denmark are of two types. One is a light coastal craft measuring 45 ft. (13.7 m) in length and 10 ft. 6 in. (3.2 m) in the beam, and is lightly decked fore and aft. The other is a larger and much more sturdily built vessel that may be similar to those sailed by the Vikings on their voyages of exploration. This ship is some 54 ft. (16.5 m) long and 15 ft. (4.5 m) in the beam.

The British ketch H.F. Bolt, *built in 1876.*

Lakatoi Traditional sailing vessel of New Guinea made of three dugout canoes fixed together with timber beams, on top of which were a bamboo deck and bamboo-framed deckhouses. The craft had two masts and was propelled by unusual claw-shaped fore-and-aft sails. The lakatoi was some 60 ft. (18 m) long and 50 ft. (15 m) in the beam. More raft than boat, it was capacious but cumbersome and slow. Steering required as many as four large oars near the stern.

Landing craft In the 18th century specially designed large, flat-bottomed rowboats were used to land men, guns, and horses in amphibious assaults. The design of landing craft scarcely changed until World War I, when the British developed armored motor barges known as X-lighters or beetles, and the Russians built engine-aft landing ships for operations in the Black Sea. Between the wars the Japanese produced landing-craft mother ships, later called landing ships, and landing craft with bow ramps for men and vehicles.

With the outbreak of World War II British and American developments were rapid: small, fast-assault landing craft; larger LCTs and LCIs for tanks and infantry respectively; and still larger LSIs and LSTs, with bow ramps, capable of beaching to land tanks. By the end of the

LASH ship for transporting floating containers, or lighters.

war a large family of specialized amphibious warfare ships had been developed. Among them were the LSDs, or dock landing ships, which carried small landing craft in a built-in dock aft, and could float them in or out. Today the U.S. Navy includes the huge *Tarawa*-class amphibious assault ships (LHAs) of nearly 40,000 tons displacement. Each can carry a reinforced Marine battalion of nearly 2,000 men with all its equipment, trucks, landing craft, and helicopters. Beneath its full-length flight deck and hangars is a large floodable docking well.

During World War II the United States developed truly amphibious landing craft, the wheeled DUKW and the tracked *Alligator*. Larger tracked landing craft have since appeared, and interesting new possibilities offered by air-cushion vehicles, which can operate equally well on land, water, or swamp, are being actively investigated.

LASH ship The abbreviation LASH stands for Lighter Aboard SHip; the vessel is a specialized CONTAINER SHIP carrying very large floating containers, or lighters. The ship is equipped with a massive gantry crane capable of lifting 500 tons. This straddles the deck, traveling along the length of the vessel on rails, and is used to load and discharge lighters over the stern. Apart from small twin funnels at the sides and a navigating bridge at the bow, the entire deck is clear, giving the crane an unimpeded run

and easy access to the hatches. The lighters each have a capacity of 400 tons and measure 61 ft. 6 in. by 31 ft. 2 in. by 13 ft. (18.74 m × 9.49 m × 3.96 m). They are stowed in the holds and on deck, and while the ship is at sea with one set of lighters, further sets can be made ready. Loading and discharge are rapid (around 15 minutes per lighter), no port or dock facilities are needed, and the lighters can be grouped into 'push tows' for transport along inland waterways.

The world's first LASH ship, *Acadia Forest*, was built in Japan, launched in 1969, and operated by the Central Gulf Steamship Corporation between New Orleans, the Dutch port of Rotterdam, and the English port of Sheerness — all three ports being linked to extensive networks of inland and intracoastal waters. Of 36,862 tons gross (43,000 tons deadweight), she is 860 ft. (262 m) long and 106 ft. (32.3 m) in the beam. Her twin diesel engines, which develop 26,000 hp, give her a speed of 20 knots. She carries 73 lighters.

See also SEABEE.

Liberty ship Mass-produced cargo ship of a simple and sturdy design constructed in the United States during World War II. Displacing 10,490 tons, and measuring 441 ft. (134.5 m) in length and 57 ft. (17.5 m) in the beam, Liberty ships were powered by reciprocating steam engines of 2,500 hp, and could cruise at 11 knots. They had two

Military landing craft.

decks, five holds, and coal-fired boilers. Prefabricated and all-welded construction methods were used because speed of assembly was vital: a record was set when one vessel was completed, from laying the keel to delivery, in only 14 days. The average construction time was, however, around 40 days. The first Liberty ship, *Patrick Henry*, was launched on September 27, 1941, and after Pearl Harbor the initial target of 200 ships was expanded. In total, 2,610 were built, including 62 fitted out as tankers, 24 as colliers, and 36 as aircraft transporters. Many Liberty ships were still in service as merchantmen in the 1970s.

During the immediate postwar years a successor to the Liberty ship, known as the Victory ship, was produced. A total of 414 were built, less austere in fittings, longer, faster (16 knots), and powered by steam turbines.

Lifeboat Small, specially designed craft for sea rescue work. Those carried aboard large ships for emergency use by passengers and crew are usually smaller than shore-based rescue craft, but they are normally equipped with emergency provisions, a water distillation plant, radio, and lights. Frequently equipped with diesel engines, they are fireproof and virtually unsinkable.

Shore-based lifeboats were first developed at the end of the 18th century. They are designed for safety and maneuverability in the roughest surf and seas. Today they are built of steel and

aluminum, or of traditional double-hulled timber construction. They are very strong and possess reserve buoyancy so that they can keep going even when partly damaged. Various self-righting devices are employed, one of the most common involving the transfer of water from one tank to another. Powerful diesel engines give speeds of about 15 knots in the largest vessels.

Lighter Flat-bottomed, barge-like craft used to carry cargo to and from ships in docks or open roadsteads. They are dumb, that is, unpowered, and must be towed or pushed by tugs. They are particularly useful in areas where shallow waters prevent seagoing vessels from berthing. Lighters are also used for over-the-side loading and discharge of cargo ships, a process which can take place while freight is loaded or unloaded at the dockside. This procedure is normally reserved for goods to be carried to or from other parts of the dock area. Special lighters in the form of floating containers are loaded with cargo on LASH SHIPS.

Lightship A vessel performing the duties of a fixed lighthouse at a site where conditions render a conventional lighthouse impractical. The first lightship, *Nore*, took up a station in the Thames estuary in 1732 and was soon followed by many others. The earliest vessels were converted sailing ships carrying a lantern at the masthead; today's specially built lightships can carry a light

A modern lightship.

of more than 1,000,000 candlepower, visible for 11 miles (17.5 km), and are also equipped with a compressed-air fog signal and a radio beacon.

In the United States and a number of other countries lightships are self-propelled vessels, most of them diesel-powered, and thus capable of returning to their stations if blown off position. Lightships in Britain and certain other countries have no engines and are towed to their positions. A 4-ton anchor is used to keep the ship at its station; the light is mounted atop a 40-ft. (12-m) tower in a special pendulum-balanced cradle. Lightships are expensive to build and man, and they may not always keep their position precisely. Where possible they are being replaced by Lanby buoys or by light towers, structures resembling oil drilling platforms.

Liner (1) An oceangoing ship belonging to a shipping company which carries freight or passengers on a regular scheduled service. Freight liners carry a wide assortment of general cargo, possibly from hundreds of companies. The system is expensive since loading and discharge are slow, and extensive handling and storage facilities must be provided at every port en route, but for small consignments freight liners provide an essential service.

The passenger liner era could be said to have begun in 1838 with the race between the paddle steamers SIRIUS and GREAT WESTERN to cross the Atlantic entirely under steam. Over the next eight years the *Great Western* plied regularly with outstanding success. In 1840 Samuel Cunard of Britain founded the Cunard Line to carry passengers and mail between Liverpool and Boston, and soon French, German, Italian, and American

British lifeboat of 1889.

The Cunard liner Queen Mary, *launched in 1934.*

lines joined the competition to provide the largest, fastest, and most comfortable transatlantic ferry service. The ship with the fastest passage time was said to hold the Blue Riband of the Atlantic. Famous liners of the late 19th century include *Scotia*, Cunard's last and most elegant paddle steamer, and the German KAISER WILHELM DER GROSSE. The early years of the 20th century saw the launching of such celebrated liners as the sister ships MAURETANIA and LUSITANIA and the ill-fated TITANIC, and during the 1930s a new generation of liners appeared setting even higher standards of design and comfort. Best known are the QUEEN MARY, QUEEN ELIZABETH, and NORMANDIE. The UNITED STATES, the world's fastest liner, was launched in 1952, and the longest, FRANCE, appeared 10 years later. During the 1960s all these giants, with the exception of the QE2, were forced out of business as more and more people began to travel by air. Today's passenger liners are smaller, and most have given up their 'ferryboat' role to become cruise ships.

(2) A word used during the great age of sail to describe a SHIP OF THE LINE.

(3) A fishing vessel taking its catch with lines carrying baited hooks instead of using nets.

Longship The oared warship of the Vikings or Norsemen. The largest longships were known as *skeids* or *drakars* and could measure up to 150 ft. (46 m) in length and 20 ft. (6 m) in the beam; their total complement was 180 men with two rowers pulling on each oar. Smaller longships, known as *skutas*, had one rower to an oar. A single square sail was set on a mast that could be lowered when the ship was under oars; the sail could be braced to windward by a spar called a *beitass*.

The Viking longships were far superior in performance to the GALLEYS of the Mediterranean. With their shallow draft they could penetrate far inland in search of plunder, yet their incomparable seaworthiness enabled them to make remarkable voyages of discovery across the uncharted stormy North Atlantic.

Lugger A small craft, usually two-masted, equipped with lugsails. They evolved early in the 18th century for fishing and coastal work where the maneuverability of the fore-and-aft rig provided significant advantages over the square rig. Their handiness and speed made them popular with privateers and smugglers; the French brought the privateer lugger to its peak of development during the Revolutionary and Napoleonic Wars. They decked the hull in to provide accommodation for up to 10 guns and a crew of 50, and they fitted a third mast at the stern with a bumkin, a stern version of the bowsprit, on which to sheet the mizzen lugsail. These French luggers were known as *chasse-marées*.

Minesweeper The first minesweepers were ship's boats, and later, fishing vessels, working in pairs and towing wire rope between them. Detached from their anchoring cables by the wire rope, the mines floated to the surface where they could be destroyed by gunfire. In the course of World War I specialized minesweepers were built and new methods of sweeping developed. The British adapted commercial trawler designs and eventually produced minesweepers capable of 25 knots to operate with the fleet; German and American vessels were based largely on tug types.

During World War II the contact mine gave way to a new class of influence mine detonated by a ship's magnetic field, the sound of her propellers, or the reduction in water pressure she causes. New sweeping techniques had to be evolved, and the highly sensitive Russian-made magnetic mine used in the Korean War rendered the steel-hulled ocean minesweeper obsolete. New classes of minesweepers were built of nonmagnetic materials, usually wood planking on nonmagnetic metal frames. (Some more modern minesweepers now have hulls made of fiberglass.) Coastal minesweepers, 150 ft. (46 m) long, and the smaller inshore minesweepers, developed from wartime motor launches, were produced. A notable advance has been the minehunter, a vessel fitted with high-definition sonar to detect mines lying on the seabed.

The Mississippi Queen, *a river steamboat with a stern paddle wheel.*

Mississippi steamboat The shallow-draft paddle steamers that carried passengers and freight on the Mississippi and its tributaries were among the most remarkable vessels in the history of steam navigation. The tortuous curves and shallow sandbars of western rivers produced a unique type of shallow-draft, high-powered craft, some of them of 5,000 tons gross. To cope with conditions on the river, the hull had to be extremely shallow, and therefore with little inherent strength. The main deck extended well beyond the hull at either side, the wide overhanging sections being known as guards. The engine and boilers were situated on this deck, contrary to the usual practice of placing machinery low in the hull, and as many as five or six upper decks were built up on tall pillars. Top-heavy and narrow-hulled, the vessel was inherently unstable, so that crates of heavy ballast had to be hauled across the deck when speeding around bends.

For the sake of lightness the engines were pushed to their limits, and steam pressures of up to 120 lb. per sq. in. (8.4 kg/cm^2) were not uncommon. British marine steam engines of the time worked at only a fifth of this pressure, and were therefore much safer but also much heavier for a given output. Boiler explosions were a constant hazard on the Mississippi steamboats. The engine turned a pair of side paddle wheels 30 to 40 ft (9-12 m) in diameter, although many later craft had a stern paddle. With rising tiers of often elaborately carved and decorated superstructure, magnificent staircases, and sumptuously appointed interiors, the river steamboats quickly developed into the floating palaces of the Mark Twain era. So phenomenal was the growth in tonnage of these craft, that they soon exceeded the steam tonnage of the entire British merchant marine, and carried twice as much cargo as all American ships engaged in foreign commerce.

Races were common, and the betting on their outcome was often on a grand scale. Bets on the most famous race of all, between *Natchez* and *Robert E. Lee* in 1870, totalled over $1,000,000. Steaming without passengers or freight, *Robert E. Lee* covered the 1,218 miles (1,960 km) upriver from New Orleans to St. Louis in a record time of 3 days, 18 hours, and 36 minutes — an average speed of almost 13½ mph (21.5 km/h). *Natchez*, with a full load, arrived 6½ hours later. Even this race could not revive the steamboat's fortunes, however. The Civil War and the coming of the railroad had already dealt the classic steamboats a death blow.

Monitor The original MONITOR, the shallow-draft craft with a revolving turret built by John ERICSSON for the Union navy, gave its name to an entire class of naval vessels built during the American Civil War. They saw some success in port blockades and on river duties, and the United States continued to build such vessels for coastal defense as late as the first decade of this century. In 1915 and 1916 the Royal Navy built shallow-draft shore-bombardment vessels called monitors; these were also used in World War II. Other navies built smaller monitors as river GUNBOATS.

Muletta Traditional Portuguese coastal and fishing craft of unusual design. It carried a single short forward-raking mast with a large lateen mainsail.

Additional triangular fore-and-aft sails were set on an angled spar at the stern; at the bow were two artemon-like square sails beneath a long bowsprit, and a spinnaker-like sail above it. The beamy hull was equipped with a stern rudder, leeboards, a rounded iron-spiked stern-post, and a brightly painted eye at either side of the bow.

Não General Spanish name for any kind of ship from late medieval times into the 16th century.

Nef French sailing merchantman and warship, essentially an enlarged version of the COG, carvel-built and three-masted. The nef was an early full-rigged ship, in use during the 15th and 16th centuries.

Outrigger A log or pole float suspended out on one or both sides of a canoe for added stability. The term is also commonly used to describe any craft equipped with an outrigger. An outrigger craft, like a multihull vessel, combines the stability of a broad-hulled vessel with the speed, due to the small immersed surface, of a narrow canoe-type boat. Outriggers are common among the traditional sailing craft of the Indian and Pacific oceans. They include the small *moro* single outrigger of Indonesia's Sulu Sea, and the much larger double outrigger *caracor* of New Guinea and the surrounding region. Both craft have a single tripod mast and a single, very long fore-and-aft sail combining characteristics of the lateen and the lug.

Packet Abbreviated form of the name packet boat, a vessel carrying passengers and mail on a regular service between two ports. 'Packets' were originally parcels of official letters and diplomatic dispatches; in the 16th and 17th centuries packet boats, or 'post barks' as they were also known, were strictly mail boats, owned or chartered by the state. Eventually they began to carry passengers and some freight, though still on official business only. With the advent of steam most governments entrusted the transport of mail to privately owned steamships. The earliest transatlantic steamers, for example, were known as Atlantic packets, although their primary purpose was to carry passengers.

Paddle steamer A steamship driven by paddles rather than by screw propellers. All early steamships had paddle wheels, either at the stern (sternwheelers) or at the sides (sidewheelers), but by the 1840s it was becoming clear that for oceangoing vessels and warships paddles had considerable disadvantages. They were vulnerable to enemy action and to heavy seas, and when the ship rolled one paddle spun uselessly in the air while the other was submerged. On calm inland waters, however, the paddle wheel's efficiency could rival that of the propeller, and paddle steamers remained popular for river transport throughout the 19th century.

Today most paddle steamers are pleasure boats; few ships of the past have survived other than excursion craft and some preserved as floating museums. However, in comparatively recent times paddle propulsion enjoyed a brief renaissance in the form of a series of diesel-powered harbor tugs, including some built for Britain's Royal Navy in the late 1950s. Paddle propulsion offers unrivaled maneuverability: the paddle gives almost as much power going astern as ahead, and by stopping one wheel or by having the paddles turn in opposite directions a paddle tug can turn almost on the spot. But the advent of bow-thruster units and of cycloidal, controllable-pitch, and shrouded propellers, has given some screw-propelled ships nearly the same degree of maneuverability.

Pinnace (1) A small, two-masted sailing ship of about 20 tons developed towards the end of the 16th century. It was square-rigged (and later schooner-rigged) and was often employed as a naval tender or scout. Many English navigators used this small craft on their voyages of discovery; Sir Humphrey GILBERT, for example, was lost in the North Atlantic when the *Squirrel*, a tiny pinnace of only 10 tons, capsized.

(2) Small boat carried on board a large sailing ship, rowed by 8, or later 16, oarsmen and occasionally carrying a single mast and sail. They were gradually replaced by diesel-powered ships' boats.

Pirogue A Spanish word borrowed from the Carib Indians to describe a dug-out canoe, particularly the double-hulled seagoing craft that European voyagers

A 17th-century Dutch pinnace, frequently used as a scouting vessel.

encountered in Central and South America in the 16th and 17th centuries.

Pocket battleship Under the terms of the Treaty of Versailles, the capital ships of the German navy were restricted to 10,000 tons and could carry guns no larger than 11 in. The intention was to limit German building to coastal defense vessels. Instead, the Germans proceeded in the 1930s to build diesel-engined ships intended for commerce raiding, unofficially dubbed pocket battleships. They were essentially armored cruisers, with the unusually heavy armament of two triple 11-in. turrets. The diesels gave an impressive range and endurance. Despite weight-saving expedients the displace-

ment was nearer 13,000 than 10,000 tons. The first of these ships, *Deutschland*, was followed by the slightly different *Scheer* and GRAF SPEE. They were intended to be faster than anything more powerfully armed, and more powerful than anything faster. By 1939, however, fast new battleships were being built by the Germans and other nations, and the Battle of the River Plate in December of that year showed that the margin of superiority over conventional cruisers was not overwhelming.

Proa A term coming from the Malay *prau*, meaning boat, and applied to all boats and ships of Malay waters. In the west, however, it often refers to a speci-

219

The pocket battleship Graf Spee *being scuttled after the Battle of the River Plate.*

fic vessel, the two-masted flying *prau* popular among pirates of the Java Sea. The craft had a frameless hull and changed little in the thousand years of its existence. Each mast carried a large fore-and-aft sail between lateen and lug in design, and there was also a jib. The flying prau was equipped with two steering oars and often mounted a single outrigger.

RoRo ship Freight ship or ferry with facilities for vehicles to drive on and off (roll-on roll-off). Equipped with large openings or ports at bow and stern (and sometimes also in the side), the ship permits rapid loading and discharge with hydraulically operated ramps providing easy access. The hull may be divided into as many as seven vehicle decks; folding or sliding internal bulkhead doors provide the necessary subdivision of the hold into watertight compartments. RoRo ships generally have twin engines with funnels at the sides to leave a maximum area of the deck clear for vehicles. The lower vehicle decks may have a headroom suitable for automobiles, while the main deck is designed for fully loaded trucks or trailers, often carrying containers. Much space is inevitably wasted in RoRo ships, but this is compensated for by speed and flexibility of handling; the system is especially valuable on short routes and for express freight. Because of their relatively low cargo loading, RoRo ships are

broad-beamed, with a high freeboard and a three- or four-deck superstructure.

Rotor ship Experimental ship invented by the German engineer Anton Flettner in 1924. The rotors, which powered the ship, were huge, funnel-like metal towers some 50 ft. (15 m) high and 12 ft. (3.6 m) in diameter. They were revolved at 100 rpm by small engines. A crosswind striking the spinning rotors was deflected to cause suction ahead of the rotors, and an area of higher pressure behind them, the two forces combining

A RoRo container ship.

to move the ship forward. Flettner claimed that the rotors would make much more efficient use of the wind than could sails. He demonstrated his ideas first in a converted SCHOONER, the *Buckau*, and later in the specially built *Barbara* of 1926. With a fair wind the latter reached 6 knots with rotors alone, and 13 knots with the assistance of the 1,000-hp engine. The rotors were less efficient than predicted, particularly when a good wind was lacking. Further development was abandoned, but today the idea is again under consideration.

Round ship General term used to describe broad-beamed merchant ships of ancient and medieval times, as distinct from the long, slender war galleys. Round ships were usually single-masted, square-rigged vessels with a length-to-beam ratio of 2 or 2½ to 1.

The rotor ship Barbara, *1926.*

Sampan General name for many small oriental boats. Most have a small raised deck at the flat stern and a pointed bow. Those designed for inland waters normally have a rough shelter or awning amidships, and are propelled by a large single oar at the stern. Coastal sampans carry one or two masts setting battened lugsails similar to those of a junk. Some small powered boats are also called sampans.

Schooner Fore-and-aft rigged sailing ship with two or more masts. The schooner was originally a two-masted vessel, with each mast setting a large gaffsail and the foremast also carrying square topsails. In addition, she always had headsails. This type of ship was referred to as the topsail schooner. Later schooners often had the square topsails replaced by triangular fore-and-aft gaff-

Sampans in Hong Kong.

topsails. These were set on every mast, and the resulting rig was known as the fore-and-aft schooner. Both types were built with three, four, and five masts, and to confuse the multiplicity of schooner rigs yet further, a two-master with square topsails on both masts also existed and was called the main-topsail or two-topsail schooner. One fore-and-aft schooner, the THOMAS W. LAWSON, was built with seven masts, known respectively as fore, main, mizzen, jigger, spanker, pusher, (the last three sometimes being termed simply numbers 4, 5, and 6), and driver. There were also a few five-masters, but these were considered oddities in their day.

Yet another variety was the staysail schooner. It carried a single triangular sail called the jib-headed spanker on the aftermast, and a pair of triangular fore-and-aft sails between each pair of masts. The upper sail of the pair, the trysail, was named after the mast ahead of it on which it was set, and the lower sail, the staysail, was named after the mast astern.

In the late 18th century, American shipwrights combined the fast and maneuverable schooner rig with the streamlined hull familiar from the Jamaica sloop to produce the BALTIMORE CLIPPER schooner, and during the 19th century a host of schooner types were created for a variety of duties. In the earlier and smaller schooners, the attraction of the rig had been its handiness in most wind conditions. However, towards the end of the era of sail, the schooner rig was adopted on large merchantmen as an economy measure — it required a smaller crew than a full-rigged ship did. (Even the

giant seven-masted *Thomas W. Lawson* had a crew of only 16). In the variable wind conditions of the Atlantic coast the rig proved ideal; the Grand Banks fishing schooners were among the finest of all sailing vessels. But from about 1880 to 1920 massive five- and six-masters were built and used for ocean trading, a role for which they were rightly considered unsuited. In strong winds and squalls the booms were apt to lash across the deck, causing several dismastings and earning the largest schooners the nickname 'man-killers.'

SeaBee Oceangoing freighters carrying floating containers (lighters), a variant of the LASH SHIP. Developed by the Lykes Bros. of New Orleans, the first SeaBee ship was built by the General Dynamics Corporation at Quincy, Massachusetts, in 1972. Named *Doctor Lykes*, she is of 20,500 tons gross, measures 876 ft. (267 m) in length, and carries 38 lighters each holding nearly 650 tons of freight. The essential difference from the LASH system is the method of loading. SeaBee ships have a submersible stern elevator capable of lifting 2,000 tons. With the elevator platform lowered, tugs maneuver the lighters into position two at a time. The platform is raised to the required level, and self-propelled transporters on board stow the lighters. The cargo area occupies almost the full length of the ship; the only superstructure is at the bow. Taking on or discharging a full load of 38 lighters takes only 13 hours.

Ship of the line During the 17th century standard tactics evolved for fighting naval battles in formation. It became apparent that broadside guns could only be used to best effect in battle by placing the ships in a line-ahead formation. At first all ships, whatever their size, took their place in this line of battle, but it was soon found that only the larger ships were sufficiently powerful to stay in this line. They thus earned the name 'line-of-battle ships' or ships of the line. In the 17th and 18th centuries the largest ships of the line were three-deckers of 100 guns. The first of these ships was the English *Sovereign of the Seas* (1637). Towards the end of the 18th century even larger ships began appearing, the Spanish being able to build the enormous four-decked *Santissima Trinidad* in the

1760s because of the size of timber available in Cuba where she was built. Later, improvements in construction techniques permitted an increase from just under 200 ft. (61 m) to 250 ft. (76 m) in length, and 120- and even 140-gun ships were being built after the end of the Napoleonic War.

Very few of these first-rates, as they became known, were built; they were extremely expensive in men and materials. Rather more second-rates, of about 90 guns, were built, these were slightly smaller three-deckers, but the backbone of the fighting fleets consisted of two-decked third-rates. Initially, these were 60- or 70-gun ships, but in the early 18th century it was found that the best combination of qualities was obtained with 64 or 74 guns. In the second half of the century most line-of-battle ships belonging to major navies were 74s; by early in the 19th century the 74 was being slowly replaced by the 80. The evolution of the ship of the line into the modern BATTLESHIP was a gradual process. At first wooden hulls were simply protected with iron armor (ironclad) and lengthened to accommodate screw propulsion. Masts, sails, and broadside guns were retained for some time.

Sloop (1) Small, fore-and-aft rigged sailing vessel with a single mast. Normally carrying a gaff-mainsail, gaff-topsail, and jib, sloops often set a variety of extra sails. These might include a total of three foresails (two jibs and a staysail), plus a jib-topsail and a square sail set on the mainmast, in addition to the gaff-mainsail. The sloop was evolved in the 18th century at the same time as the CUTTER, which it closely resembled in design and use. The Bermuda or Jamaica sloops that traded between the West Indies and America's eastern seaboard pioneered the streamlined V-section hull from which the CLIPPER hull later evolved.

(2) The word sloop to describe a warship first came into use about 1700, to cover smaller fighting ships of less than 20 guns. These were ships that were not rated, that is, which had no captain, but only a lieutenant in command. Sloops of this period were usually two-masted, with what would later be known as brig or ketch rig. The smallest complement of guns was originally eight, but after the middle of the century this was increased

to 12, at about the same time that the first three-masted, ship-rigged sloops were developed. During the American War of Independence two-masted sloops classed as brig sloops appeared. The three-masted vessels were normally known as ship sloops, and the biggest were virtually miniature FRIGATES.

Sloops were maids-of-all-work, tackling any job that did not need the bigger frigates. Even the introduction of steam and of metal hulls did not alter their appearance significantly, because for much of the 19th century sloops were mainly employed in distant parts of the world where the ability to cruise under sail was still important. By the end of the century, however, no more of these colonial vessels were being built.

In World War II a new class of Royal Navy ships engaged in antisubmarine warfare took the designation of sloop. These were escort vessels midway in size between frigates and corvettes.

Smack Term now used to describe a fishing vessel of any type, whether powered or using sails. Originally, the smack was a small inshore fishing boat rigged as a CUTTER or KETCH.

Snow Two-masted European merchant sailing ship almost identical in rig to the BRIG. In addition to its two square-rigged masts, however, the snow generally carried a short trysail mast stepped immediately aft of the mainmast. This arrangement permitted the gaff-mainsail to be raised and lowered without any danger that the hoops attaching it to its mast would foul the square mainsail. The largest two-masted merchantmen of the 16th to the 19th century, some snows carried as much as 1,000 tons of cargo.

Submarine A naval vessel capable of underwater operation for long periods of time. Experiments with vessels capable of operating underwater were made at least as early as the 1620s, but the first actually used in combat was David BUSHNELL's Turtle of 1776. Shaped like an upended turtle, constructed of wood, and carrying one man, it had one hand-cranked screw for propulsion and a second for diving, a rudder, and a hand-pump arrangement for controlling buoyancy. Though an attempt to fix a mine on a

The Resolution, *one of the Royal Navy's four Polaris submarines launched in 1967.*

British warship during the American Revolution failed, the *Turtle* can claim to be the first effective submarine.

In 1801 Robert Fulton built the *Nautilus*, the first submersible to take on the characteristic fish-like shape of modern craft. The earliest successful use of the submarine came during the Civil War, when the *H.L. Hunley* sank the Federal sloop *Housatonic* with a spar torpedo. Many of the features of modern submarines — including the use of water ballast, horizontal stabilizers for diving, and electric batteries for propulsion underwater — were all embodied in a succession of boats built by the Irish-born American John P. HOLLAND. By the turn of the century his ninth submarine, the *Holland*, was accepted by the U.S. Navy. Further Holland vessels were ordered by the Royal Navy; other navies followed with designs of their own.

World War I proved the effectiveness of the submarine in dramatic fashion. After the German navy adopted unrestricted submarine warfare early in 1917, U-boats very nearly succeeded in closing the Atlantic to Allied shipping. It was only with the introduction of Allied convoys and the development of the depth charge and other antisubmarine weapons that the menace was overcome. World War II once again saw the vital North Atlantic supply routes nearly cut, with wolf-pack tactics and the use of the snor-

kel marking major advances. In the Pacific, U.S. submarines were responsible for the destruction of two-thirds of all the Japanese shipping and naval vessels sunk in the war.

The range, duration, and virtual immunity to detection of the nuclear-powered submarine marked a revolution in naval strategy. The first nuclear submarine, the NAUTILUS, was launched in 1954 and four years later became the first ship to travel to the North Pole, relying solely on its inertial navigation system. In 1960 the *Triton* circumnavigated the world underwater. In hull design these early nuclear submarines still broadly resembled their predecessors, which spent the largest part of their time on the surface. But with the launching of the *Albacore* and *Skipjack* at the end of the 1950s a new streamlined, tear-drop hull shape was adopted. The hunter-killer submarines based on this design can reach speeds of more than 45 knots.

When the the *George Washington* was launched in 1959 the submarine came of age as the most powerful warship the world has known. Carrying 16 Polaris ballistic missiles, it was armed with a greater destructive power than all the weapons used in World War II combined. The substitution of the multiple-warhead Poseidon for Polaris missiles in the 1970s gave the U.S. ballistic-missile submarine force over half the strategic warheads in the nation's nuclear arsenal. The first submarines of the new *Ohio* class, now under construction, are each being equipped with 24 Trident missiles possessing a range of over 4,000 miles (6,500 km). With a displacement of 18,700 tons when submerged, they are the largest undersea craft ever built.

The development of the submarine has opened striking new possibilities for peaceful oceanographic research. In the past 20 years a variety of deep-diving submersibles have been developed for salvage and rescue as well as research. The BATHYSCAPHE *Trieste*, which reached a depth of 35,800 ft. (10,900 m), was followed by a series of craft for deep-sea rescue. The U.S. Navy's Deep Submergence Rescue Vehicle (DSRV) can descend to depths of more than 5,000 ft. (1,525 m) to rescue 24 men at a time from a damaged submarine. The Deep Submergence Search Vehicle (DSSV) *NR-1*, which can dive to at least 20,000 ft. (6,100 m), is the first nuclear-powered noncombatant submarine. Numerous smaller craft have been developed by many of the world's navies and also find a role in deep-sea oil exploration.

Tainu Oceangoing double canoe of the South Pacific, sailed by the people of Polynesia in their great transpacific migrations. Some 70 ft. (21 m) long, these craft had beautifully decorated sternposts rising 20 ft. (6 m) from the hull, and a pair of large, claw-shaped sails. The hulls of the two dugout canoes were built up with planking for additional freeboard and storage space. A large cabin was built on the deck joining the two hulls together.

Tanker BULK CARRIER designed to transport liquid cargo. Specialized tankers carry such liquids as asphalt, wine, molasses and liquefied natural gas, but the largest and the overwhelming majority transport petroleum products, either crude oil, from oil fields to refineries, or the refined products (notably gasoline) from the refinery to centers of distribution. Oil tankers vary in size from small coastal vessels some 200 ft. (60 m) long and of 1,500 tons deadweight, through medium-sized ships of 60,000 tons, to the giant VLCCs (very large crude carriers) and ULCCs (ultralarge crude carriers). These, the largest

The U.S. Navy's Deep Submergence Rescue Vehicle, DSRV-2.

mobile objects ever made by man, are over 1,200 ft. (365 m) long. The largest of all is the French BATILLUS (542,400 tons deadweight, and with a draft of over 90 ft. or 27 m). Much larger tankers have been planned, but with the present drop in demand *Batillus* may remain a record size for some time to come.

A tanker is essentially an enormous floating tank; the oil is carried next to the hull. For safety and convenience the cargo space is divided into a number of separate tanks by athwartships and longitudinal bulkheads. Some 60 percent of the tanker's length is used for carrying oil. Fuel, stores, and ballast are carried in

The 190,600-ton oil tanker Esso Bernicia, *1968.*

holds at the bow. Engine, machinery, accommodation, and the navigating bridge are invariably at the stern, so that the working areas of the ship are away from the cargo. The oil is isolated from the rest of the ship by empty watertight compartments known as cofferdams.

The characteristic appearance of a tanker arises from its very long flush deck and its raised superstructure aft. The deck is unobstructed by cargo-handling gear or hatches, since loading and discharge are through pipes. Openings in the hull are therefore small and easy to seal, and the tanker can safely be loaded to a lower freeboard than most other ship types. A raised walkway or 'flying bridge' runs the length of the ship, carrying a multitude of pipes and service lines and providing a safe passage for the crew in rough weather, when the deck is awash.

Tankers have grown to such enormous size because the bigger the ship, the more economic it is to operate. Most have a single power plant and propeller, and may therefore be rendered helpless by a comparatively minor mechanical fault. These giant ships are in any event difficult to maneuver. The stopping time may be as much as 20 minutes, during which time the ship may travel up to 5 miles (8 km).

Torpedo boat Spar torpedoes, explosive charges fixed on the end of long poles and carried over a boat's bows, were used during the American Civil War. However, the true torpedo boat came into being as a result of Robert Whitehead's invention of the locomotive, or self-propelled, torpedo in the late 1860s. The appeal of a weapon that would enable a small boat, no more than a steam launch, to sink the largest battleship was considerable. The first effective torpedo boat, the LIGHTNING, was launched in 1876, and with a speed of 19 knots she was highly successful and widely copied. By the next decade most of the world's navies possessed torpedo boats, and the British Admiralty embarked on a search for an effective answer to the new menace. The result was the DESTROYER, a vessel as fast as a torpedo boat, and which could also launch torpedoes itself. On account of their cheapness and agility many navies continued to build torpedo boats into the beginning of this century.

The development of the internal combustion engine and its use in fast racing motorboats led to the birth of a new class of torpedo boat. This took place during World War I, when the British firm of Thornycroft developed a coastal motorboat capable of 40 knots, which dropped its torpedo over the stern. The Italians developed their slower, but equally effective MAS boats at the same time. During the interwar years the motor torpedo boat (MTB) was improved in range and seaworthiness. Among the torpedo boats of World War II were the large, powerful German S-boats, and the extremely fast American PT-boats. Several European navies were also building what were in effect small destroyers but were confusingly called torpedo boats, though several times the size of the MTBs. They were the direct descendants of the earlier steam torpedo boats.

In the years since World War II the torpedo boat as a type of naval vessel has largely given way to the more versatile fast patrol boat or strike craft. The aim of the designers, however, is much the same as it was in the days of the earliest torpedo boat: to produce the smallest, fastest possible craft capable of sinking whatever it meets, however large. The weapon able to strike such a blow is more likely today to be a surface-to-surface missile.

Tramp As distinct from the LINER, which operates a scheduled service on a specific route, the tramp ship carries general or bulk cargoes wherever business takes it. Its ancestor was the sailing merchant adventurer, loading whatever goods were available at the home port, and on arrival abroad looking for markets and for new cargo to load and sell elsewhere. Today shipowners seeking cargoes and shipping companies looking for carriers conduct their business through brokers. The most important center for such negotiations is the Baltic Exchange in London. Rates can vary from day to day, depending on supply and demand.

Trimaran Multihull boat with three hulls, or with a central hull and large outrigger-like floats at either side. Compare CATAMARAN.

Trireme A GALLEY with three banks of oars, the most formidable warship of the Mediterranean world from the beginning of the 5th century BC until medieval times. The Greeks developed the trireme from the two-banked BIREME; it was a vessel some 130 ft. (40 m) long including its 10-ft. (3-m) ram, and was manned by 170 rowers seated in three ranks. In short bursts the trireme was capable of speeds of up to 8 knots. The metal ram or beak was the vessel's principal weapon; on the heavy Roman triremes it was supplemented by large catapults. The Romans also employed the *corvus*, a hinged wooden bridge or gangway, to board enemy vessels.

The first torpedo boat, HMS Lightning, *launched in 1876.*

Tug A small vessel designed to tow or push large ships or LIGHTERS (dumb barges). Tugs have very powerful diesel engines, which usually occupy the bulk of the hull, and either twin rudders or variable thrust, shrouded, or cycloidal propellers for maximum thrust and maneuverability. The conventional harbor or short-haul tug has a high bow and a short superstructure forward, and can be up to 250 tons with a 2,500-hp engine. The specialized towing equipment can compensate for sudden changes in tension and has a quick-release safety device.

Tugs are an essential feature of docks and ports, where they maneuver large ships into their berths. Most ports also have a specialized firefighting tug, while tugs used for towing tankers are equipped with extensive firefighting gear and equipment for dealing with oil spills. Pusher tugs, with specially strengthened bows, are also used to push enormous trains of barges on the rivers and inland waterways of North America. Ocean-going salvage tugs, designed for heavy-duty work, can be up to 2,000 tons with engines of 15,000 hp. In addition to providing assistance to ships in distress, these large tugs are engaged in such work as towing drilling rigs and oil production platforms.

Umiak Large open Eskimo boat used for transport and for whaling. The literal meaning of the word is 'woman's boat.' The solid timbers of its frame are lashed together with hide thongs, and the craft is covered with sealskins. It is commonly about 30 ft. (9 m) long and 6 ft. (2 m) in the beam, large enough to carry a family and its possessions. The craft is double-ended and propelled by rowers or by a single square sail set on a mast stepped amidships. Like the CORACLE, the equivalent vessel of Celtic regions, the umiak is steered by oars.

Urca (1) Spanish sailing ship of the 16th century used as a naval auxiliary. In her rigging, the urca resembled a scaled-down version of the galleon. (2) A Spanish flat-bottomed craft of the 17th and 18th centuries designed for local trade, with a square or lateen rig, and of a tonnage of about 300. They were generally armed with about six guns.

The Danish steam tug St. Canute, *built in 1931 as harbor tug, icebreaker, and firefloat for Odense.*

Victory ship See LIBERTY SHIP.

Wherry (1) Small sailing barge characteristic of the Norfolk Broads of eastern England. Its tall mast is positioned near the bow and carries a single gaff-mainsail lacking a boom. The mast is pivoted and counterbalanced so that the craft can pass under bridges. (2) An open rowboat used to carry passengers along the Thames in 17th- and 18th-century London.

Windjammer A general term used to describe a large sailing merchantman, especially one of the giants of the last days of sail.

Xebec Fast Mediterranean sailing ship in use from the 16th to the 19th century, and particularly favored by privateers and pirates, among them the Barbary corsairs. The xebec was of shallow draft, and had three masts and a bowsprit. Originally a lateen-rigged vessel, square sails were later set on the foremast and, when conditions were favorable, on the mainmast as well. A lateen rig was substituted when sailing close to the wind, which necessitated a large crew. Other notable features of the xebec included a highly decorated and overhanging stern and a turtle deck covered with gratings. The turtle deck, shaped as its name suggests, allowed water shipped on board to flow away freely, and the gratings enabled the crew to maintain a firm footing when the deck was awash.

Yacht Deriving its name from the Dutch JACHT, the modern yacht is a pleasure craft used for cruising or racing, with a deck and a cabin to provide shelter and accommodation for crew and passengers. The word yacht was also used to describe a vessel of state used to carry royalty or other notables, hence the description of the British monarch's 5,769-ton *Britannia* as a royal yacht.

Yawl Small two-masted sailing craft with a fore-and-aft rig. The vessel is rigged like a KETCH with gaff and gaff-topsail, but the smaller mizzen carries only a spanker, which is generally smaller than that of the ketch. In addition, the mizzen is stepped abaft the rudder-head and is usually sheeted to a short bumkin. Like the ketch, the yawl has a bowsprit and one or more foresails. Originally used for fishing and coastal trading, the yawl has more recently proved popular for single-handed ocean voyaging. A modern yawl-rigged yacht has triangular sails in place of the traditional four-sided gaffsails.

Modern racing yachts.

Great Men
of the Sea

Albuquerque, Alfonso d' (1453-1515) Portuguese naval and military commander, second Governor-General of India, who transformed a precarious foothold of trading posts and warehouses into a chain of fortresses and naval bases that controlled the Indian Ocean. Albuquerque had been sent out to the east in 1502 and 1506; his appointment as Governor-General came in 1508. He seized Goa in 1510 and made its excellent harbor the base for Portuguese operations in the Indian Ocean. By taking Malacca (1511) he gained control of the key bottleneck on routes to China and the Spice Islands. The recapture of Hormuz (1515) established a hold on the Persian Gulf. Only in an attempt to seize Aden (1513) and block the spice route through the Red Sea did he meet failure. Albuquerque was the ablest naval strategist of his day; in a few short years he had created a Portuguese monopoly of the spice trade with a permanent fleet in eastern waters. He died of a heart attack when he learned that he was to be superseded as a result of intrigues within the Portuguese court.

Amundsen, Roald (1872-1928) Norwegian polar explorer, leader of the first expedition to navigate the Northwest Passage, and the first man to reach the South Pole. Amundsen had studied medicine before going to sea and joined the *Belgica* as first mate on the expedition (1897-99) that became the first to winter in the Antarctic. He used his medical knowledge to save his companions from scurvy. He then bought the 47-ton converted fishing smack, *Gjøa*, in which he and his crew of five sailed secretly to avoid creditors in June 1903. After wintering at King William Island and King Point, *Gjøa* completed the navigation of the Northwest Passage from east to west in September 1906.

Amundsen then planned to use Nansen's ship FRAM for an attempt on the North Pole, but with the news in 1909 that PEARY had succeeded in reaching that goal, Amundsen turned his attention to the South Pole and sailed in August 1910 for Antarctica. Only after leaving did it become known where he was heading; he had told no one except his brother of his change of plans. After wintering in the Ross Sea he set out with four companions and 52 sled dogs on October 20,

1911. He reached the South Pole on December 14, leaving a flag and a message for the rival British expedition led by SCOTT, which reached the Pole 34 days later. Amundsen and his companions returned to their base in only 38 days with food and supplies to spare.

Between 1918 and 1921 Amundsen attempted to reach his original goal, the North Pole, by drifting in the Arctic ice in the specially built polar ship *Maud*. He completed a navigation of the Northeast Passage but his attempt on the Pole did not succeed. Amundsen then turned to aviation. An attempt in 1925 to reach the Pole in two Dornier Wal flying boats failed just short of success; the following year he finally succeeded in the airship *Norge*, captained by the Italian Umberto Nobile, and reached the North Pole two days after Robert E. Byrd's successful flight. Amundsen lost his life in June 1928 when his aircraft went missing in the Arctic while searching for Nobile, who had crashed north of Spitsbergen in the airship *Italia*.

Anson, George (1697-1762) British naval hero whose reforms at the Admiralty helped make possible the achievements of the Royal Navy in the Seven Years' War. Anson's greatest single feat, however, was his epic voyage around the world in his flagship *Centurion* (1740-44). In September 1740 he set sail with a

squadron of six small, poorly equipped warships, with instructions to capture one of the Spanish treasure ships that sailed between the Philippines and Mexico. Anson lost several ships rounding Cape Horn but went on to raid settlements on the coast of Chile. Over half his crew died of scurvy, others of starvation, but he succeeded in crossing the Pacific in the *Centurion*, his one remaining ship, and captured a Spanish treasure galleon off the Philippines. He arrived back in England in June 1744, parading a treasure worth £500,000 through London. He rose rapidly in the service, was created a baron in 1747 and was First Lord of the Admiralty from 1751 to 1756 and again from 1757 to 1762. He was an able administrator, reforming numerous aspects of naval discipline and organization, and was responsible for introducing the system of 'rating' ships. His strategy of blockading the French fleet at Brest during the Seven Years War was an important key to British victory.

Baffin, William (1584-1622) English navigator, one of the greatest of all Arctic explorers. In 1612 he sailed as chief pilot with Captain James Hall on a search for the Northwest Passage along the coast of Greenland. In 1615 he set sail in Hudson's former ship, *Discovery*, with Robert Bylot as chief pilot, to explore

Anson's ship Centurion *in battle against a Spanish treasure ship, June 1743.*

Hudson Strait and Southampton Island in search of a channel leading east. The following year, again with Bylot, Baffin sailed into what is now known as Baffin Bay and discovered the three sounds that lead west from it. He thought, however, that they were merely bays and that no route out of Baffin Bay existed. To succeeding generations even the existence of 'Baffin's Bay' became dubious, and when Captain James Ross duplicated Baffin's voyage two centuries later, confirming his discoveries, he too thought Baffin Bay had no outlet. From 1617 until his death at the siege of Hormuz in the Persian Gulf, Baffin was in the service of the East India Company, making surveys of the Red Sea and the Persian Gulf.

Bainbridge, William (1774-1833)
American naval officer famous for his capture of the British frigate *Java*, one of the most notable victories of the War of 1812. He began his career at the age of 15 in the merchant marine and became an officer in the newly established U.S. Navy in 1798. He was given command of the sloop *Retaliation* but was captured by two French frigates. As commander of the *Washington*, Bainbridge suffered high-handed treatment by the Dey of Algiers that led the United States to declare war on the Barbary States. In 1803 he commanded the frigate *Philadelphia* in a blockade of Tripoli. His ship grounded on an uncharted reef and he was again taken prisoner. Released in 1805, he commanded merchant vessels before rejoining the navy in 1812.

Bainbridge played an important part in persuading President Madison to allow the 16 frigates and sloops of the U.S. Navy to venture out to sea against the 600-strong British fleet, and he was given command of the famous frigate CONSTITUTION. His duel with the *Java* took place on December 29, 1812, off the coast of Brazil. Bainbridge was wounded twice in the encounter, and the wheel of his ship was shot away, but he was able to compel the *Java* to surrender.

Barbarossa (1482-1546)
Barbarossa (Red Beard) was the name given by Europeans to Khair-ed-Din, a Barbary pirate who came from a family of corsairs and in 1518 became its head in succession to his brother Aruj (also known as Barbarossa). He offered homage to the Otto-

Bainbridge scored a decisive victory when his ship Constitution *captured the British frigate* Java *off the coast of Brazil in 1812.*

man Sultan and used the reinforcements he obtained to capture Algiers from the Spanish in 1529; subsequently Algiers became the main center of Barbary pirate activity. Sultan Suleiman the Magnificent recognized Barbarossa's talents and in 1533 appointed him High Admiral of the Ottoman fleet. He extended his conquests to include the rest of the Barbary coast and twice defeated Christian fleets commanded by Andrea Doria, thus giving the Turks virtual control of the Mediterranean.

Barents, Willem (1550-97)
Dutch navigator, who gave his name to the sea east of North Cape. In 1594 he was second-in-command of a fleet under Jan van Linschoten, sent to find the Northeast Passage. Barents' ship reached the west coast of Novaya Zemlya but was halted by thick ice. In 1595, in company with Linschoten, he took a fleet of seven ships back to Novaya Zemlya, but having started out too late in the year he once again encountered an impenetrable barrier of ice which prevented him from entering the Kara Sea.

In his voyage of 1596-97 Barents succeeded in rounding Novaya Zemlya, but then ice set in and Barents and his crew were forced to spend the winter there, the first Europeans to winter successfully in the far north. Their quarters, built of driftwood, where they survived by trap-

ping bears and foxes, were later discovered in 1871. In June 1597 they abandoned their ship, which was hopelessly damaged by the ice, and reached the mainland in two small boats. Barents, however, died on the way. His accurate charts and weather observations proved of great value to later expeditions.

Barney, Joshua (1759-1818)
American naval hero of the Revolution and War of 1812. He went to sea at the age of 12 and his later numerous exploits during the Revolution led to his being captured three times by the British. Twice he was exchanged; on a third occasion he

Barents' Arctic voyage of 1596-97.

escaped from prison and made his way to France. In 1782 he captured the British ship *General Monk* off Cape May. In 1794 Barney was nominated one of the six captains of the newly established U.S. Navy. Angered at being placed fourth on the list, he joined the French navy, with which he sailed as captain and Chef de Division until 1802.

At the outbreak of the War of 1812 he undertook a daring privateering voyage which lasted three months, in the course of which he accounted for 18 enemy merchant ships and took 217 prisoners. He finally accepted a commission as captain in the U.S. Navy in 1814, and with inadequate resources (three small gunboats and ten barges) was assigned the defense of Chesapeake Bay against a British landing. He had to scuttle his small fleet when the British disembarked, but he rushed his 500 men to Bladensburg on the road to Washington. There they held the center of the line against the British until the cowardice of the militia left the sailors and marines outflanked. Barney himself was wounded and captured.

Barron, James (1768-1851) American naval officer, notorious for his part in the Chesapeake affair of 1807. As Commodore of the Mediterranean Squadron, he had only just left Hampton Roads in his flagship CHESAPEAKE when he was challenged by the British frigate *Leopard* with a demand to surrender alleged deserters. On Barron's refusal the *Leopard* opened fire. Stores still covered the *Chesapeake*'s decks and, unable to clear his ship for action, Barron was forced to submit. The British boarded and took off a number of men, several of them American citizens. Barron returned to face a court-martial; he was suspended for five years and consequently joined the French navy. When he eventually returned he was refused a new command. He accused Stephen DECATUR, who had sat on his court-martial, of barring his return to active service. In 1820 Barron challenged Decatur to a duel and killed him.

Barry, John (1745-1803) American naval officer rivaled only by John Paul JONES in his successes during the American Revolution, and often called the father of the U.S. Navy. Born in Ireland, Barry was a Philadelphian merchant shipmaster. He was commissioned captain of the brigantine *Lexington* in March 1776. In April he captured the tender *Edward*, the first British vessel taken by a commissioned American ship. In 1780 he was given command of the frigate *Alliance*, with which he was sent on a diplomatic mission to France. En route he took several prizes, but his most notable exploits came in his last cruise with the *Alliance* of 1782-83. Discovering that a British convoy had been scattered by severe winds, he proceeded to chase and capture four of its ships. Returning from France via the West Indies, he fought the last naval action of the War of Independence, successfully beating off three British frigates in a pitched battle off the coast of Florida in March 1783. In 1794 Barry was recalled to service and nominated senior captain of the new U.S. Navy. In this role he supervised construction of the frigate *United States*, which he commanded in the undeclared naval war with France of 1798-1800.

Beatty, David, 1st Earl (1871-1936) British admiral in command of the Royal Navy's battle-cruiser fleet at the Battle of Jutland in 1916, and later Admiral of the Fleet. After distinguishing himself commanding a Nile gunboat in the Sudan campaign (1896-98) and serving in China during the Boxer Rebellion (1900), Beatty was promoted to captain at the unusually early age of 29. Promoted to rear admiral in 1910, he became naval secretary to the First Lord of the Admiralty, Winston Churchill, and was then put in command of the battle-cruiser squadron of the Grand Fleet. After a daring raid into the Heligoland Bight early in the war, he scored a somewhat less impressive victory over four German battle cruisers at the Dogger Bank in 1915, which was marred by a combination of signal and gunnery errors enabling three of the German ships to escape. Although much criticized for the serious losses incurred by the risky deployment of his forces at Jutland in 1916, he nonetheless achieved the desired aims of keeping the scouting German battle cruisers away from the British fleet while luring the combined German fleet into a vulnerable position. Promoted to Commander in Chief of the Grand Fleet in 1916, in succession to JELLICOE, he went on to become Admiral of the Fleet and then First Sea Lord (1919-1927).

Admiral Sir David Beatty (1871-1936).

Bell, Henry (1767-1830) Scottish engineer, pioneer of the passenger-carrying steamboat in Europe. After serving in a shipyard at Bo 'Ness on the Firth of Forth in Scotland, and then with an engineering firm in London, he settled at Helensburgh on the Firth of Clyde. As early as 1800 he experimented with a small steam-powered boat, studied Symington's steam tug CHARLOTTE DUNDAS, and met the American steamboat pioneer Robert FULTON. Eventually he raised the funds to commission the shipbuilders John Wood & Sons of Port Glasgow to build the COMET. Bell himself designed the 4-hp single-cylinder steam engine. In August 1812 he inaugurated Europe's first regular passenger steamboat service, with the *Comet* plying between Glasgow, Greenock, and Helensburgh. He later extended the service up the west coast of Scotland. *Comet* was wrecked in 1820 and lack of funds prevented her replacement. Bell built a number of smaller steam ferries and designed the engine of the AARON MANBY, but despite the importance of his pioneering work died almost destitute.

Blake, Robert (1599-1657) English naval officer and pioneer of naval organization and tactics. He distinguished himself as a soldier on the parliamentary side in the English Civil War (1642-49) and was appointed one of three 'generals-at-sea' in 1649. In 1649-50 he hunted and destroyed Prince Rupert's royalist fleet and in 1651 captured the Scilly Isles from the Royalists. During the First Anglo-Dutch War he commanded the Channel Fleet against the Dutch admiral,

Robert Blake (1599-1657).

Maarten TROMP. In 1655 he was sent to the Mediterranean, where he triumphed over the Barbary pirates, and in 1657 he destroyed a Spanish fleet of 16 vessels at Santa Cruz, Tenerife, without the loss of a single ship. As the introducer of the Fighting Instructions of 1653, he laid down the tactics and the line of battle followed by the Royal Navy well into the 18th century. His *Articles of War* provided the basis of naval discipline.

Bligh, William (1754-1817) British naval officer chiefly remembered as captain of the BOUNTY at the time of the famous mutiny. He entered the navy in 1762 and served as sailing master of the RESOLUTION on Captain Cook's final voyage of 1775-79. Bligh was given command of the *Bounty* in 1787. The mutiny occurred off the Friendly Islands on April 28, 1789, and its causes have been variously ascribed to Bligh's supposed brutality and to the attractions for the crew of a life on a Pacific Island. Bligh and his 18 supporters survived a voyage of over 3,500 nautical miles (6,500 km) in an open boat, reaching Timor in the East Indies on June 12. In his subsequent career he distinguished himself at the Battles of Camperdown (1797) and

Copenhagen (1801). His period as Governor of New South Wales (1805-08) was ended by a mutiny in the so-called Rum Rebellion and he was sent back to England under arrest. Bligh was made a rear admiral in 1811 and vice admiral in 1814. An able officer and navigator, Bligh was a man of short temper but probably not as tyrannical a figure as later legend portrayed him.

Boscawen, Edward (1711-61) British naval hero famous for his part in the Seven Years' War. He joined the navy in 1726, became a captain in 1737, and took part in the capture of Porto Bello (1739) and in the attack on Cartagena (1741). Commanding the 60-gun *Dreadnought* in 1742, he engaged two French ships in the Bay of Biscay and earned the nickname 'Old Dreadnought.' He took part in ANSON's victory off Cape Finisterre in 1747 and in the same year became Commander in Chief in the East Indies. He was made a Lord Commissioner of the Admiralty in 1751. His most notable later exploits include his command of naval operations at the capture of the fortress of Louisburg on Cape Breton Island in 1758 and his scattering of a major part of the French fleet at Lagos Bay on the coast of Portugal in 1759. In his operations in Quiberon Bay in 1760 he blockaded French shipping and he

made it impossible for a planned invasion of England to take place.

St. Brendan (c. 484-578) Irish monk and hero of the medieval tale *Brendan's Voyages (Navigatio Brendani)*. In this account he is credited with having reached the 'Land of Promise' after a long ocean voyage in an open boat made of ox-hide. His journey took 8 years and he was accompanied by 17 monks. Although the story has affinities with numerous pagan myths, there is evidence of a genuine knowledge of seamanship behind it, and the 'Land of Promise' has been tentatively identified with the Canaries, Iceland, and America itself. That such a long oceanic voyage in an open skin coracle was at least feasible was demonstrated in 1977 by Tim Severin, who successfully sailed from Iceland to Newfoundland in the 'Brendan boat.' Several voyages in search of St. Brendan's Island were made by medieval sailors, and the island found a place on maps as late as the 18th century.

Brunel, Isambard Kingdom (1806-59) British engineer and ship designer, probably the greatest and most original figure of the Victorian age of engineering. At the age of 27 he was appointed Chief Engineer of Britain's Great Western Railway (GWR), which was to have its

Mutineers on the Bounty *setting Captain Bligh adrift, 1789.*

terminus at the western port of Bristol. He turned his attention to shipbuilding in 1835, suggesting that the GWR extended its route from Bristol to New York with a steamship service. As a result, he designed the first true transatlantic steamship, the GREAT WESTERN (1838). After the success of the *Great Western* on regular passenger runs, Brunel went on to design and build the first oceangoing iron-hulled screw steamship, the GREAT BRITAIN (1843). Dwarfing all earlier vessels, she has been described as the forerunner of all modern ships. Brunel's third ship, the ill-fated GREAT EASTERN (1858), was designed for the Australian trade and was capable of carrying enough coal for a return voyage. She remained the world's largest ship for decades to come. Brunel died of a stroke shortly before *Great Eastern*'s maiden voyage.

The sinking of the Cumberland *at Hampton Roads, March 8, 1862. Buchanan was the victorious commanding officer of the ironclad* Virginia.

Buchanan, Franklin (1800-74) American naval officer who became admiral and senior officer of the Confederate States Navy. He began his career as a midshipman in 1815 and became Superintendent of the U.S. Naval Academy at Annapolis on its foundation in 1845. Between 1852 and 1854 Buchanan was in command of the *Susquehanna*, flagship of Matthew C. PERRY's fleet on its voyage to Japan. When the Civil War broke out Buchanan was commander of the Washington Navy Yard. Thinking his native state of Maryland would secede, he resigned his commission, then found it impossible to regain it and so joined the Confederate States Navy. He was in command of the ironclad *Virginia*, the former MERRIMACK, when she sank the *Cumberland* and *Congress* in Hampton Roads on March 8, 1862. However, he was wounded in the action and was ashore having treatment during the *Virginia*'s famous duel with MONITOR the following day. He was promoted to admiral in August 1862 and commanded the Confederate forces at the Battle of Mobile Bay in 1864. His flagship, the ram *Tennessee*, fought on heroically after the rest of his squadron had been destroyed or captured, but Buchanan was eventually forced to surrender to the superior Union fleet of David FARRAGUT.

Bushnell, David (1742-1824) American inventor, pioneer of the submarine.

Bushnell's one-man *Turtle* of 1776 was the first submersible craft to attack an enemy ship. *Turtle*'s egg-shaped hull was held upright in the water by a lead keel, and buoyancy was controlled by admitting seawater into two internal ballast tanks. Propelled by two hand-cranked screws, *Turtle* carried a mine containing 150 lb. (68 kg) of gunpowder, designed to be attached beneath the enemy vessel's hull by a boring tool and equipped with a 30-minute clockwork fuse. The attempt to sink the *Eagle*, a British warship in New York Harbor, was a failure because of copper sheathing on the ship's hull, something Bushnell had not foreseen. Two more attacks on British ships failed because of sharp lookouts kept on board, but the *Turtle* is still considered to be the earliest effective submarine. At the end of the Revolutionary War Bushnell put aside his experiments (he had joined the Corps of Engineers) and became a successful doctor in Georgia.

Byng, John (1704-57) British admiral executed for neglect of duty. With little active experience he was put in command of a fleet sent in 1756 to relieve British forces on Minorca, then under siege by the French. After an inconclusive engagement he decided his fleet was inadequate and departed, leaving the garrison to its fate. Public outrage at the loss of Minorca led to Byng's arrest and court-martial. He was found guilty of

neglect of duty in battle, a crime which carried the automatic death penalty. The court strongly recommended mercy and did not expect its sentence to be carried out, but the government, probably anxious for a scapegoat, let the execution by firing squad go ahead. This prompted Voltaire's famous comment in *Candide* that the English had from time to time to execute an admiral '*pour encourager les autres*' (to encourage the others).

Cabot, John (c. 1450-99) John Cabot (Giovanni Caboto) was an Italian sailing in the service of England who made the first recorded voyages to North America since the days of the Vikings. He was born at Genoa, later moved to Venice, and settled in Bristol sometime between

The shooting of Admiral Byng, 1757.

1484 and 1490. In March 1496 Cabot obtained Letters Patent from King Henry VII, instructing him to discover, explore, and occupy unknown lands in the name of the king. He sailed from Bristol in the tiny *Matthew* on May 2, 1497, and after 53 days he made a landfall, probably on the coast of Nova Scotia. Believing it was part of Asia, he returned with a second expedition in May 1498, and after reaching Greenland he sailed south down the North American coast. Nothing is known of him subsequent to this voyage.

Cabot, Sebastian (c. 1483-1557) John Cabot's second son, Sebastian, apparently accompanied his father and two brothers on the voyage of 1497 and may also have gone on the second voyage the following year. He was already a cartographer to Henry VIII in 1512 and became Chief Pilot (*Pilot Mayor*) of Spain in 1518. He returned to England briefly, and from 1526 to 1530 commanded a Spanish expedition, intended to sail to the Pacific by way of South America. Instead of following instructions he spent three years exploring the mouth of the Rio de la Plata and fell into disfavor in Spain. He returned to England in 1548 and received a royal pension. In 1551 he founded a company of Merchant Adventurers in Bristol, England, and sent out expeditions in search of the Northeast Passage; among these were the voyages of Sir

Sebastian Cabot (1483-1557).

Hugh WILLOUGHBY and Richard CHANCELLOR. Sebastian Cabot thus forms a link between the early Spanish voyages of discovery and the exploits of the Elizabethans.

Cartier, Jacques (1491-1557) French navigator and discoverer of the St. Lawrence River, whose voyages provided the basis for French claims to Canada. In 1534 he was given command of an expedition to search for the Northwest Passage. After reaching Newfoundland with his two ships, he passed through the icy Belle Isle Strait into the Gulf of St. Lawrence, landed on the Gaspé peninsula to take possession for France, and reached Anticosti Island at the mouth of the great river before returning to France. The following year he sailed with three ships up the St. Lawrence as far as the present site of Quebec, then went on in two longboats to the Lachine Rapids near what is now Montreal. He and his men wintered on the St. Lawrence and took back reports of a Kingdom of Saguenay 'rich and wealthy in precious stones.' Cartier made a third voyage to the St. Lawrence in 1541. A force of soldiers and colonists led by Seigneur de Roberval was to have joined him, but as they did not appear Cartier abandoned his mission and returned home, meeting up with Roberval off Newfoundland. A later expedition by Roberval proved, in fact, that Saguenay did not exist.

Champlain, Samuel de (1567-1635) French explorer famed as the 'Father of New France.' Champlain had already sailed with a Spanish expedition to the West Indies in 1599 before being appointed geographer to a French expedition to Canada in 1603. In 1604 he returned to Canada on a second voyage, surveyed the coast of North America as far south as Martha's Vineyard, and helped establish a colony at Port Royal. In 1608 he commanded the voyage that founded a settlement at Quebec, then went on the following year to find the lake to which he gave his name. In his last major voyage into the interior of Canada, he ascended the Ottawa River and arrived at Georgian Bay on Lake Huron in 1615. His alliance with the Huron Indians antagonized the Iroquois, who helped the English capture Quebec

in 1629. Champlain was sent to England as a prisoner but was released in 1632 and returned to Quebec, which was once again in French hands.

Chancellor, Richard (d. 1556) English navigator who opened British trade with Russia and laid the foundations of the Muscovy Company. He was appointed pilot general to Sir Hugh WILLOUGHBY's expedition to find the Northeast Passage in 1553. He lost sight of Willoughby's ship in a storm off the Lofoten Islands, and after Willoughby failed to appear at the appointed rendezvous Chancellor sailed on alone in the *Edward Bonaventure*, entering the White Sea and arriving at what is now Archangel. Together with some of his officers, he set off on a 1,500-mile (2,400-km) journey to Moscow and back in horse-drawn sleighs. Czar Ivan IV (Ivan the Terrible), anxious to break out of his isolation and establish new trade links, treated Chancellor with great hospitality and gave him a letter to Queen Mary granting favorable terms for English trade. Chancellor returned to his ship and sailed back to England in 1554. The result was the establishment of the Muscovy Company, with a monopoly of trade with Russia. Chancellor arrived in Moscow on a second visit in November 1555, but on his return journey he was lost together with most of his crew in a shipwreck off the Scottish coast.

Chichester, Sir Francis (1901-72) English solo yachtsman and aviator, who circumnavigated the world single-handed in the yacht GIPSY MOTH IV. Chichester was born in England but emigrated to New Zealand as a young man. Beginning in 1929 he made a series of pioneering flights in a Gipsy Moth biplane, among them the second solo flight from England to Australia and the first solo crossing of the Tasman Sea from east to west. At the outbreak of World War II Chichester returned to England, where he performed important services in the field of astronavigation. After the war he became a map publisher, took up ocean racing in the early 1950s in the yacht *Gipsy Moth II*, and in 1960 won the first transatlantic single-handed race in a new yacht *Gipsy Moth III*, sailing from Plymouth to New York in 40 days. Chichester set out on his famous circumnavigation in *Gipsy Moth IV* on August 27,

1966. He returned to Plymouth 274 days later on May 28, 1967, and shortly afterwards was knighted at Greenwich by Queen Elizabeth II, with the very sword Elizabeth I had used to knight that other circumnavigator, Sir Francis DRAKE. In 1971, in *Gipsy Moth V*, Chichester crossed the Atlantic from Portuguese Guinea to Nicaragua, a voyage of 4,000 nautical miles (7,400 km), in 22 days.

Cochrane, Thomas, 10th Earl of Dundonald (1775-1860) British naval commander whose turbulent and unconventional career is one of the most colorful in the annals of the Royal Navy. Cochrane gained distinction at an early age in his command of the brig sloop *Speedy*, which captured the much larger Spanish frigate *El Gamo* in a famous battle in 1801. His cruises in the frigates *Pallas* and *Impérieuse* were equally successful. Cochrane was an elected Member of Parliament and his criticisms of senior officers and demands for political reforms antagonized his superiors and won him numerous enemies. The result was an end to his employment at sea.

In 1814 he was convicted of manipulation of the Stock Exchange and was imprisoned, expelled from Parliament and dismissed from the Royal Navy. In 1817 he accepted command of the Chilean navy in the war of independence against Spain; his brilliant tactics helped ensure the liberation of Peru and Chile from Spanish rule. From 1823 to 1825 Cochrane served with the Brazilian navy in the war of that newly independent country against Portugal, and he returned to Europe to command the Greek navy in the war of independence against Turkey.

In 1832 Cochrane regained his commission in the Royal Navy; he championed the use of steam propulsion for warships and concerned himself with numerous innovations in ship design and marine engineering. He commanded the Royal Navy's American and West Indies station between 1848 and 1851, and only his advanced age kept him from participating in the Crimean War.

Columbus, Christopher (1451-1506) Italian-born navigator sailing in the service of Spain and generally regarded as the discoverer of America. It is almost certain that the Vikings landed in the

Cochrane's fireship attack at the Battle of Basque Roads, 1809; one of his many notable naval engagements.

New World five centuries earlier (see Leif ERICSSON), but it was Columbus' discoveries that began the exploration and settlement of the Americas.

Columbus was born in Genoa and went to sea at the age of 14. When the Genoese ship on which he was serving was sunk by the French off Portugal, he went to Lisbon where his brother Bartholomew was a cartographer. He became a merchant and a master mariner, and his growing conviction that one could reach the Indies by sailing west was not unique; it was his persistence and determination to realize his dream that made him unique among his contemporaries. In 1484 he tried to persuade King John II of Portugal to finance such a voyage but the proposal was turned down. Columbus went to Spain and after years of futile efforts finally won the backing of the Spanish monarchs. He was given three ships, the *Santa Maria*, *Pinta*, and *Niña*, and he sailed from Palos on August 3, 1492. After calling at the Canary Islands the expedition headed west. On October 12, 1492, they sighted land, San Salvador (probably Watling Island) in the Bahamas. Columbus believed himself to be near the coast of China and sailed southwestward, making landfalls on Cuba and Hispaniola, where the *Santa Maria* was wrecked on Christmas Day. The *Pinta* and *Niña* arrived back at Palos on March 15, 1493.

Columbus was created Admiral of the Indies and given a second fleet of 17 ships, which sailed from Cadiz on Sep-

tember 25, 1493. He arrived off Dominica on November 3 and sailed on to Hispaniola, where he expected to find the sailors he had left to search for gold on his first voyage. They had vanished without a trace. Columbus founded a new settlement nearby at Isabela, and after sending most of his ships home with Indian captives and news of his latest findings, he discovered Jamaica. He sailed back to Spain in 1496, arriving on June 3. Although there were many complaints against his administration of the settlement of Isabela, he was allowed to form a third expedition at royal expense. This set sail on May 30, 1498, and resulted in the discovery of Trinidad and the exploration of the northern coast of the South American mainland. On Columbus' arrival at Hispaniola he found the colony in an uproar: the settlers had rebelled against his imposed rule and he was consequently sent home in irons.

On his return to Spain Columbus was restored to his title and revenues but prohibited from having anything more to do with the running of the colony. He was allowed, however, to undertake a fourth voyage to try to find a way through the Caribbean to what he was sure would be the Indies. He sailed from Cadiz on May 11, 1502, and explored much of the coast of central America. Disasters ensued; he was shipwrecked on the coast of Jamaica for a year and finally returned to Spain in bad health on November 7, 1504. He spent his last years in bitter obscurity.

Cook, James (1728-79) British navigator, the first and probably the greatest figure in the age of scientific exploration. Cook was a farm laborer's son and was apprenticed to a COLLIER owner in 1746. Six years later he became a mate on one of the colliers. In 1755 he enlisted in the Royal Navy as an able seaman. Cook had a natural aptitude for mathematics and navigation and gained rapid advancement. He played an important part in a survey of the St. Lawrence during the war against France, and after the fall of Quebec spent several years charting the Newfoundland coast. His careful observations of an eclipse of the sun led to his appointment by the Royal Society as leader of an expedition to Tahiti to observe the transit of Venus. Promoted to lieutenant, he obtained the Whitby collier *Earl of Pembroke*, renamed ENDEAVOUR, which he knew would be suitable for this, his first scientific expedition. After the work at Tahiti was completed, Cook was directed by the Admiralty to search for Terra Australis Incognita, the great continent believed to exist in southern waters, and to ascertain whether New Zealand, last visited by Abel TASMAN, might be part of that continent. Joseph Banks and one other naturalist accompanied the expedition.

Cook sailed on August 25, 1768, and after rounding Cape Horn he arrived at Tahiti on April 10, 1769. After observing the transit of Venus he made a search for a continental landmass to the south and then sailed for New Zealand. After charting the two islands Cook sailed on to Australia, landed at Botany Bay, and proceeded up the east coast. Twice *Endeavour* was wrecked on the Great Barrier Reef, but Cook headed north and passed through the Torres Strait, thus establishing beyond doubt that New Guinea was not a part of Australia. He arrived back in England in July 1771.

The following year he was given command of a second expedition to pursue the search for a southern continent still further. He was promoted to commander and set sail on July 13, 1772, in another converted Whitby collier, RESOLUTION, accompanied by the smaller *Adventure*. On this voyage he took a copy of John HARRISON's fourth chronometer to determine his longitude. He twice penetrated south of the Antarctic circle, the first

Captain Cook's ship Resolution, *a converted collier which he took on his third and last voyage of exploration (1776-79).*

explorer ever to do so, but did not find Terra Australis Incognita and rightly concluded that even if such a continent did exist, it must be uninhabitable and therefore of little political or economic interest to Britain at that time. *Adventure* then sailed home while Cook in *Resolution* visited and surveyed most of the islands of the central and eastern Pacific to the south of the equator. He returned to the high southerly latitudes and sailed east past Cape Horn, discovering the South Georgia Islands. He returned to England on July 29, 1775; his expedition was the first to circumnavigate the globe from west to east.

After being promoted to post-captain, he sailed for the Pacific for the third and last time on July 1, 1776. He retained *Resolution* and was accompanied by another converted collier, *Discovery*. He was instructed to seek the western end of the Northwest Passage. In January 1778 he discovered the Hawaiian Islands and then sailed on to the west coast of North America. His ships were refitted in Nootka Sound, and after surveying the southern coast of Alaska he penetrated the Bering Strait but was turned back by ice. In January 1779 he returned to Hawaii for further refitting and was greeted with gifts and ceremonies befitting a Polynesian god. The priests urged the natives to make large contributions, which, after a period of nearly a month, caused some resentment on the part of the inhabitants. Cook left on February 4,

but unfortunately the *Resolution* sprung her foremast and he was forced to return two days later. Relations with the natives were now at a crisis point. After the theft of one of Cook's boats, he set off on February 14 to try and take the chief of the village as a hostage for its return and lost his life in the ensuing hostilities.

Cousteau, Jacques-Yves (b. 1910) French oceanographer and undersea explorer, renowned for his books and films. Cousteau served in the French navy from 1930 to 1957. During World War II, together with Emile Gagnan, he developed the first aqualung device which made free diving possible to a depth of 150-180 ft. (48-55 m) and led to its development as a major new sport. He also invented a camera sled for filming on the seabed. In 1945 Cousteau helped

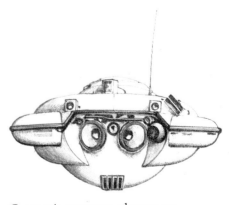

Cousteau's soucoupe plongeante.

establish the French navy's undersea research group at Toulon and later helped to test Auguste Piccard's BATHYSCAPHE, as well as developing a two-man *soucoupe plongeante* (diving saucer) of his own. Cousteau's oceanographic expeditions have resulted in a succession of stunning films and television series; he has also been involved in the 'pre-continent' program to enable divers to spend long periods on the seabed.

Cunningham, Andrew Browne, 1st Viscount (1883-1963) British Admiral of the Fleet responsible for a series of outstanding victories in the Mediterranean in the first stages of World War II. Cunningham joined the Royal Navy in 1898; during World War I he commanded a succession of destroyers, and was later captain of the battleship *Rodney*. In 1937 he was promoted to the rank of vice admiral and from 1939 to 1942 was Commander in Chief of the British Mediterranean Fleet. Cunningham's brilliant tactics were responsible for the crippling of the Italian fleet by air attack at Taranto (November 1940) and the mauling, without loss to his own ships, of an Italian squadron in the Battle of Cape Matapan (March 1941). In 1942-43 Cunningham was in overall command of Allied naval forces taking part in the landings in French North Africa, Sicily, and Italy, and from 1943 until he retired in 1946 he was First Sea Lord and Chief of Naval Staff, responsible for British naval strategy in all theaters of operation.

Dampier, William (1652-1715) English navigator and buccaneer, best known for his exploration of the coasts of Australia, New Guinea, and New Britain (which he discovered to be an island and named). Dampier went to sea at an early age, served on an East Indiaman, and fought in the Third Anglo-Dutch War before joining English buccaneers in the Caribbean. In 1683 he set out on a pirate voyage in the Pacific that was eventually to take him around the world before he again reached England in 1691. He had visited Australia and China and been marooned on the Nicobar Islands, and the account of his experience, which he published in *A New Voyage Round the World* (1697), gained him the attention of the British Admiralty.

He was sent on an official voyage of exploration to Australia in 1699, in command of the fifth-rate ship *Roebuck*. After surveying most of the west coast of Australia he refitted at Timor, going on to explore New Guinea and New Britain. Discontent among the crew, combined with the poor condition of his ship, forced him to set sail to England. On the way home *Roebuck* foundered off Ascension Island, and Dampier and his crew returned to England in an East Indiaman. He was court-martialed for the loss of his ship and was never again employed by the Royal Navy.

He sailed on two further privateering expeditions, however. The first (1703-7) was a failure and is chiefly remembered as the voyage during which Alexander Selkirk (the real-life Robinson Crusoe) was marooned on Juan Fernandez Island. Shortly after his return to England Dampier set out again on another privateering voyage, not as commander, but as navigator to Woodes Rogers. This was a success, the booty taken amounting to £200,000; on his return home in 1711, Dampier had circumnavigated the globe for the third time. Dampier was a navigator of genius and an author of some talent, but his incompetence as a leader of men and his tyrannical temper were legendary. When Woodes Rogers' ships called at Juan Fernandez to rescue Alexander Selkirk, the castaway saw Dampier on board and had to be dissuaded from going ashore again.

Davis, John (c. 1550-1605) English navigator and Arctic explorer, one of the most distinguished seamen of his day. Davis made three voyages in search of the Northwest Passage (1585, 1586, 1587). On his first expedition he 'rediscovered' Greenland, lost since the decline of the Norse settlements, and sailed up its western coast, crossing to Baffin Island and exploring Cumberland Sound. On his final voyage he managed to push through the strait that bears his name into Baffin Bay, making extensive surveys and adding greatly to knowledge of the Arctic. In 1588 Davis commanded the *Black Dog* against the Spanish Armada, and in 1592, as navigator to Thomas Cavendish on an ill-fated privateering voyage, he discovered the Falkland Islands. After sailing with Sir Walter RALEIGH to Cadiz in 1596-97, he made three voyages to the East Indies, the last two in the service of

the East India Company. He was killed by Japanese pirates near Singapore.

Davis was the author of a book on the Northwest Passage, *The Worldes Hydrographical Description*, and an extremely useful manual on navigation, *The Seamans Secrets*. He was also inventor of the backstaff or Davis' quadrant, which enabled the navigator to read solar altitude (and thus determine latitude) without having to look directly into the sun's blinding rays. It was the last great advance in navigational instruments made during the Age of Discovery and was not superseded until well into the 18th century, when Hadley's reflecting quadrant was introduced.

Decatur, Stephen (1779-1820) American naval officer, hero of the war against the Barbary pirates of Tripoli, and distinguished for his bravery in the War of 1812. Decatur saw service as a lieutenant in the undeclared naval war against France (1798-1800) and achieved fame in operations against the Barbary pirates. In 1804, as commander of the schooner *Enterprise*, he decided to enter the harbor of Tripoli to destroy the frigate *Philadelphia*, which had fallen into enemy hands. He and his volunteers took a captured pirate ketch alongside the *Philadelphia* under cover of darkness, set her ablaze, and escaped under heavy enemy fire with only one man wounded. Decatur was promoted to a captaincy and awarded a sword of honor by Congress.

He saw further action in operations against Tripoli, and then, as commander of the frigate *United States* early in the War of 1812, he captured the Royal Navy's *Macedonian* off Madeira. A British blockade kept him in port until January 1815, when he put out to sea from New York in the frigate *President*. She was grounded and damaged in a gale, but Decatur was still able to outrun three British ships and maul a fourth, the frigate *Endymion*, before being forced to surrender. Later in 1815 Decatur led a squadron of 10 ships into the Mediterranean and forced the Barbary pirates of Algiers, Tunis, and Tripoli to end their predations on American shipping. He was appointed one of the three naval commissioners in 1815 and held the post until he was killed in a duel with James BARRON, who held him responsible for his disgrace and suspension from duty.

The burning of the Philadelphia *at Tripoli. For this exploit Decatur was awarded a sword of honor by Congress and promoted to captain.*

Dewey, George (1837-1917) American naval commander, hero of the Battle of Manila Bay. Dewey graduated from Annapolis in 1858, served under David FARRAGUT on the lower Mississippi in 1862-63 and under David Porter in attacks against Fort Fisher off Wilmington, North Carolina, in 1864-65. By 1896 he had reached the rank of commodore; the following year he sought a return to sea duty and was put in command of the U.S. Asiatic Squadron. When the Spanish-American War broke out he was at Hong Kong, where he received instructions to attack the Spanish fleet in the Philippines. He sailed into Manila Bay early on May 1, 1898, and proceeded to destroy the entire Spanish fleet, at a cost of only eight men wounded. Dewey became a national hero and Congress created the special post of Admiral of the Navy for him in 1899.

Diaz, Bartholomew (c. 1455-1500) Portuguese navigator, leader of the first expedition to round the Cape of Good Hope and enter the Indian Ocean. In 1487 he was given command of an expedition to continue the exploration of the coast of West Africa in search of a sea route to India. Diaz sailed from Lisbon in August with two small caravels and a storeship, passed the southernmost point reached by previous explorers, and battled down the coast of what is now Namibia in the teeth of contrary winds and currents. Leaving his storeship behind, Diaz stood off from the coast to seek more favorable winds and sailed south for 13 days before turning east and then north. He reached land about 200 miles (320 km) east of the Cape on February 3, 1488, and continued east and northeast along the coast of South Africa as far as the mouth of the Great Fish River. He soon realized he had rounded the southern tip of Africa without sighting it and that the way to India now lay open. His officers and men persuaded him, however, to turn back, and it was on his homeward journey that he erected a pillar at the great cape he had been seeking, naming the place the Cape of Storms; however the King of Portugal, realizing that this meant that his dream of reaching the east was now within his grasp, later renamed it Cape of Good Hope. Twelve years later, while taking part as second-in-command in a voyage to India led by Pedro Cabral, Diaz was lost at sea in a storm off the Cape.

Dönitz, Karl (b. 1891) German admiral, creator of the U-boat fleet of World War II, and for a brief period after Hitler's death, German Führer. Dönitz had had experience commanding U-boats in World War I and after the war he laid plans for a new German submarine fleet, even though the Treaty of Versailles prohibited Germany from building submarines. After Hitler came to power, Dönitz was made commander of the German submarine force, in 1936. He was instrumental in developing anti-convoy tactics that included the 'wolf pack' system, in which U-boats patrolled a wide area, in constant contact with each other, and converged for a massed attack. He also revived the tactic of attacking on the surface under cover of darkness, taking advantage of the U-boat's higher surface speed, low silhouette, and sonar 'invisibility.' In 1943 he was made Commander in Chief of the German navy after his predecessor, Erich Raeder, had resigned in protest against Hitler's orders to decommission the major warships and land their guns for coast defense. An ardent Nazi, Dönitz was chosen by Hitler as his successor. He received a 10-year sentence of imprisonment at the Nuremberg Trials.

Drake, Sir Francis (c. 1543-96) English admiral, the most famous seaman of his day, who circumnavigated the world in one of the most successful privateering voyages ever made. Drake went to sea as a young man, and in 1567-68 captained the *Judith* in a slaving voyage commanded by his cousin John HAWKINS. Only *Judith* and Hawkins' own ship returned to England after the squadron was attacked by the Spaniards in San Juan de Ulúa (near Veracruz, Mexico). He spent the next several years as a privateer on the Spanish Main. Among his famous exploits were the taking of the town of Nombre de Dios on the Isthmus of Panama and the burning of Porto Bello. He captured a mule train carrying silver across the Isthmus and saw the Pacific, which he vowed he would one day sail upon.

In 1577 Drake assembled a fleet of five small ships, including his flagship *Pelican*, later renamed GOLDEN HIND. The ostensible purpose of the voyage was peaceful exploration; the real aim was to raid and plunder Spanish settlements on the west coast of South America. By the time he had passed through the Strait of Magellan into the Pacific, only the *Golden Hind* remained of the original five ships, but Drake raided settlements and took rich prizes along the unprotected coasts of

Chile and Peru, including the treasure ship *Cacafuego*. He sailed north, landed near what is now San Francisco, and named the region New Albion. He decided that the only safe way home was to cross the Pacific and return via the Cape of Good Hope. He arrived back at Plymouth on September 26, 1580, the first Englishman to circumnavigate the world, and was knighted by Queen Elizabeth I on board the *Golden Hind*.

In 1585 Drake was given command of a fleet of 29 ships with which he sacked Spanish settlements in the Caribbean; in April 1587 he destroyed 26 Spanish ships at Cadiz, a feat he called 'singeing the King of Spain's beard,' and which helped put back preparations for the Armada by a year. When the Armada did appear in 1588, Drake was vice admiral of the English fleet, captaining the *Revenge* and taking a major part in the battle. His last command was in 1595, when he was sent with Hawkins on what proved to be an unsuccessful voyage to the Caribbean to repeat the feats of 10 years earlier. Hawkins died in November off Puerto Rico and Drake succumbed to yellow fever and was buried at sea off Porto Bello.

Ericsson, John (1803-89) Swedish-American engineer and inventor, designer of the ironclad MONITOR, and a pioneer of screw propulsion. After an early career in the Swedish army he moved to England, where he worked on ideas for an improved steam engine and designed a steam locomotive. He also put forward a plan for a steam-powered warship with its engines below the waterline and safe from shell fire, and in 1836 he was awarded a patent for a screw propeller.

To demonstrate his ideas he built a small screw-propelled ship, the *Francis B. Ogden*, and his work won him a fifth part of the British Admiralty's £20,000 prize. When the Royal Navy rejected his marine screw he moved, in 1839, to the United States and designed the engines and screw of the world's first screw-propelled warship, *Princeton*. In 1848 he became a U.S. citizen. After the outbreak of the Civil War the U.S. Navy sought a design for an armored warship and Ericsson replied with the *Monitor*. Launched in January 1862, the *Monitor*'s design represented a radical break with the conventional idea of a warship, and she featured the major innovation of a

revolving gun turret. Ericsson became a national hero with his ship's success. He spent the rest of the war designing further monitors, and his last years were occupied with numerous projects including the design of torpedoes.

Ericsson, Leif (c. 970-1020) Norse explorer, whom the sagas describe as the discoverer of Vinland, and who is now generally regarded as the first European to make a landing in the Americas. He was a son of Eric Thorvaldson (Eric the Red), who founded the first Viking settlement in Greenland in 982. Leif was born in Iceland, grew up in Greenland, and went to Norway in 999. In Norway he discovered Christianity and carried the faith back to Greenland.

Sometime between 1000 and 1002 (according to an account in the *Flatey Book*) he organized an expedition to investigate a sighting of land to the southwest of Greenland made by Biarni Heriulfsson, who had been blown off course on a voyage in 986. Another account (the saga of *Eric the Red*) has Leif making his discoveries after losing his way on his return from Norway in 1000, but in any event he landed at three points on the North American coast: Helluland (the land of flat stones), Markland (Woodland), and Vinland (Vineland). These have been tentatively identified with Baffin Island, Labrador, and Newfoundland, but they may well lie farther to the south. Leif brought back grapes and timber to Greenland, and Thorfinn

Karlsefni set off on an expedition with four ships and 160 men and women to settle in Vinland. The settlement was abandoned after only a few years.

Farragut, David Glasgow (1801-70) American naval commander, hero of the Battles of New Orleans and Mobile Bay during the Civil War. Farragut went to sea as a midshipman at the age of 10 and by the outbreak of the Civil War had seen nearly 50 years of service in the U.S. Navy. Although a Southerner by birth, his sympathies were with the Union, and he was given command of the West Gulf blockading squadron in January 1862, with instructions to ascend the Mississippi and capture New Orleans. Failing to silence the two Confederate forts that controlled the river below New Orleans, Farragut decided to run his fleet past them under cover of darkness. He succeeded, suffering only minor losses, on April 24, 1862. The next day he defeated a Confederate flotilla and anchored off a defenseless New Orleans. The forts surrendered on April 28 and Union troops entered the city on May 1.

The following year Farragut aided Grant's capture of Vicksburg by running the batteries of Port Hudson and preventing supplies from reaching the Confederates from the south. His next target was Mobile, the headquarters of blockade runners in the Gulf. On August 5, 1864, he forced his way into Mobile Bay with the assistance of a flotilla of monitors. The leading monitor, *Tecumseh*, was des-

Farragut's attack on Mobile, August 1869.

The first all-big-gun battleship Dreadnought, *brainchild of Admiral Sir John Fisher.*

troyed by a Confederate mine (then known as a torpedo) and Farragut's fleet was thrown into confusion, drifting with the tide towards the guns of Fort Morgan. Shouting 'Damn the torpedoes, full speed ahead,' Farragut took instant action, sailing his flagship boldly across the rows of mines, followed by the rest of his ships. He captured or destroyed the entire Confederate fleet, including the ironclad *Tennessee*, gallantly commanded by Franklin BUCHANAN. The forts surrendered soon after and Mobile Bay was sealed. Farragut returned to New York a hero and the rank of vice admiral was specially instituted for him. Two years later he was made an admiral, the first in the history of the U.S. Navy.

Fisher, John Arbuthnot, 1st Baron (1841-1920) British admiral and naval administrator whose reforms and innovations were crucial in maintaining British command of the sea in World War I. Fisher entered the navy in 1854, and after active service in the Crimean War, he commanded the battleship *Inflexible* at the bombardment of Alexandria (1882). He then served as Director of Naval Ordnance and Torpedoes (1886-91), and was Third Sea Lord and Controller from 1892 to 1897, Second Sea Lord 1902-3, and First Sea Lord 1904-10.

In his first shore appointments Fisher played an important role in the development of the torpedo and the destroyer and in the radical improvement of naval gunnery. During his controversial period as First Sea Lord — professional head of the navy — he was responsible for con-

struction of the DREADNOUGHT, the first 'all-big-gun' battleship, which rendered all existing battleships obsolete. He also introduced the new class of *Invincible* battle cruisers and presided over the change to the use of oil as fuel. Equally important were his reforms in naval training and staffing, including the 'nucleus crew system' and a redistribution of the fleet that concentrated its forces in home waters.

Fisher was an unorthodox figure who made many enemies inside and outside the service, but he was concerned above all to transform the tradition-bound Royal Navy into a force capable of meeting the emerging threat of Germany as a naval power. After the outbreak of war in 1914, which he had accurately foretold, Fisher was reappointed First Sea Lord and at once initiated a crash construction program. After disagreement over conduct of the Dardanelles campaign, he resigned in 1915.

Fitch, John (1743-98) American pioneer of steam navigation, originator of the first regular steamboat service. Apprenticed to a clockmaker and brass founder, and later making a career in land surveying, he became interested in steam navigation in 1785.

After finding financial backing in Philadelphia and obtaining exclusive rights to operate steamboats on the waters of several states, he built his first boat in 1786. This strange craft, 45 ft. (13.7 m) long, was propelled by 12 vertical paddles, 6 on each side of the hull, which were 'rowed' back and forth under steam

power. Encouraged by the limited success of this vessel, which he demonstrated before members of the Federal Constitutional Convention, Fitch went on to build an improved steamboat which he called *Experiment*. This 60-ft. (18-m) vessel was driven by paddles at the stern and could reach 8 knots.

In 1790 he inaugurated the world's first regular steamboat service, carrying passengers and freight on the Delaware River between Philadelphia and Trenton, N.J., a distance of over 30 miles (48 km). The service was reliable and kept to a timetable but proved a commercial failure. Fitch obtained U.S. and French patents for his steamboat but failed to achieve financial backing. A trip to France in an attempt to arouse interest there in his work was unsuccessful, and although Fitch made further experiments on his return with a small screw-propelled steamboat, he eventually committed suicide, a bitter and disappointed man.

Franklin, Sir John (1786-1847) English navigator and explorer of the Canadian Arctic. Franklin entered the Royal Navy in 1801 and served at the Battles of Copenhagen and Trafalgar. He commanded two overland expeditions (1819-22 and 1825-27) that surveyed 1,200 miles (1,900 km) of coastline from Cape Beechey, Alaska, to well beyond the Coppermine River. After serving as Governor of Tasmania (1836-43), Franklin was given command of the two ships *Erebus* and *Terror* in an expedition to discover the Northwest Passage. Franklin set sail on May 13, 1845, and entered Lancaster Sound on the eastern coast of Baffin Bay some two months later but was never seen again.

A 12-year search for Franklin soon began; it involved some 40 expeditions and added enormously to knowledge of the region. With the discovery in 1859 of the expedition's records and the bodies of some of its 129 members, the whole tragedy at last became clear. Franklin had wintered at Beechey Island at the western end of Lancaster Sound and then eventually headed south until stopped by ice in Victoria Strait off King William Island. Franklin had died the following year, and the survivors finally abandoned ship in April 1848 to head south. None lasted more than a few miles.

Frobisher, Sir Martin (c. 1535-94) English navigator, one of the greatest seamen of his age, and the first to sail to the Arctic in search of the Northwest Passage. Frobisher had gone to sea at an early age, and, perhaps under the influence of Sir Humphrey GILBERT, had become interested in the possibility of a Northwest Passage to the Indies. In 1576 he was given command of an expedition of two ships — *Gabriel* (25 tons) and *Michael* (20 tons) — and a tiny pinnace. He made a landing on the southeast coast of Baffin Island after a storm in which the *Michael* deserted and the pinnace was lost. Frobisher sailed on in the *Gabriel* and entered the mouth of Frobisher Bay, which he took to be a strait, before ice and bad weather forced his return.

Frobisher brought back with him a sample of 'black earth' which was wrongly thought to contain gold. As a consequence, Queen Elizabeth lent him the *Aid*, a 200-ton ship of the navy, and herself subscribed to the expedition. Accompanied by the *Gabriel* and *Michael*, Frobisher set sail in 1577. The search for the Northwest Passage was forgotten; he returned in September with some 200 tons of ore. On a third expedition in 1578 he took 15 ships and planned to establish a settlement of 100 men. Many vessels were scattered by storms, and Frobisher entered Hudson Strait before returning to Frobisher Bay and loading still more ore. On his return the ore was found to be valueless and his career was under a cloud until 1585, when he sailed in the *Primrose* as vice admiral of Sir Francis DRAKE's expedition to the Indies.

Frobisher was knighted for his part in the defeat of the Armada, in which he had commanded the *Triumph*, England's largest man-of-war. In 1590 and 1592 he took part in attempts to capture the Spanish treasure fleet. He died as a result of wounds sustained while helping to dislodge Spanish forces that threatened the French port of Brest.

Fulton, Robert (1765-1815) American inventor whose steamboat CLERMONT (1807) was the world's first commercially successful steam-powered vessel. Born in Lancaster Co., Pennsylvania, Fulton became a skilled gunsmith before turning his talents to painting portraits and landscapes. In England and France his paintings received some attention, but his interest soon shifted to canal engineering and then to the designing of a submarine. He submitted plans to the French government in 1797 and eventually received a grant of 10,000 francs to build the *Nautilus*. She was cigar-shaped, some 21 ft. (6.5 m) long and propelled underwater by a hand-cranked propeller. The *Nautilus* performed well, actually sinking naval vessels in tests, but neither the French nor the British government was interested.

Meanwhile, Fulton had turned his attention to steamboats. With the American Minister to France, Robert Livingston, as his partner, Fulton launched a steamboat on the Seine in Paris in 1803. He then returned to the United States and with Livingston's support built the *Clermont*, which began her historic voyage on August 17, 1807. Fulton followed this success with numerous other steam-powered vessels for the Hudson and the waters around New York, and also drew up the plans for the first steamboat on western waters, the *New Orleans*, built at Pittsburgh in 1811. In the last years of his life Fulton designed the steam-powered warship DEMOLOGUS for the defense of New York in the War of 1812.

Gama, Vasco da (c. 1460-1524) Portuguese explorer, commander of the first European expedition by sea to India. He set sail on July 8, 1497, to pioneer the sea route around the Cape of Good Hope, which had been discovered by Bartholomew DIAZ nine years earlier. Da Gama set out with the 120-ton three-masted *nãos São Gabriel* and *São Rafael*, the 50-ton caravel *Berrio*, and a storeship. His *nãos* were armed and they carried goods for trade; the journey was as much a commercial embassy as a voyage of exploration. Da Gama sailed to the Cape Verde Islands and then headed boldly out into the Atlantic, sighting the coast of South Africa after 13 weeks at sea, during which he covered 4,500 miles (7,250 km), the longest passage yet made by European seamen out of sight of land. He rounded the Cape of Good Hope, 100 miles (160 km) farther south, on November 22, 1497, and sailed up the coast of East Africa to Malindi, where he found a Gujerati pilot, Ahmed Ibn Majid, who knew the route to India. Da Gama and his ships arrived at the Indian port of Calicut on May 20, 1498. Despite the hostility of local Moslem traders he was able to depart with a cargo of pepper and cinnamon on August 29, 1498. Because so many sailors had died of scurvy during the long passage of the Arabian Sea, Da Gama burned the *São Rafael* at Malindi, and finally returned to Lisbon on September 9, 1499. He was rewarded handsomely for his achievements and was sent out three years later to India in command of a fleet of 14 ships, equipped for a demonstration of force. After exacting tribute, bombarding Calicut, and defeating an Arab fleet — the first naval battle for European control of the east — he returned home in December 1503 with a rich cargo of spices. Appointed Viceroy of India in 1524, he died at the port of Cochin shortly after his arrival.

Gilbert, Sir Humphrey (c. 1537-83) English navigator and explorer, half-brother of Sir Walter RALEIGH, and founder of the first English colony in the New World. Gilbert saw wide service as a soldier on the European continent and in Ireland, and in the mid-1560s wrote his famous *Discourse* discussing the possibility of a Northwest Passage to China and the Indies. In 1576 this work was published and almost certainly helped encourage the voyages of Martin FROBISHER and John DAVIS. But by this time Gilbert had become interested in colonizing a part of the American continent, on the pattern of English plantations in Ireland with which he was associated.

In 1578 he obtained vaguely worded Letters Patent from Queen Elizabeth I authorizing him to found such a colony, but his first expedition (1578-79) was a disaster, with his fleet scattering and turning back in mid-Atlantic. Four years later, however, Gilbert managed to equip a second, more ambitious colonizing venture. He sailed from Plymouth on June 11, 1583, with a fleet of five ships. He arrived at St. John's, Newfoundland, on August 3 and took possession of the region in the name of the queen. He soon sailed southward to explore the coast, but with the loss of his largest ship, combined with other misfortunes, he decided to head back to England. Gilbert insisted on returning in the smallest of his fleet, *Squirrel*, a tiny pinnace of 10 tons, and he was lost in a storm off the Azores.

Grasse, François Joseph Paul, Comte de (1722-88) French admiral who made possible the American victory at Yorktown, the single most decisive battle of the Revolutionary War. Appointed commander of the French Atlantic Fleet in February 1781, he scored a victory over Admiral Sir Samuel Hood and took the British Island of Tobago. Washington then requested him to sail north to Chesapeake Bay to aid in the campaign against General Cornwallis. A British fleet under Admiral Sir Thomas Graves, bringing reinforcements to Cornwallis, met de Grasse's ships off Cape Henry on September 5 and was forced to turn back to New York. The French thus secured command of Chesapeake Bay and Cornwallis had no choice but to surrender on September 18.

De Grasse was, however, later defeated by Admiral Sir George RODNEY at the Battle of the Saints, which took place between Guadeloupe and Dominica on April 12, 1782. The French admiral was taken prisoner; on his return to France he was acquitted at a court-martial but banished from court, his naval career at an end.

Grenville, Sir Richard (1542-91) English naval commander, captain of the REVENGE in the hopeless battle against the Spanish fleet that has become one of the most celebrated actions in naval history. Grenville was a cousin of Sir Walter RALEIGH and commanded the expedition of seven vessels that took the first settlers to Raleigh's ill-fated colony on Roanoke Island in 1585. Returning with supplies the following year, he found the colony mysteriously deserted.

Grenville was wealthy enough to supply three ships to the fleet to oppose the Armada, and himself commanded a small naval force off Ireland, in an attempt to capture one or two Spanish ships. In 1591 Grenville was named vice admiral and second-in-command of a fleet commanded by Lord Thomas Howard. The expedition sailed to the Azores to intercept a homeward-bound Spanish treasure fleet. The English ships were surprised by a superior Spanish fleet and Grenville's flagship, the *Revenge*, was unable to escape in time. In the ensuing action, which lasted 15 hours, Grenville was wounded and died aboard the Spanish flagship a few days later.

Harrison, John (1693-1776) English clockmaker, inventor of the first reliable marine chronometer, which made possible the accurate and simple determination of longitude at sea. The Board of Longitude, created by an Act of Parliament in 1714, offered a £20,000 prize for an accurate means of calculating longitude. Harrison made various attempts to win the prize. His fourth chronometer, little larger than a pocket watch, easily met the Board's requirements in trials in 1762 and 1764, but he was paid in full only in 1773, having spent many years embittered by lack of recognition. A copy of his successful chronometer was used by COOK on his second voyage of exploration; at the end of a three-year circumnavigation Cook's calculated longitude was only 8 miles (13 km) in error.

Hawkins, Sir John (1532-95) English admiral, the architect of the Elizabethan navy. In 1562-63 and 1564-65 he made two highly successful slave-trading voyages to the West Indies, but his third voyage of 1567-68, accompanied by Francis DRAKE, ended with the loss, through Spanish treachery, of four of the original six ships which had started the voyage. Hawkins became Treasurer of the Elizabethan navy in 1577 and Comptroller in 1589. As a member of the Navy Board, he was responsible for the introduction of new 'low-charged' GALLEONS, carrying fewer but heavier guns and far faster and more maneuverable than the conventional ships of his day. His new fleet successfully beat off the Spanish Armada of 1588, during which Hawkins himself commanded the *Victory* and was knighted for his services. In 1595 he sailed with Drake on a raid to the West Indies, but died off Puerto Rico before action began.

Henry the Navigator (1394-1460) Third son of King John I of Portugal and patron of the Portuguese voyages of exploration that ultimately led to the discovery of the sea route to India around the Cape of Good Hope. Prince Henry gained military renown at the conquest of Ceuta in Morocco in 1415; this became Portugal's first overseas possession and marks the beginning of his interest in exploration. As Governor of the Algarve in southern Portugal, he gathered about him experts in navigation, cartography, and astronomy at the Vila do Infante near Sagres. From 1420 until the time of his death he sent out small but frequent expeditions that gradually mapped the west coast of Africa as far south as Sierra Leone and also discovered Madeira and the Azores. The impetus of these discoveries continued after Henry's death and led to the discovery of the Cape of Good Hope by Bartholomew DIAZ in 1488 and to the first voyage to India in 1497-99.

Heyerdahl, Thor (b. 1914) Norwegian anthropologist and explorer whose keen

Thor Heyerdahl on his raft Kon-Tiki.

interest in transoceanic migrations of peoples led to a series of remarkable expeditions in vessels that ancient voyagers might have used. As a member of a scientific expedition to the Marquesas Islands in 1937-38 he began to develop the theory that the first settlers of Polynesia had migrated from South America. After World War II, to test the practicality of this theory, he built the balsa-wood raft KON-TIKI, using only such binding materials as would have been available to ancient Indian tribes. On April 28, 1947, he made a landing on the Tuamotu Islands, having successfully completed the 4,300-mile (6,900-km) voyage from Peru in 101 days, thus proving the feasibility of his theory.

Heyerdahl next turned his attention to early Egyptian voyages and attempted to build a craft of papyrus reeds, of the kind that the ancient Egyptians might have used. RA, named after the Egyptian sun god, was the result, but in an attempt to cross the Atlantic the boat broke up in heavy seas. Undeterred, Heyerdahl built *Ra II*, and in 1970 successfully crossed the Atlantic from Morocco to Bridgetown in the West Indies.

In 1977 Heyerdahl built the reed boat *Tigris* on the pattern of ancient Sumerian craft and although he successfully sailed down the Persian Gulf, he burned the *Tigris* at Djibouti as a protest against the political situation in the Horn of Africa.

Holland, John Philip (1841-1914) Irish-born American inventor, designer of what is generally considered the world's first fully practical submarine. As a schoolteacher in Ireland Holland had already drawn up plans for a submarine before he emigrated to the United States in 1873. Two years later he tested his first boat and in 1881, with funds from Irish nationalists in America, he launched his successful *Fenian Ram*. These early models pioneered many features that have become standard on modern submarines, including horizontal rudders for diving under power.

In 1895 the U.S. Navy ordered a submarine from Holland's newly established Torpedo Boat Company, but the resulting *Plunger* was not a success, largely because of alterations insisted upon by naval authorities. Holland returned the navy's money and financed his next submarine, the *Holland*, himself. Launched

at Elizabeth, N.J., in 1898, it was an outstanding success. The *Holland* was 53 ft. 10 in. (16.4 m) long, displaced 15 tons, and was armed with Whitehead torpedoes. For underwater propulsion the *Holland* used an electric motor run on a battery; on the surface a gasoline engine supplied power. She was purchased by the U.S. Navy in 1900 and became the prototype for submarines ordered from Holland by many of the world's navies. Holland's company, which later became the Electric Boat Company, has continued to this day to build most U.S. Navy submarines.

Howard of Effingham, Charles, 2nd Baron (1536-1624) Lord High Admiral of England, commander of the English fleet in the defeat of the Spanish Armada (1588). Howard was at the start of his career mainly a courtier and diplomat, and he won his position of Lord High Admiral in 1585 largely because he was a member of an illustrious family, three of whom had already been Lord Admirals. Nonetheless, he proved a masterful Commander in Chief of the first great fleet England had ever assembled.

In December 1587, as the Spanish fleet gathered at Lisbon, he hoisted his flag aboard the *Ark Royal* and made sure, through personal inspection of the ships, armament, and stores, that the fleet was ready for battle. Howard joined Sir Francis DRAKE and the advance squadron at Plymouth in May 1588, and he, Drake as vice admiral, and Sir John HAWKINS as rear admiral, were the principal members of the English council of war. His prudent and cautious tactics, partly forced upon him by circumstances, were not so opposed to the plans of his more brilliant and experienced commanders as later accounts have made out. His refusal to play into the hands of the enemy by fighting at close quarters, together with his ability to coordinate the talents of his subordinates, played a large part in the English victory. Howard was joint commander with the Earl of Essex of the expedition that sacked Cadiz in 1596; he remained Lord High Admiral until 1619.

Howe, Richard, Earl (1726-99) British naval officer, victor over the French in the battle that became known as 'The Glorious First of June.' Howe entered the navy at the age of 14, and as

commander of the *Dunkirk* captured the French warship *Alcide* at the mouth of the St. Lawrence on June 8, 1755. He went on to distinguish himself in the famous defeat of the French fleet off Quiberon Bay in 1759, in which he led the line in the *Magnanime*.

At the outbreak of the American Revolution he was appointed to command the North American station, and with his brother, General Sir William Howe, in charge of British troops in the colonies, he was instructed to negotiate a reconciliation with Congress. Nothing came of the talks he undertook, and he aided his brother in the taking of Philadelphia and beat off a French fleet in its attempt to take Newport, Rhode Island. Howe resigned his command in 1778; four years later, in command of the Channel Fleet, he successfully relieved besieged Gibraltar in the face of a far superior French and Spanish fleet.

In 1793, at the personal request of the king, he once more took up active command of the Channel Fleet. In his defeat of the French Admiral Villaret de Joyeuse off Ushant on 'The Glorious First of June' 1794, he captured six French ships and destroyed a seventh through highly unorthodox tactics and without any losses of his own. After this first naval engagement of the French Revolutionary War, Howe was forced into retirement by ill health, but he was called back to quell the mutiny at Spithead in 1797. Through his popularity with the men, he succeeded in pacifying the mutineers. Howe also played a large part in the adoption of improvements in signaling methods.

Hudson, Henry (d. 1611) English navigator and Arctic explorer, discoverer of Hudson Bay. In 1607 he was employed by the English Muscovy Company as captain of the *Hopewell* on a voyage in search of the Northeast Passage. Finding his way up the east coast of Greenland barred by ice, he sailed east along the barrier of the pack ice as far as Spitsbergen and on his return journey discovered Jan Mayen Island. His reports of the large number of whales in that area sparked off the Arctic whaling industry.

The following year he set out again, this time exploring the Barents Sea in search of a passage eastward, but once again ice forced him to turn back. Late in

Lord Howe's defeat of the French at 'The Glorious First of June,' 1794.

1608 he entered the service of the Dutch East India Company and in April 1609 he sailed once more for the Barents Sea in *Half Moon*. After encountering ice, and facing a mutinous crew who feared having to winter in the Arctic like Willem BARENTS, Hudson decided instead to search for a westerly route to China across the Atlantic. He entered Chesapeake Bay and Delaware Bay and then sailed up the Hudson 150 miles (240 km), as far as what is now Albany, in a vain search for a route to the Pacific. His voyage provided the basis for the Dutch claim to the region, but on his return journey to Holland he put in at an English port and he and the other Englishmen on the *Half Moon* were detained and forbidden to serve the Dutch.

In April 1610 Hudson set out in command of an English expedition in the *Discovery*, once more in search of a passage to China. He entered Hudson Strait, between Greenland and Labrador, and through it reached Hudson Bay. He explored the eastern shores of Hudson Bay and wintered in the southwestern corner of James Bay. The following June the crew, led by Henry Greene, mutinied and sailed for home after setting adrift Hudson, his young son, and seven others in a small boat without food or water.

Hudson and his companions were never seen again.

Hull, Isaac (1773-1843) American naval hero of the War of 1812, commander of the CONSTITUTION in her famous victory over the *Guerrière*. Hull went to sea at the age of 14 and was commissioned a lieutenant in the newly established U.S. Navy in 1798. During the war against the Barbary pirates of Tripoli, he distinguished himself as commander of the *Enterprise* and the *Argus*; in 1806 he was promoted to captain and in 1810 was given command of the frigate *Constitution*.

Soon after war was declared, in 1812, Hull slipped out of Chesapeake Bay and eluded a squadron of seven British ships in a remarkable chase that lasted three days. On August 19 he encountered the British (ex-French) 48-gun frigate *Guerrière*, and in half-an-hour's close action dismasted the British ship and forced her to surrender. It was in this engagement that the *Constitution* gained the nickname 'Old Ironsides' from her crew. Hull's victory gave a much-needed boost to American morale, and it proved to be the first of a series of victories by America's tiny fleet of frigates that destroyed the myth of British invincibility at

sea. Hull later served as one of the first three naval commissioners and was Commodore of the U.S. Pacific Squadron (1824-27) and Mediterranean Squadron (1839-41).

Jellicoe, John Rushworth, 1st Earl (1859-1935) British admiral in command of the Grand Fleet at the Battle of Jutland in 1916. Jellicoe entered the Royal Navy in 1872 and won rapid promotion in a career in which he specialized in gunnery. As Assistant to the Controller (1902-03), Director of Ordnance (1905-07), and Third Sea Lord and Controller (1908-10), he assisted Sir John FISHER in his far-reaching reforms of the Royal Navy and was closely associated with the building of the DREADNOUGHT and the subsequent naval construction race with Germany. Jellicoe's abilities so impressed Fisher that he decided the younger man was the best candidate for Commander in Chief of the Grand Fleet in the event of war — 'admiralissimo when Armageddon comes' in Fisher's words. Jellicoe had a brief period in command of the Atlantic Fleet, and then of the Second Division of the Home Fleet, before returning to the Admiralty as Second Sea Lord (1913)

At the outbreak of war he was given command of the Grand Fleet at Scapa Flow. His cautious tactics at the Battle of Jutland, the one great engagement between modern battle fleets in European waters, were criticized at the time, but the German High Seas Fleet never again ventured from port. Appointed First Sea Lord at the end of 1916, he was adamant in his pessimistic belief that the introduction of merchant convoys was impracti-

Admiral Sir John Jellicoe (1859-1935).

cable at the time, but a later analysis of transatlantic sailings convinced him that it would be possible, and in April 1917 he presided over the introduction of an ocean convoy system which proved a total success in the face of Germany's unrestricted submarine warfare. Jellicoe was replaced as First Sea Lord late in 1917. After the war he was promoted to Admiral of the Fleet and went on to serve as Governor-General of New Zealand (1920-24).

Jervis, John, Earl St. Vincent (1735-1823) one of the greatest British admirals. He first achieved fame in 1782 when, commanding the third-rate *Foudroyant*, he captured the French first-rate *Pégase* without the loss of a single man. During the Revolutionary War with France (1793-1801) he commanded the naval expedition to the West Indies that captured the French possessions of Martinique, St. Lucia, and Guadeloupe. In 1795, at the age of 60, he was appointed Commander in Chief in the Mediterranean and two years later, with a fleet of 15 ships, defeated the Spanish fleet off Cape St. Vincent in an action in which he was outnumbered in ships and guns by a margin of two to one. In 1799 he returned to England after a breakdown in health, but recovered to become first Lord of the Admiralty. A superb administrator, Jervis was tireless in stamping out inefficiency and fraud in the naval dockyards, in training the fleet for the great battles which lay ahead, and in reforming the medical service of the navy in its fight against scurvy and typhus, the two great scourges of the lower deck.

Jervis is perhaps best known for his selection of Horatio NELSON, over the heads of senior admirals, to command the Mediterranean Squadron, which crushed the French fleet at the Battle of the Nile in 1798. Although a stern disciplinarian, Jervis was a man of great justice and humanity and is remembered for the many battles he fought for the introduction of pensions and other benefits for seamen and their families.

Jones, John Paul (1747-92) Scottish-born American naval hero of the Revolutionary War. He went to sea at the age of 12, and after killing a mutinous crewman in self-defense on the island of

John Paul Jones' remains being taken from the port of Cherbourg, France, to the USS Brooklyn *for return to the United States.*

Tobago in 1773, he fled to America, changing his name from John Paul to John Paul Jones. After successful and daring voyages as commander of the *Alfred* and the *Providence* in the first years of the American Revolution, he was promoted to captain in 1777 and given command of the sloop *Ranger*, in which he cruised in waters around the British Isles. He took numerous prizes and engaged in several spectacular shore raids; the *Drake*, which he captured off Ireland in April 1778, was the first warship taken by the continental navy.

Hailed as a hero on his arrival in France, he was given command of a combined French and American squadron. This included his own ship, the converted French East Indiaman BONHOMME RICHARD, and the new U.S. frigate, *Alliance*. He intercepted a Baltic convoy escorted by the British warships *Serapis* and *Countess of Scarborough*, and the ensuing battle off Flamborough Head on September 23, 1779, has become one of the most famous engagements in American naval history. After a grueling gun battle which lasted for more than three hours, *Serapis* caught fire and surrendered. Jones received less than full recognition from Congress for his victory; he spent much of his life after the war in France collecting the prize money due his squadron. In 1788-89 he served as a rear admiral commanding the Russian fleet in the Black Sea against the Turks,

but intrigue robbed him of credit for his victories and he died in Paris an embittered and broken man. Later he came to be regarded as the U.S. Navy's founding father, and in 1905 an escort of American warships returned his remains to the United States; his tomb in the U.S. Naval Academy at Annapolis has become a national shrine.

Le Maire, Jacob (1585-1616) Dutch navigator, who with his pilot Willem Schouten discovered a new route to the Pacific around Cape Horn. He was the son of Isaac Le Maire, originally a director of the Dutch East India Company, who had decided to try and break its monopoly of Dutch trade with the east. The company had been given sole rights to voyages via the Cape of Good Hope and the Straits of Magellan. Isaac Le Maire was certain that other routes must exist, and recalled that Sir Francis DRAKE had suggested that Tierra del Fuego was not part of a great southern continent but an island, to the south of which a passage could be found. With instructions to seek this route, Jacob Le Maire and Schouten set sail with two ships, *Hoorn* and *Eendracht*, on June 14, 1615. Although *Hoorn* was lost by fire, *Eendracht* succeeded in making her way south of Tierra del Feugo and on January 29, 1616, rounded the promontory to which the name Cape Hoorn was given. On arrival at Ternate, the Governor of the Dutch East India Company refused to believe that Le Maire had discovered a new route to the Pacific, an unbefitting end to this pioneering voyage.

Magellan, Ferdinand (1480-1521) Portuguese navigator, sailing in the service of Spain, who was commander of the first circumnavigation of the world. Magellan was born of a noble family and was a page at the Portuguese court. From 1505 to 1512 he served in Portugal's new empire in the east, and was present at the capture of Malacca, the key to the control of the spice trade. According to some authorities he may actually have visited the Spice Islands (the Moluccas) in 1511. After his return from India he fought in Morocco, but accusations of financial irregularities led to his fall from favor at court, and in 1517 he finally offered his services to Spain. He proposed to seek a western (and therefore Spanish) route to the Moluccas, through a passage that would lead from the Atlantic into the Pacific. Despite Portuguese opposition his plan was accepted and Magellan set sail on September 20, 1519, with five ships (the flagship *Trinidad, San Antonio, Concepcion, Vittoria,* and *Santiago*) and 268 Spanish crew members.

After sailing down the coast of South America and repairing storm damage at Rio de Janeiro, Magellan pressed on to Port San Julian on the barren and treeless coast of Patagonia, where he decided to winter. Several of the ships' companies mutinied and Magellan, after he had regained control, executed one ship's captain and marooned another. *Santiago* was wrecked further down the coast and, during the terrifying passage through the straits that now bear Magellan's name, *San Antonio* turned back for Spain. The straits were passed in 38 days in a masterly feat of seamanship and Magellan sailed boldly out into the Pacific, the first man to enter that ocean from the Atlantic. After 99 days his ships reached Guam where they reprovisioned: food had run so short on the voyage that sailors were reduced to a diet of rats and leather. Magellan pressed on to the Philippines, but was killed on Mactan Island on April 22, 1521, after an attempt to conquer the island in the name of Catholicism.

Juan Sebastian del Cano, the senior surviving captain, then took command. The *Concepcion* had to be scuttled, but *Vittoria*

and *Trinidad* reached the Moluccas where they took on a cargo of precious spices. The *Trinidad* set off for Mexico but only four of her crew ever reached Spain. Del Cano, returning by the Cape route, arrived back in Spain in the *Vittoria* on September 8, 1522, with a crew of only 31, the first men to sail around the world.

Mahan, Alfred Thayer (1840-1914) American naval officer and historian, whose works on the decisive importance of sea power had an enormous impact on the policies of the great naval powers of his day. Mahan saw active service in the Civil War and became a lecturer and then President (1886-89, 1892-93) of the newly established Naval War College at Newport. From his lectures came two of the most influential books of the age, *The Influence of Sea Power upon History, 1660-1783* (1890) and *The Influence of Sea Power upon the French Revolution and Empire, 1783-1812* (1892). Mahan's argument for the importance of control of the sea as the decisive factor in warfare and international politics gained an audience that included the German Kaiser Wilhelm II and Theodore Roosevelt.

Maury, Matthew Fontaine (1806-73) American naval officer, one of the founders of the modern science of oceanography. Maury entered the U.S. Navy as a midshipman in 1825, and in 1842 he was appointed Superintendent of the Depot of Charts and Instruments (which eventually became the U.S. Naval Observatory and Hydrographic Office). His research into ocean winds and currents, which he pursued by systematically collecting observations from ships' masters, led to a series of wind and current charts for the world's oceans. Combined action by the principal maritime nations followed as a result of an international conference at Brussels in 1853, which Maury attended as U.S. representative. Two years later, and by now a figure of international repute, Maury published *The Physical Geography of the Sea*, the first great classic of the science of oceanography. As a native of Virginia, Maury reluctantly resigned his commission at the outbreak of the Civil War, and from 1862 to 1865 was an agent for the Confederacy in England. Before his return to the United States in 1868, when he

became a professor at the Virginia Military Institute, he served briefly as Commissioner of Immigration for Emperor Maximilian, hoping to establish a colony of ex-Confederates in Mexico.

McKay, Donald (1810-80) Nova Scotia-born American shipbuilder, responsible for a series of world-famous CLIPPERS that make him one of the greatest of all designers of sailing ships. McKay came to New York as an apprentice ship's carpenter in 1827; by 1845 he had a shipyard of his own at East Boston where he built some of the largest and fastest ships of his day. His first clipper, the revolutionary *Staghound* (1850), was followed by the FLYING CLOUD (1851), *Sovereign of the Seas* (1852), and other clippers intended for the route to California around Cape Horn. The *Sovereign of the Seas* so impressed James Baines, head of Liverpool's Black Ball Line, that in 1853-54 he ordered four clippers for the Australia trade — LIGHTNING, CHAMPION OF THE SEAS, *James Baines*, and *Donald McKay*. The GREAT REPUBLIC, launched in 1853 and originally registering 4,555 tons, was the largest wooden sailing ship ever built. By the end of the 1850s McKay's shipyard was forced to close through lack of orders, but during the Civil War he built a number of iron warships, among them the monitor *Nausett*. His last great sailing ship, *Glory of the Seas*, was built in 1869.

Mountbatten of Burma, Louis Francis, 1st Earl (1900-79) British Admiral of the Fleet and statesman. Mountbatten entered the Royal Navy in 1913, specialized in radio communications after World War I, and was given his first command, the destroyer *Daring*, in 1934. On the outbreak of World War II he was put in command of the 5th Destroyer Flotilla and distinguished himself in several epic actions as captain of the *Kelly*. Appointed Chief of Combined Operations in 1942, he was responsible for commando operations in Norway and France. In October 1943 Mountbatten became Supreme Allied Commander, Southeast Asia, in charge of the operations against Japan that brought the reconquest of Burma. After a period as Viceroy and later Governor-General of India (1947-48), during which the subcontinent received its independence,

Fridtjof Nansen (1861-1930).

Mountbatten resumed his naval career to become Fourth Sea Lord (1950-52), Commander in Chief in the Mediterranean (1953-54), and First Sea Lord (1955-59). In 1956 he was promoted to Admiral of the Fleet, and from 1959 to 1965, as Chief of Defence Staff, he supervised the reorganization of the separate armed services into a single Ministry of Defence. He was killed by a terrorist bomb in August 1979, while on his yacht off the coast of Ireland.

Nansen, Fridtjof (1861-1930) Norwegian scientist and Arctic explorer. Nansen's first major Arctic venture was the first crossing of the Greenland ice cap, made in 1888. He then decided to test his controversial theory that the Arctic ice drifted westward from Siberia to Spitsbergen. A ship frozen into the ice could provide an ideal base for scientific observations and at the same time a means of reaching the Pole. Nansen raised the money to build the 402-ton schooner FRAM, specially constructed to lift free of the ice rather than be crushed by it. He set out with Otto Sverdrup and 11 others, and was frozen into the ice off Siberia on September 22, 1893. Important scientific work was carried out and on March 14, 1895, Nansen set off by sled with one companion for the North

Pole. On April 8 they had to turn back only 226 miles (364 km) short of their goal. After wintering in Franz Josef Land they were picked up by a British expedition and returned to Norway in August 1896. A few days later Nansen found the *Fram*, which had left the ice, as he had predicted, near Spitsbergen.

Nansen's expedition accumulated a monumental amount of information about all facets of the Arctic, and Nansen devoted much of the next two decades to scientific research as Professor of Oceanography at Christiana (Oslo) University. He also served as Norway's first minister to Britain, and after World War I he headed the Norwegian delegation to the League of Nations. His work in famine relief and the repatriation and care of prisoners of war and displaced persons earned him the 1922 Nobel Peace Prize.

Nelson, Horatio, 1st Viscount (1758-1805) British naval hero of the wars against Revolutionary and Napoleonic France, the greatest figure in the history of the Royal Navy. Nelson went to sea at the age of 12, became a lieutenant in 1777, and was given command of his first ship when still only 20. After

service on the North American station and in the Caribbean during the American War of Independence, he was given command of the frigate *Boreas* and sent to the West Indies. At the start of the wars against France he was captain of the 64-gun *Agamemnon*. During service in the Mediterranean he distinguished himself as a leader of genius; he lost the sight of his right eye at the siege of Calvi in Corsica.

In 1797, at the Battle of Cape St. Vincent, his bold initiative in leaving the line of battle played an important part in the British victory. Even rasher was his unsuccessful assault on Tenerife the following year, which led to the loss of his right arm. Now a rear admiral, and sailing in his flagship *Vanguard*, Nelson received his first independent command and soon became a national hero by destroying the French fleet at the Battle of the Nile in 1798. After a period at Naples and Palermo, where his well-known liaison with Lady Hamilton began, came the victory over the Danish fleet at the Battle of Copenhagen, the occasion when he disregarded the signal to disengage given by his admiral, Hyde Parker, with the remark: 'I have only one eye — I have a

Nelson receives the surrender of the San Josef *at the Battle of St. Vincent, 1797.*

right to be blind sometimes.'

In May 1803 he took command of the Mediterranean Fleet in his flagship VICTORY, charged with the blockade of the French fleet in the port of Toulon. In the spring of 1805, during bad weather, the French escaped him, an event that eventually led to the Battle of Trafalgar on October 21, 1805. Nelson achieved the greatest naval victory of the age against a combined French and Spanish fleet, but at the moment of victory he was killed by a marksman's bullet. An inspired leader and tactician, Nelson remains the most famous of all British naval commanders.

Nimitz, Chester William (1885-1966) American naval officer, commander of the Pacific Fleet and the Pacific Ocean area in World War II. Nimitz graduated from Annapolis in 1905 and served as Chief of Staff to the commander of the U.S. submarine force in the Atlantic during World War I. In 1939 he became Chief of the Bureau of Navigation, and in December 1941, shortly after the Japanese attack on Pearl Harbor, he was appointed to command the U.S. Pacific Fleet in succession to Admiral H.E. Kimmel. Nimitz headed American naval forces throughout the war; although he never commanded at sea, he displayed quiet confidence and brilliant strategic deployment, and a genius for selecting the right subordinates. In 1944 he was promoted to Fleet Admiral, the U.S. Navy's highest rank, and in his flagship MISSOURI he participated in the Japanese surrender in Tokyo Bay. From December 1945 until he retired from the navy two years later Nimitz served as Chief of Naval Operations.

Nordenskjöld, Nils Adolf Erik (1832-1901) Swedish Arctic explorer and scientist, leader of the first expedition to navigate the Northeast Passage (1878-79). Nordenskjöld was a trained geologist and a professor of mineralogy, and between 1858 and 1873 he carried out a series of scientific voyages and surveys of Spitsbergen and Greenland. After two reconnaissance voyages as far as the mouth of the Yenesei River in 1875 and 1876, he set out in 1877 in command of a converted whaler, the *Vega*, to navigate the Northeast Passage. Aided by unusually favorable ice conditions he managed

to reach the Chukchi peninsula only 120 miles (190 km) from the Bering Strait before he was forced to halt by the winter. The following year he continued his voyage without difficulty and arrived in Stockholm on April 24, 1880, having circumnavigated the Eurasian continent. On his last Arctic expedition of 1883 he sailed through the great ice barrier off the southeast coast of Greenland, the first navigator to accomplish this feat.

Peary, Robert Edwin (1856-1920) American Arctic explorer, leader of the first party to reach the North Pole. Peary became a civil engineer in the U.S. Navy in 1881, and after surveying a route for a canal across Nicaragua, made his first sled journey in Greenland in 1886. In 1891-92 he led an expedition to northern Greenland that confirmed Greenland was an island. He returned for further exploration and scientific work in 1893-95, 1896, and 1897. In 1898 he made public his intention of reaching the Pole, and in July 1905 set sail in the *Roosevelt*, specially built for Arctic exploration. His sled party was forced to turn back less than 200 miles (320 km) from the Pole, but Peary set out once again for the Arctic in the *Roosevelt* in August 1908. From his starting point at Cape Columbia on Ellesmere Island, Peary, together with his black dog-driver Matthew Henson and four Eskimos, reached the North Pole by sled on April 6, 1909. Peary retired from the navy with the rank of rear admiral in 1911.

Perry, Matthew Calbraith (1794-1858) American naval officer and diplomat, responsible for opening Japan to the west. The younger brother of Oliver Hazard Perry, he entered the navy in 1809 as a midshipman, commanded the navy's first steamship, the *Fulton*, led the African Squadron in the suppression of the slave trade, and fought in the Mexican War, carrying out the bombardment of Veracruz. Perry is best remembered, however, for his two visits to Japan. In 1852 he was ordered to take command of the East India Squadron and led an expedition to establish diplomatic relations with Japan. He arrived in lower Tokyo Bay in July 1853 with four ships, including the steam frigates *Mississippi* and *Pennsylvania*. He carried a letter from the President to the Emperor, and after

five weeks of waiting with a 'resolute attitude,' refusing to depart, he finally succeeded in having the presidential letter in its gold casket ceremonially received by court officials in a tense confrontation.

Perry returned in February of the following year and anchored his squadron off Yokosuka. A quarter-size steam railroad and a telegraph, presents for the Emperor, were demonstrated on shore, and finally, on March 31, the Treaty of Kanagawa was signed. Two ports were open to trade, and, most significantly, a U.S. consulate was established. Japan's traditional isolation was broken; further concessions were soon extracted and the discredited feudal regime was toppled in the so-called Meiji Restoration. Perry prepared a three-volume official account of his expedition and lectured widely on America's role in the Far East.

Perry, Oliver Hazard (1785-1819) American naval officer, victor of the Battle of Lake Erie (1813). Perry joined the navy in 1799 and served in the Mediterranean against the Barbary pirates. In 1813 he was ordered to Erie, Pennsylvania, to command a fleet of nine vessels being built on the shores of the lake. On September 10, 1813, he left Put-in-Bay on Bass Island and engaged a British squadron commanded by Robert Barclay. After his flagship *Lawrence*, a 500-ton brig, was reduced to a virtual wreck, Perry transferred to the sister ship, *Niagara*. With the wind freshening he was at last able to close on the British ships to put his superior short-range fire power to use. The entire enemy flotilla surrendered — the occasion for Perry's famous message to General William Henry Harrison: 'We have met the enemy and they are ours.' Perry's victory was acknowledged by Congress and he was promoted to captain. In 1819 he was sent on a special expedition up the Orinoco River which resulted in his death from yellow fever.

Raleigh, Sir Walter (c. 1552-1618) English adventurer, courtier, and man of letters, one of the most brilliant figures of the Elizabethan Age. Raleigh was the half-brother of Sir Humphrey GILBERT, and in 1578 he captained the *Falcon* on Gilbert's unsuccessful first expedition to found a colony in the New World. In

1580-81 he served in Ireland, and on his return became the reigning favorite at court, showered with riches and honors. In 1584 he took over Gilbert's patent and sponsored the colonizing expeditions to America that resulted in the ill-fated 'lost colony' on Roanoke Island. Raleigh eventually fell out of favor with the queen and was prevented from sailing on expeditions to intercept the Spanish treasure fleet. In 1595 he led an expedition up the Orinoco in search of the gold of El Dorado, and the following year his tactical skill helped save the British expedition against Cadiz. After the accession of James I in 1603 he was sentenced to death, unjustly, on a charge of treason, but at the last moment was reprieved, only to find himself imprisoned in the Tower of London for the next 13 years of his life. It was while in confinement that he wrote his famous *History of the World*. In 1616 he was released to command another expedition to Guiana in search of gold. It was a failure, compounded by an attack on the Spanish settlement of San Thomé while Raleigh was ill in Trinidad. Raleigh had had express orders not to clash with Spanish interests, and he was arrested on his return to England and executed.

Rickover, Hyman George (b. 1900)

American naval officer, champion of nuclear propulsion, and father of the atomic submarine. Rickover was born in Russia and came to the United States with his parents in 1906. He graduated from Annapolis in 1922; during World War II he was head of the electrical division of the Bureau of Ships. After two years at Oak Ridge studying nuclear engineering he returned to the Bureau of Ships in 1947 convinced that the construction of a nuclear-powered submarine was a practical possibility. His plans were approved, and he became head of the navy's nuclear propulsion program, in charge of the design and construction of the new submarine. His single-minded determination resulted in the launching of the *Nautilus*, as the new vessel was called, in 1954. In January of the following year the *Nautilus* began her sea trials under nuclear power, becoming the first ship to be propelled by atomic energy. While remaining in the navy, Rickover also helped design the first U.S. nuclear power station for the Atomic Energy

Sir Walter Raleigh and his men burning the town of San Josef, Trinidad, during his expedition in search of El Dorado, 1595.

Commission. He was closely involved in the development of further nuclear submarines and surface vessels and developed the missile-firing submarines of the Polaris program. Rickover was made a rear admiral in 1953 and vice admiral in 1959.

Rodney, George Brydges, 1st Baron (1719-92)

British admiral famous for his victory over the French at the Battle of the Saints in 1782; the final naval battle of the American War of Independence and one which secured Britain's West Indian colonies. Rodney was commander of the *Eagle* in the famous victory of Sir Edward Hawke over the French off Ushant in 1747, and he was promoted to rear admiral in 1759. As Commander in Chief of the Leeward Islands station in 1761, he captured St. Lucia, Grenada, and St. Vincent from the French. In 1779 he was once more appointed Commander in Chief in the West Indies. On the voyage to relieve Gibraltar and take up his command, he captured a Spanish convoy off Cape Finisterre and defeated a Spanish squadron off Cape St. Vincent in the famous 'Moonlight Battle.' In 1781 he captured the Dutch island of St. Eustatius, and on April 12, 1782, met a French fleet commanded by Admiral de Grasse in the Battle of The Saints off Dominica.

Rodney threw the French fleet into disorder by daringly sailing into gaps in the enemy line of battle and engaging from the opposite side. Among the French ships taken was the 104-gun *Ville de Paris* with de Grasse himself aboard, but had Rodney continued in pursuit of the disorganized fleet, the victory might have been even greater.

Ruyter, Michael Adriaanszoon de (1607-76)

Greatest of all Dutch ad-

Admiral Rodney (1719-92).

mirals, the outstanding commander of the Second and Third Anglo-Dutch Wars. De Ruyter went to sea at the age of 11 and through most of his career until the wars with England was a merchant captain. In the First Anglo-Dutch War (1652-54) he distinguished himself on numerous occasions by his courage, fighting under the Dutch admiral Maarten TROMP. After operations against the Barbary pirates and fighting in the Baltic in support of Denmark against Sweden, he was made Lieutenant Admiral of Holland in 1665. In the Second Anglo-Dutch War (1665-69) he won victory in the Four Days Battle of 1666, and the following year carried out a daring raid up the Thames to surprise the British fleet at anchor in the Medway. He destroyed or captured 16 ships and towed home to Holland the flagship *Royal Charles* as a prize. During the Third Dutch War (1672-74) he performed even greater services in the face of the combined fleets of England and France. Through his tactical skill he was able to hold the enemy to a draw at the Battles of Solebay (1672) and Texel (1673), saving the Dutch Republic from invasion and hastening peace with England. He continued the war against France in the Mediterranean and was fatally wounded while defeating a French fleet commanded by Admiral Duquesne off Sicily.

Scott, Robert Falcon (1868-1912)
British naval officer and Antarctic explorer, leader of the second party to reach the South Pole. In 1899, as a lieutenant-commander, he met Sir Clements Markham, Secretary of the Royal Geographical Society, who recommended him for the command of the British National Antarctic Expedition. He sailed in the specially built *Discovery* in August 1901, and for two successive seasons explored King Edward VII Land, which he discovered, and Victoria Land. Scott's expedition was one of the first to work from a settled base; together with Ernest Shackleton and E.A. Wilson he set out on a sled journey in 1902 that was the first to penetrate any distance into the interior. Scott returned to naval duties in England in 1904, but five years later was chosen to command another Antarctic expedition in pursuit of the South Pole. Scott sailed in the converted whaler *Terra Nova* in June 1910, learning at

The Discovery, *which Scott took to the Antarctic in 1901.*

Melbourne that the Norwegian Roald AMUNDSEN was also heading for the Pole. Scott reached Antarctica on December 31, 1910, and after establishing supply bases set out on November 1, 1911, for the Pole. From the foot of the Beardmore Glacier and across the polar plateau he and his four companions had to pull their sleds themselves, unlike Amundsen, who relied on dogs. They reached the Pole on January 17, 1912, only to find that Amundsen had beaten them by 34 days. Their return journey of 800 miles (1,300 km) was dogged by unexpectedly bad weather; they were weakened by illness and a badly chosen diet, and they finally died only 11 miles (18 km) from a supply depot they were unable to reach in the blizzard. The tent with Scott's diaries, his body, and those of his two remaining companions was found the following November. That Scott's heroic journey was one of the greatest in the annals of polar exploration is indisputable; recently, however, his leadership and planning have come under question.

Semmes, Raphael (1809-77)
American naval officer famous as commander of the Confederate ships *Sumter* and ALABAMA, in which he raided Union merchant shipping and sank, took as prizes, or destroyed 100 vessels. Semmes joined the U.S. Navy in 1826 as a midshipman and fought in the Mexican War. When the Civil War broke out he resigned his commission to join the Confederate Navy. In command of the commerce raider

Sumter he took 18 prizes, chiefly in the South Atlantic and Caribbean, before being bottled up at Gibraltar in January 1862. Semmes was promoted to the rank of captain and given command of the *Alabama* in August 1862. A two-year cruise during which he took more than 80 prizes made him a hero of the Confederacy. On June 19, 1864, he engaged the Union steam sloop *Kearsarge* in a 70-minute battle that forced the *Alabama* to surrender. Semmes and many of his crew were rescued by British and other neutral ships before the *Kearsarge*'s boats could reach them. On returning to the Confederacy he was given the rank of rear admiral in command of the James River squadron defending Richmond. When the city was evacuated he blew up his ships, and together with his men joined the forces of General Joseph Johnston, still fighting in North Carolina in the last weeks of the war.

Shackleton, Sir Ernest Henry (1874-1922)
British Antarctic explorer. Shackleton's first voyage to the Antarctic was as third lieutenant on Commander Robert SCOTT's first expedition of 1901-04. He was invalided home in 1903 but in 1908 returned to Antarctica in the *Nimrod* in command of a British expedition that was one of the most successful in the history of Antarctic exploration. Its culminating achievement was an

Shackleton's ship Endurance, *which was crushed in the Antarctic ice in 1915.*

attempt to reach the Pole, in which Shackleton and three others discovered a route onto the polar plateau and came within 97 miles (156 km) of their goal. Shackleton was knighted on his return to England in 1909.

Five years later he left Britain in command of another expedition, with the aim of crossing the Antarctic continent by way of the Pole. His ship *Endurance* was caught in the pack ice of the Weddell Sea and drifted for more than nine months before being crushed in October 1915. Shackleton evacuated his men onto an ice floe and the following April, when it broke up, the expedition used *Endurance*'s boats to reach Elephant Island in the South Shetlands. Shackleton then set out with five companions in a 22-ft. (6.7-m) open boat for South Georgia, which they reached after an epic 850-mile (1,370-km) voyage. He crossed the mountainous unmapped island to a whaling station where he found help and finally managed to rescue the entire party. In 1921 Shackleton sailed in the *Quest* in command of another Antarctic expedition. He died at South Georgia of a heart attack and was buried there.

Slocum, Joshua (1844-1910) Nova Scotia-born American sea captain who made the first single-handed voyage around the world. Slocum went to sea at the age of 12 after running away from home, and after a colorful and adventure-filled career as merchant captain, he was wrecked with his wife and sons off the coast of Brazil in 1886. From what was left from his bark, the *Aquidneck*, he built a 35-ft. (10.6-m) canoe which he named *Liberdade*, in which he and his family returned safely to New York after a voyage of over 5,000 nautical miles (9,000 km). The *Liberdade* is preserved

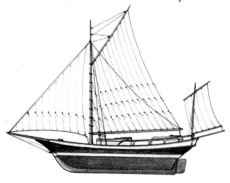

Slocum's Spray, *a 37-ft. (11.3-m) yawl.*

today in the Smithsonian Museum in Washington, D.C.

In 1895 Slocum sailed from Boston in the *Spray*, a sloop he had largely rebuilt himself, and circumnavigated the globe via Gibraltar, the Straits of Magellan, Australia, and the Cape of Good Hope, arriving at Newport, Rhode Island, in 1898. His account of his adventures, *Sailing Alone Around the World* (1900), has become a seafaring classic. In November 1909 Slocum set out on another single-handed voyage in the *Spray* and was never heard of again. The *Spray* was an unusually sturdy vessel, and Slocum a highly skilled seaman; his fate remains a mystery to this day.

Tasman, Abel Janszoon (c. 1603-59) Dutch navigator and explorer, discoverer of Tasmania, New Zealand, Tonga, and Fiji. In 1633 he entered the service of the Dutch East India Company, and in 1642 he was given command of an expedition to determine whether the 'Great South Land' (Australia), already visited by several Dutch navigators, was part of the great continent supposed to exist in the southern hemisphere, and to explore adjacent waters in the Indian Ocean and Pacific. He set sail in August 1642 in the *Heemskerck* and *Zeehaen*, and after heading west from Batavia (the modern Djakarta) into the Indian Ocean, he turned south and then east, finally making a landfall on November 24, 1642. He named his discovery Van Diemen's Land, in honor of the Governor-General of the Dutch East Indies; it was later renamed Tasmania. He sailed along its southern shores, not realizing it was an island separated from Australia, and headed further east. He reached New Zealand, which he believed was part of the great southern continent, on December 13. He returned to Batavia by way of Tonga, Fiji, the Solomons and New Guinea, having circumnavigated Australia, but never actually sighting its shores.

In 1544 Tasman was sent on a second expedition to discover whether New Guinea and Tasmania were part of Australia or separate islands. With his three ships, *Limmen, Zeemeeuw,* and *Brak,* he explored the northwest coast of Australia but failed to penetrate the Torres Strait. His voyage was a disappointment to the East India Company, but he remained in its service until 1658.

Edward Teach (Blackbeard).

Teach (or Thatch), Edward (d. 1718) English pirate, known to history as Blackbeard. Teach had probably been a privateer in the West Indies before turning to piracy at the end of the War of the Spanish Succession (1701-13). In 1717 he captured a French merchantman and turned her into a warship of 40 guns named *Queen Anne's Revenge*. From bases in the Carolinas and the Bahamas he carried out raids on shipping and shore settlements and became notorious for his treachery and cruelty. He apparently shared his booty with the Governor of North Carolina, Charles Eden, in return for protection, but his activities so enraged the people of the colony that they appealed to the Governor of Virginia for help. Two sloops, manned by men of the Royal Navy, were sent out, and Teach was shot dead in a hard fight after his ship was boarded in the James River. His head was cut off and 12 of his crew hanged from the yardarms.

Tirpitz, Alfred von (1849-1930) German admiral, the most influential figure in shaping German naval policy in the years before World War I and the creator of the High Seas Fleet. Tirpitz joined the Prussian navy at the age of 16, was given his first command in 1879, and rose rapidly in the service. In 1897 he was appointed Secretary of State of the Imperial Navy Department, a post he held for the rest of his active career. His bold advocacy of naval expansion made a great impression on the Kaiser, and the result was a series of naval laws that transformed the German navy from a coastal defense force into a battle fleet intended to challenge British naval supremacy.

Tirpitz was a skilled manipulator of public opinion and a powerful figure in the Anglo-German naval rivalry that marked the years before World War I. Although appointed Grand Admiral in 1911, he had no real control over actual naval operations after the outbreak of war.

Disappointed at his powerlessness, and finding his call for unrestricted submarine warfare unheeded, he resigned from his post in 1916.

Togo, Heihachiro (1847-1934) Japanese admiral, victor over the Russians at the Battle of Tsushima Strait, and his country's greatest naval hero. Togo entered the fledgling Japanese navy at an early age and was sent to England in the 1870s for further training. He first achieved fame as commander of the cruiser *Naniwa* in the war against China (1894-95); soon after he was made a rear admiral and in 1904 was appointed Commander in Chief of the Combined Fleet, with his flagship the battleship MIKASA. After directing the blockade of the naval base of Port Arthur and inflicting heavy damage on the Russian squadron based there, Togo skillfully intercepted the Russian Baltic fleet in the Tsushima Strait on May 27-28, 1905. Commanded by Vice Admiral Zinovi Rozhestvensky, the Russians had left the Baltic seven months earlier and were within a few hundred miles of their goal of Vladivostok when Togo attacked. The Russian fleet, many of its vessels old and slow, and handicapped by a convoy of auxiliaries, was totally annihilated and command of the sea passed to the Japanese. The sharp, decisive victory broke Russia's power in the Far East and brought her to the conference table. Togo was later made Chief of Naval Staff and a member of the Supreme War Council, and he became Japan's most respected elder statesman.

The Four Days Battle (June 1666); de Ruyter commanded the victorious Dutch fleet in this battle of the Second Anglo-Dutch War, in which Cornelis Tromp also served.

Tromp, Maarten Harpertszoon (1597-1653) Dutch admiral, leading commander of the First Anglo-Dutch War. Tromp entered the navy in 1622. By 1637 he had been made Lieutenant Admiral of Holland. Two years later he defeated a force of Dunkirk privateers and won a victory over a much superior Spanish fleet that marked the passing of Spanish sea power. In the spring of 1652 he exchanged fire with an English fleet under Robert BLAKE in an incident that marked the beginning of the Anglo-Dutch War. He was able to win control of the Channel after his victory over Blake off Dungeness on November 30, 1652, but the Dutch supremacy was short-lived. The inferiority of the Dutch fleet became apparent in a series of encounters early in 1653. Tromp joined in the attack on the English fleet under Monck at Scheveningen on July 31, 1653. He was defeated and mortally wounded, but the engagement broke the blockade of Dutch ports and was the last battle of the war. His son, Cornelis Tromp (1629-91), was an admiral in the Second and Third Dutch Wars, and served under de Ruyter in the Four Days Battle (June 1666).

Verrazzano, Giovanni da (1485-1528) Florentine navigator who sailed in the service of France and apparently made the first recorded voyage along the length of the eastern seaboard of what is now the United States. In 1523 he persuaded the King of France to sponsor a voyage in search of a new passage to the Pacific. Verrazzano, in his ship *Dauphine*, reached the coast of North America somewhere between Florida and North Carolina and turned northward, sailing probably as far as Newfoundland. He entered New York Harbor, the first European to do so, and brought back reports of a narrow neck of land separating the Atlantic from another great sea; identifying Pamlico Sound, behind North Carolina's Outer Banks, with the Pacific. Verrazzano set out again in search of a passage to the Pacific in 1527, but his activities were limited to bringing back a cargo of wood from Brazil. With the profits he was able to mount a third expedition which sailed in the spring of 1528. He reached the coast of Florida and sailed south as far as the Lesser Antilles. On one of the islands, probably Guadeloupe, he was killed by Carib cannibals as he waded ashore.

Vespucci, Amerigo (1454-1512) Florentine navigator whose name in its Latin form, Americus, was given to the New World. Vespucci was employed by the

Amerigo Vespucci (1454-1512).

banking family of the Medicis, and was sent in 1491 or 1492 to be its agent at the Spanish port of Seville. There he met many voyagers, probably including Columbus, and studied navigation and geography. Accounts of his own voyages are secondhand and contradictory, but it now seems that he sailed on two expeditions to the New World, rather than four as previously thought. On the first, in 1499-1500, he sailed with Alonso de Ojeda, a companion of Columbus, and independently voyaged along the northern coast of South America from the Gulf of Maracaibo at least as far as the mouth of the Amazon.

In 1501-02 he led a second expedition, this time in the service of Portugal. He sailed to Brazil and then southwestward as far as the Rio de la Plata and possibly Patagonia. Vespucci's two voyages between them covered nearly the entire Atlantic coast of South America and revealed the vast size and continuity of the continent. He became convinced that his discoveries were not a part of Asia but a 'New World.' The German cartographer Martin Waldseemüller proposed the name America for the new southern continent in 1507, and the suggestion took hold among later mapmakers. Largely through Mercator's influential maps later in the century the name was extended to North America as well. Vespucci himself returned to Spain in 1505 and three years later was appointed the first occupant of the important post of *Pilot Mayor*, responsible for training and licensing navigators and interpreting new discoveries.

Wilkes, Charles (1798-1877) American naval officer and Antarctic explorer. Wilkes joined the navy as a midshipman in 1818 and in the 1830s became Superintendent of the Depot of Charts and Instruments, which was to develop into the Naval Observatory and Hydrographic Office. In 1838 he was given command of the U.S. Exploring Expedition to survey the South Pacific and Antarctic. Wilkes set sail from Norfolk with six ships and a large body of scientists. After surveying Samoa and nearby islands he made two thrusts south into Antarctic waters. During January and February 1840 he sailed 1,500 miles (2,400 km) along the coast of what is now called Wilkes Land, sighting land several times and becoming convinced that an Antarctic continent lay behind the pack ice. After further survey work in the Pacific and a highly important visit to the coast of the Oregon country, he returned home via the Cape of Good Hope in June 1842, having circumnavigated the globe. At the outbreak of the Civil War Wilkes was given command of the cruiser *San Jacinto*, with orders to hunt the Confederate commerce raider *Sumter*, captained by Raphael SEMMES. By stopping the British mail steamer *Trent* on the high seas to remove two Confederate envoys, Wilkes precipitated a serious diplomatic crisis that nearly involved the United States in war with Britain, but he became a national hero in so doing.

Willoughby, Sir Hugh (d. 1554) English soldier who was appointed captain general of the first expedition in search of the Northeast Passage, sent out by the English Company of Merchant Adventurers, whose master was Sebastian CABOT. With Richard CHANCELLOR as his chief pilot or navigator, Willoughby set sail from London with three ships, *Bona Confidentia, Bona Esperanza,* and *Edward Bonaventure*, on May 22, 1553. They encountered a gale as they were rounding North Cape and Chancellor in *Edward Bonaventure* was separated from the other two vessels, eventually making its way towards what is now Archangel. Willoughby pressed on but encountered bad weather and contrary winds. He finally anchored at Arzina, a harbor on the Kola peninsula, where he was forced to spend the winter. He and his entire crew, unequipped for Arctic conditions, perished from cold and starvation. In 1555 Chancellor put in at Arzina and collected Willoughby's log and papers, which gave an account of the expedition's last months.

Yamamoto, Isoroku (1884-1943) Japanese admiral, Commander in Chief of the Combined Fleet and planner of the attack on Pearl Harbor. Yamamoto saw action in the Russo-Japanese War and in the 1920s became closely involved in the new field of naval aviation. He was instrumental in Japan's withdrawal in 1934 from the naval agreements that curtailed the size of her fleet, but he was opposed to war with the United States, which he believed was too powerful an adversary. In August 1939 he was appointed Commander in Chief of the Combined Fleet, and finding himself unable to halt the drift to war, he ordered his staff to study the possibility of a carrier-borne surprise attack on the U.S. Pacific Fleet at Pearl Harbor. Yamamoto knew it was a strategic gamble, and it was only approved, with reluctance, in September 1941. All three U.S. carriers were away from port at the time and escaped attack; at the Battle of Midway the following year the Japanese fleet lost four of its carriers and its best pilots to American carrier-borne aircraft. In April 1943 the aircraft in which Yamamoto was flying, after having taken personal command of the struggle to secure New Guinea, was shot down in an ambush by American fighters.

The attack on Pearl Harbor, December 7, 1941, masterminded by Admiral Yamamoto.

253